CLASSICAL MEMORIES/MODERN IDENTITIES
Paul Allen Miller and Richard H. Armstrong, Series Editors

Ancient Sex

New Essays

EDITED BY

RUBY BLONDELL AND
KIRK ORMAND

THE OHIO STATE UNIVERSITY PRESS · COLUMBUS

Copyright © 2015 by The Ohio State University.
All rights reserved.

Library of Congress Cataloging-in-Publication Data
Ancient sex : new essays / edited by Ruby Blondell and Kirk Ormand. — 1 Edition.
   pages cm — (Classical memories/modern identities)
 Includes bibliographical references and index.
 ISBN 978-0-8142-1283-7 (cloth : alk. paper)
  1. Sex customs—Greece—History. 2. Sex customs—Rome—History. 3. Gender identity in literature. 4. Sex in literature. 5. Homosexuality—Greece—History. I. Blondell, Ruby, 1954– editor. II. Ormand, Kirk, 1962– editor. III. Series: Classical memories/modern identities.
 HQ13.A53 2015
 306.7609495—dc23
                    2015003866

Cover design by Regina Starace
Text design by Juliet Williams
Type set in Adobe Garamond Pro
Printed by Thomson-Shore, Inc.

Cover image: Bonnassieux, Jean-Marie B., Amor clipping his wings. 1842. Close-up. Marble statue, 145 x 67 x 41 cm. ML135;RF161. Photo: Christian Jean.
Musée du Louvre
© RMN-Grand Palais / Art Resource, NY

Bryan E. Burns, "Sculpting Antinous" was originally published in *Helios* 35, no. 2 (Fall 2008). Reprinted with permission.

∞ The paper used in this publication meets the minimum requirements of the American National Standard for Information Sciences—Permanence of Paper for Printed Library Materials. ANSI Z39.48-1992.

9 8 7 6 5 4 3 2 1

For Jack, in memoriam

CONTENTS

List of Illustrations   ix

Acknowledgments   xi

INTRODUCTION   One Hundred and Twenty-Five Years of Homosexuality
                 Kirk Ormand and Ruby Blondell   1

CHAPTER ONE   Vaseworld: Depiction and Description of Sex at Athens
                 Holt N. Parker   23

CHAPTER TWO   Lesbians Are Not From Lesbos
                 Kate Gilhuly   143

CHAPTER THREE   Pederasty and the Popular Audience
                 Julia Shapiro   177

CHAPTER FOUR   What Is "Greek Sex" For?
                 Nancy Worman   208

CHAPTER FIVE   Lusty Ladies in the Roman Imaginary
                 Deborah Kamen and Sarah Levin-Richardson   231

CHAPTER SIX   The Illusion of Sexual Identity in Lucian's
                 Dialogues of the Courtesans 5
                 Sandra Boehringer   253

CHAPTER SEVEN	Sculpting Antinous: Creations of the Ideal Companion	
	Bryan E. Burns	285
EPILOGUE	Not Fade Away	
	David M. Halperin	308

Contributors   329
Index Locorum   333
General Index   337

ILLUSTRATIONS

CHAPTER ONE

FIGURE 1.1A	Bearded man with youth holding rooster	42
FIGURE 1.1B	Bearded man touches chin of youth carrying deer	43
FIGURE 1.2	Man and youth interfemoral intercourse, four male–female couples	47
FIGURE 1.3	Man and youth in interfemoral intercourse, youth behind them	49
FIGURE 1.4	Ithyphallic youths	51
FIGURE 1.5	Bearded male engages in interfemoral sex with youth	52
FIGURE 1.6	Naked males in Scythian hats	61
FIGURE 1.7	Komast facing left holding a wreath	62
FIGURE 1.8A	Youth prepares to penetrate a woman	64
FIGURE 1.8B	Three naked youths in pursuit of two naked women	65
FIGURE 1.9	Youth prepared to mount ithyphallic youth sitting in chair	67
FIGURE 1.10	Man on couch, singing "O most beautiful of boys"	78
FIGURE 1.11	Man lifts woman's leg	89
FIGURE 1.12	On couch, youth masturbates	91

FIGURE 1.13A	Two threesomes of a man irrumating a woman	92
FIGURE 1.13B	Intercourse from behind	92
FIGURE 1.13C	Tondo of the above; youth with kylix and walking stick	93
FIGURE 1.14A	Dionysus with kantharos	99
FIGURE 1.14B	Same composition; youth and man further apart	99
FIGURE 1.15	Graffito on black-glazed stand of a dog sodomizing a man	101

CHAPTER SEVEN

FIGURE 7.1	Drawings of Antinous restored as Heracles, Ganymede, and Hylas	290
FIGURE 7.2	The Belvedere "Antinous"	295
FIGURE 7.3	The Capitoline "Antinous"	296
FIGURE 7.4	The San Ildefonso group	303

ACKNOWLEDGMENTS

We, the editors, would like to thank several people who made this work possible. First, it is our pleasure to recognize David Halperin (who also contributed an epilogue to this book) and the late Jack Winkler, whose work served as an inspiration for the APA panel that preceded this collection, and for the volume as a whole. This volume is dedicated to Jack, whose loss to the field remains an absence that cannot be filled. We hope that this collection of essays will be a fitting tribute to his influence on classical scholarship.

We also thank the contributors to this volume, who have worked tirelessly on their essays, put up with our editing, and waited patiently for the various pieces of this work to come together. And while we're at it, the editors would like to thank each other—good friends and excellent co-conspirators.

Numerous people have provided less direct but no less necessary support. Kirk thanks Denise McCoskey, Alex Purves, Brooke Holmes, Joy Connolly, and Nancy Rabinowitz for their ongoing friendship and encouragement. He also thanks his spouse, Gayle Boyer, and his two great kids, Ella and Kevin Boyer, all of whom are smarter than him and better-looking. Ruby, likewise, is grateful to all those who supported her during this lengthy process, especially her cocktail buddies (you know who you are), and her spouse, Douglas Roach, who is still the world's best boyfriend.

We also thank Tom Cooper for his continued support of the Oberlin Classics Department and for helping with production costs, and the Classics Department at the University of Washington for financial assistance. Thanks as well to the anonymous readers for the Press for helpful comments and suggestions, and our editors at the Press, for their fine work on the volume as a whole.

INTRODUCTION

One Hundred and Twenty-Five Years of Homosexuality

KIRK ORMAND and RUBY BLONDELL

The final decades of the twentieth century saw a revolution in the study of ancient Greek and Roman sexualities. In 1976 the first volume of Michel Foucault's *The History of Sexuality* initiated a complete reconfiguration of the very notion of sexuality as a product of recent social, political, and discursive practices. K. J. Dover's groundbreaking book, *Greek Homosexuality,* which appeared in 1978, placed our understanding of ancient Greek sexual practices on a more secure basis, and was one of several works that led to Foucault's reassessment of his multivolume project, resulting in the much-delayed publication of his volume 2 (subtitled *The Use of Pleasure*) in 1984. In this volume Foucault developed a notion of ancient Greek discourse about sex that was organized around a principle of masculine self-control and not, as has been the case for the last 120 years or so in the modern West, around a preoccupation with the sex of one's object of desire. Foucault's insights were, in turn, reapplied to the ancient world by classical scholars, most notably in a series of important books published in 1990: David Halperin's *One Hundred Years of Homosexuality,* John J. Winkler's *Constraints of Desire,* and *Before Sexuality: The Construction of Erotic Experience in the Ancient Greek World,* edited by Halperin, Winkler, and Froma Zeitlin. The approach adopted in these books was not universally accepted; but they introduced many classicists to queer theory for the first time and revolutionized ancient sexuality studies as a field.

Prior to the modern period, as Halperin explained in *One Hundred Years of Homosexuality* (citing the work of American historian George Chauncey), "homosexuality" was not thought of as

> clearly distinguished from other sorts of non-conformity to one's culturally defined sex-role: deviant object-choice was viewed as merely one of a number of pathological symptoms exhibited by those who reversed, or "inverted," their proper sex-roles by adopting a masculine or a feminine style at variance with what was deemed natural and appropriate to their anatomical sex. Political aspirations in women and (at least according to one expert writing as late as 1920) a fondness for cats in men were manifestations of a pathological condition, a kind of psychological hermaphroditism tellingly but not essentially expressed by a preference for a "normal" member of one's own sex as a sexual partner. (1990: 15–16)

In other words, sexuality, as a telling, essential element of one's psychological makeup, simply did not yet exist, either in medical discourse or in the popular imagination. Instead, various forms of abnormal sexual desire were conceptualized in terms of a failure to achieve one's proper gender role.

The historicizing of the very concept of homosexuality produced a major shift in academic discussion of ancient sexual behavior, regulation, and ideology by questioning the universality of modern sexual categories. This led Halperin, Winkler, and others, following Dover and Foucault, to attempt, rather, to understand ancient Greek and Roman sexual discourse on its own terms. To borrow the common anthropological terminology used by Holt Parker (one of our contributors), they attempted to produce a more *emic* view of ancient Greek and Roman sex—that is, a view that is grounded as far as possible in the perspective of the cultures under discussion, drawing upon their assumptions and perceptions, whether explicit or implied, rather than those that have erroneously come to seem "natural" or unquestionable in our own eyes. As a result, they stimulated the growth of a vibrant field of study despite, and in part because of, the considerable controversy surrounding certain aspects of the models they employed and promulgated. Their work challenged even those who disagreed with them to articulate their opposition and develop alternatives.

With time, however, controversy calcified into more predictable patterns of disagreement, which generated a certain amount of wheel-spinning, with opponents (especially Thomas Hubbard, James Davidson, and scholars following their work) attempting to undermine these now influential models, and partisans (e.g., Craig Williams, Kirk Ormand) rising to their defense. Our desire in putting together this book is not to rehash these debates, which have started to seem stale even to some of their participants, but to move on to a new set of questions now that the dust has more or less settled. This volume is not a retrospective of the past thirty years, or an assessment of the influence of Dover and Foucault, or a survey of scholarship on ancient sexuality.[1] Thirty-five years after Dover, it is time to move on. Our purpose is, then, to point to future directions by presenting a collection of fresh work in the field that exemplifies where ancient sexuality studies is now and where it is going. Before introducing our contributors, however, it is necessary to sketch our understanding of the importance of the Foucauldian turn and its transformation of the field, and our reasons for asserting that the ancient sexuality wars of recent decades are, in effect, now over.

THE FOUCAULDIAN TURN

Foucault made two radical claims in his final work, the revolutionary but incomplete *History of Sexuality*. The first has, for the most part, been ignored by classicists. The second, which Foucault did not develop until volume 2 of the *History*, was largely borrowed from Dover, and has been the topic of seemingly endless debate and considerable confusion of categories. Let us turn to the second claim first. Our treatment of this topic will be necessarily cursory, as this is ground that has been well covered elsewhere.

Proposition 2: The Greeks and Romans Were Not Gay

Building on Dover's *Greek Homosexuality*, Foucault argued in volume 2 that the ancient Greeks (and, as he discussed in volume 3, the Romans) did not divide the world of sexual identities into homo- and heterosexual. In many contexts, indeed, it seems to matter little to the writers of ancient Greek history, philosophy, oratory, or comedy whether a man was interested in having sex with an attractive younger man or an attractive woman.

---

1. Several useful surveys already exist. See Williams 2010; Ormand 2008; Sissa 2008; Skinner 2005; Hubbard 2003; Nussbaum and Sihvola 2002; Rabinowitz and Auanger 2002; McClure 2002; Larmour, Miller, and Platter 1998; Hallett and Skinner 1997. On the "sexuality wars" in Classics, see now the excellent discussion in Holmes 2012, ch. 2.

Rather, as Foucault explained at some length, the Greeks were concerned with the question of whether the desiring man—the citizen-subject of sexual desire—was sufficiently able to master his desires, rather than being mastered by them:

> The notion of homosexuality is plainly inadequate as a means of referring to an experience, form of valuation, and a system of categorization so different from ours. The Greeks did not see love for one's own sex and love for the other sex as opposites, as two exclusive choices, two radically different types of behavior. The dividing lines did not follow that kind of boundary. What distinguished a moderate, self-possessed man from one given to pleasures was, from the view point of ethics, much more important than what differentiated, among themselves, the categories of pleasures that invited the greatest devotion. To have loose morals was to be incapable of resisting either women or boys, without it being any more serious than that. (Foucault 1985: 187)

Concurrent with this set of ideas, however, is another, complicating restriction. While the ancient Greeks (and Romans) thought it quite normal for men to want to have sex with younger men, the sometimes unspoken rules of Greek gender-formation dictated that men should not be penetrated, and should never desire to be penetrated. Foucault does not discuss this at great length (although see Foucault 1985: 194); it is primarily the observation of Dover (1989: 100–111). Dover's work was elaborated on at length by Halperin and Winkler, and in a passage that has been much quoted (usually for the purposes of attack) Halperin (1990) explained the relationship of sex to the dominant categories of social life in Athens as follows:

> Sex is not only polarizing, however; it is also hierarchical. For the insertive partner is construed as a sexual agent, whose phallic penetration of another person's body expresses sexual "activity," whereas the receptive partner is construed as a sexual patient, whose submission to phallic penetration expresses sexual "passivity." Sexual "activity," moreover, is thematized as domination: the relation between the "active" and the "passive" sexual partner is thought of as the same kind of relation as that obtaining between social superior and social inferior . . . hence, an adult, male citizen of Athens can have legitimate sexual relations only with statutory minors (his inferiors not in age but in social and political status): the proper targets of his sexual desire include, specifically, women, boys, foreigners, slaves. (30)

Simply put, of much greater importance for ancient Greek sexual morality than the gender of a man's object of desire was his adherence to relevant norms of age, gender, social status, and citizenship. A free, adult, male citizen of Athens was expected to behave in a sufficiently masculine way: penetrating rather than penetrated, and, equally important, maintaining an adequate level of control over his potentially rampant sexual desires.

This formulation did not meet with universal approbation. Indeed, almost from the moment that Dover's *Greek Homosexuality* was published, and especially after Foucault's volume 2 was taken up by his followers within ancient studies, the idea that the ancient Greeks (and Romans) did not organize individual identity through the sexually determined categories of "gay" and "straight" came in for attack by classicists.[2] But one of the most important critiques of Foucault's and Halperin's approach appeared from outside of Classics, in Eve Sedgwick's now fundamental work *The Epistemology of the Closet*. There, Sedgwick (who was also a follower of Foucault and who had initially saluted *One Hundred Years of Homosexuality* for its "fine weave of scholarship, [its] breadth and daring of theoretical gesture" [from the back cover of Halperin 1990]), argued that the insistence on the alterity of the past flattens out the present and its relation to that past: "But an unfortunate side effect of this move has been implicitly to underwrite the notion that 'homosexuality as we conceive of it today' itself comprises a coherent definitional field rather than a space of overlapping, contradictory, and conflictual definitional forces" (Sedgwick 1990: 45).[3] Sedgwick's project, as she explicitly stated, was to denaturalize the *present* as well as the past, an operation that stems from Foucault's insights, but that uses them precisely to destabilize past and present understandings of nonnormative sexuality (Sedgwick 1990: 48).

Within the field of Classics, by contrast, critics have largely assumed that "homosexuality as we know it today" is a coherent definitional field, and they proceed from there. Most frequently the disagreements with Foucault, Dover, and those who developed their ideas further have taken one of two forms: either the argument is made that we can find evidence of individuals in the ancient world who have clear sexual preferences (e.g., who prefer young men rather than women) or evidence is raised to prove that the ancient Greeks or Romans did, in fact, show clear signs of homophobia

---

2. See, among many other works, J. Davidson 2001 and 2007; Hubbard 1998 and 2000; Richlin 1993; Thorp 1992; Cohen 1991.

3. Halperin responds to this critique with a revision of his own arguments in Halperin 2002; see especially 10–13.

(and hence must have been thinking in terms of homo- and heterosexual).[4] But the first argument is largely irrelevant: the presence of sexual preferences does not prove the existence of *sexuality* as Foucault articulated the term unless a particular kind of social meaning is ascribed to those preferences (on which, see further below). And the second argument also founders: virtually all the examples of "homophobia" that are adduced prove, on close inspection, to target more narrowly specific instances of gender-deviance: men are criticized as effeminate and sexually passive, women are attacked when they "do what men do in bed," and the like.[5] This is not proof that the Greeks and Romans were thinking with our modern sexual categories, but rather that they were thinking with their own. As Holt Parker (1997) expressed it more than fifteen years ago, "By the fifth time one has made the qualification, 'The passive homosexual was not rejected for his homosexuality but for his passivity,' it ought to become clear that we are talking not about 'homosexuality' but about passivity" (22).

The most vociferous and influential critic of the Foucauldian model has been James Davidson, who takes Foucault to task not least for his acceptance of Dover's "active–passive model" of ancient Greek sex (see esp. J. Davidson 2007: 127–45). In Davidson's view, the system of sex that Dover described was largely a product of Dover's own feverish imagination. The Greeks were not so obsessed with penetration as we have been led to believe; moreover, such a reading of the Greeks fails to take into account the real and therefore meaningful emotions that Greek men and their younger beloveds felt for one another:

> Is it conceivable that behind the modern festival of sodomania, another kind of repression has been at work? Is there denial in all this truth telling? Is it possible that these nice classicists—not all of them straight, not all of them men—who are so keen on anal rape in Crete, and who imagine poetical descriptions of drowning men being forcibly sodomized by the sea, are not quite the cool, gay-friendly scholars they purport to be? What if it is not Love that has been marginalizing sodomy, but sodomy that has been used to marginalize Love? (J. Davidson 2007: 147)

In other words, the description of same-sex desire in antiquity through the "penetration model" becomes, for Davidson and his followers, an attack on gay love. Davidson's use of rhetorical questions in this passage hides the

---

4. Richlin 1993 is a particularly clear example of both modes of argument. See also Taylor 1997.
5. See, e.g., Ormand 2009: 82–83.

underlying assumption of his argument: namely that what is at stake in the discussion of ancient Greek sexual practice is specifically the presence—or absence—of gay people in ancient Greece. This matters, rather bluntly, because what we think of ancient Greek same-sex relationships has pervasive effects on gay politics in the modern West today. Davidson made this aspect of his argument more clear in an earlier work. Arguing against the system of domination and passivity described by scholars such as Halperin and Winkler, Davidson concludes:

> We should require an entirely new array of texts and images from classical Greece before sex as "zero-sum competition" is allowed to stalk our texts once more. At worst it represents an obnoxious myth-making of sexual intercourse as essentially dominating, and of gay sex as gestural and instrumentalizing, motivated by a quite self-conscious and opportunistic desire to undermine the already strongly contested identity of a sexual minority. At best it has been a distraction. (J. Davidson 2001: 49)[6]

In order for Davidson's argument to work, however, we have to accept two of its premises: we must privilege the described emotional depth of ancient same-sex relationships over their sexual organization, and we must understand that the practitioners of such relationships were, somehow, really gay. Of these two steps, there is considerable virtue in the first. Domination and submission have to do with the social structuration of sexual categories: they do not tell us what it felt like to be in love and they do not capture the emotional tone of the pederastic relationships described by Plato and mocked by Aristophanes, and it is surely our responsibility as scholars to tease out the ethical and emotional bounds of those relationships. Indeed, we would argue that Foucault's insights give us precisely the perspective and tools that we need in order to perform these analyses. At the same time, we believe (with Foucault) that greater historical definition is needed. Implicit in Davidson's assumptions is a notion of sexuality as dependent on the depth and authenticity of emotion, as an expression of love; such a definition is a product of the same modern discourse of romance that produces hetero- and homosexuality, but again, it tells us little about the sexual categories of the ancient Greeks and Romans. Greek men might really, truly, and deeply have loved their beloved "boys"; but that does not make their system of sexual signification ours, nor does it obliterate the operative social distinction between men and boys in ancient

---

6. See the useful discussion of this passage in Holmes 2012: 105–6.

Greece and Rome, nor does it make those ancient men gay. We would do well to remember Sedgwick's warning that what we mean by "homosexual" is less coherent than we often think; but understanding the current matrix of conflicting social discourses that constitute modern sexuality will not be assisted by insisting that we are just the same as the Greeks and Romans.

Proposition 1: Sexuality Is a Correlative of Modern Discourse

Despite the considerable furor over questions of category—should we think of Greek men as "active" and "passive" rather than as "straight" and "gay"?—the more radical claims made by Foucault in volume 1 of the *History* have been largely unexamined by classicists.[7] That more radical claim is that sexuality *per se* did not exist—could not have existed—in *any* society, *anywhere*, much before the nineteenth century because sexuality is the result of the modern deployment of a particular set of discourses that came into being relatively late in the history of the West. Foucault (1978) finally defines sexuality, nearly halfway through volume 1:

> "Sexuality": the correlative of that slowly developed discursive practice which constitutes the *scientia sexualis*. The essential features of this sexuality are not the expression of a representation that is more or less distorted by ideology, or of a misunderstanding caused by taboos; they correspond to the functional requirements of a discourse that must produce its truth. (68)

Sexuality, on this understanding, is constituted in part by its function in grounding a modern system of power/knowledge that makes possible new ways of governing human subjects. The question of whether one's sexual orientation is a product of inborn genetic factors ("nature") or social upbringing ("culture") plays a tactical role in upholding such a system, and should not be considered a disinterested mode of investigation into the cause of a biological or social phenomenon. Sexuality is not a transhistorical apparatus into which all human beings are plugged, either at birth or at puberty.

---

7. Exceptions are Halperin 1990, 1995, 2002; Winkler 1990. The point is reflected in the title of Halperin et al. 1990. Miller 1998 is critical of Foucault, but deals seriously with his analysis of discourse. J. Davidson 2007: 163–204 discusses Foucault's discursive analysis, but largely discredits it through parodic description rather than argument. Holmes 2012: 92–110 provides an unusually clear discussion of Foucault's discursive thesis and its implications in modern debates about sexual identities and laws restricting same-sex acts.

Sexuality is not even *caused* by discourse (*pace* J. Davidson 2007: 190); it is simply the *correlative* of a specific, particularly powerful and pervasive discursive practice which was not in existence before the nineteenth century, but which has defined individuals ever since.

What does it mean to say that sexuality is a correlative of discourse? Discourses are notoriously slippery social and linguistic phenomena. Any given discourse consists of a socially defined structure of speaking about the world, a formal system for the production of true and false statements, such that it both describes the world in a certain way and implicitly delimits what aspects of the world are meaningful *within* that discourse. Of particular significance for Foucault is the idea that each discourse implicitly defines what "truth" is within its own boundaries. To take a rather simple example, legal discourse can determine whether killing another human being is justified or whether it is accidental, premeditated, or due to temporary insanity (with very real effects on the guilt of the perpetrator). But legal discourse, unlike certain modes of philosophical discourse, cannot evaluate different modes of living happily. Conversely, philosophical discourse can discuss whether the killing of an individual is morally or ethically right or not, which may have legal implications; but philosophical discourse is unconcerned with whether such an act is *legal* or not. No one person or institution controls the creation, destruction, or deployment of individual discourses, and indeed it is one of the advantages of discourse analysis that it recognizes the ways in which discourses exist both inside and outside of institutions of power, and can cross between such institutions. Psychoanalytic discourse, for example, is meaningful in both medical and legal institutions, with different effects in each.

The radical claim that Foucault makes in volume 1, then, is that sexuality as we understand it did not come into being until the advent of psychiatric and other forensic discourses made it possible; until, in Foucault's phrase, emerging procedures for the will to knowledge concerning sex "caused the rituals of confession to function within the norms of scientific regularity" (1978: 65). The development of this new discourse allowed, as Foucault and others have shown, a new mode of medical and legal control over personal subjectivity, the deployment of a category of sexual *identity* as a way to classify, understand, treat, and, of course, oppress individuals.

The work of Arnold Davidson is particularly illustrative here: Davidson has argued that "sexuality" as it is understood in the modern West did not come into being until the notion of *perversion* "emerged as the kind of deviation by which sexuality was ceaselessly threatened" (2001: 57). That is, the developing discipline of sexology in the nineteenth century (Davidson focuses especially on the work of Havelock Ellis and Richard von Krafft-Ebing) constituted sexuality as a key, internal, psychological state, in large part through defining the mechanisms that might render that psychological state abnormal. Such reasoning may run counter to our intuitive sense of how we live—most of us think of ourselves as having a deeply inborn sexuality, whether perverse or not—but there is considerable evidence to suggest that before the developments of nineteenth-century psychiatry, with its links to criminology, forensic law, and medicine, that is, before the birth of these new *discourses and practices* of the self, people simply did not think that way.

Because power in Foucault's conception is highly mobile, fluid, and dynamic, discourses can easily backfire or produce unanticipated, inverse effects. So discourses that aim to regulate behavior can also function to create the modes of being that they set out to categorize and repress. Foucault also makes this point late in volume 1:

> There is no question that the appearance in the nineteenth-century psychiatry, jurisprudence, and literature of a whole series of discourses on the species and subspecies of homosexuality, inversion, pederasty, and "psychic hermaphrodism" made possible a strong advance of social controls into this area of "perversity"; but it also made possible the formation of a "reverse" discourse: homosexuality began to speak in its own behalf, to demand that its legitimacy or "naturality" be acknowledged, often in the same vocabulary, using the same categories by which it was medically disqualified. There is not, on the one side, a discourse of power, and opposite it, another discourse that runs opposite it, another discourse that runs counter to it. (1976: 101)

In other words, the medical categorization of homosexuality as a perversion, with a set of identifiable psychic origins and a "diffuse causality" into every aspect of an individual's being, *also* brought about the possibility of self-identification as gay. Oppression of homosexuality as a perversion and gay pride rallies are politically opposed aspects of the same discourse.[8]

This runs, as we say, counter to the intuitive understanding of self that most people have. It may well seem absurd to argue that something as ephemeral as a mode of speaking can constitute entire new ways of being. But a discourse is more than a mode of speaking, which should be thought

---

8. On this function of discourse, see also Ian Hacking's discussion of "dynamic nominalism," summarized in A. Davidson 2001: 57.

of as no more than one of its effects; and Foucault's analyses allow us to see how discourses function to enable otherwise untenable forms of power and thereby to produce particular styles of life. Arnold Davidson has discussed at length a rather telling test case; shortly after the first volume of the *History of Sexuality* came out, Foucault was challenged in a conversation by one of his colleagues, Alan Grosrichard. Grosrichard suggested that a seventeenth-century treatise titled *On the Use of the Whip in the Affairs of Venus* constituted evidence for medical awareness of psychological perversion earlier than Foucault's chronology would allow (A. Davidson 2001: 54–55). Although Foucault did not follow up on this conversation, Davidson does, and his findings are revealing.

A. Davidson has found the treatise in question, in fact titled "On the Use of Flogging in Medical and Venereal Affairs, the Function of the Reins and the Loins," by John Henry Meibom and dating to 1629 or 1639.[9] After confirming that there are men in the world who appear unable to develop an erection or achieve sexual satisfaction without being whipped, Meibom turns to examine what the cause of this disorder could be. He considers, and rejects, both astrological causes and a continuation of bad habits from childhood. Instead he comes to the conclusion, as Davidson summarizes, that "the most adequate explanation of these strange cases . . . can be found by examining the physiology and anatomy of the reins [kidneys] and loins" (A. Davidson 2001: 58). Davidson quotes Meibom at length:

> For it is very probable that the refrigerated parts grow warm by such stripes, and excite a heat in the seminal matter, and that the pain of the flogged parts, which is the reason that the blood and spirits are attracted in greater quantity, communicate heat also to the organs of generation, and thereby the perverse and frenzical appetite is satisfied. Then nature, though unwilling, is drawn beyond the stretch of her common power, and becomes a party to the commission of such an abominable crime. (A. Davidson 2001: 59)

Though Meibom uses the word "perverse" to describe his patients' "appetite," it is clear from the quotation above that he does not view the *cause* of the patient's impotence to be psychological perversion in the modern sense; rather, an unnatural coldness of the patient's genitalia can only be

---

9. Originally written in Latin, the treatise was translated into several modern European languages, including an English translation by George Sewell apparently published in 1718. Davidson quotes from the Sewell translation.

satisfied through the physiological application of heat, and the appetite is "perverse" in the literal sense of being "turned" away from normal practice (see A. Davidson 2001: 62–63). Here "nature" must be "stretched" through flogging ("an abominable crime") in order for the patient to perform in a way that, for the normal individual, would be considered "natural." The patient's fantasies, desires, erotic scenarios do not come into it: we know nothing about them, because they are simply not relevant to the physiological, rather than psychological, condition that is at issue in this text.

By way of contrast, Davidson cites Krafft-Ebing's *Psychopathia Sexualis*, first published in 1886. Krafft-Ebing draws a useful distinction between those who are *masochists* (a psychological state) and those "weakened" individuals who need flagellation for physical, rather than psychological, reasons:

> It is not difficult to show that masochism is something essentially different from flagellation, and more comprehensive. For the masochist the principal thing is subjection to the woman; the punishment is only the expression of this relation—the most intense effect of it he can bring upon himself. (trans. and quoted A. Davidson 2001: 62)

The difference from Meibom here is striking. In Krafft-Ebing's formulation, two entirely new sets of ideas have made an appearance: first that this perverse behavior could have an entirely psychological cause, of which the failure to perform sexually is only a tangentially related symptom; and second, that the person who needs flogging to perform sexually because he is a masochist is a *kind of person*, rather than an individual suffering from a physiological deficiency—in Foucault's terms, "a species."

This digression into seventeenth-century medicine may seem unnecessary. It provides, however, a particularly clear example of what is meant by the proposition that sexuality is a correlative of discourse. Before Krafft-Ebing's important formulation of the psychological category of *masochism*, we can reasonably say that masochists *did not exist*. At least, they did not exist in medical discourse and could not be treated by psychiatric means. There existed a class of men who required flagellation to perform sexually, but not only did they not self-identify as masochists, the medical institutions and discourses of the time viewed their problem as primarily physiological, and sought, in fact, to treat it through the proper application of whippings. There is no mention in the works of Meibom of attempts to "cure" this physiological deficiency; it is simply an ongoing physical condition to be managed in order that the patient perform normally. Of course, once Krafft-Ebing produces the category of masochism, defined in psychological terms, it becomes possible to see people in all times and places as potentially falling under it: modern sexual categories are discursively constructed so as to be universally applicable, which is one of the reasons we have such a hard time discerning their limited historical purview.

In broader terms, recognizing the emergence of a discourse of perversion in the nineteenth century makes it impossible to speak of "sexuality" in the ancient world, at least in the full modern sense of the word, that is, the sexually centered psychological core of every human being on the planet. That is not to deny, of course, that the ancient Greeks and Romans had their own discourses about sex, sexual behavior, and perhaps even something like a sexual identity. (It is in such terms that the language of "sexuality" and "identity" should be understood throughout this book.) It is, however, to insist on examining those discourses in their own terms, rather than assuming that they are congruent with, or necessarily even analogous to, our own, historically specific discourses.

Foucault's ideas are not, to be sure, beyond criticism. Scholars have labored to correct distortions in his work and supply its deficiencies. But his overall theoretical framework and its implications for approaching the study of ancient sexualities seem to us incontrovertible. We would argue, moreover, that this point has been conceded (albeit inadvertently) even by his most strident critics. Despite James Davidson's pugilistic stance, on closer examination the picture he presents in its place does not demolish the Foucauldian framework but operates within it. To quote Victoria Wohl, "Davidson presents himself as a critic of Foucault, but the very guiding principles of his book are Foucaultian [sic], not only the emphasis on discourse (as he acknowledges, xxi–xxii) but also the idea of pleasure as a key element in the struggle for self-mastery within a culture that prized moderation (the entire book might well be titled, after Foucault, 'The Moral Problematization of Pleasures'). This is a common phenomenon: the spirit of Foucault's work mobilized to critique the letter" (Wohl 2002: 15n30).

In his most recent book, at the end of his chapter on Foucault's discursive method, J. Davidson himself ironically confirms the central thesis of Foucault's *History of Sexuality,* volume 1, albeit inadvertently. Faced with the difficult question of how such a scholar as Foucault could have produced the allegedly wrongheaded volumes that he did, he takes a brief trip into psychoanalysis, which leads him to two astonishing conclusions: Foucault wrote as he did because he was anti-Semitic and because he was a closeted gay man (J. Davidson 2007: 200–204). Leaving aside the highly questionable nature of Davidson's evidence for both propositions, this conclusion completely, though presumably inadvertently, exemplifies Foucault's claim that sexuality functions as the truth of the modern subject, as the ground of the subject's very being:

> Thus sex gradually became an object of great suspicion: the general and disquieting meaning that pervades our conduct and existence, in spite of ourselves . . . a general signification, a universal secret, and omnipresent cause, a fear that never ends. And so, in this "question" of sex . . . we demand that sex speak the truth . . . and we demand that it tell us our truth, or rather, the deeply buried truth of that truth about ourselves which we think we possess in our immediate consciousness. (Foucault 1976: 69)

For Davidson, Foucault's sexuality has become exactly this sort of truth-producing truth, a fact that, once revealed, legitimizes the very view of history that his scholarship purports to rebut. As Wohl has suggested, we are all Foucauldians now.

THE ESSAYS IN THIS VOLUME

In our view, the field has now reached a new stage, in which the insights of Dover, Foucault, and their followers have been successfully incorporated into the mainstream of ancient sexuality studies. As a result, a new wave of scholarship on ancient sexuality is emerging, no longer preoccupied with these debates. Our contributors show varying levels of agreement and disagreement with the work of those scholars who, in the 1990s, forced a re-evaluation of the fundamental terms of the field. But all of them, though not all to the same degrees and not all in the same ways, are grounded in the basic understanding that what we think of as sexuality is a product, or a correlative, of discourse. Rather than worrying about whether the Greeks and Romans "really were gay," our authors have moved into a post-Foucauldian mode, and are concerned, rather, with exploring the ways that Greek and Roman discourses about sex functioned within their respective cultures.

This strikes us as an important development, in two ways. First, the recognition that the ancients cannot be understood simply through our categories of sexuality raises important questions: if Socrates did not have sexuality, what did he have? How did Sappho think about, and represent, the relation of desire to the surface of the body? The Greeks and Romans had their own discourses about sex, and as every discourse operates according to its own internal rules, in conjunction with the institutions within which it operates, those discourses have their own logic, their own grammar, and their own set of effects. The essays in this volume are united in a shared methodological commitment to teasing out the shape and function of ancient discourses about sex. To be sure, these ancient discourses have a strong historical relation to modern discourses about love, friendship, sexuality, and sexual orientation.[10] But they also function in their own historical context in particular ways, and the post-Foucauldian moment allows our authors to analyze those functions with, in our view, a new and salutary historical specificity.

Second, and perhaps somewhat paradoxically, by moving beyond the debates that have beset Foucault's contributions to the field, the essays in this volume are also able to move beyond some of the polarizing effects of those debates. Holmes has recently made this point effectively:

> But the terms in which the debates unfolded can feel like forced disjunctions: acts *or* identities; sexuality *or* gender; penetration *or* self-mastery; the past as continuous with the present *or* the past as completely alien . . . The challenge for those who study the past is to resist this kind of narrowing as much as possible without forfeiting the hope of making resonant, effective connections between the past and the present. (2012: 109–10)

We think that in their very specificity and historical grounding, the essays in this book succeed in moving beyond these polarizations, and allow us to see new aspects of ancient sexuality both as they functioned in ancient Greece and Rome and as they have affected modern discourses about the desiring subject.

OUR AUTHORS are a diverse crew, ranging from distinguished senior scholars of ancient sexuality and culture (Parker, Halperin) to established members of the next generation, who have already published important work in the field (Boehringer, Worman, Gilhuly, Kamen), to rising scholars with a bright future ahead of them (Levin-Richardson, Shapiro). All of them bring to bear their experiences as students and scholars whose intellectual formation occurred at different times ranging from the 1980s to the present. Our volume is thus firmly grounded in the intellectual milieu of the

---

10. See Halperin 2002, especially ch. 4.

late twentieth century, while providing a forum for the first generation of twenty-first-century scholars.

All of our contributors have research interests in varied aspects of ancient culture, as opposed to focusing narrowly on the history of sexuality. This breadth reflects the coming-of-age of sexuality studies as part of the Classics curriculum. It both grounds our understanding of ancient sexuality within a broader and deeper cultural context and integrates sexuality studies with other areas of Classics, to the mutual benefit of both. The essays here cover a range of issues that are central to the understanding of ancient sexuality. They draw upon literary, artistic, and historical sources and exploit new kinds of evidence (such as graffiti). There is coverage of classical Greeks (Gilhuly, Shapiro, Worman, Parker), Romans (Kamen/Levin-Richardson, Burns), and imperial Greeks (Boehringer). Scholarly pieties are challenged by many of our contributors (Kamen/Levin-Richardson, Parker, Shapiro, Worman). Areas of research that are currently lively and influential in Classics generally are well represented, notably the use of material culture (Kamen/Levin-Richardson, Parker, Burns), reception (Gilhuly, Burns) and imperial Greek (Boehringer). Our collection is also remarkable for the attention it pays to female sexuality (Boehringer, Gilhuly, Kamen/Levin-Richardson), the neglect of which has been one of the more legitimate complaints about Foucault's work on antiquity. Male sexualities are, of course, still central to many of the essays.

We see a fertile degree of overlap in our various contributors' subject matter, concerns, and approaches, and have therefore chosen not to organize the essays into any particular set of conceptual categories. Rather, we present them in a loosely chronological order, allowing readers to find their own modes of intersection among them. We start with the longest essay in the collection, Holt Parker's "Vaseworld: Depiction and Description of Sex at Athens." It is fair to say that Parker's piece is a monumental reassessment of one of the most important sources of our evidence for ancient sex, namely Greek vase painting, and particularly of the ways in which the visual evidence for various forms of sexual behavior in ancient Athens differs from the evidence of our textual sources. It has long been the case that Athenian black- and red-figure pottery has been taken to provide realistic illustrations of lived sexual experience, rather than demonstrating its own set of generic and stylistic conventions.[11] Parker demonstrates, through a careful analysis of nearly every known pot depicting homoerotic activity

---

11. This point has recently been made by Lear and Cantarella 2008. Parker's essay here reaches several points of disagreement with Lear and Cantarealla on the meaning of specific iconographic themes; see ch. 1 that follows.

in the corpus, that this assumption simply will not hold. In particular, his study calls into question the often-alleged "practice" of an *erastes* presenting his *eromenos* with a "love gift" in the form of a hare, a small deer, or a cheetah; Parker suggests that this common motif on vases, never mentioned in our literary sources, is more likely a visual reference to the relationship between lover and beloved as a form of erotic "hunt." At the same time, Parker's exhaustive analysis shows that many previous scholars' assumptions about "intercrural" sex are supported by the evidence from vase painting and not, as has recently been asserted, thrown into disarray by one or two exceptional vases. Finally, Parker suggests that what we tend to think of as a particular subject of ancient vases—namely the erotic—is perhaps better understood as only one element of the vase-painters' tendency to depict various aspects of "the good things in life."

In "Lesbians Are Not from Lesbos," Kate Gilhuly contributes to the geography of sexuality as well as its history through an examination of the discursive history of the island of Lesbos. She challenges the typically unexamined modern assumption that the island's association with female–female desire results, simply and directly, from the fact that Sappho was born there. Rather, this association is the result of a complex and extended nonlinear process, involving not only the reception of Sappho and Lesbos in Greek and Roman texts but also geographical stereotypes predating Sappho, the thematics of Athenian comedy, the discourse surrounding "new" music, and the representation of the courtesan. The lesbian identity of Lesbos was produced, she argues, not by history or geography—the contingent fact of Sappho's birth—but by discourse, above all the discourse of the comic stage.

Julia Shapiro examines the often-asserted claim that the Greek practice of pederasty was considered an exclusive province of the elite, and criticized as amoral by the lower and middle classes. Through a careful analysis of some of the most-often cited sources, she comes to the conclusion that pederasty itself is rarely, if ever, the target of popular criticism. Rather, the depictions of pederasty in legal speeches and Old Comedy—generally agreed to appeal to audience members from a broad range of statuses—suggest that pederasty, if done properly, was regarded as a respectable and, indeed, enviable form of behavior. Although members of the middle and lower classes would not have had the material resources to engage in the activities that characterize such relationships (*symposia*, elaborate courtship of wealthy youths), they nonetheless appear to participate aspirationally in a common ideology that considers desire for young men natural, and proper pederastic courtship a hallmark of civilized behavior.

Though critique of the wrong sort of pederasty does certainly exist, and can be used to attack members of the elite classes, "condemnation of aristocrats for homoerotic misbehavior should not be assimilated to a blanket condemnation of all homoerotic (and specifically pederastic) behavior." In this regard, Shapiro articulates with new precision the attitudes of texts addressed to nonelite audiences regarding the elitist practice of pederasty.

In another essay dealing with ancient Greek men, Nancy Worman argues that Athenian discourse about sex is just that: social discourse, with the particular aim of regulating male citizens' behaviors in nonsexual contexts. In particular, she notes that the metaphorical use of body parts to indicate behavior is not necessarily intuitive, or as sexually inflected as it has been taken. Words denoting open bodily orifices, for example, suggest a concern with excesses of behavior rather than, as might be expected, a suggested feminization of the male so designated. Even more important, she shows a careful linkage in oratory and in comic works between accusations of anal penetrability and inappropriate lack of control, particularly of oral behaviors such as public speaking. Many of the passages that have been taken as providing evidence for male sexual behavior in ancient Athens are, she argues, metaphors in a larger game of social surveillance and control; as such, they point to ideals of masculine behavior in Athens, but cannot be taken as evidence of actual sexual practices.

Turning to evidence from Rome, Deborah Kamen and Sarah Levin-Richardson use the material evidence of graffiti from Pompeii as a starting point for investigating ancient discourses about specific sexual practices. In particular, they demonstrate that our modern alignment of the terms active/passive with penetrating/penetrated is not always operative in antiquity. They argue that the subject of the Latin verb *fello* (to perform fellatio) should be understood as *active* because of her (or his) active and desiring participation in a sexual act. Through a careful discussion of comparanda and of the descriptions of similar sexual acts, they conclude that a *fellatrix*, though active, should be distinguished from a *tribas* as well as from the object of an *irrumator* in the Roman imagination.

In her contribution, "The Illusion of Sexual Identity in Lucian's *Dialogue of the Courtesans 5*," Sandra Boehringer revisits a work that is unique in our surviving ancient sources for its extended and detailed account of sex among women. Most studies of this dialogue have focused primarily on the "masculine" character of Megilla, either arguing that Lucian is applying the male *erastes–eromenos* model to women (in order to make same-sex desire legible to an ancient audience) or reading Megilla in anachronistic modern terms as a "butch" lesbian. Boehringer argues that such approaches are mistaken; the dialogue portrays, rather, a pastiche of ancient clichés about women, sex, and gender. Lucian is not offering us an alternative sexuality, or revealing one that has been suppressed by other authors, but amusing his sophisticated audience by creating a fantastical picture through a manipulation of conventional erotic tropes that ultimately do not add up to a coherent subjectivity.

"Sculpting Antinous: Creations of the Ideal Companion," by Bryan E. Burns, is the only essay in the book to have been previously published. We have chosen to include it because it exemplifies two fields within Classics that have recently taken on a new vibrancy: the cultural interpretation of material objects and the later reception of antiquity. The emperor Hadrian memorialized his beloved Antinous in numerous statues after the latter's untimely demise, thus launching the youth on a long career as an icon of classicizing male beauty and a touchstone in the formation of gay identities. Burns explores the youth's shifting persona as an emblem of homoeroticism in a wide range of Victorian and twentieth-century texts, fruitfully juxtaposing scholarly writing and historical fiction with poetry and drama to demonstrate a persistent fascination with the sculpted Antinous as an elusive object of desire.

We end with an epilogue by David M. Halperin, whose eminence in the field and distinctive intellectual trajectory—from Classics to Foucault to contemporary gay identities—give him a unique vantage point from which to survey the developments of recent decades. Halperin offers his personal reflections on the state of the field that he was instrumental in founding more than twenty years ago and his hopes for the future. We find his contextualizing of his own historical moment both helpful and bracing—as he begins with the question "are today's solutions tomorrow's problems?" and outlines the ways in which the movement that came to be known as The New Historicism has seemed, at times, an impediment to the inquiries it hoped to provoke.

Halperin concludes his piece with a brief discussion of a new development in queer theory, namely "queer temporality," a movement that insists on our ability to make connections, to see continuities in modes of identity across vast expanses of time. In keeping with what we see as the post-Foucauldian shape of this volume, Halperin resists the apparent dichotomy that such an approach might be seen to create in opposition to his own historicist work:

> I have responded to some of these critiques by arguing that historicism is not incompatible with queer temporality. Identification is motivated by

the erotic appeal of difference and distance as much as by a sense of shared identity, so it is not blocked or baffled by a recognition that same-sex behaviors in the past were differently organized from the dominant ways in which they are organized in many modern societies today.

There is much to unpack here, not least Halperin's implicit suggestion that the work we do is motivated not only by scholarly curiosity, but by a form of erotic attraction to the subject of our study. We think the essays collected here provide an array of attractive approaches, exemplifying scholarly desire in the best sense of that idea. The authors here move beyond recent binaries to present historicist readings of sex in ancient Greece and Rome that need not prevent moments of identification and political mobilization. While we insist on the historical specificity of discourses, we hope these essays will contribute to the shifts in force relations that Foucault called for forty years ago:

> We must not expect the discourses on sex to tell us, above all, what strategy they derive from, or what moral divisions they accompany or what ideology—dominant or dominated—they represent; rather we must question them on the two levels of their tactical productivity (what reciprocal effects of power and knowledge they ensure) and their strategical integration (what conjunction and what force relationship make their utilization necessary in a given episode of the various confrontations that occur). (Foucault 1978: 102)

In short, as Halperin points out, studies of ancient sexuality are always on some level concerned with our own sexualities. We hope that the studies presented here will illuminate the former, even as we use them, in part, to negotiate the "conflicting . . . definitional forces" of modern sexual subjectivity.[12]

BIBLIOGRAPHY

Boehringer, Sandra. 2007. *L'homosexualité féminine dans l'Antiquité grecque et romaine*. Paris.

Cohen, David. 1991. *Law, Sexuality, and Society; The Enforcement of Morals in Classical Athens*. Cambridge.

Davidson, Arnold I. 2001. *The Emergence of Sexuality: Historical Epistemology and the Formation of Concepts*. Cambridge, MA.

---

12. Quotation from Sedgwick 1990: 45.

Davidson, James. 2001. "Dover, Foucault, and Greek Homosexuality: Penetration and the Truth of Sex." *Past and Present* 170: 3–51.

———. 2007. *The Greeks and Greek Love: A Radical Reappraisal of Homosexuality in Ancient Greece*. New York.

Dover, Kenneth J. 1989 [1978]. *Greek Homosexuality*. New York.

Foucault, Michel. 1978 [1976]. *The History of Sexuality*. Vol. 1, *An Introduction*. Trans. R. Hurley. New York.

———. 1985 [1984]. *The History of Sexuality*. Vol. 2, *The Use of Pleasure*. Trans. R. Hurley. New York.

———. 1986 [1984]. *The History of Sexuality*. Vol. 3, *The Care of the Self*. Trans. R. Hurley. New York.

Gilhuly, Kate. 2009. *The Feminine Matrix of Sex and Gender in Classical Athens*. New York.

Hallett, Judith and Marilyn Skinner (eds.). 1997. *Roman Sexualities*. Princeton.

Halperin, David M. 1990. *One Hundred Years of Homosexuality and Other Essays on Greek Love*. New York.

———. 1995. *Saint Foucault: Towards a Gay Hagiography*. New York.

———. 2002. *How to Do the History of Homosexuality*. Chicago.

Halperin, David M., John J. Winkler, and Froma I. Zeitlin (eds.). 1990. *Before Sexuality: The Construction of Erotic Experience in the Ancient Greek World*. Princeton.

Holmes, Brooke. 2012. *Gender: Antiquity and Its Legacy*. Oxford and New York.

Hubbard, Thomas. 1998. "Popular Perceptions of Elite Homosexuality in Classical Athens." *Arion* 6.1: 48–78.

———. 2000. "Pederasty and Democracy: the Marginalization of a Social Practice," in T. Hubbard (ed.), *Greek Love Reconsidered*, 1–11. New York.

———, (ed.). 2003. *Homosexuality in Greece and Rome: A Sourcebook of Basic Documents*. Berkeley.

Larmour, D. H. J., P. A. Miller, and C. Platter (eds.). 1998. *Rethinking Sexuality: Foucault and Classical Antiquity*. Princeton.

Lear, Andrew with Eva Cantarella. 2008. *Images of Ancient Greek Pederasty: Boys Were Their Gods*. London and New York.

McClure, Laura (ed.). 2002. *Sexuality and Gender in the Classical World*. Malden, MA.

Miller, P. Allen. 1998. "Catullus Consciousness, the 'Care of the Self,' and the Force of the Negative in History," in D. H. J. Larmour, P. A. Miller, and C. Platter (eds.), *Rethinking Sexuality: Foucault and Classical Antiquity*, 171–203. Princeton.

Nussbaum, Martha and Juha Sihvola (eds.). 2002. *The Sleep of Reason: Erotic Experience and Sexual Ethics in Ancient Greece and Rome*. Chicago.

Ormand, Kirk. 2009. *Controlling Desires: Sexuality in Ancient Greece and Rome*. Westport, CT.

Parker, Holt N. 1997. "The Teratogenic Grid," in Judith P. Hallett and Marilyn B. Skinner (eds.), *Roman Sexualities*, 47–65. Princeton.

———. 2001. "The Myth of the Heterosexual: Anthropology and Sexuality for Classicists." *Arethusa* 34: 313–62.

Rabinowitz, Nancy S. and Lisa Auanger (eds.). 2002. *Among Women: From the Homosocial to the Homoerotic in the Ancient World.* Austin.

Richlin, Amy. 1993. "Not Before Homosexuality: The Materiality of the *Cinaedus* and the Roman Law Against Love Between Men." *Journal of the History of Sexuality* 3: 523–73.

Sedgwick, Eve. 1990. *The Epistemology of the Closet.* Berkeley.

Sissa, Giulia. 2008. *Sex and Sensuality in the Ancient World.* New Haven.

Skinner, Marilyn B. 2005. *Sexuality in Greek and Roman Culture.* Malden, MA.

Taylor, Rabun. 1997. "Two Pathic Subcultures in Ancient Rome." *Journal of the History of Sexuality* 7: 319–71.

Thorp, John. 1992. "The Social Construction of Homosexuality." *Phoenix* 46: 54–61.

Williams, Craig. 2010 [1999]. *Roman Homosexuality: Ideologies of Masculinity in Classical Antiquity.* New York.

Winkler, John J. 1990. *The Constraints of Desire: The Anthropology of Sex and Gender in Ancient Greece.* New York.

Wohl, Victoria. 2002. *Love Among the Ruins: The Erotics of Democracy in Classical Athens.* Princeton.

Worman, Nancy. 2008. *Abusive Mouths in Classical Athens.* New York.

CHAPTER ONE

Vaseworld

Depiction and Description of Sex at Athens[1]

HOLT N. PARKER

We are obsessed with Greek painted pots, not for any intrinsic value—although their intrinsic value is a matter of fierce debate—but because they survive (and in prodigious numbers) and so are our principal source of visual information. Images are at the heart of the study of ancient sexuality. "There is no fuller record," writes Boardman, "of man the lover in any other medium or period of Greek art" (1975: 219). Indeed, the goal of combining philology and archaeology, text and image, has perhaps been more vigorously pursued here than in other parts of the discipline. Yet, despite a considerable body of theory on the "reading" of images,[2] there is still a strong tendency to use the images found on Greek vases as "illustrations" of Greek sexual customs.[3] Kilmer,

---

1. The principal vases are listed in the catalog (with numbers in bold). Vases not in the catalog are generally cited by numbers from the Beazley Archive (BA), which provides a convenient way to access other bibliography and illustrations, some of which for reasons of space are omitted.
   A note on vocabulary: I have used where necessary English's rather impoverished vocabulary of primary obscenities, not for their shock value but to reflect as accurately as possible the meanings of Greek and Latin words and concepts, which euphemism tends to distort.
2. E.g., Schmitt-Pantel and Thélamon 1983; Vickers 1983; Beard on "Undermining the Stereotype" (1991: 26–30); Ferarri 2002: 1–7; 2003; Steiner 2007. Oakley 2009 for a survey of recent work.
3. E.g., Guerrieri 2007: 40 (on Louvre G13): "During the symposium the banqueters, now possessed by orgiastic frenzy from overindulgence in wine, lose all restraint and indulge in episodes of unrestrained sex. Scenes like these are not rare on the cups used at banquets. That clearly means

for example, writes (1997: 36–37): "I think it very likely—at the very minimum, it is an economical proposition—that the differences in presentation of homoerotic relationships reflect some difference in the experience of homoerotic relationships in the two time periods represented by the two disparate sources of evidence [that is, between early pots and the works of Plato]." Kilmer's "economical proposition" is a single (and nuanced) example of what is elsewhere a rather naïve tendency to say, "Look, here's a picture that doesn't square with DoverFoucault,[4] so they must be wrong," leaving us free to remake Greek sexuality in our own image.[5]

That is, the decorations on pots are too often taken as both *representations* (as if the unmediated depiction of practices) and *representative* (as if offering an accurate cross-sample of what people actually did).[6] This "snapshots of Athenian life" approach tends to ignore the facts that even our snapshots are controlled, selected, cropped, manipulated, intended to convey one *picture* of reality and not another.

A third mistake is to assume that what we find is what there was. Our picture of Athenian pottery production is heavily skewed by the survival of pots in large numbers as grave goods in Etruria. There were more papyri than are found in Oxyrhinchus. There were more pots than are found in Italy.

Oddly enough, for this view of Greek pots as documentary evidence, even mythological scenes are used as illustrations of what the Greeks actually did. So Kilmer offers three images of Zephyr (or Eros, we cannot be

---

that sexual manifestations were familiar events on these occasions, well beyond the limits suggested by 'good manners.'" Such scenes are in fact quite rare. See below.

4. Davidson 2001, 2007: 122–66. Lear 2014: 122: "For a time a kind of Dover–Foucauldian orthodoxy dominated studies of pederasty." The rhetorical strategy that offers a straw-man blend of Dover and Foucault is well worth examining.

5. E.g., Hubbard 2003a: 4–5; 2014: 130: "Dover's (1978) groundbreaking survey of the visual evidence for Greek homosexuality unfortunately neglected numerous scenes that did not fit his assumed model of relations that were always age-differential and hierarchical." This is incorrect. Dover discusses at length "the possibility of homosexual relationships between coevals" (1978: 86–87), covering many of Hubbard's examples. A full review of the evidence offered for "Peer Homosexuality" is forthcoming.

6. See, for example, the criticisms of Ferarri 2002: 1–7; 2003. Stewart takes as one of his four starting points (1997: 8): "Though Greek art may look broadly naturalistic and therefore lifelike, it actually offers more insights into ideology than reality. In other words, we have no unmediated access to gender construction in ancient Greece." Oakley 2009: 616: "In general, an increasing number of scholars no longer see the images merely as illustrations of ancient life but as cultural constructs that have their own language that needs to be decoded so as to understand the social and cultural values and beliefs that they reflect." Also Oakley 2013: 144: "Only a little over ninety Attic black-figure examples are known from the twenty thousand or more Attic black-figure vases that have come to light. Thus, it would appear that they were not intended to represent scenes of daily life, revealing true Athenian sexual mores, but rather that many of the paintings were meant to amuse."

sure which) carrying off a beardless youth under the heading "Male homosexual intercrural copulation, both standing, face-to-face."[7] Hubbard offers Eros in pursuit of a beardless youth as images of "Age-Equal Adolescent Interactions," and Dionysus seated with a bearded man under the heading of "Age-Equal Adult Interactions."[8]

Cantarella and Lear's *Images of Ancient Greek Pederasty* offers a welcome warning and corrective, but we still lack an overview of the visual evidence for sexuality in general, not just pederasty. Dover's *Greek Homosexuality* is broader than its title but still partial. Kilmer 1993 is limited to red-figure.[9] Sutton limits his data to heterosexual acts (1992: red-figure; 2009: black-figure). Lynch (2009) makes a controlled sondage limited to heterosexual intercourse on red-figure.

Pots were not painted to illustrate texts, and the world they depict is different in many interesting respects.[10] My essay briefly examines seven such disparities (interfemoral intercourse, male–male anal intercourse, age reversal, courting gifts, group sex, fellatio, and cunnilingus) between two

---

7. Kilmer 1993: 17–18, R603, R574, R595.1, noting that "because the wind god is shown flying, his mortal partner does not have to stand on the ground: this allows the god much more freedom of movement than is possible for his mortal counterparts."

8. Hubbard 2003b; "interactions" is usefully vague. Hubbard 2014: 131: "By depicting Eros himself as a beautiful youth, Greek artists acknowledge that youths can themselves be desiring subjects." We can test the logic: "By depicting Dike herself as a beautiful youth, Greek artists acknowledge that young women can be lawyers." Rather as Berg 2010: 77 notes on the image of Eros in Plato's *Symposium,* "Agathon's whole conception of Eros is based upon the identification of Eros with that which it desires." So, too, Nichols 2009: 54: "The ones who are alike are Love, who is young, and the young, whom Love loves. Agathon's speech is not about human lovers and beloveds, but about the 'god' and his favorite." Hubbard immediately continues, "the categories erōmenos and erastēs really make no sense with Eros, as he simultaneously embodies both." Quite right, and therefore he is not much of a guide to what actual *human* lovers and beloveds did.

9. Somewhat flawed; see Von Bothmer 1995.

10. Topper 2012: 3–4: "In fact, it is remarkable that although modern studies generally define the symposium as a communal after-dinner party at which men reclined on couches in an andron, drank mixed wine and were entertained, and eventually participated in a kōmos, no definition consistent with this description emerges from the pictures. The symposiasts on the vases recline on couches, on the ground, and outdoors; they are old men, mature men, young men, women, barbarians, heroes, satyrs, and gods; they drink alone and in the company of others; they drink wine mixed in kraters and neat from wineskins; and the subsequent kōmos may include a variety of activities and participants." The problem is fundamental: "If so many practices depicted on the vases fit so poorly with what we believe the Athenians did at their symposia, then by what criteria should we define an image of a symposium?" Topper's solution to the differences is "a rejection of the premise that contemporary Athenian life is known to be the subject of (or inspiration for) any image under consideration. . . . One of the goals of this project is to move beyond the mode of thinking that posits myth and contemporary life as the only options for interpreting the sympotic scenes" (2012: 4 and 5). Instead, the subject matter may be a mythic and foundational "sympotic past" (2009; 2012: 5–9).

distinct types of evidence, each with its own stylizations: the world of Athenian literature and the world of Athenian pottery. Vaseworld, as we may call it, has its own set of interpretive conventions, about which we are largely ignorant. This article, therefore, is mainly aporetic. I hope simply to point out that some of our interpretations are much less secure than we would like to think.

PRELIMINARY REMARKS

Before we look at the discrepancies, three problems need to be mentioned briefly. (1) It is sometimes supposed that the erotic scenes on pots were the exclusive property of, or directed at, the Athenian elite. (2) It is also sometimes supposed that, on the contrary, Attic erotic pots were intended primarily or exclusively for export, principally to Etruria. (3) Some pots appear to be more "realistic" than others.

The first notion rests on three interrelated ideas: (a) price, (b) pederasty, and (c) potation.

(a) Whether painted pottery was expensive or not can have considerable implications for what scholars see as the pots' place both at home and abroad. This is a highly contentious subject. For example, Oakely states: "Attic clay vases were luxury items."[11] On the other hand, Vickers and Gill conclude: "It is no longer possible to maintain that the trade in painted pottery was a 'luxury' trade."[12] Others seek to split the difference: "Vases, though luxury goods, commanded modest prices by comparison to those asked for bronzework."[13] One of the greatest experts has asserted all three positions.[14]

(b) There is a persistent idea that "homosexuality"—by which is usually meant the custom of pederasty—was confined to the Athenian upper

---

[11]. Oakely 2003: 510. So, too, Neer 2002: 213: "Clay vessels were the signal luxury good of Athens."

[12]. Vickers 1985: 128: "down-market consumption"; Vickers and Gill 1994: 92. Sparkes 1996: 143: "So pots were cheap in monetary terms, but could of course be valuable to their owners and to families in a way that had nothing to do with money"; Reusser 2002: 119: "so kann die attische Keramik in Etrurien nicht als Luxusware bezeichnet werden." Gill 1994: 103: "Pots, of course, had some value—even if low," with a hard look at the use of the word "luxury"; so, too, Vickers 1986: 162.

[13]. Cartledge 1983: 14. Snodgrass 1980: 127: "almost a luxury trade."

[14]. Boardman 1991: 79: "among the cheapest decorated objects of the day"; 1996: 126: "Decorated vases were cheap on the home market, but not *that* cheap"; 2004: "a semiluxury." Perreault (1986: 171) neatly splits the difference: "les plus 'luxueuses' de ces importations de 'demi-luxe.'"

classes.¹⁵ The reasons for this notion are varied. One, beginning with the Victorians, has been to protect the golden Greeks from charges of immorality.¹⁶ Others have more to do with our own ideologies, identity politics, anxieties, and a discourse of "decadence" than with the facts. However, one important reason is the nature of the data. We may be led by elite written sources into thinking that a desire to have sex with (or on or in) boys was confined to the elite. However, the evidence that pederasty was a custom of Athenian society as a whole is unmistakable.¹⁷

(c) This view is reinforced by a form of circular argument from the visual evidence: decorated pottery was sympotic, the symposium was elite, therefore the pederastic scenes on the pottery were a custom confined to the elite. However, not all decorated pottery was solely for use at the symposium, nor were pots with erotic decoration exclusively sympotic.¹⁸ Nor was decorated symposium ware the exclusive property of the rich.¹⁹ The phrase "the elite symposium" has become fossilized.²⁰

---

15. Ehrenberg 1962: 180; Shapiro 1981a, 1992; Golden 1984: 320; Ober 1989: 250, 253, 257–58, 263; Bremmer 1990; Todd 1990: 166; Thornton 1997: 195–96; Hubbard 1998, 2000, 2006, 2010: 127, 2014: 129, 138; Steiner 2002: 354–55; Yates 2005; even Dover (1964: 36–39; 1989: 149–52) tends to view pederasty as the prerogative of the rich.

16. On the Victorians, see Jenkyns 1980: 280–93, Dowling 1994: 155–68, Goldhill 2011.

17. See the criticisms of Halperin 1990: 91 (but cf. Halperin 1986, 1990: 4), Wohl 2002: 6–7. Parker 2011: 129–31 for a review.

18. By sympotic I mean used in the preparation or consumption of *wine* at symposia (since any vase of any shape might be incidentally present at a symposium). For nonsympotic pottery with erotic scenes: two tripod pyxides: (a) BF. c. 540, Amasis P. (BA 14701; DeVries 2.12); (b) BF, c. 550 (Beazley Archive 7285; DeVries 2.106). The Beazley Archive under the word "erotic" lists 4 alabastra, 1 aryballos, 1 ball, 1 bowl, 1 lebes, 16 lekythoi, 3 plaques, 5 plates, and 5 pyxides.

19. Again, the evidence is spotty but decisive. Fragments of four red-figure kraters were found at the houses of probably prosperous country farmers at Vari and Dema (c. 430 BCE) in Attica. One fragment at Dema shows "symposium with kottabos, and B[acchus], maenad and other figures," with a youth and a bearded man on a kline. See Jones et al. 1962: 88, 100; 1973: 384, 396. Whitley (2001: 361): "Excavations of houses in the Attic countryside have uncovered only meagre finds, mainly of 'black-glazed' pottery. Still, fragments of red-figure kraters were found at both the Vari House (fig. 13.19) and the Dema House, suggesting that symposia of some kind must have taken place there.... The following hierarchy can be proposed. At the bottom rung was the small 'citizen's house' like the one in the Piraeus, with an andron that could only fit three couches and direct evidence only for the use of black-glazed pottery. Above this are the Vari House, the Dema House and the houses found near the Agora, with larger andrones. The quantity of red-figured pottery, particularly kraters, found in and around the Agora strongly suggests that many must have been used in private as well as public symposia. At the top end of the scale is the house like the one at Menander street, where metal vessels must surely have been used." Nor was the Etruscan symposium the exclusive property of the elite: Reusser 2002, 1:119–23, Avramidou 2006: 575.

20. So Węcowski 2014, *The Rise of the Greek Aristocratic Banquet,* where the possibility of a nonaristocratic banquet is defined out of existence (8): "I would provisionally define the symposion as a culture-oriented drinking occasion of Greek élites, as opposed to 'casual and commercial wine

However, not all symposia were elite events, as Socrates pointedly remarked: even ordinary shopkeepers have them.[21] Hobden points to the evidence and rightly complains (2009: 276): "Yet, in analyses of the sympotic phenomenon, these non-aristocratic events are virtually ignored, as if, without aristocratic participation, they were not true symposia."

So, on the one hand, the argument is made that the pots show normal (elite or not) Athenian behavior. On the other, it has been claimed that Attic pots with erotic decoration were exclusively intended for export, catering not to Athenian tastes but to those of the customers. This, too, is a very contentious matter.[22] For now, I think it can be said that there is no

---

consumption' in ancient Greece and communal drinking by non-élites"—I find the use of "commercial" interesting, and wonder what Sappho would have made of it; (10) "No doubt, non-aristocratic groups of citizens did organize drinking parties in Greek cities and elsewhere. But the question is whether they ought to be called 'symposia.' I think they should not, as granting them this title would require ignoring the cultural and literary aspects of the symposia—its defining features"—Plato would now agree (see next note), and what to do with the skolia to Harmodius and Aristogeiton?; (11) "However we define the 'sympotic group,' it must therefore be characterized as a 'leisure class' of the archaic and early classical period. Mechanisms for social advancement by non-aristocrats, who become successful enough to join in this group, represent another issue, because acceptance by the group permanently removed them from the ranks of non-élite citizens." This a fine example of Flew's "No True Scotsman" fallacy.

21. Pl. *Protag.* 347c–e: τοῖς συμποσίοις τοῖς τῶν φαύλων καὶ ἀγοραίων ἀνθρώπων. Obviously, the rich could give fancier symposia than the poor, but that no more means that the custom of drinking with one's friends was confined to the upper class than ancient (or modern) dinner parties are confined to the aristocracy. For early times, our evidence is, again, spotty, and most of it comes from sources that we might label "elite," "aristocratic," or the like (without delving too deeply into what we mean by those terms), Alcaeus, Sappho, Theognis, Xenophanes, etc. Yet, we have clear examples of people in "modest circumstances" having drinks parties, which is all a symposium is. Hesiod is the most obvious (*Works and Days* 744–45):

μηδέ ποτ' οἰνοχόην τιθέμεν κρητῆρος ὕπερθε
πινόντων· ὀλοὴ γὰρ ἐπ' αὐτῷ μοῖρα τέτυκται.

Nor ever put the ladle on the mixing bowl
when people are drinking: a destructive fate has been fixed for that.

This is a symposium, pure and simple. The reason for the superstition is unclear (West 1978: 340). Beltrami (1897) took it to mean that the host must not hint to the guests that the party is over. For the non-elite symposium, see Murray 1983a and 1983b: 198; Pellizer 1990: 181; Stein-Holkeskamp 1992: 43–45; Eder 1998: 130; Fisher 2000; Shapiro 2000b: 318; Wilkins 2000: 202–13; Whitley 2001: 361–63; Pütz 2003: xii, 119, 155; Hammer 2004; Lynch 2007 and 2011: 172–73; Wilkins and Hill 2006: 177–78; Topper 2009: 4–5, 22–23 and 2012: 9; Yatromanolakis 2009; Hobden 2009: 275–77 and 2013: 11–15, 38; Corner 2010, esp. 353–60; Nevett 2010; 62.

22. Erotic content on Attic pots intended to satisfy Etruscan taste: Brommer 1984: 181 (on the basis of four examples); Sutton 1992: 8; Lewis 1997; Lewis 2002: 116–29; Lewis 2003; La Genière 2006, 2009; Lynch 2009, 2011: 175. Lewis (2003: 189–90) has taken this line of argument to its

solid evidence for this view. Attic vases (both black-figure and red-figure) with erotic scenes of various types have been found all over the Mediterranean world, including Attica and Athens itself. Comparison with Chinese import pottery is often made but a better model might be Japanese Ukiyo-e prints ("pictures of the floating world'): though collected in the West and collected for their sexual content, the sex they show is Japanese sex (Lambourne 2005).[23] What needs to be explained is not the number of erotic vases in Etruria, but the much larger number of courting vases, which are

---

conclusion and now claims that nearly all Attic pottery was in fact made for the Etruscans, and specifically that the sexual scenes represent Etruscan orgies and not Athenian symposia. There is little basis for this idea, which confuses survival with cross-section. Most erotic vases are found in Etruscan tombs because most vases are found in Etruscan tombs. For detailed criticisms, see Lissarrague (1987b: 268, "Il ne semble pas que l'on puisse conclure que les vases érotique sont destinés aux Etrusques pornophiles"); Spivey 1991; Miller 1997: 2, 68–71; Stissi 1999; Hastrup 1999; Osborne 2001; Boardman 2001: 55, 226, 236–39; Reusser 2002: 149–50; Lee 2003; Stansbury-O'Donnell 2006: 37–39; Steiner 2007: 234–36; Rasmussen 2008; Dipla and Paleothodoros 2012: 210. Sutton 2009: 77 (on black-figure heterosexual acts): "In the Archaic period, when most of the red-figure scenes were painted, the vast majority with known provenance came from Etruria, raising the prospect of special production for the Etruscan market. From the black-figure scenes it quickly became clear that . . . the theme is widely distributed through Greek and Etruscan lands" and (85): "These vessels found a wide market throughout the Greek and Etruscan world. More stem from Etruria than any other region, but this distribution demonstrates that representations of heterosexual lovemaking in the Archaic period were not produced chiefly for export to Etruria, as the distribution of red-figure had suggested. The theme enjoyed popularity throughout the Greek world, with examples found around the Aegean and at colonies spread from the Crimea to Egypt, Sicily, and south Italy. Athens itself has yielded ten examples, only one from mortuary context." Rasmussen 2013: 678: "Apart from exceptional products such as the Perizoma Group, most of the Athenian imagery is neither tomb- nor Etruria-specific. . . . The idea of an Etruscan hanging around the port of Tarquinia for the latest shipment of pornographic pots from Athens, because these images harmonized with his views of death, seems an unlikely scenario."

23. Mehren, who argues *for* Tyrrhenian and Nikosthenic amphorae "as export ware for Etruria," and Miller, who argues *against*, both hit the nail on the head. Mehren 2001: 50: "Several scholars believe the subjects to be purely Greek, but considering the shape and the potential customers, it would have been strange if the selective iconography was not intended to suit Etruscan taste. Like the Tyrrhenian amphorae, the genre scenes display a selection of motifs common on Attic black-figure in the Archaic period: fighting warriors, athletic competitions, komos, standing and seated persons, and erotic couples." Miller 1997: 2: "The fact that the wares of Attic vase-painters were often exported to the West is less important in this regard than the fact that the vases were produced in Attica." On the "fine line to be drawn here between (i) the simple *selection* of a certain subject matter within the potter's workshop (i.e. customer targeting, so to speak) or later in the process of distribution, which would be nonetheless treated indifferently by the Athenian painter and, on the other hand, (ii) the actual *alteration* of iconographic content in connection with the demands of an external market," see Ulieriu-Rostás 2013: 12–13, who summarizes: "Only a few clear cases of conscious adaptation *ab initio* to the local markets have been identified to date in the Attic output. Most of these regard vase forms, while only two or three sixth-century series of vases show alteration of the iconographic content in response to Etruscan conventions." See also the diagram of production and distribution, p. 15.

concerned with an Athenian custom, said by Athenians to be uniquely Athenian, and unknown to the Etruscans as far as we can tell.[24]

The third point is the most fundamental problem of interpreting Greek vases: What do we mean by "realistic"? This problem is acerbated by the idea (at least as old as Winkelmann) that Greek art was devoted to the "ideal."[25] Himmelmann, in a book titled *Realistische Themen in der griechischen Kunst der archaischen und klassischen Zeit*, offered this as a starting point (1994: 2): "The simplest definition of realism in art is an image that is true to nature." However, even defining as "realistic" any image that breaks no law of physics does not help, for Himmelmann continues, "When one considers early Greek art from this point of view it often turns out that a given work of art is simultaneously realistic and unrealistic."[26] Even Boardman's broad distinction of "Scenes of Reality" and "Scenes of Myth" breaks down at once.[27] In an ordinary workshop scene—for Himmelmann, the very type of realistic presentation—Athena herself and two Nikes offer crowns to everyone except the sole figure of a woman artisan

---

24. Pl. *Symp.* 182b. See below. E.g., the delicate kiss in Paris, Louvre, G278 (BA 204415). We might imagine the Etruscans having a taste for vivid depictions of intercourse, but why should they care about scenes where a man is offering a boy a rabbit? If the Athenians were producing vases for Etruscan tastes, it is odd that we see so few examples of male–male anal intercourse. We may choose to disregard Theopompus's claim that the Etruscans were especially given to boys and enjoyed both active and passive roles (*FGrH* 115 F 204 = Athenaeus 12.517e–18b), but the Athenian strictures on depiction of anal intercourse (see below) seem not to be observed by the Etruscans (so the Tomb of the Bulls and the Tomb of the Chariots, contrasting with the modest youth and bearded man sharing a couch in the symposium scene in the Tomb of the Diver). The preliminary sketch of the right-hand couple shows that the youth being penetrated was originally going to be a woman (his coloring is much lighter, but not lighter than the large figure of Troilus), while the left-side threesome in the Tomb of the Bulls shows that it was originally going to be a foursome, with the man on his knees fellating another man (Bonfante 1996: 162; Giuliano 1969: 11–12, fig. 11; Oleson 1975: 197n72; Wit 1929), so violating another apparent Attic taboo (see below). One might make a case that funerary art is different, but as Oleson noted (ibid.): "Designation of the groups as 'apotropaic' . . . is insufficient." Equally odd, if Attic production was intended to satisfy Etruscan taste in erotica, is the relative lack of such scenes in Etruscan pottery, even though the Etruscans were eager imitators of Corinthian and Attic vases, to which they gave their own particular twist (Spivey 1997: 35–39, 66–72). The Etruscans were not averse to sex on pots, at least ones featuring satyrs and maenads (e.g., Tragliatella oinochoe, c. 600, New York, Metropolitan Museum of Art, Inv. 22.139.83, Painter of Munich 833, c. 530–525; or Vienna, Kunsthistorisches Museum 3577, Eagle Painter, c. 520). In general, see Bonfante 1996, 2013; Rasmussen 2013: 672–74.

25. Hence the title of the important collection by Cohen 2000: *Not the Classical Ideal.*

26. "Die einfachste Definition von Realismus in der Kunst wäre naturgetreue Darstellung. . . . Betrachtet man nämlich frühgriechische Kunst unter diesem Gesichtspunkt, so stellt sich häufig heraus, daß ein bestimmtes Kunstwerk zugleich realistisch und nichtrealistisch ist." Also pp. 7–8.

27. Ferrari 2002: 1; Topper 2012: 2. Lissarrague and Schnapp 1981: 277: "The two halves of the sundered body of the 'Science of Antiquity' were thus permanently apportioned. To the historian of literature, the images of myth; to the archaeologists, daily life, the *realia*."

tucked in the corner.²⁸ On the other hand, Exekias has the Dioscuri come home to the family dog and servant.²⁹ As will be seen, Greek depictions of sexual activity are as highly stylized as any other iconographic tradition and offer a pictorial language of their own.

INTERFEMORAL INTERCOURSE

Our first case is paradigmatic for the rest, for there seems to be a near perfect complementarity between written and painted evidence. Dover sums up the problem that the Greek sexual code of conduct created (1989: 103–4):

> If an honorable *eromenos* [i] does not seek or expect sensual pleasure from contact with an *erastes*, [ii] begrudges any contact until the *erastes* has proved himself worthy of concession, [iii] never permits penetration of any orifice of his body, and [iv] never assimilates himself to women by playing a subordinate role in a position of contact, and if at the same time the *erastes* would like him to break rules (iii) and (iv), observe a certain elasticity in his obedience of rule (ii), and even perhaps bend rule (i) a little on occasion, in what circumstances does a male in fact submit to anal penetration by another male, and how does society regard his submission?

Dover continues:

> There seems little doubt that in Greek eyes the male who breaks the "rules" of legitimate eros detaches himself from the ranks of male citizenry and classifies himself with women and foreigners. . . . It is not only by assimilating himself to a woman in the sexual act that the submissive male rejects his role as a male citizen, but also by deliberately choosing to be the victim of what would be, if the victim were unwilling, hybris.

We might change the question here to: "In these circumstances, what are an honorable *eromenos* and an honorable *erastes* to do?" The answer is, "Something other than 'penetration of any orifice of his body.'" In other words,

---

28. Himmelmann 1994: 10 (and Abt. 6 on p. 12): Vicenza, Banca Intesa 2, Leningrad Painter, ARV 571.73, 1659; BA 206564. See Himmelmann 1994: 7–14, 23–48 on *Banausen*. He quotes (1994: 7) Beazley's summation of the Foundry Painter: "non è un realista nel senso di tanti moderni; è un realista greco" (Beazley 1966: 60).

29. Himmelmann 1994: 13: Vatican, Museo Gregoriano Etrusco 16757, ABV 672.3, 145.13, 686, Para 60, Add 40, BA 310395.

the Athenians came up with their own solution to a perennial problem in sexual relations: how to have sex (orgasm) that does not quite count as "sex" (the real thing). Archilochus, the seducer, said (196a.13–15): "There are many delights of the goddess / for young men / apart from the divine thing."[30] The lexicographer Hesychius (drawing on some lost ancient commentary) laboriously explains (in case you didn't get it): "apart from the divine thing: other than intercourse." For girls, this is frottage, rubbing the penis on the pubic mound but not actually penetrating.[31] For boys, it takes the form of interfemoral intercourse:

> The *erastes* and *eromenos* stand facing one another; the *erastes* grasps the *eromenos* round the torso, bows his head on to or even below the shoulder of the *eromenos,* bends his knees and thrusts his penis between the *eromenos*'s thighs just below the scrotum.[32]

The analogy of young men and women dating in the 1950s and before can help us understand the contradictions in pederastic courtship, contradictions of which the Athenians themselves were fully aware (Pl. *Symp.* 182a–85c).[33] So, just as a good girl in the 1950s might allow some "heavy petting" without losing her reputation but would not "go all the way," so a

---

30. τ]έρψιές εἰσι θεῆς / πολλαὶ νέοισιν ἀνδ[ράσιν / παρὲξ τὸ θεῖον χρῆμα. So Hsch. παρὲξ τὸ θεῖον χρῆμα· ἔξω τῆς μίξεως: Degani 1975; Burnett 1983: 88 (n. on line 15). Not marriage, despite Gentili's desperate defense (1988: 185n34).

31. The situation in Archilochus has been misunderstood. She has asked him to hold off from sex completely (1: πάμπαν ἀποσχόμενος). If he can't, she offers a substitute who is willing. He proposes a compromise, something less than intercourse (15: παρὲξ τὸ θεῖον χρῆμα). He would prefer to get inside her vagina, past the labia (21: πυλέων), but will instead go only as far as the grassy garden (σχήσω γὰρ ἐς ποη[φόρους κ]ήπους), i.e., her pubis. At the end: "And touching her whole beautiful body, / I shot my [white? hot?] force, / just touching her blonde [hair]" (ἅπαν τ]ε σῶμα καλὸν ἀμφαφώμενος / λευκ]ὸν ἀφῆκα μένος / ξανθῆς ἐπιψαύ[ων τριχός). He is not proposing *coitus interruptus* (rightly Degani 1974: 119, 121; Marcovitch 1975; Van Sickle 1975a: 14, 1975b: 152n45; Burnett 1983: 88, 89, 95–96) nor interfemoral intercourse (since 1. he's laying her down and 2. plans to ejaculate on, not under, her pubis) but what in American high schools used to be known as a "dry-hump."

32. Dover 1989: 98; Dover termed it "intercrural," but interfemoral is more accurate; German *Schenkelverkehr.*

33. Dover 1964: 31: "We have only to substitute 'girl' for 'boy' in Pausanias's speech, changing the gender of pronouns and adjectives where appropriate, and we have a recognisable description of the operation of the notorious 'double standard' in a predominantly heterosexual society with a high degree of female emancipation"; Dover cited a newspaper poll of the day (*The Observer,* May 5, 1963, p. 30) and Mead 1950: 290. See also Dover 1973: 67, 1974: 215; 1989: 88–91. Cohen (1987: 19 = 1991: 197) rightly compares Laclos's *Les liaisons dangereuses* and the game of gallant courtship.

good *eromenos* could allow interfemoral intercourse, but not penetration.³⁴ Cohen sums up:

> In Athens an ideal solution was offered to the dilemma of the zero-sum game of honour, an ideal indicated by the descriptions of chaste courtship in the *Phaedrus, Symposium* and other texts. According to this ideal, an equilibrium was reached whereby the *erastes* and *eromenos* could both maintain their honour. The *erastes* was granted "favours" by his *eromenos*, but the *eromenos* stopped short of granting (or appearing to grant) favours which would dishonour him (that is, as Dover and Foucault argue, the *eromenos* only allowed intercrural intercourse and never anal penetration).³⁵

There seems to be considerable confusion on this point, some of it, I fear, self-generated. Cantarella thinks Dover naïve for assuming that Greeks did not bugger their beloved boys.³⁶ Davidson accuses (not too strong a word) Dover of "sodomania" for thinking that they did.³⁷ Lear seems doubtful that interfemoral intercourse was an actual practice (2014: 107):

> Vase painting is often more explicit about sex than textual sources, and it is tempting to treat it as direct evidence for sexual practices. For example,

---

34. Strato *AP* 12.22 speaks euphemistically but unmistakably of "getting inside" (τὸ λαβεῖν ἔνδον). Similar attitudes are easily found: oral sex is widely viewed as not *real* sex by American teenagers and at least one former president.

35. Here again, it is interesting to see the fusion of Foucault with Dover. In fact, Foucault (1985, 1986), reflecting the delicacy of his sources, never spells out exactly what acts are alluded to, and never uses "intercrural" or "interfemoral." Cf. Cohen 1991: 197–98.

36. Cantarella 1992: 24–26: "It has recently been maintained that Athenian sexual morality did not envisage sodomy in the pederastic relationship. According to the findings of Sir Kenneth Dover, anal intercourse (which never appears when intercourse between adults and *paides* is depicted on vases) seems to be reserved for relations between adults . . . Does this finding necessarily mean that anal intercourse was socially prohibited in the case of *paides*? Might one not assume that the iconography represented images better suited to highlighting the affective aspect of the pederastic relationship, almost as if to point out and emphasise the importance and nobility of this relationship, contrasting it with the purely physical one which linked two adult lovers? . . . In the light of these pieces of evidence [treated below], so diverse and far from each other in time and yet so consistent, how could it be thought that the pederastic relationship did not envisage (and should not envisage) anal penetration of the *pais*?" What precisely is meant by "envisage" is unclear.

Dover said nothing of the sort (1989: 99–101: "We may well suspect a divergence between homosexual copulation in vase-paintings and what an erastes actually hoped to achieve"). What he did say was (1989: vii): "I know of no topic in classical studies on which a scholar's normal ability to perceive differences and draw inferences is so easily impaired; and none on which a writer is so likely to be thought to have said what he has not said or to be charged with omitting to say something which he has said several times."

37. Davidson 2001, esp. 7–20; 2007: 99–134.

many scholars have considered intercrural scenes as proof that the Greeks actually practiced intercrural intercourse. Vase painting is, however, not documentary photography, but an artistic genre; through a language of repeated elements, it presents a certain vision or version of practices, just as literary genres do. In general, it presents a highly idealized vision of elite males and their activities. In this light, it is best to ask why vase painters preferred to represent intercrural rather than anal intercourse. The answer is probably that the former allowed them to portray the erōmenos as upright and uninvolved in the sex act: this corresponds to Greek ideals.

This, however, is almost exactly what Dover said and which has been ignored (1989: 101):

> An interesting contrast between heterosexual intercourse and the intercrural activity ascribed to erastes and eromenos by the vase-painters suggests itself. The woman is almost invariably in a "subordinate" position, the man "dominant"; the woman bent over or lying back or supported, the man upright or on top. In intercrural copulation, on the other hand, the eromenos stands bolt upright, and it is the erastes who bows his head and shoulders.

I think we can strike a middle ground between "This is a picture of what they actually did" and "This is coverup for what they really did." We might again evoke the 1950s and '60s. Married couples in plays and movies were almost always shown in twin beds.[38] We would be wrong to assume that no married couples slept in a single bed. We would be equally wrong to assume that no married couples slept in twin beds and that twin beds were an idealized piece of elite funiture or something invented to cover up the coarser reality.

Some of the thinking is muddled because people are not talking about the same things. We need to distinguish three levels: (1) What the Greeks did. (2) What the Greeks could talk about. (3) What the Greeks could not talk about, that is, things that would get them talked about.

(1) We have to give up on the first. We can never know what the Greeks actually did in the privacy of their own rooms. (We cannot know what our friends and contemporaries are doing, even in this age of surveys and surveillance). (2) In the fifties, good girls could do a lot, depending on

---

38. Both the Hollywood Hays Code and the British Board of Film Censors forbade men and women in bed together.

their families, their upbringing, their standards, and the depth of the relationship. And if a couple went a bit further, even if some suspected, the consequences might not be bad, provided no one talked about it.[39] So in Athens, good boys could grant their lovers certain "favors." If a boy granted more than this in private, we will never know.[40] (3) But we can see the power of what could and could not be spoken in a number of little incidents. In a famous anecdote, the tyrant Periander openly asked his *eromenos*, "Aren't you pregnant yet?" What had been private penetration became public shame, and the boy reasserted his honor by killing his betrayer.[41] In *AP* 12.179, Strato cleverly promises not to boast and then boasts:

> I swore to you, Zeus, that never not even to myself
>   would I say out loud what Theudis said I could have (*labein*).
> But my disobedient soul rejoicing has flown up
>   in the air and cannot contain the good.
> No, I will say it, please forgive me: He gave in! (*pepeisthai*)
>   Father Zeus, what pleasure (*kharis*) is there in good luck that no one
>   knows?[42]

Plato *Symposium* 183c7–d2 and *Phaedrus* 231e–32a, 234a show how powerful gossip was as a control on public or publicly known behavior.

Socrates famously exhibited superhuman self-control when it came to boys, even the irresistible Alcibiades (Pl. *Symp.* 217a–22b). We would be wrong to smirk and think we know that no one really behaved that nicely.[43] Did the Greeks despise boys that yielded? Some presumably did not,

---

39. See John Updike, "Village Sex II," in *Villages: A Novel* (2004) for a depressing picture of sex (or not) in the fifties.

40. Halperin 1997: 47; 2002: 148: "The protocols of Athenian paederasty were carefully designed and stylized so as to spare the boy the effeminizing humiliation of bodily penetration and thereby to prevent his future status as an adult man from being compromised in advance. Respectable erotic relations between men and boys preserved the social fiction that the man fucked the boy only between the legs, never in the ass—or, God forbid, in the mouth. It was not a question of what people actually did in bed (the boy was conventionally assumed, I suppose, to be anally receptive to his older lover, although De Vries has plausibly suggested to me that some high-minded lovers may not in fact have required their boyfriends to go through with the act of anal sex); rather, it was a question of how they behaved and talked when they were out of bed." See Ludwig 2002: 50–52, 229–34 for clear statements.

41. Plutarch (*Amatorius* 768F): Περίανδρος δ' ὁ Ἀμβρακιωτῶν τύραννος ἠρώτα τὸν ἐρώμενον εἰ μήπω κυεῖ, κἀκεῖνος παροξυνθεὶς ἀπέκτεινεν αὐτόν.

42. Maxwell-Stuart 1972: 219 for an appreciative reading.

43. Dover 1989: 156n7, citing Lucian (*Philosophies for Sale* 15). So, too, Amphis 15 KA: "Say what? Do you expect me to believe *this*, that there's a lover, who's in love with a ripe boy, and is a lover of his *character*, and ignores his looks? How dumb do you think I am? I don't believe it, any

but others clearly did and said so.[44] Periander had contempt for his *eromenos* because he put out. Even Pausanias, that romantic lover, says boys should not be caught too quickly (*Symp.* 184a5–6). Aeschines advises the jury (1.195): "Those who are hunters of young men who are easily taken, tell them to turn to foreigners and resident aliens. That way they won't be deprived of their choice, but won't harm you." Athenian boys, it is clear, should play hard to get. Just as the hunter passes by the wounded hare or doe,

> So is my desire: it knows how to pursue what flees,
>   but what lies in the middle of road, it flies by.
> (Callimachus *AP* 12.102).

Easy boys, says Strato, are no challenge (*AP* 12.200):

> I hate kisses that are hard to get and battling
>   words and strong opposition with the hand.
> And yet, someone who wants it straightaway when he's in my arms
>   and offers it wholesale, I don't want him at all;
> rather, one who's in between the two, the kind who knows
>   how not to offer and to offer.

So here we have our first disjunction between written and visual evidence. The literary sources have some praise for boys' thighs, but surprisingly little (in comparison to lips or eyes, that is). The first three all come from a single passage in Athenaeus (13.602c) on pederasty. So, Solon 25:

> ἔσθ' ἥβης ἐρατοῖσιν ἐπ' ἄνθεσι παιδοφιλήσῃ,
> μηρῶν ἱμείρων καὶ γλυκεροῦ στόματος.

> while one loves a boy in the desirable flowers of youth desiring thighs and sweet mouth.[45]

Aeschylus, *Myrmidons,* fr. 135 and 136 Radt, (over the dead body of Patroclus):

---

more than I believe that a poor man who keeps bugging the rich, isn't out to get something." Cf. Strato *AP* 12.228 (quoted below).

44. Dover 1989: 140, as the vocabulary shows: "a liking for dalliance with a handsome adolescent boy did nothing to diminish the seducer's contempt for the seduced."

45. Also in Plutarch *Amatorius* 751b; Apuleius *Apology* 9, showing its popularity.

σέβας δὲ μηρῶν ἁγνὸν οὐκ ἐπῃδέσω,
ὦ δυσχάριστε τῶν πυκνῶν φιλημάτων

"You showed no respect to the holy glory of thighs giving a sad return for all my kisses."[46]

μηρῶν τε τῶν σῶν εὐσεβὴς ὁμιλία

"the reverent intercourse with your thighs."[47]

Sophocles, *Colchian Women*, fr. 345 Radt (Zeus and Ganymede):

μηροῖς ὑπαίθων τὴν Διὸς τυραννίδα.

"With your thighs setting aflame the royal power of Zeus."

A sympotic poem of Anacreon (407) recalls Ben Jonson's "Song. To Celia":

ἀλλὰ πρόπινε
ῥαδινοὺς ὦ φίλε μηρούς

"But pledge me, my dear, your slim thighs."[48]

And his imitators in the Anacreonta 17.30–37 paint a portrait of Bathyllos, the perfect boy:

μεταμάζιον δὲ ποίει   30
διδύμας τε χεῖρας Ἑρμοῦ,
Πολυδεύκεος δὲ μηρούς,
Διονυσίην δὲ νηδύν·
ἁπαλῶν δ' ὕπερθε μηρῶν,
μαλερὸν τὸ πῦρ ἐχόντων,   35
ἀφελῆ ποίησον αἰδῶ
Παφίην θέλουσαν ἤδη.

---

46. Also Plutarch *Erotikos Amatorius* 751c; *How to Tell a Friend from a Flatterer*, 61a.
47. From Ps.-Lucian *Amores* 54.14. The last word is corrupt.
48. The adjective "slim, tapering" seems out of tune with the depictions of boys on vases which tend to show them with rather bulky thighs. Dover 1989: 70.

Make his chest and twins hands those of Hermes; his thighs, of Polydeuces, and his stomach of Dionysus. But above his tender thighs, which hold raging fire, make a simple modesty already wanting the Paphian goddess.[49]

Dioscorides (*AP* 12.37) praises Sosarchus of Amphipolis whose thighs are more honeyed than Ganymedes'. Theomnestus, the champion of pederasty in Pseudo-Lucian's *Amores* (53), describes a "ladder of pleasure": sight, touch, kiss, embrace, fondling; then:

when Eros has gained such power, it ignites a warmer business and after making its overture from the thighs, as the comic poet said, strikes the thing itself.[50]

Boys' thighs are also the focus of attention in a series of poems stretching from Simonides to Hellenistic and later poets who work variations on the theme of warning beautiful but hard-hearted boys that their power and perfection will soon be over when their youthful thighs begin to sprout adult hairs.[51]

Though not a great number of passages, these make clear that a boy's smooth thighs were an erogenous zone to adult males.[52] And yet there is, to the best of my knowledge, no direct mention much less description of

---

49. The word αἰδώς "modesty" in the concrete sense of τὰ αἰδοῖα "the pudenda" is as old as Homer (*Il.* 2.262). Here, we should notice that the *erastes* is hoping for a sexual response from the *eromenos*, specifically his penis but that hoped-for response is colored by the choice of noun "his modesty." Plautus's Alcumena (*Amph.* 840) similarly prays for *pudicitiam et pudorem et sedatum cupidinem* ("modesty and respect and a *calm* desire"). DeVries 1997 overstated both the idea that *eromenoi* were expected to feel nothing (hence the tendentious "frigid" in his title) and the evidence for a specifically sexual response.

50. τοσαύτης τυχὼν ἐξουσίας ὁ ἔρως θερμοτέρου τινὸς ἅπτεται πράγματος· εἶτ' ἀπὸ μηρῶν προοιμιασάμενος κατὰ τὸν κωμικὸν αὐτὸ ἐπάταξεν. The comic poet is unknown. Adesp. 465 KA. Here, thighs are only a way station to the goal of anal intercourse.

51. Simonides elegy 21 (West) interestingly written from the boy's perspective; see West 1993: 11–12; Bartol 1999 for a different reading. Later variants in rough chronological order: *AP* 12.31 (Phanias 1), *AP* 9.326 (Automedon 10), *AP* 12.36 (Asclepiades of Adramyttium); cf. *AP* 12.176 (Strato), [Lucian] *Amores* 26. Tarán 1985. However, the sign that a boy's time is over is the sprouting of hairs, and not just on the thighs.

52. Dover 1989: 70. More indirect are: Achilles Tatius's *Leucippe and Cleitophon* 8.9.3, where the good Nikostratos intimates in a series of double entendres that the evil Thersander, as a youth had "homerized a lot" (ὁμηρίζων μὲν τὰ πολλά, which Goldhill [1995: 100] cleverly translates as "'thigh to thigh research"). Probably the same type of innuendo at Strato, *AP* 12.247 (on Meriones). The pun on Homer at *AP* 11.218 (Crates) refers to cunnilingus: Richlin 1992: 49. One might also cite *AP* 12.161 (Asclepiades 20) where, despite a damaged text, Dorkion ("Little Fawn"), who dresses like a boy to entice the ephebes, shows a little thigh.

interfemoral intercourse.[53] In many ways, this is not surprising. The Greek sources, apart from comedy, are properly reticent about what exactly people are doing with and to each other and prefer euphemism and indirectness, referring rather to "favors." The main verb is χαρίζω (LSJ I.3. "in erotic sense, grant favours to a man"). Such favors included kisses and embraces, but a scholiast to Pindar has to spell it out: "'Grant favors' properly means 'have intercourse.'"[54]

The verb διαμηρίζω, often taken as meaning "I get a thigh job," in fact clearly means "part the thighs," as LSJ rightly (if in decent obscurity) defined it: "*femora diducere, inire,*" that is, "spread the legs"—the exact opposite of what is required for interfemoral intercourse[55]—and is used of

---

53. Davidson (2001: 26; also 2007: 478) refers to *Knights* 424, 484 as "one of the rare textual references to intercrural sex"; both are explicitly about anal penetration.

54. Scholia to *Pythian* 2.78a: χαρίζεσθαι γὰρ κυρίως λέγεται τὸ συνουσιάζειν. Examples: Plato *Phaedrus* 227c, 230e–34c (the speech of Lysias), *Symposium* 182a, 182a–c, 183d, 184ab, 184de, 185ab, 217a, 218d, *Euthd.* 282b. Henderson 1991: 160. Dover 1989: 44, 48, 53–54, 83 on the general indirectness of the texts. It is this politeness of the Greek and Dover's clear philological explanations of exactly what was at stake (e.g., 1989: 91) that seem to drive Davidson mad (2001; 2007: 101–21, 478–79). Thornton, confronting the euphemisms of the texts, turns splenetic (1997: 205–6): "Having surveyed these encomia of 'just' or 'chaste' eros, the modern reader no doubt wonders exactly what these pederastic couples were doing under their cloaks. Were the 150 couples of the Theban Sacred Band sodomizing one another on the eve of Chaeronea? Was Solon celebrating buggery in his poetry?" He is oddly at odds with himself. On the same page he writes of Pausanias's speech in *Symposium* (the most idealized of all portrayals of pederasty): "Is 'noble way' to be understood as 'without physical gratification'? It seems unlikely, since the verb Pausanias uses over and over—'gratify' (*charizesthai*)—clearly is a euphemism for sex. . . . Pausanias has found a way to valorize an otherwise despised relationship by sneaking it into the accepted pederastic ideal. No wonder those rubes in Aristophanes figured pederasty was a highfalutin pretense for buggery." On the next page he maintains that "in the idealized pederasty of the literary remains . . . physical consummation is taboo" (206).

55. Dover 1989: 98: "The original specific word for this type of copulation was almost certainly *diamērizein,* i.e. 'do . . . between the thighs (*mēroi*).'" Lear (2008: 108) also takes *diamērizō* as interfemoral male + male. This idea was examined long ago by Vlastos (1987: 96n56): "There is no textual evidence for the supposition (*GH,* p. 98) that the word used here, διαμηρίζειν, was 'almost certainly' the original term for intercrural copulation or that it ever meant anything but genital intercourse with females or anal with males, as it uncontroversially does in Zeno Stoicus (H. von Arnim, *SVF* 250 and 251, ap. Sextus Empiricus, *Hypotyp.* 3.245, *Adv. Math.* 11.190). Its three earliest literary occurrences are in the *Birds*. In [1254] it refers unambiguously to vaginal copulation, as Dover recognizes. I submit that it must refer likewise to the usual type of intercourse in the other two occurrences as well: Euelpides, declaring, ἐγὼ διαμηρίζοιμ᾽ ἂν αὐτὴν ἡδέως (699), could hardly be lusting after *ersatz* gratification. And if it were agreed that the word is used to signify phallic penetration in 699 and then again in [1254], as it is by Zeno in the Stoic fragments cited above, we would have no good reason for supposing that in 706 Aristophanes has shifted to a different sense which is never unambiguously attested in a single surviving Greek text and is not required by its immediate context: no reason is discernible in the text why the birds' vaunted power to fulfil men's longings should accord to their favourites something less than the usual thing." The often-repeated word *διαμήριον (as if a technical term for "thigh job"; e.g., Davidson 2007: 426, 478;

both male and female objects, a fact on which even Hesychius remarks.[56] It may have began life as a comic coinage on the innocent δια-μερ-ίζω, "divide, distribute." Women's thighs are praised as well, but we never read about or see depicted interfemoral sex with women.[57] This is part of Pausanias's argument in the *Symposium* (181c) that sex with women always involves hybris, that is, violation of bodily boundaries.[58]

As if to fill the gap left by the literary evidence, where we do find interfemoral intercourse between men and youths is the world of vases (10, fig. 1.1a and 1.1b).[59] But these scenes need to be put in perspective. First, erotic scenes even broadly defined are in fact rather rare compared to the total body of Attic painted pottery. (Our focus on them sometimes makes it seem as if Attic figural pottery had no other subject.) Second, even within the world of courting and symposium, nudity and nature, scenes with explicit sex acts are relatively uncommon. "Scenes of consummation are so rare in vase-painting as to be inherently exceptional."[60] Beazley in a short but important article divided man–boy scenes into three classes that have formed the framework for all subsequent discussion, and which need some re-examination. In Type α:

Lear 2008: 108, originating from Dover 1989: 98) does not exist and morphologically could not mean "a between-the-thigh-ing." It is supposedly attested on a lost vase (BA 306425, ABV 664, 665, Para 317) known only from an imperfect engraving after a sketch: Stackelberg 1837: 6–7, pl. XII.3; Lear. A detailed treatment in Parker (forthcoming).

56. Hsch. δ.1162: διαμηρίσαι· τοῦτο καὶ ἐπὶ παίδων ἀρρένων καὶ θηλείων ἔλεγον. E.g. Ar. *Birds* 1254–56:

ἀνατείνας τὼ σκέλει διαμηριῶ
τὴν Ἶριν αὐτήν, ὥστε θαυμάζειν ὅπως
οὕτω γέρων ὢν στύομαι τριέμβολον

After I've pulled your legs apart, I'll even get between your thighs, Iris, and you'll be amazed at how an old man can still get a hard-on like three battering rams.

57. Even though it might be thought an obvious (if unreliable) form of birth control. See Dover 1989: 99; Bremer 1987, 39, 47–51. For praise of women's thighs, see, e.g., Alcaeus 45, Ibycus 339, Anacreon 439, Arist. *Lys.* 552, Rufinus AP 5.36, [Lucian] *Amores* 14–15 (the famous story about the stain on the thigh of the Cnidian Aphrodite, where, too, the thigh is a substitute for something preferable).

58. Hsch. δ.1162.

59. Thornton objects (1997: 205): "A more widely accepted view is that the pederastic lover had 'intercrural' intercourse with his beloved—he rubbed his penis between the boy's thighs while both were standing. Postures of lovers on vase-paintings seem to support this idea, as do the few references to thighs in pederastic poetry. . . . Such intercourse presumably avoided the shame of penetration and thus avoided the charge of 'outrage' while allowing the older active partner to achieve orgasm. This evidence, however, is slight and depends on reading into the fragments their lost context." A good point, but reading into fragments their lost context is precisely what classicists are supposed to do.

60. Lear 2008: 106. So too Kilmer (1993: 15): "Clear instances of male homosexual copulation are rare, as are scenes of imminent homosexual copulation."

α) "a man stands to right with bent knees, chin slightly raised, his left forearm raised with the hand touching the chin of a boy who stands facing him, and his right arm extended downwards towards the boy's middle . . . This is a popular scene in Attic black-figure vase-painting; and the chief group recurs, with comparatively slight variations, on many vases. The bent knees of the wooer, and the 'up and down' position, as I shall call it, of his arms, are regular. The boy stands still, and not infrequently grasps one of the man's arms, usually the raised one." (1947/1989: 4)

β) "There are black-figured pictures of a man presenting a cock to a boy, and a good many of a boy holding the cock which he has been given by the man. In most of them it is made plain that the wooer hopes for a prompt recompense. The groups vary, but many of them closely resemble those of our type α" (1947/1989: 14). Beazley counted only scenes where a rooster is being presented but all subsequent scholars expanded the type to include any kind of "love token" (a concept we will be questioning below).

γ) "The moment depicted is later than in Types α and β, and the two figures are interlocked. Type γ is stable: there is little variation from one picture to another" (1947/1989: 19). All of the vases that Beazley listed are of interfemoral intercourse (not anal).

So we have twenty-seven black-figure vases clearly featuring interfemoral sex.⁶¹ These include five based on DeVries's detailed descriptions (25, 29, 32, 33, 35).⁶² Six others are damaged or fragmentary at the crucial part

---

61. For interfemoral intercourse, Dover listed only six in black-figure: (1) B114*, (2) B130, (3) B250*, (4) B482, (5) B486*, (6) B534. See the Catalog. This list can be expanded using the catalogs of DeVries (in Lear 2008: 194–233), Hupperts (2000, 1: 385–446), and the Beazley Archive. See the Catalog.

Other notices present four difficulties: (1) Some scholars have adopted Beazley's γ class, but used it to indicate any sort of sexual contact; so, for example, Hupperts's number Z200, listed as γ, shows male–male anal intercourse. (2) This combines with the fact that in some cases both DeVries's and Hupperts's lists are simply passing on information; for example, DeVries no. 3.42 repeats Beazley's typo of Villa Giulia 1932 for 1392, as do Dover and Hupperts. Thus in the absence of explicit description or a photograph it is not always possible to determine exactly what activity is going on. (3) It is possible to confirm some of these items on the Beazley Archive, but the descriptors of COURTING and EROTIC are used in no precise manner. (4) Older descriptions can be as unhelpfully euphemistic. So Von Bothmer 1951: 56: "A and B, man embracing boy." This is BA 330691, ABV 519.10, Para 256, labeled "man courting boy," but there is no available image to see how far the embracing had got.

62. DeVries's list uses c' (Beazley's γ) consistently to mark interfemoral intercourse; cases of anal intercourse are noted separately; and Lear's edition of the list gives a precise definition: "scenes which, as Beazley says, are 'later' in the courtship, in which the lovers have a kind of intercourse, with the *erastes*' penis between the *eromenos*' thighs." DeVries's notes (or other descrip-

FIGURE 1.1A. Cat. 10. London, British Museum, 1865.1118.39. Painter of Berlin 1686, c. 550–540. (l) Bearded man with youth holding rooster; (m) Interfemoral intercourse, bearded man dancing; (r) Youth touching chin of bearded man holding rooster. © Trustees of the British Museum.

FIGURE 1.1B. Cat. 10. London, British Museum, 1865.1118.39. (l) Bearded man touches chin of youth carrying deer. (m) Interfemoral intercourse, dancing bearded man; (r) Youth touches chin of bearded man carrying rooster; hanging dead hare and fox.

(often the bottom of the cup and so more liable to damage) but are unmistakable and show the two figures in the same stance ([2], [6], [7], [8], [36], [37]); a seventh ([28]) is heavily abraded, but "outside, the upper part of the couple is preserved" (Beazley 1947/1989: 21 y 14), while an eighth ([38]) preserves only the heads, but the composition makes the subject certain.[63] Three other cases we might consider "imminent," that is, with the *erastes* figure in the posture for interfemoral intercourse but the penis not shown between the boy's thighs ([20], [21], [27]).

There is also an interesting vase from the Shelby White and Leon Levy Collection (**A**).[64] The kalpis is unprovenanced and unattributed, having "appeared suddenly on the Swiss art market."[65] The composition is curious. So Shapiro in the first publication (2000a:18):

> Two kinds of intercourse are rather pointedly juxtaposed. At the right, a bearded *erastês* is engaged in intercrural intercourse with a stationary *erômenos* who neither resists nor willingly acquiesces. At the left, a boy bends over to be penetrated anally by a much bigger, more muscular youth. This is the only vase known to me on which anal intercourse forms part of a courting scene rather than a *kômos*.[66] The unexpectedness of the act is evident. It has certainly drawn the attention of a youth at the center of the scene, who brought a hare as a love gift, but now finds himself suddenly without a partner. Perhaps the object of his affection is the very boy who has been abruptly overpowered by a much stronger youth. The manner in which the boy braces himself against the fictive wall of the picture panel may be paralleled on many contemporary red-figure scenes of copulating heterosexual couples (e.g. Dierichs 1993: 74, fig. 131)[67] but is unique in this context. The bearded/beardless distinction may once again offer a clue to interpretation. While the

---

tions) are sufficiently detailed to show autopsy, and these I have marked "*non vidi.*" A sixth case, DeVries 3.45, seems to be "imminent," but the description is not clear enough to be included in the catalog. Both DeVries and Schauenburg (1965: 850n1) give the number as Athens 19297 but I have not been able to trace this on the Beazley Archive or elsewhere.

63. A ninth kylix is likely, but too little (except for feet) remains to be sure: Rome, Villa Giulia, 9872 (BA 9025438, Hupperts z253).

64. N. B. the picture has been printed reversed, and it is clear from the descriptions (bearded man to right or left) that everyone is working from the same photograph.

65. Golden 1984: 315n32. *Exposition Marie Laforet, S. A. Genève, 12 Juin 1980; vente publique*, no. 17; Shapiro 2000: 18–19; Sutton 2000: 187; Lear 2008: 116–17, fig. 3.8.

66. So too Sutton (2000: 186–87): "Indeed, only one preserved Attic vase—the kalpis in the Shelby White and Leon Levy collection (Fig. 7.2)— presents male–male anal intercourse in the idealized context of courting."

67. Oxford, Ashmolean 1967.305. BA 204435, ARV 408.37, Para 371, Add 232.

one bearded man in the scene demonstrates the "proper" means of consummating his desire, the less experienced and more impetuous youth violates the behavioral norm.

The beardless figure in the middle is very odd. He seems to have been bunged in from a different vase. No one knows what to make of him; indeed he seems not to know what to do with himself. Scholars are uncertain if he is intended to represent a youth who has received a gift or a hopeful *erastes* offering a gift. Sutton (2000: 186–87) calls him "a central *erastes* holding a hare by the ears"; Lear (2008: 116) labels it "a scene of mixed courtship iconographies" and the central figure a "youth"; so too Hubbard (2003b): "The youth in the center has brought a hare as a gift, but has no one left to give it to." The central youth's body and left arm holding the hare are oriented to the right, while his head is turned around to the left looking over (not at) the heads of the interfemoral couple. His right arm is bent at the elbow to fill in the triangular space. The bearded *erastes* engaged in interfemoral intercourse appears to be standing on tiptoe and on top of the youth's feet (normally, of course, the *erastes*' feet when they overlap with the *eromenos*'s feet do so on the outside). I can find no good parallels to these oddities of composition.

Some of the scenes of interfemoral intercourse seem to be given a naturalistic setting in a gymnasium.[68] And the gymnasium was a favorite place to meet and see beautiful boys.[69] Yet, of course, we do not imagine that the gymnasia were filled with couples having interfemoral intercourse.[70] Quite the opposite in fact.[71] However, we have to be more cautious about assigning a precise setting based on what Lear calls "props" (2008: 26–29). For example, a skyphos by Amasis (53) seems to show all the clues—arybaloi and wreaths hanging from the walls—but in the middle of each side there stand two naked women both holding wreaths, one of whom

---

68. Black-figure seems to provide fewer visual clues about setting: 4 (arybolos). Red-figure: 43, 44; "imminent," marked with an arybolos: 42; "imminent," marked with a net bag: 45. See Bérard and Durand 1989: 31–34 for the gymnasium setting.

69. E.g., Ar. *Peace* 762–63, *Clouds* 972–78; Pl. *Chrm.* 154a–c, *Euthd.* 273a–74c, *Lysis* 206e, *Symp.* 255b, *Laws* 636ab (disapprovingly); Aesch, *In Tim.* 10 (supposed laws of Solon); Phaenas fr. 16 ap. Parthenius Ἐρωτικὰ παθήματα 7; Plut. *Dem.* 24, *Erotikos* 751f–52a; *AP* 12.34, 12.192, 12.222; Ath. 13.602d; Dover 1989: 54–55.

70. Though Alcibiades (Pl. *Symp.* 217 BCE) implies that getting off away from others was not an impossibility.

71. [Theog.] 2.1335–36: gym, then home for sex; Aiskhines *In Tim.* 135, 138: he ought to be ashamed of making himself a nuisance (ὀχληρός) in the gymnasium; cf. Pl. *Lysis* 207b. One might cite the much later (mid second century BCE) Gymnasium Law from Beroia in Macedonia: *SEG* 27.261: Gauthier and Hatzopoulos 1993.

is being presented with a hen by a naked bearded man. Despite this picture, women, even naked hetairai, could not be found in the gymnasium (Lear and Cantarella 2008: 129). It can also be unclear how far a scene is intended to stretch. So on 4: on either side of the couple one youth holds an arybolos, another a lyre, but as we read around the continuous band we come to two naked dancing male figures and a clothed woman. Wreaths, therefore, do not unequivocally indicate athletic victory, nor do aryboloi, nor strigils, and so forth. We find the same "gym kit" (bag, sponge, strigil) on a kylix by Douris (**B**), where a man is entering a woman from behind (the famous ἔχε ἥσυχος "Keep still"). In another quasi-realistic setting the couple are surrounded by two cloaked hunters with spears and dogs; the *erastes* is engaged in interfemoral intercourse and yet has managed to hold onto his shaft (**14**).

In virtually every instance of interfemoral intercourse in black-figure the copulating couple is shown with or flanked by other men, who are frequently shown dancing.[72] There are two exceptions where the lovers are flanked by animals ([**8**], **11**). The other exceptions, where we can be sure, are the White and Levy kalpis, where two copulating male couples flank the central figure with his hare, and an "orgy" where one bearded man–youth couple engaged in interfemoral sex stands on the left of four man–woman couples in a variety of sexual positions (**26**, fig. 1.2). Frontisi-Ducroux takes such figures as voyeurs within the fiction of the frame and as a means of incorporating or directing the outside viewer's vision (1996: 90):

> Ever since black-figure painting, erotic scenes may be framed by static observers whose attentive gaze extends the gaze of the individual to whom the image is addressed while indicating the specular quality of courtship and of amorous revels.

However, what is interesting is precisely the framing figures' *lack* of engagement. The bodies of flanking figures are oriented towards or away from the couple; their heads may or may not be facing the same way as their bodies. The postures are rather widely various.[73] There is no clear eye

---

72. Lear 2008: 31–32: "Framing figures are a common motif in vase-painting, particularly in black-figure, and their relationship to the scene is often, as here, ambiguous." Lear raises the possibility that they might be competitors for the youth or merely symbols of the "exciting nature of the central action" or both, but not the possibility that they might be neither, but simple formal elements. See Kaeser in Vierneisel and Kaeser (1992: 151–56) on "Zuschauerfiguren" and Schäfer 1997: 76–81 on "der Symposiast als Zuschauer."

73. Both flanking figures turned away: **15**, **17**, **24**, **30**.
    Both flanking figures turned towards: **2**, **12**, **19**, **22**, **27**, [**38**].

FIGURE 1.2. Cat. 26. Berlin, Antikensammlung F1798. Unattributed. c. 530. (l) Man and youth interfemoral intercourse, four male–female couples. bpk, Berlin / Art Resource, New York.

contact in any and only one likely case of interaction between the "observers" and the "observed," but what is meant is uncertain. On a skyphos from Olbia (18, fig. 1.3) we see three youths (L, facing R), the rightmost of whom seems to be embracing the back, not of the *eromenos*, but of the *erastes*. The youth stands slightly apart from the couple, no erection visible, but his left arm disappears behind the couple while his right hand rests on the *erastes*' thigh, apparently under the *erastes*' hand where it grips the *eromenos*'s upper thigh. Far from illustrating "specular quality," most

> One towards, other away: 3, 9, 10, 14, 20, [21], 23 (L: naked male facing away to another naked male, with a rooster in between; R: dancing female facing in toward couple).
> Single figure, turned away: 5.
> Three (L) towards, thee (R) away: 18.
> Three couples (leftmost with "up and down" gesture, two in interfemoral) flanked by (L) dancer turned towards, and (R) man holding rooster turned towards: 1.
> Isolated couple with man–woman intercourse to R (broken to left): 16.
> Isolated by columns: 34.

loving couples seem lost in a world of their own with no interaction from the flanking figures. The wide variety of orientations shows that we are not looking at a depiction of social practice (were we tempted to think so) but at a stylized way of filling up space. The armorial animals (**8**, **11**) show this clearly.

Stewart, describing the Berlin "orgy" vase (**26**, fig. 1.2; cf. **Q**), warns us against facile readings (1997: 161):

> Yet these pictures are not a sixth-century Kinsey report, and drop heavy hints that they are not always to be taken literally. One doubts that Athenian men often stood inline to copulate, often held their partners unsupported in midair, often had group sex in vineyards conveniently furnished with symposion couches.

Lear explicates what may be the iconography (2008: 111):

> Indeed, one could view the vase as presenting a dictionary of sexual positions. In this dictionary, however, there is only one position for pederastic intercourse: intercrural. That, we would claim, is the message of this scene—on this point—and the implicit message of the courtship-related intercrural scenes illustrated above: intercrural intercourse is the only means of consummation for pederasty, or for decent, courtship-based pederasty.

But suddenly in red-figure there is a set of changes. First, the pool shrinks to only eight examples (**39–46**), of which only two are certain (**43**, **44**), plus three likely fragments (**39–41**).[74] Kilmer labels seven scenes as depicting "imminent" or "preparation for" interfemoral intercourse; too a subjective call, I fear. I would prefer that we apply the stricter definition used above: the *erastes* in the posture but his penis not actually between the other's thighs, which gives us three examples (**42**, **45**, **46**). There may be times when we *think* we can be pretty sure what the *erastes hopes* will happen, but opening up every kiss and hug to the label "imminent" intercourse makes the category too wide.[75] Kilmer also includes three mythological

---

74. Dover (1989) listed two: **42** (R573) and **43** (R502), and even here the first is only "imminent." Besides the mythological cases (below), Kilmer (1993: 16–21) listed only two certain examples for red-figure: **43** (R502) and **44** (R371).

75. Lewis 2002: 112: "More than any other theme, the sexual makes interpreters unwilling to accept scenes as they are, and too wiling to create stories around them—about what will happen or has just happened in the scene." Besides **42** and **43**, Kilmer's other "imminent" cases are R27

FIGURE 1.3. Cat. 18. St. Petersburg, Hermitage, O.1912.272. P. of the Carlsruhe Skyphos, c. 540–530. Man and youth in interfemoral intercourse, youth behind them touches the couple. Flanked by dancing men and women. © The State Hermitage Museum, St. Petersburg. Photo: Svetlana Suetova, Konstantin Sinyavsky.

scenes (1993: 16–18), where Eros or perhaps Zephyros carries off a youth. These are dubious evidence of human behavior at best, and it is far from clear that they were intended to show interfemoral sex.[76]

And some are meant to be funny (**C.**, fig. 1.4). It is odd to have this vase solemnly discussed as evidence of, for example, "age-equal" homosexuality, or interfemoral intercourse.[77] It is not interfemoral—it is not physically possible. It is not evidence of anything, except the painter's skill and imagination.

Second, in red-figure we find a new convention: the couples are shown alone. The exception is this pelike by the Eucharides Painter (**44**, fig. 1.5).

(DeVries 3.65 = BA 200100): youth and boy kissing; R36 (DeVries 3.85 = BA 30685): taller youth embracing and touching the penis of shorter; R142 (DeVries 3.60 = BA 200641): "preparation for a kiss," touching the boy's penis; and R196 (DeVries 3.72 = BA 200977): 4 youth and boy couples in various "stages" of courtship.

76. Kilmer claims Berlin F2305 (R595 = DeVries 4.144 = BA 205366) as an example of interfemoral posture but notes (2002: 130): "The winged immortal, oddly innocent of erection, and given very small genitals." The artist has taken pains to show that this is not interfemoral intercourse: the left thighs are pressed together but the right ones are apart, revealing the god's genitals (contra Lear and Cantarella 2008: 156). So, too, Boston, Museum of Fine Arts 95.31 (R574 = DeVries 4.137 = BA 205271), where the god's penis cannot be seen but the thighs do not overlap. In fact, we can see that the god's horizontal posture is the same as in Florence, Museo Archeologico Etrusco 91456 (BA 200931, ARV 108.27, Add 173; see Cohen 1997: 148–49). However, on Boston 13.94 (R603 = DeVries 4.173 = BA 9017565), Eros/Zephyros has an erection that seems to penetrate the thighs and the clothing as well (Dover 1989: 98). Boardman (Boardman and La Rocca 1978: 100) consequently argues that these figures should be viewed as vertical.

77. Lear 2008: 117: "anal sex, though . . . not in intercourse." Hubbard 2003a: 20: "Similarly, figure 15 [**C**] shows seven age-equal youths engaged in a wild naked dance combined with sexual horseplay: one youth, who stares directly at us, as if inviting us to join, places his penis between the buttocks of two others, while another ithyphallic youth approaches from the left with outstretched arms, perhaps offering himself to be fellated by the youth next to him, but clearly intending to join the fun in some form." In fact one cannot see the standing youth's penis. Hubbard (2014: 131): "Sometimes the horseplay turns to what we might call sexual experimentation." This scene cannot be used as an example of regular behavior or even "sexual experimentation." Hubbard also labels a cup by the Brygos Painter (London, British Museum E71, BA 203927*) as "Youth Plays Kottabos With Another's Anus" (2003b) or just "sexual horseplay" (2014: 131, fig, 8.2). It is neither. Hubbard is less certain in the text (2003b): "Could it be a crude game of kottabos?" No, it could not. The British Museum online catalog says that the left figure "gestures with his right hand (the hand is missing)." There is no room for a cup. BM: "On the right is a komast in an extraordinary pose. He is bent over and seen from behind so that, in extreme foreshortening, between his splayed legs appear his anus, his testicles and penis, and his belly, and to the left his shoulders and the back of his head." The other side may be horseplay, but not sexual. BM: "On the left a youth kneels on a couch with a backrest, as he wields a wineskin over his head. . . . In the centre dances a naked youth." It does look as if the kneeling youth is trying to brain the dancer with his wineskin—the ancient equivalent of a pillow fight, perhaps. http://www.britishmuseum.org/research/collection_online/collection_object_details.aspx?objectId=399225&partId=1

FIGURE 1.4. Cat. C. Turin, Museo di Antichità 4117. Exterior unattributed, c. 525–500. Ithyphallic youths. Two bumping buttocks while a third stands behind them, guiding. Draped and naked youth dancing. Photo courtesy of the Soprintendenza per i Beni Archeologici del Piemonte e del Museo Antichità Egizie (Dr. Patrizia Petitti).

The setting is marked as a gymnasium by the race course turning point stele, the suspended sponge, alabastron, and strigil. The odd squatting figure to the right of the couple, his eyes cast down and away, has been variously interpreted, most often as a slave.[78] Frontisi-Ducroux, having argued for "the specular quality of courtship," now claims that "the explicit negation of the spectator is no less significant." She continues, examining this vase:

> This is exhibited by a pelike that shows intercrural intercourse occurring under a half-open cloak, without any visual exchange. Seated at the base of a column, a little sleeping slave holds his master's staff. His averted head joins with his being asleep to underline his status as a nonwitness and confers a furtive character on this encounter. Is this to suggest that

---

78. Keuls (1985: 293–94; fig. 264, 265) suggests: "A second youth sits on the ground in a dejected pose; perhaps he is the man's slave, jealous of his master's attentions to another." So, too, Kilmer 1993: 16.

FIGURE 1.5. Cat. 44. London market. Eucharides P., c. 480–470. (l) Bearded male engages in interfemoral sex with youth; gymnasium setting is suggested. (r) At their feet a youth squats, face averted.

the seduction of young men is not entirely beautiful to see? Or, rather, does this conjunction of the shown and the nonseen indicate that what the image shows us is not the precise act as it actually unfolds?[79]

In this group, one vase seems to show that even interfemoral intercourse may have been regarded (by the *eromenos,* or someone speaking for him, in any case) as giving in too easily. Boston, Museum of Fine Arts 65.873, is a fragment of a red-figure kylix by Onesimos (**D**). To the left, a bearded man, slightly bent at the waist, wearing a wreath and an elaborate fillet, with his cloak thrown off his right shoulder exposing his torso, is reaching around and behind the shoulder of another figure. We can see the tip of a nose and chin and lips. The figure is smaller and undoubtedly male, wearing a red ribbon. The *erastes* is too far away to be engaged in interfemoral intercourse,[80] but from his mouth comes the word ἔασον, "Let (me)." From the youth's lips: οὐ παύσει; "Please stop" (the polite future, as the grammar books say).

Can we then, despite all these stylized and unrealistic attributes, read the figures as evidence of a praxis, a real way that real Athenian men had (not quite) real sex with real Athenian boys? I think, with due caution, we can, and this is because of the centrality of the human figure to Greek art. As Lissarrague and Schnapp note (1981: 282):

> In the Greek imaginary,[81] space comes from the represented subject, from the representation of the human body. The body of persons—men and women, gods and goddesses, monsters—is at the center of representation. Landscape barely exists; spatial décor is only suggested. The city, with its roads, its places, its fountains, is strangely absent. All indicators of space—indoors or out, town or country—are uncommonly rare. A colonnade or a step suggests a building; a piece of furniture, an interior. The setting of the image has the almost abstract purity of modern theater. This curious abstraction of space gives its place over to human representation.[82]

---

79. Davidson (2007: 436, 437) captions the scene: "A friend or attendant looks away or misses what is happening while he dozes off." In the main text he speculates: "Another Stripling [part of Davidson's invented terminology] crouches on the ground, with his head in his hands turned away and his eyes closed. Is he just napping while his friend or his slave-master has a bit of fun, as many have suggested? Or is this 'to suggest that the seduction of young men is not entirely beautiful to see'?" The other side, seldom illustrated or discussed, shows a youth with a garland playing the aulos accompanied by a young woman playing *krotala* (castanets). A walking stick and sponge (?) lean on the right side of the frame.

80. Contra Lear 2008: 183–84, fig. 7.2: "the man's head is at the level of the youth's shoulder and we would therefore argue that the scene is instead one of intercrural intercourse."

81. Used in the generalized Lacanian sense of a culturally shared set of images.

82. "Dans l'imagerie des Grecs l'espace procède du sujet figuré, de la représentation du corps

They sum up this central distinction with epigrammatic brevity (1981: 285): "The abstraction of the setting of the representation is the reason for the naturalism of the subject."[83] We might reverse this: "The naturalism of the subject is the reason for the abstraction of the setting of the representation." And yet the presence of "gods and goddesses, monsters," however human (sometimes) their actions, should warn us to proceed carefully. So too should an example of an unnatural stylization of a natural sexual action, which I have not seen discussed.[84] In what may be a stylistic convention of the Triptolemos Painter, several scenes, where a man is having sex with a woman while she reclines on her back on a couch, show the man's knees not as pressing into the mattress but as straddling and gripping the outside of the frame of the couch; in fact his knees are sometimes shown projecting outside and below the level of the couch. Such a posture is not, I suppose, impossible, but it would require extraordinary stamina. It is not likely to be the actual way Greek men bedded Greek women (**E–G**, cf. 57, below).[85]

So what accounts for the decrease in the number of representations of men getting a thigh job? Did Athenian men discover the chemistry of red-figure painting and lose interest in femoral frottage at about the same time? Did the move from flanking figures to couples in isolation mark a change from scopophilia and/or exhibitionism to modesty and privacy (somehow obtainable in the gymnasium)? Here a change in forms of presentation is more likely than a change in experience.

ANAL INTERCOURSE

On the other hand, when the sources, both literary and popular, are explicit, they assume that anal penetration is the only form of intercourse between males.[86] It is always possible to insult an adult male adversary by calling

---

humain. Le corps des personnages—hommes ou femmes, dieux ou déesses, monstres—est au centre de la figuration: le paysage n'existe guère, le décor spatial n'est que suggéré. La cité avec ses rues, ses places, ses fontaines est étrangement absente. Les indicateurs d'espace—dedans ou dehors—ville ou campagne—sont d'une rare discrétion. Une colonnade ou un gradin suggèrent un édifice, un meuble, un intérieur, le cadre de l'image a la pureté presque abstraite du théâtre moderne. Cette curieuse abstraction de l'espace donne toute sa place à la figuration humaine." Cf. Bérard and Durand 1989: 30. On the concept of space in Attic pottery, see Dietrich 2010.

83. "L'abstraction du cadre de la figuration est la raison du naturalisme du sujet."

84. But cf. Keuls 1985: 168, who does not quite grasp the picture.

85. Contrast Berlin, Staatliche Museen, Antikensammlung F2052 (lost), BF cup, c. 530 (BA 14936); or the woman's knees on Brussels, Musées Royaux (BA 200192; Dover R351), mentioned below.

86. E.g., Ar. *Knights* 639, 877–80; *Thesm.* 35, 50, 59–62, 1115–24; Eubulus fr. 120 KA, Eupolis 77;

him καταπύγων "one who takes it in the ass," εὐρύπρωκτος "with a wide-asshole," and a variety of similar insults,[87] but this assumption holds true for pederastic relations as well.[88] Aristophanes, with characteristic bluntness, mentions excrement (*Peace* 11, 724).[89] [Lucian] *Amores* 27 is unusually direct in speaking about the pain that the boy feels from anal intercourse (cf. Theoc. 5.41, Strato *AP* 12.211), while Aristotle (*Nic. Eth.* 1148b29–33) notes that those who were violated (*hubrizō*) as boys may develop a disposition towards being mounted through habituation.[90]

Dover noted the disparity in the evidence (1989: 204, in the postscript):

> For example, the fact that comedy assumes anal penetration to be the normal mode of homosexual intercourse suggests that the vase-painters' overwhelming preference for the intercrural mode is highly conventional, and I would not resist such a suggestion.

As far as I know now, there are only four example of males in the act of anal intercourse with males on Attic pottery, all in black-figure, all with difficulties of interpretation.[91] There are none in red-figure. There are another four

---

cf. Dioskorides 7 (*AP* 5.54), Marcus Argentarius (*AP* 5.116); Strato 12.6–7, 12.22 (taking it inside), 12.240, 245. Dover 1989: 99, 145 for the evidence: "In Greek comedy it is assumed, save in *Birds* 706 (see above), to be the only mode . . . and when Hellenistic poetry makes a sufficiently unambiguous reference to what actually happens on the bodily plane, we encounter only anal, never intercrural, copulation." The exception is Dover's misunderstanding of *diamērizō* (see above). See also Henderson 1991: 53.

87. Henderson 1991: 209–15; Parker 2011: 135. Both Hubbard and Davidson wish to avoid the plain sense of *katapugōn*. Hubbard (1998: 51, 58–59) tries to make *katapugōn* mean its exact opposite. Hubbard (2003a: 84) renders it tendentiously (and meaninglessly) as "anal": "Titas, the Olympic victor, is anal" (this is Athens, c. 525–500 BCE: *SEG* 16:38; Lang 1976: 12, C 5). His footnote reads, "The Greek word here is *katapugon* (oriented toward the buttocks). It seems to be used of both active and passive participants in anal sex." Both parts are incorrect, and Hubbard gives no evidence. Davidson speaks (1997: 161) about the "bizarre sexual monsters called katapugōn and kinaidos," which he glosses as "sexual degenerates" (167). Davidson (2007: 60–64, 467–68) uses "debauchee," and wishes to see only "lewdness, lack of sexual restraint, general degeneracy." He cites Bain 1991: 67, Lombardo 1985, Milne and Bothmer 1953, none of whom support him.

88. E.g., Ar. *Wasps* 1070, *Wealth* 152–59. Rhianus 1 (*AP* 12.38), Meleager 90 (*AP* 12.33).

89. The giant dung beetle wants to be fed dung from a prostituted boy (*paidos hētairēkotos*); for this precise use of *hetaireō*, see Dover 1989: 20–22. The point, however, may not be a contrast between an unpenetrated good *eromenos* and a penetrated prostitute, but simply the joke that only a prostitute can provide "well-ground" (*tetrimmenēs*) dung.

90. Cf. [Arist.] *Problemata* 4.26 (879a36–80a5). See Dover 1989: 168–70. Thornton (1997: 104) by lumping both active and passive roles into "homosexuality" misunderstands the thrust of the passage, but correctly sums up: "Today's *kinaidos* is yesterday's *eromenos* or 'boy-favorite.'"

91. Hupperts (2000: 404; z200) lists as an example a "phiale" (more properly a pinax) from Neapolis in Thrace (modern Kavala), Sanctuary of the Parthenos, c. 510, Kavala Archaeological Museum A 1104, illustrated in *Eros grec* 1989: nr. 59 (no description). The pinax, however, is from a

examples of what we might more loosely term preparation for anal intercourse, one in black-figure. There are also several cases which have been claimed as anal intercourse or preparation for it that are not.[92] As Kilmer noted, "There seems to have been a strong taboo against depiction in the visual arts of anal intercourse between males."[93] Rather, less a taboo than a preferred setting.

So besides the conveniently contrasting scenes on the White-Levy kalpis (**A**), we have two so-called Tyrrhenian amphorae (**47, 48**). The Tyrrhenians are interesting and anomalous within the corpus of Attic black-figure pottery.[94] They are early (c. 570/65–545) and contain some of the first erotic scenes on Attic pottery. We may also be able to see something of the introduction and rise of erotic imagery. "From Corinth come the komasts—the jolly, bottom-slapping dancers with their sunburnt faces and chests, naked or in red tunics, and sometimes joined by women. They appeared on many Corinthian vases, but not so often on cups as they do in Athens."[95] The figures were taken up by the eponymous Komast Group (c. 585–570) and feature on certain Siana cups (c. 565–560).[96] From there komasts were introduced as a decorative frieze by the Timiades Painter or the Goltyr Painter. Overall komasts are the most common scene on Tyrrhenian amphorae, followed closely by chariot races. The erotic scenes, however, are not characteristic of komast painters in general nor the Tyrrhenian group as a whole but only certain painters, notably the Timiades Painter and the Guglielmi

---

workshop on Thasos, the island opposite: Lazaridis 1969: 94. The pinax is nonetheless interesting. On the left, a beardless youth bent at the knees and waist, facing left, supporting himself with his right hand on his knee. His left arm goes behind, possibly touching the back of the figure behind him. This is an adult man (traces of a beard line), also bent. His left hand holds the youth's torso; his right hand guides his erect penis into the youth's buttocks. This seems to be only instance where the act of man–youth anal intercourse is presented simply. Sutton 2000: 188n25 identifies this as "heterosexual." This example is useful to remind us that Athens was not the only source of pottery, that erotic imagery, even pederastic imagery, occurs elsewhere, and that the rules of representation may vary from place to place and time to time.

92. See Appendix.

93. Dover 1978: 99; Kilmer 1993: 23. For red-figure, Kilmer (1993: 22–26) lists only four examples and only when anal intercourse is "imminent": R243 (**C**, not anal, see above), R954 (**46**, leading to interfemoral or anal?), R1155 (**53**, threatened, the Eurymedon vase), and R1127 (satyrs, BA 275638).

94. "Tyrrhenian" from the large numbers found in early excavations in Vulci (1828–); see Kluiver 2003: 11–15 for the history of study. These finds tend to distort the picture of Tyrrhenian vases. In particular the oft-repeated assumption that they were "meant" (though in what sense?) for an Etruscan market is unwarranted. See Kluiver 2003: 120–22, "Why did the Etruscans buy Tyrrhenian amphorae?" For the erotic scenes, ten out of one hundred seventy-one examples, see Mayer-Emmerling 1982: 152–57.

95. Boardman 1974: 18. See also Beazley 1951: 18; Smith 2010.

96. Smith 2010: 33–73, esp. 43.

Painter (Kluiver 2003: 100). The komast scene had its own arc: "The theme's popularity rose in the early years of 'Tyrrhenian,' peaked in about 555–550 BC, and then declined" (Kluiver 2003: 99). In short, we are not looking at a reaction to an Etruscan market's demand for lewd pottery, but a short-lived genre scene used by a few Attic painters.[97]

Kluiver notes a further difficulty in reading the erotic scenes as illustrations of any social reality (2003: 99–100):

> It is curious that satyrs sometimes participate in "Tyrrhenian" komoi and erotic scenes, especially those made by the Timiades Painter. . . . Reversely, ordinary men are sometimes found in "Tyrrhenian" pictures which are predominantly populated with satyrs and maenads. . . . The "Tyrrhenian" painters simply ignored the tenuous boundary between the real and the mythical.

The first two examples are amphorae by the Guglielmi Painter, one in Orvieto (47), the other in Montpellier (48).[98] Sutton describes the action on the Orvieto vase (2000: 185–86):

> A column-krater at the right identifies the occasion as a kōmos. The scene is divided in the center by a hefty man with a large flaccid penis who looks toward the left and gestures toward the right. He is framed by contrasting pairs of male figures. Toward the left, a long-haired man bends over and pats his rump invitingly as he turns back to face a man approaching with phallus ready.[99] Toward the right, by contrast, a bearded man is violently penetrated by another. Presented as a victim, he is smashed to the ground in a crumpled position. The aggressor, who seems to have a lighter beard, may be younger. The depiction of sexual relations between two male figures is rare in orgy scenes. . . . This black-figure vase painting, with a flaccid, impotent man juxtaposed with another in extreme excitement,

---

97. Kluiver 2003: 20: "The 'Tyrrhenian' amphorae fit into the evolution of Attic vase-painting. As remarked, traces of the influence of Sophilos can be detected in the work of Prometheus Painter, who established the 'Tyrrhenian' amphora. And the *later* 'Tyrrhenian' painters were followed by Nikosthenes, who adapted some elements of the Attic tradition in which they worked."

98. Musée Languedocien 149bis. Attribution to the Guglielmi Painter by A. F. Laurens (see Kluiver 1996: 21, no. 202; 2003: 166, no. 202). Caution must be used since the vase is heavily reconstructed (including shards that belong elsewhere) and repainted before 1836. Oddly Kuiver (2003: 77) does not notice the significance of both vases being attributed to the Guglielmi Painter.

99. The buttock-slapping on this and other komast vases has been thought to indicate "receptivity to anal intercourse" (Lear 2008: 125; Hupperts 1988: 262–63). The gesture, however, is common on all type of komast vases; it is merely part of the dance. See Smith 2010: index, s.v. "slapping, bottom."

contrasting pairs of buggers, and a woman abandoned on the fringes of the action, is surely intended as a humorously lascivious depiction of depraved social Others.

Lear comments (2008: 124–25):

> A scene of anal intercourse, with reversed age-roles: a youth (though possibly with a short beard)[100] penetrates a bearded adult anally. It may also be a scene of potential group sex: it is unclear whether the other figures are watching the central action or waiting in line for a turn. The *krater* (mixing bowl for wine and water) at far right sets the scene at a symposium or kōmos, a possible setting for pederastic courtship,[101] but all courtship elements are missing. No gifts are present, nor is any other symbol or gesture of courtship. There are no elements connecting the scenes to the gymnasium or hunting. . . . All of the standing males have large penises. They are erect, except for the pendulous, flaccid one of the central fat/deformed figure, which is either circumcised or has its foreskin retracted, an element that appears elsewhere only in comic scenes.

Lear reads this scene of drunken excess against the depiction of Dionysus and satyrs on the other side: "Thus, it would seem that the figures on side A not only engage in Satyr-like behavior: the painter sees them as equivalent to Satyrs."[102] As always, if you want to know what is forbidden, look at satyrs.[103]

Kilmer reads this all quite differently (1997: 48):

> Even the single case of black-figure homoerotic anal penetration presented here challenges the belief that anal penetration of one male by another

---

100. The hatchings for the beard are visible.

101. "Setting" is perhaps incorrect. Rather, courting male figures are sometimes flanked by komastic dancers.

102. I find this line or reasoning plausible, but I would add a note of caution. All arguments for what Lear calls a "decorative program," linking the imagery of one side of a vase to the other, or inside to outside, run into the difficulty that type-scenes are freely repeated and mixed-and-matched on all sorts of pottery; different sides may even be by different painters (rightly noted by Lear 2008: 27). Any argument for linking then has to make a strong case that *this* time it is justified; see Lewis 2002: 112. So on this vase (48), the drunken orgy on one side is matched with Dionysius on the other. On the Montpellier amphora by the same painter (47), the other side of the continuous frieze shows a simple kōmos with one ithyphallic figure at the end; while 23 (see above) shows interfemoral intercourse on one side and Achilles playing draughts with Ajax (one of the most common motifs in vase painting) on the other.

103. Lissarrague 1990b; Lear 2008: 120–21, 125.

was such a shameful thing for the penetrated partner that it could never be visually represented. For the Gugliemi [*sic*] Painter (and for his client, who need not have been Greek) this taboo was certainly not operating in the anticipated way.

The same Tyrrhenian amphora by the Gugliemi [*sic*] Painter also provides the single case of anal penetration of an adult male by a youth. While this scene does not on its own provide a new orthodoxy, it does raise the possibility that two current orthodoxies about "sexuality" in the Athenian world need to be re-examined: first, that homoerotic sex is always to involve the elder acting on the younger partner; second, that for the archaic Athenians, "sexuality" was not divided into "males," "females," and "homosexuals," but into those who penetrate and those who are penetrated, the latter considered as social inferiors of the former. If the younger can penetrate the older, even this once, the value system posited for late fifth/early fourth centuries cannot have held for the time when our Tyrrhenian vase was painted.

Claims of "orthodoxy" aside, this is, to be blunt, naïve. The unstated assumption here is that this image must reflect reality. First, of course, no one has ever claimed "that anal penetration of one male by another was such a shameful thing for the penetrated partner that it could never be visually represented," merely that it was a shameful thing for the penetrated partner. The important thing is not to be that represented person. One need only substitute "verbally" for "visually" to see the error: comedy and invective are full of descriptions of buggered men. Second, the idea that a value system cannot be in force if even a single image contradicts it is very curious. That the image might be intended as a deliberate flouting of conventions, that it might be outrageous, shocking, funny, or silly, never occurs.[104] Again, the model of Old Comedy might help clarify what is being claimed. Far from showing that a value system cannot have held

---

104. Beard 1991: 30: "Visual images can subvert as much as establish and uphold norms." For Kilmer's overvaluation of single scenes, see below. Hupperts (1988: 257) is equally convinced that these images somehow constitute evidence of real practice: "In the sixth century the paederastic relation was not the only form of homosexuality. In my view the scholars haven't paid enough attention up till now to vases that make clear that other forms of homosexual practice must have existed"; that "must have" is the giveaway. The Tyrrhenian amphorae (262–64) "give evidence for another aspect of homosexual love in Greek culture of the sixth century." Whatever they show, it isn't love. On the Orvieto amphora (48), "At any rate the action of the copulating men shows clearly another form of homosexual practice. So far the examples. I think I have shown enough vases to justify my conclusion that paederasty wasn't the only form of homosexual practice in Attica of the sixth century."

sway when a play shows people violating it, the play shows precisely how strongly the system was valued. However, the most interesting thing about this passage is not the idea that a single image invalidates an entire set of customs, but that, if we can wish certain types of evidence away, things automatically revert to *our* sexuality, expressed somewhat oddly as "'males,' 'females,' and 'homosexuals.'"[105]

The Guglielmi Painter's second vase (48) is equally over the top. A kōmos is in progress. From the left four naked men, in increasing order of excitement it seems, approach a couple: the man is taking the woman from behind as she supports herself with one hand on a krater placed on the floor.[106] On the other side of the krater (Shapiro 2000a: 16):

> The couple on the right clearly consists of a bearded man bending over to ladle some wine and a youth perhaps playfully taking advantage of the man's vulnerable position to insert his penis. Not only do these scenes on Tyrrhenian vases seem to violate the rule just enunciated, viz. that anal intercourse between males is never depicted, but they do so doubly, since the passive partner has a full beard and the active one appears to be beardless. In fact it is this apparent role reversal which proves that the whole scene is far removed from the world of *erastês* and *erōmenos* as we know it from the vases discussed above. It is simply a riotous drunken revel, or *kōmos* (note the large bowl for wine) at which all inhibitions have broken down.[107]

A third vase confirms the readings of scenes of male–male intercourse as outrageous, for we have a scene of "daily life" involving daring young men and the flying trapeze (49, fig. 1.6).[108] On each side a couple is framed by naked males wearing iconic Scythian hats. Both make use of a stool. On the obverse a woman (traces of white paint) lies on her back on the stool, her legs up in the air, while a man penetrates her.[109] On the reverse we find two beardless figures (Sutton 2000: 188–90):

---

105. That is, I might well be mistaken in my analysis of, say, Navaho sexuality. But to assume that once I have correctly understood it, it will turn out to be exactly the same as my own, reveals either essentialism or parochialism.

106. Laurens (1984: 47, 49n7) rightly identifies the first figure to the left of the mixing bowl as female ("la seule représentation féminine de tout le vase"); so too Hupperts (2000: 113).

107. See also Lear 2008: 125–26.

108. The swinging couple has been misread, principally because of its preposterous subject matter, as male–female by Dierichs (1993: 52–54, fig. 91a–b; 2008: 55–56, fig. 41a–b) and Stewart (1997: 159).

109. For the pose, one can compare the similar little master band-cup also by Hermogenes (16), where the male–female couple flanks a decorous man–youth couple engaged in interfemoral intercourse.

FIGURE 1.6. Once Riehen, Switzerland, collection Heinz Hoek. Unattributed, c. 555–535. (l and r) Naked males in Scythian hats, flanking a male figure swing down to penetrate another male, bent over and holding on to a stool. Photo after Hornbostel 1980: 85, no. 53.

[An] active male lover who swings from a strap or trapeze to penetrate his male partner who bends over obligingly, supporting himself on the stool as he looks back to face his lover. Lest there be any doubt about the gender of the bending figure, his testicles are shown clearly beneath his buttocks.[110] Here the framing dancers, both facing right, echo the ridiculous action of the flying lover, as they too hang from straps performing suggestive pelvic thrusts. . . . The deliberate contrast of the cup's two sides seems intended to ridicule buggery as an Other practice.

Another Tyrrhenian vase is imminent, but so very imminent that we might include it in the count. On the neck of an amphora by the Timiades Painter (50, fig. 1.7), we see three male bearded figures. On the left, a komast facing left holding a wreath, while in the center a man wearing a traveler's hat (*petasos*) stands bent at the waist. Both are wearing short tunics. On the right, a naked male touches the thigh of the bent-over man with his left hand, while his right guides his penis, which is almost touching the man's buttocks. This does not seem to be a case of komasts overlapping in the same pictorial space, and no other komast is shown in this bent-over stance.[111] Below, on the shoulder, there are four male–female couples. All the men are naked, all the women clothed. At the far left, a single male komast dancer, then a bearded male with one arm in the air; the other clasps the waist of a woman, slightly bent over, who guides the man's penis for intercourse from behind. Their faces are close, as if about to kiss, and there seems to be eye contact. The central couple is damaged. He seems

---

110. Cf. from Dover (1989), R140, R243 (**C**), R462, R498, R954 (**46**), R1047.
111. Smith (2010: 43, 60) discusses the amphora but not the goings-on on the neck.

FIGURE 1.7. Once Kurashiki, Ninagawa Museum 22. Timiades P., c. 570–560. Upper register: (l) Komast facing left holding a wreath. (c) Man wearing *petasos* stands bent at the waist. (r) Naked male guides his penis towards central figure's buttocks. Lower register: (l) Komast dancer, 4 male/female couples. Image after Simon 1982: 49.

to be in the same posture as his fellow to the left. His face is also near his partner's, but she is shown dancing. The third couple balances the one of the right. The beardless man penetrates the woman from behind. His left hand cups her breast and his right rests on her thigh. On the far right by the handle, male and female komasts. Her back is turned towards him, but he is not shown erect. The reverse shows a pair of dancers, man and woman, flanked by two male dancers, bodies turned to the outside, faces to the inside. Here is it hard to make a case for a contrast between decorous and indecorous sex.

The three scenes in red-figure are more difficult to read. The first is a frequently discussed kantharos by Nikosthenes as potter (51, fig. 1.8a and 1.8b). Our primary interest (for now) is on the pair of figures to the left of side A. There is considerable debate about whether the figure about to be pulled down onto the youth's erect penis is a boy or a girl.¹¹² Dover, Reinsberg, Lear, and Hubbard take the figure as a youth;¹¹³ Peschel, Kilmer, and Rabinowitz as female.¹¹⁴ Hupperts (2000: 205, no. RS4) gives a "non liquet." I originally assumed the figure was male; now I am less certain. I would draw attention to three points: (1) the breast line of the figure in question is drawn with the two scooping lines on the chest, and the line of the breast extends a little ways past the body line: the drawing resembles the breast of the first female figure on the reverse (contrast the drawing of the chest of the male figure at the far right); (2) the figure has lines running down the neck, apparently indicating a pendant of some kind: both the women on the reverse have these lines, while none of the men do;¹¹⁵ and (3) if the second figure is female, then we have three youths and two women on both sides. Given the uncertainties of even identification, proper interpretation may forever elude us. But I think we would be safe in saying that these scenes of excess, resembling the orgy of the Pedieus Painter (73, fig. 1.13a and 1.13b),¹¹⁶ were not meant to be realistic or normative.¹¹⁷

Equally puzzling is the image on a bell crater by the Dinos Painter (46, fig. 1.9), though at least we are sure of the sexes of those involved.¹¹⁸ This is one of the latest images of explicit sexual behavior in Athenian red-figure.¹¹⁹ A beardless youth sits in a chair, erect. Another beardless youth prepares to

---

112. On the difficulties of so seemingly simple a matter, see Kilmer 1993: 180–86.
113. Dover 1989: 86–87: "a squatting youth, becoming impatient while some of his friends are engaged in heterosexual activity, tries to pull another youth down on to his erect penis." Reinsberg 1989: 205, fig. 49a–c. Lear 2008: 119: "The list of elements present in vase 3.10, for instance, that are present in no pederastic scene is a long one." Hubbard 2014: 131: "a wholesale bisexual free-for-all (Boston 95.61 = Dover 1978, fig. R223), where the youths are as likely to penetrate one another as the female prostitute in the scene."
114. Peschel 1987: 66–68; Kilmer (1993: 25; also 41, 182–83) notes other difficulties: "In my view the passive partner there is intended to be a woman, but if the scene should prove to be homosexual, the copulation could still as easily be intercrural as anal; it is imminent, not actual; and the partner who is about to be penetrated has not adopted a subordinate position." Rabinowitz 2002: 142–45 (fig. 5.23).
115. Not, I think, mentioned before.
116. Paris, Louvre G13, discussed below.
117. Lear 2008: 118–19: "These scenes represent group activities of a festive or orgiastic nature, and they relate, iconographically, to a broad set of scene-types that include Satyr scenes and kōmos scenes. In fact, it may be that by concentrating on the presence of anal intercourse in these scenes, we are missing their more general value for our study."
118. However, Vermeule (1969: 12) identified the standing figure as female (the scrotum and tip of penis can be seen), and Schauenburg (1972: 6) identified the figure behind the door as a youth.
119. Brendel 1970: 39–42, and following him, Blanckenhagen (1976: 37) and Kilmer (1982: 110n32; 1993: 45) takes the scene as directly based on an oenochoe by the Shuvalov Painter (M): a young woman prepares to straddle a young man in a chair. In both, one foot is placed on the chair itself: in 46 it is the left foot nearest the viewer; in M it is the right (hidden) foot.

FIGURE 1.8A. Cat. 51. Boston, Museum of Fine Arts 95.61. Nikosthenes Painter, Nikosthenes as potter, c. 520–510. Youth prepares to penetrate a woman (?). Second youth preparing to insert a wine skin mouth into woman bent over to fellate a youth, who raises a slipper. Photograph © 2015 Museum of Fine Arts, Boston.

FIGURE 1.8B. Boston, Museum of Fine Arts 95.61. Three naked youths in pursuit of two naked women. Photograph © 2015 Museum of Fine Arts, Boston.

straddle him. Both are naked; both wear spiky crowns. Since his legs are on the outside of the seated youth, anal intercourse rather than interfemoral is probably intended. The figures to their right are mysterious. After a thin Doric column, a bearded man stands looking on, wearing a crown with ribbons. Peering over the lower half of a Dutch door is a woman. Keuls read this as a scene in a male brothel (though the action seems to be outdoors).[120] Blanckenhagen (1976) came up with a remarkable reading. He began by comparing crowns on two choes, and on a silenus on a vase that Simon identified as depicting the holy marriage ceremony (*hieros gamos*), held on the night of the second day of the Anthesteria (the *Choes* "jugs"), where the wife of the *archon basileus* (often called by a modern title the *basilinna*) was married behind closed doors to Dionysus.[121] This led him to another depiction supposedly of the "basilinna" behind an open valve door,[122] and from there to a depiction of a drunken reveler banging on a Dutch door (an *exclusus amator*?).[123] From all this he concludes that the scene on the London vase must show a lost comedy with two boys making a blasphemous mockery of the rite.[124] However, there is nothing to connect this krater with the Anthesteria, much less any putative lost play about it. Equally unconvincing is DeVries's reconstruction, where the odd crowns are those of the Athenian torch-race, the Lampadedromia,[125] making the male watcher "possibly the gymnasiarch in charge of the torch-racing."[126]

Last, we have the disputed testimony of the Eurymedon vase (52). Whatever the identification of the penis-clutching left figure (Athenian hoplite, hunter, sailor) or the bent-over left figure (Thracian, Scythian), the

---

120. Keuls 1985: 293, fig. 263: "Given these derogatory associations of anal penetration, one may safely assume that in most cases where it takes place between ordinary adult males, it implies male prostitution. This is clearly the case in the scene depicted in Figure 263, even though the customer and the male prostitute appear to be of roughly the same age. A youth is about to mount another, who is seated on a chair. On the right a mature man and a woman are leaning on a cottage door, watching the scene in what is surely a male brothel."

121. Agora P 7685 (BA 10223) and Paris, Louvre CA21 (BA 217494; Hoorn 1951: no. 822). Skyphos by Penelope Painter, Berlin F2589 (BA 219002, ARV 1301, Para 472): the crown of the silenus in no way resembles those on **46**. For the ceremony, see Arist. *Ath. Pol.* 3.5; Dem. 59.73–78; Pickard-Cambridge 1988: 10–12; Simon 1983: 96–97; Avagianou 1991: 177–98; Dillon 2001: 101–4.

122. Tarquinia, Museo Nazionale Tarquiniese RC4197 (BA 213726, ARV 1057, Para 445.96). Matheson (1995: 191) for the likely argument identifying the figure as Ariadne.

123. New York, Metropolitan Museum, 37.11.19 (BA 539).

124. That the action on the krater is set at the Anthesteria is accepted by Kilmer (1993: 24); Lear (2008: 177) is rightly skeptical. Torch-races marked not just the Anthesteria, but also the Aianteia, Epitaphia Hephaisteia, Panathenaea, Prometheia, and Theseia.

125. Cf. Harvard, Arthur M. Sackler Museum 1960.344 (BA 213533); Simon 1983: 53, 64. pl. 22.2.

126. In Lear 2008: 229 (no. 263). Lear is again rightly skeptical.

FIGURE 1.9. Cat. 46. London, British Museum F65. Youth prepared to mount ithyphallic youth sitting in chair. A bearded man with festive crown looks on (?). A woman stands behind an open Dutch door. © Trustees of the British Museum.

inscription indicates a threat of anal rape; κύβδα is the *vox impropria* for rear-entry intercourse.[127]

In sum: Despite a valiant effort to find them, there seem to be no pictures of a man having anal intercourse with a youth on an Athenian vase.[128]

---

127. Miller 2010, who covers fully the preceding bibliography. Based on autopsy in 2004 and with a drawing made by Eric Csapo, she reads: ΕΥΡΥΜΕΔ[Ο]ΝΕΜ[Ι]ΚΥΒΔ[Α]ΕΠΕΣΤΗΚΑ, that is, with normalized spelling in the Ionic alphabet, Εὐρυμέδων εἰμί. κύβδα ἐπέστηκα. "I am Eurymedon. I stand at the ready, bent over." This has the advantage of restoring the attested adverb κύβδα (in place of Schauenburg's invented *κυβά[δ]ε) but at the expense of a psilotic verb prefix. Yet, might this be part of the joke? The speech of the Scythian bowman in Aristophanes' *Thesmophoriazusae* is characterized by an inability to make aspirates (Willi 2003: 203–4), and perhaps a kind of "stage-Scythian" was already a running joke around 460 (something rike our pletend Japanese confusion of r and l)? For κύβδα's sexual usage, see Henderson 1991: 22, 169–70, 178.

128. Of course, that fact could be changed tomorrow by a new discovery. Lear 2008: 84: "As will be seen in chapter 3, anal intercourse is not as firmly excluded from pederastic iconography as most

The few surviving depictions of male–male anal intercourse tend to present the deed as something anomalous, outrageous, or ridiculous, while the surviving literary texts present it as the natural and most desirable outcome in a pederastic relationship.

This stylization—shielding the *eromenos* from the crudity of debasing penetration—should not surprise us. We would be incorrect to infer from sculpture and painting that no woman had pubic hair before 1866.[129] *Playboy* offers a useful parallel. Playmates were not shown with pubic hair until 1971, always carefully posed and airbrushed. They remained objects of erotic reverie but were never shown in explicit sex acts, which were reserved for the more degrading worlds of *Penthouse* and *Hustler*.[130]

Here is one of the many places where the attempt to impose our notions of homo- versus hetero- on the ancient material does a grave disservice to our understanding of Greek culture. Not only does our category of "homosexuality" confound the vital distinction between active and passive, penetrator/penetrated, but it confounds two totally different sexual objects: smooth young boys (whom everyone wanted to have sex with) and hairy grownup men (whom no one wanted to have sex with). An adult man buggering an adult man was not a matter of "homosexuality"; it was a matter of insult, contempt, ridicule, punishment, drunken mistake, or desperation.[131]

AGE REVERSAL

The two amphorae by the Guglielmi Painter bring us to the third point. "It was shocking if an *erastes* was younger than his *eromenos*."[132] Talk of *erastes* and *eromenos* is too polite perhaps: shocking when younger fucked older. So the Guglielmi Painter shows us a beardless man taking a bearded man (**47**) and a lightly bearded man taking a bearded man (**48**). The Timiades Painter shows us a bearded man just about to take another bearded man (**50**). Do these pictures sound the death knell for our way of understanding the structures of Athenian pederasty?[133] Hardly, since the point of these

---

scholars since Dover have believed." However, as Lear's own examples show, neither is it celebrated as are interfemoral intercourse with boys or intercourse with women.

129. Gustave Courbet, *L'Origine du monde*, Paris, Musée d'Orsay, RF 1995 10.

130. Acocella 2006; Pitzulo 2011, where the word "wholesome" appears nine times.

131. E.g., Ar. *Thesm.* 1118–24; Eubulus 118 KA; Theoc. 5.39–43, 116–19; *AP* 9.317. It is odd that there is such resistance to this idea on the part of some scholars in a society in which the term "bitch," taken from pimp and prison slang, has become ubiquitous.

132. Dover 1989: 87, citing Xenophon *Anab.* 2.6.28. See also Plato *Phdr.* 240c–d and Xenophon *Symp.* 4.23–24. See Golden's postscript 1984: 321–22.

133. Kilmer 1997: 45: "Two things which we have seen scholars treat as major taboos in the visual

scenes is precisely to be shocking. The nuanced readings of Shapiro, Sutton, and Lear, where these scenes represent comic excess, drunken behavior over the krater, acts that belong to the "world of Satyrs," is the right way to see these vases.[134] They belong, therefore, to the same category as the depiction of men vomiting, or urinating, or defecating: a funny, outrageous thing to come swimming up from the bottom of your cup.[135]

COURTING AND COURTING GIFTS

So-called courting scenes (and at the start we need to question this label) make much of "love gifts" (and we need to question that, too): hares, roosters, and so forth, yet they are barely mentioned in any literary source. Only twice, only in Aristophanes, and neither passage is clear testimony of an established custom.[136]

The chorus of *Birds* sing of their noble help to mortals (703–7):

ἡμεῖς δ' ὡς ἐσμὲν Ἔρωτος
πολλοῖς δῆλον· πετόμεσθά τε γὰρ καὶ τοῖσιν ἐρῶσι σύνεσμεν·
πολλοὺς δὲ καλοὺς ἀπομωμοκότας παῖδας πρὸς τέρμασιν ὥρας
διὰ τὴν ἰσχὺν τὴν ἡμετέραν διεμήρισαν ἄνδρες ἐρασταί,
ὁ μὲν ὄρτυγα δοὺς ὁ δὲ πορφυρίων' ὁ δὲ χῆν' ὁ δὲ Περσικὸν ὄρνιν.

We are the children of Eros; that's clear from many things. We fly and help lovers. Men in love have spread the legs of many beautiful boys who had sworn not to until the end of their bloom[137] with the aid of our power. One gives a quail; another a coot;[138] another a goose; another a rooster.

---

arts for Attic craftsmen are here violated. First, there is clear anal penetration, not the intercrural copulation which normally stands in as the visual substitute for that [an interesting assumption in itself]. Second, the person doing the penetrating is obviously younger than the penetrated person, reversing the relationship which we have been conditioned to anticipate." "Conditioned" is tendentious.

134. Shapiro 2000: 161; Lear 2008: 124–25; Sutton 2000: 185.
135. Dover 1989: 182; Sutton 2000: 193–4.
136. Koch-Harnack (1983: 22) cites only *Birds* and a passage in the Suda (μ 497 Adler s.v. Μέλητος; cf. κ 251, for the fact that ὁ καλός can mean the *eromenos*), which is, in fact, a selection from Aelian (fr. 69 Hercher, pp. 219–20). This story is not about love gifts as such but rather about a boy setting nearly impossible tasks on his lover (rather like Schiller's "Der Handschuh"). However, it does show that certain roosters could be worth stealing. Lear (2008: 238n39) also lists Aristophanes *Knights* 904–9 and 1104–99 (food as bribes to Demos), neither of which is relevant.
137. See Dunbar 1995: 303–4. That is, they swore to remain untouched until they were grown up and no longer under siege.
138. Technically the purple gallinule (*Porphyrio porphyrio*), but let's not quibble. It is interest-

Here the list has an obvious avian slant. However, there are no gifts of quail, coot, or goose from lover to beloved depicted on Attic vases.[139] The other passage is Aristophanes *Wealth* (149–59), where Khremulos is disabused of his innocence by his slave Karion:

ΧΡ. καὶ τάς γ' ἑταίρας φασὶ τὰς Κορινθίας,
     ὅταν μὲν αὐτάς τις πένης πειρῶν τύχῃ,
     οὐδὲ προσέχειν τὸν νοῦν, ἐὰν δὲ πλούσιος,
     τὸν πρωκτὸν αὐτὰς εὐθὺς ὡς τοῦτον τρέπειν.
ΚΑΡ. καὶ τούς γε παῖδάς φασι ταὐτὸ τοῦτο δρᾶν
     οὐ τῶν ἐραστῶν ἀλλὰ τἀργυρίου χάριν.
ΧΡ. οὐ τούς γε χρηστούς, ἀλλὰ τοὺς πόρνους· ἐπεὶ
     αἰτοῦσιν οὐκ ἀργύριον οἱ χρηστοί.
ΚΑΡ. τί δαί; ΧΡ. ὁ μὲν ἵππον ἀγαθόν, ὁ δὲ κύνας θηρευτικάς.
ΚΑΡ. αἰσχυνόμενοι γὰρ ἀργύριον αἰτεῖν ἴσως
     ὀνόματι περιπέττουσι τὴν μοχθηρίαν.

KR. And the courtesans of Corinth, they say, whenever a poor man tries to hit on them, pay no attention. But if it's a rich man, they immediately turn their ass his way.
KAR. The boys, too, they say, do the same thing, not for their lovers' sake but for money.
KR. Not good boys, just whores! Good boys don't ask for money.
KAR. What do they ask for?
KR. Maybe a good horse, or hunting dogs.
KAR. Probably because they're ashamed to ask for money, so they cover up their badness with a word.

Here the point is not the animal itself but—like a girl's best friend, the diamond—its fungible value. Again there is a disjunct between written and

---

ing that this and the goose are not game birds. Quail and rooster are fighting birds. Cf. Pl. *Lysis* 211e where Socrates declares that quail and rooster, horse and dog, and even gold are less desirable than a friend. These gifts then are all desirable things but not specifically erotic, love-gifts, or associated only with youths. Csapo (1983: 21) claims that cockfighting was particularly associated with the young, but the texts he cites do not bear him out. However, birds for boys became a trope in the Second Sophistic for a lost Golden Age of non-gold-digging boys: cf. the epigram by Glaucus [of Nicopolis?] *AP* 12.44 (Gow and Page 1965: 2, 287), Dio Chrys. 66.11; cf. Strato *AP* 12.212 for rising costs. See below.

139. Barringer 2001: 90. A quail is depicted on a white ground lekythos by the Syriskos Painter (Berlin, Antikensammlung, F2252 = BA 202736), but in the lap of a woman. Geese are common but not in an erotic or courting scene.

painted sources. There are no horses or dogs being given as gifts to youths on vases.¹⁴⁰ Still, the passage does imply that dogs or even horses might be something that a "good" boy could ask for and not damage his reputation over much.¹⁴¹ In neither passage is there any mention of the most common prop on vases, a hare.

In fact, the literary sources are rather sparse on the entire subject of what Beazley labeled "courting."¹⁴² Obviously no source says, "First approach the boy making the up and down gesture (α), next offer him a rooster (β), and then slip your penis between his thighs (γ)," but the whole notion of a courtship narrative (a linear flow of events) is a pattern that Beazley and then others placed on visual evidence.¹⁴³ We have many scenes in literary sources of men looking at and talking to beautiful boys, and of the extremes to which a man in love with a boy will go to win him (e.g., Pl. *Symp.* 182d–83b), but apart from these two passages, there is little about gifts, and nothing about animal gifts.¹⁴⁴

The most complete study of the data, Koch-Harnack's *Knabenliebe und Tiergeschenke* (1983), despite a cursory survey of symbolic associations, insists on a literal reading of almost all scenes, and concludes that "the erotic meaning of animals in courting scenes stems from their actual use in

---

140. For a later gift of a dog to a beloved, see Theoc. 5.106, but this is among shepherds. Horses and dogs are depicted in vase painting, even in scenes with men and youths, but none are clearly being handed over as are roosters, deer, and panthers. Koch-Harnack 1983: 63.

141. The range and subtleties of gift-giving codes may be seen in an example from Emily Post's *Etiquette* of 1922 (virtually unchanged in 1945), a time marked by "an unreserved frankness of young women and men towards each other": "If the bridegroom-elect has plenty of means, she [the fiancée] may not only accept flowers but anything he chooses to select, except wearing apparel or a motor car or a house and furniture—anything that can be classified as 'maintenance.' It is perfectly suitable for her to drive his car, or ride his horse, and she may select furniture for their house, which he may buy or have built. But, if she would keep her self-respect, the car must not become hers nor must she live in the house or use its furniture until she is given his name. He may give her all the jewels he can afford, he may give her a fur scarf, but not a fur coat. The scarf is an ornament, the coat is wearing apparel. . . . It would be starting life on a false basis, and putting herself in a category with women of another class, to be clothed by any man, whether he is soon to be her husband or not."

142. Lear 2008: 38: "Despite the great importance of pederasty as a theme in the remains of Greek literature, the actual modalities of courtship are hardly mentioned outside of comedy."

143. Koch-Harnack 1983: 66–77 with six carefully delineated steps: Initial Approach/Address, Showing the Gift, Signals of Understanding, Handing Over the Gift, The *Eromenos* Holding the Gift, Reciprocity–Sexual Intercourse.

144. Of course, gifts and briberies might be part of a dishonorable attempt at seduction of boys or women, e.g., Plutarch, *Demetrius* 24.2: the story of Democles the Beautiful, who "was never caught by any of the men who tried gifts, threats, everything" (ὡς δὲ πολλὰ πειρώντων καὶ διδόντων καὶ φοβούντων ὑπ' οὐδενὸς ἡλίσκετο) and who committed suicide rather than be raped by Demetrius.

real courtship rather than any inherent quality."¹⁴⁵ Koch-Harnack's approach is to combine Plato on the teaching role of pederasty and Xenophon on the teaching role of hunting and argue that the hunt was the primary way for lovers to educate boys in manly *arete,* and that this is illustrated on Greek vases.¹⁴⁶ The goal of the gift givers, it seems, is pedagogic before it is pederastic. The cocks are for cockfighting, the live hares and deer are there to be released for practice hunting (Koch-Harnack 1983: 80–82, 122–24). She claims that the leopards (or cheetahs, or panthers) were real presents and were used as hunting cats (105–12). The dead hares are gifts (or bribes) of food (155); the dead foxes (less tasty) serve a "purely didactic function" (93).¹⁴⁷ Unfortunately, this literal reading of the vases rapidly becomes preposterous. We might believe that a trained fighting cock would make a nice present,¹⁴⁸ but the idea that men could be seen in Athens and environs handing over adult stags to young boys so they could release them for hunting strains belief (and is unknown to Greek hunting).¹⁴⁹ Nor did the Greek hunt with or for cheetahs, leopards, or other large cats. Leopards, et cetera, did not exist in Attica.¹⁵⁰ On the more mundane level, we hear no stories of lovers taking their beloveds out on a hunt, even though that would seem to be a good way to get a boy alone.¹⁵¹

Some are willing to pull social inferences (or confirm existing presuppositions) by taking these scenes as depictions of daily events.¹⁵² However,

---

145. Sutton 1985: 183.
146. Koch-Harnack 1983: 54: "Wert der Jagd al Erziehungsmittel." Schnapp (1997) gives a much more careful and subtle reading.
147. So that Hoch-Harnack 1983: 94 (no. 47, fig. 28; BA 350505)—showing a bearded man making an up-and-down gesture to a beardless youth, flanked by a dead hare and a dead fox—is read as "Liebesdienste im Austaush gegen Erasten-Pädagogik" ("Sexual favors in exchange for a lover's teaching").
148. Though in fact no one ever says so. Aristophanes mentions the rooster but not that it was a fighting cock. There are very many descriptions of or references to cockfighting in ancient Greece, and the sexual symbolism of defeat and buggery is clear (Dem. *Against Conon,* 54.7–9, for a vivid instance), but no one ever ties it to pederasty, perhaps for that very reason. Saying or implying "If you let me, I will despise you. You will be a loser, like the defeated/buggered rooster in a cockfight" is not a winning approach to seduction. See Schneider 1912, Csapo 1993.
149. We need to specify exactly what we are being asked to believe: that men hunted live stags, captured them (in nets?), transported them, kept them in cages (?), and then released them for practice hunts. There is no indication of a wild setting in the depictions of deer being held by *erastai*.
150. Barringer 2001: 90. That Athenian children kept cheetahs as pets has become something of a truism, despite the urgings of common sense and the silence of the texts.
151. Contrast the story of Aphrodite and Adonis. It is interesting to note that in Ephorus's telling of the Cretan abduction ritual, the hunting together comes after the abduction (*FGrH* 70 F 149).
152. Hubbard (2003a: 9): pederasty "was primarily an upper-class phenomenon, at least in Athens; only men with a certain amount of wealth, leisure, and education were in a position to provide boys with the attention and courtship gifts they might expect, whether tangible or intangible."

the more informed readings of Schnapp, Barringer, and Lear call this simple reading into question.[153] Hunting was a common metaphor for sexual pursuit (of women as well as boys),[154] and Schnapp (1989: 81) refers to "this social construct of the imagination." What we have is not a transcription or depiction of reality but a series of overlapping associations and metaphors: hunting overlaps with war, hunting overlaps with training, training overlaps with pederasty, and a series of analogic equivalences is set up. So Schnapp (1989: 79–80): "The game is an unambiguous social marker, the sign of an age-class and social rank that gives value to the erotic relationship: the lover is to the beloved as the hunter is to the hunted. The artist plays on the hunting metaphor with the same agility as Plato, for whom the philosopher hunts words (*onomata thereuein*) and is a hunter of the truth (*thereutes tes aletheias*)."

This alone explains the extremely limited range of animals: roosters, hares, some deer, a handful of panthers, and what is probably a swan.[155] The reason is not that these were proportionally the most common "gifts" offered to persuade youths to have sex.[156] Instead, they are symbolic. The limited range of animals reflects a limited range of desirable traits. Barringer sums up (2001: 101):

> The various animal gifts presented by the *erastes* to the *eromenos* in Attic vase painting possess qualities associated with the giver and receiver; *erastai* should be virile and fight for their *eromenoi*, whereas *eromenoi* should be attractive and difficult to catch.

I think we can read at least one vase (54) as a parody of vase painting's own conventions. On one side we see a youth, sometimes identified as Pelops, in open mantle apparently running away. On the other side Poseidon, armed with trident, is running holding out a fish (Lear 2008: 149). What else would the sea god have to offer?[157]

Exactly how much might a hare cost?

153. Schnapp (1989; 1997, esp. 247–57, 318–54), Barringer (2001: 70–124), and Lear (2008: 38–52). Barringer (2001: 70–71): "Pederastic courtship vase paintings borrow iconography from hunting scenes to create the metaphor of courtship as hunting. Animal gifts, most commonly hares and cocks, but also deer and felines underscore the metaphor."

154. Dover 1989: 87–88 for sources.

155. For the burning question of hares vs rabbits, see Schnapp 1997: 342–47. Lear 2008: 238n40 counts 100 roosters and 70 hares in DeVries's list.

156. Koch-Harnack 1983: 63 assumes that frequency of representation reflects frequency of the type of animal gift.

157. Cf. a red-figure pelike with a satyr holding out a hare to tightly-wrapped seated youth: St. Petersburg, Hermitage, ST1721 (BA 206009).

Nor should we forget that similar gifts are offered to women on vases (e.g., **53**; Schnapp 1989: 78–79). This fact only reinforces the idea that the gifts are essentially signs, attributes to identify the scene, since there was no "courtship" of women in Athens. Citizen girls were off-limits; slaves were not courted, while courtesans and whores were unlikely to be persuaded by a rabbit, however nice.[158] And hares are not the exclusive attribute of love. Children, including girls, are shown with them evidently as pets on tombstones and funeral lekythoi.[159]

It is a serious error to mistake these images for reality. Hunting game is a metaphor for hunting boys, but of all the images of sex with boys only two seem to place it in a context of hunting: **[8]** (flanking dog and hare; throwing stick for hares, λαγωβόλον) and **14** (spears and leashed dogs).[160] We are justified in concluding that in black-figure at least, precise location was not a primary concern for erotic scenes. In real life, a dead fox or a live cheetah would make a lousy gift. We therefore need to distinguish more rigorously the things that have been labeled "gifts" from the things that Lear (2008: 28–29) more correctly labeled "props."

Lear and Cantarella rightly explain the prevalence of certain animals in the visual sources by the painter's need to use a symbol for the courting relationship. This is so, but it does not explain the lack of attention in the literary sources. That is, the things we label "courting gifts" probably were not. The more bizarre offerings, such as panthers, or stags,[161] all force us to realize that these scenes are symbolic, not representational.

---

158. Cohen (1987: 17) misses the point that there was no need or opportunity for courtship with women: "Given this ambivalent view of the sexual identity of boys [male but not adult male, and hence associated with the female], it is not surprising that in Attic vase-painting courtship of boys and courtship of women were depicted in an almost identical manner. Apart from one major difference (the depiction of the sexual consummation of courtship), the stages, gestures, rituals and gifts of courtship were much the same whether the object was a boy or a woman."

159. Neils and Oakley 2003: 191; Kavvadias 1890–92: no. 794 = Conze 1893–1922: 2, 201, no. 937, pl. clxxxvi; Kavvadias 1890–92: 898 = Conze 1893–1922: 2, 221, no. 1036, pl. ccviii (hare curled in the palm of youth's hand). The Cheramyes kore with a hare, c. 560, dedicated in the Samian Heraion, Berlin Staatliche Museen inv. 1750: Freyer-Schauenburg 1974: 27–31, no. 7, pl. 7–8; Karakasi 2003: no. 7 and 9A.

160. For the same composition as **8**, cf. BA 350505 (Para 72.2, Add 49), with dead hare and fox framing an up-and-down gesture. The mere presence of dog(s) does not indicate a hunting scene. Other lesser possibilities of "courting" in a hunting situation are: (1) DeVries 2.59 (BA 320395): youth with stag, dead hare suspended, dead fox at far right; but the youths are holding wreaths and flank a dancing man. (2) DeVries 3.24 (BA 302651) dog and vines, flanked by dancing men. (3) DeVries 4.102 (BA 203813; R502) shows a dog and the *eromenos* holding a hare by the ears, but the location is marked as a gymnasium by turning post, etc. (4) DeVries 2.12 (BA 14701) is uncertain. One person holds an aryballos and (apparently) a spear; a figure with a dog holds a hare.

161. "Not easy to carry," as Dover notes (1989: 92).

In other words, in real life if you wanted to chat up a boy in ancient Athens, it was not likely that you would hand him a baby panther, miniaturized stag, or a full-sized rooster and say, "I have a nice cock for you." So was there a time when boys could be had for a quail?[162] Only in Cloud-cuckoo-land or that pleasant vale of Sicily where a dove would get you a shepherdess and pan-pipes would get you a boy's kisses.[163]

Lear and Cantarella label this exchange of animals that signals pederastic predation as a form of synecdoche: "the representation of a whole by a part of that whole . . . a common technique in vase iconography," which, they write, is "the center of our interpretive method" (2008: 26, 32). So, for example, the gymnasium can be represented by a herm, an athlete's gym-kit, the racetrack's turning post (Bérard and Durand 1989: 33–34). More properly, perhaps, this type of prop ought be labeled metonymy, and this pedantic distinction has some important implications. Synecdoche implies the reality of the object, an actual part of whatever we are referring to; that is, synecdoche is inherently indexical. Metonymy, as substitution, is inherently symbolic (Andrews 1990: 61). The metonymic object is not an arbitrary substitution, but neither is it necessarily "real." A ladder leaning up against an upper window in cartoons is a metonym for "elopement"; yet it is doubtful that anyone has ever actually eloped that way.

So I am afraid I cannot follow Lear and Cantarella down the bunny trail of synecdoche (2008: 26): "Synecdochic elements abound, however, in every kind of vase-painting. Certain elements can, furthermore, be detached from the scene-type in which they habitually occur and become a kind of symbol for that scene-type or for its subject." This is clearly a slippery argument unless bound by careful rules. The same element will mean something quite different in a different context.[164] In short, without a handbook of iconography we are like to err. A lamb may indicate Christ, St. Agnes, John the Baptist, or the sacrifice of Isaac, John the Baptist, Christ, or St. Agnes. And sometimes a hare is just a hare.

Koch-Harnack (1983: 83–89) had claimed that the basic triad of lover–gift–beloved could be "reduced" to just a youth or just a man (calling them *eromenos* or *erastes* merely begs the question). For her, a kylix by Douris (55) "removes any doubt about the meaning of the hare in representations of a youth by himself."[165] The kylix shows on the outside two sets of three

---

162. As later poets fondly imagined: Glaucus *AP* 12.44; cf. Strato *AP* 12.212.
163. Theoc. 5.96, 133–34; cf. Virg. *Ecl.* 2 (where country gifts count for little in country matters).
164. Bérard and Durand 1989: 26: "We may stress once more that it is always the combination of elements that is significant in each case."
165. Koch-Harnack 1983: 84: "Um jeden Zweifel an der Bedeutung des Hasen in Einzeldarstel-

bearded men standing in front of three tightly wrapped seated youths; hanging auloi, bags, and a lyre, indicate a school scene. One man in each set of three pairs holds out a hare. On each side is written: "Beautiful, beautiful, Hippodamas." In the interior, running around the rim, is a repetitive set of ten men standing in front of similarly wrapped and seated youths, none with "gifts"; hanging sponges and aryballi indicate the gymnasium. The tondo features a seated youth, casually draped, with a hare in his lap and the same gym-kit on the wall.

Lear follows this same chain of sand (2008: 32–34):

> Beazley's scene-type b', the courting-gift scene, is overall the most common type of pederastic scene. These scenes have a particular relationship to synecdoche. In a sense, they themselves are a synecdoche. There is little evidence for gifts in pederastic courtship outside of vase-painting; indeed there are only four references to it in textual sources, all in comedy.[166] In any case, giving gifts can only have been one step in a courtship, not to speak of an entire relationship. Yet in the world of vase-painting, these scenes were for many years the main image of pederasty: this scene-type is a part which represents the whole of pederasty.

The main image certainly, but not the whole, since we do have scenes of "consummation" in interfemoral intercourse. However, I am not persuaded by the next move:

> Further, the animals which were commonly given by *erastai* to *eromenoi* in these scenes—of which the commonest are the fighting-cock and the hare or rabbit—are so associated with pederasty in vase-painting that they serve as a kind of synecdoche for pederasty: they break loose from their original significance as props with a concrete role in courtship scenes and become an independent indicator of pederastic interest.

Lear then reads the cup in the same way as Koch-Harnack had (2008: 34):

> It is beyond doubt that there is a programmatic connection between the tondo and the scenes on the sides: in the frieze, the *erastai* put hares on the youths' laps, and here we see a youth with a hare on his lap. In effect,

---

lungen auszuräumen, wird auf einer Schale des Douris im Louvre (Kat. 33, Abb. 20) außen und und innen das gleiche Thema behandelt. . . ."

166. In fact, two, as we have seen: n. 132 above.

the tondo scene, although more carefully painted, is a synecdoche from the frieze. We do not see the *erastes,* but he is unnecessary to convey the scene's meaning. The scenes in the frieze make clear where hares come from, and here the youth has a hare.

The hare was a prop on the outside, a synecdoche on the inside. This is a reasonable argument, but I am less certain, especially in other cases. So, to confine ourselves to the works of Douris (**56**), we find an almost identical youth with a rabbit on his lap (A) and another youth writing in his tablets (B) on the exterior of a cup; but in the tondo, a young woman, with her dog, throwing her head back and singing with her barbiton. She has nothing to do with pederasty or the youth or the hare.[167]

One can certainly make a case that *one* of the *possible* meanings of a hare is desire,[168] but the fact that X is shown with Y in one vase does not guarantee that X means the same thing when X is shown with Z on a different vase.[169] Lear moves from an image (**I**, fig. 1.10) of a man singing "O most beautiful of boys," which may be from the *Theognidea,*[170] and petting a live hare on the ground beneath his couch, to a kylix by Makron showing just a boy with a *dead* hare on the wall behind him (**J**), to another kylix by Makron where we have nothing but bearded men with a dead hare on the wall and a dog on the floor (**K**). Lear concludes that "a hare is enough to convey the existence of a lover, *erastes* or *eromenos,* in the world of vase painting," and therefore concludes that these men must be talking about their beloveds.[171] Yet the tondo of **K** shows a bearded man talking with a young girl, who is reaching out to grab his stick (the end of a couch is nearby).[172]

---

167. That inside and outside are not necessarily related is shown by Athens, Agora Museum, P24113 (BA 202142), with a youth crouching next to a hare (I), and outside, the battle between Achilles and Memnon (A) and Dionysus (B).

168. The best evidence is **H**: a trio of flying youths bearing a fillet, a flower, and a hare, the first labeled ηιμερος "desire." This is the B side of the famous name vase of the Siren Painter (Odysseus and the Sirens). Barringer (2001: 95) tellingly cites Xen. *Cyn.* 5.33: "There is no one who, on seeing [a hare] tracked, spotted, chased, and captured, would not forget what it was that he desired."

169. Buitron-Oliver (1995: 23) on Douris and "Men and Youths": "Some of these cups have tondos with subjects drawn from mythology, not obviously related to the exterior scene": and vice versa.

170. Ὦ παίδων κάλλιστε [Theognis] 2.1364. Dover 1989: 10: possibly just a generic tag.

171. Lear (2008: 35), agreeing with Koch-Harnack (1983: 97) that the dead hare is sufficient to indicate that the men are "talking about their *eromenoi.*"

172. Cf. Vienna, Kunsthistorisches Museum, 3698 (BA 204875), with men and youths, one holding a hare (A, B), while the tondo shows an undraped youth looking at a girl holding two sprigs.

FIGURE 1.10. Cat. I. Athens, National Museum, 1357. Man on couch, singing "O most beautiful of boys," petting a hare below. Image courtesy of the American School of Classical Studies in Athens.

At this point, we must make an appeal to what I would like to call "scientific iconography." I mean "scientific" in the Popperian sense of falsifiable. When advancing a hypothesis we need to look for counterexamples. And in fact, hares show up in any number of places:[173] they are very com-

---

173. A random selection: A hare accompanies Apollo and the Muses: Ferrara, Museo Nazionale di Spina, T127 (BA 215539) and London, British Museum, 1917.7–25.2 (BA 217933). The Muse Tragoidia holds a thyrsus and hare, while Dionysus pours wine into baby Kōmos: Compiègne, Musée

mon in mourning scenes;[174] they pop up between men and women;[175] children play with them on choes, where there is no erotic interest;[176] and they are used merely to fill up space.[177] As Lear rightly noted: "Hares occur in hunting scenes as well as pederastic scenes and are not invariably a marker for pederasty."[178] With that, I think, goes most of the argument. One could argue with equal cogency that a hare signals a man grieving for his dead son.[179] A hare might give rise to thoughts of pederasty, or a wide variety of things, but only when combined with other markers.

Vivenel, 1025 (BA 213708). Even the eponymous Hare Hunt Painter: Brussels, Musees Royaux, A2323 (BA 203428).

174. A sample: woman with a hare in a mourning scene on a white-ground lekythos: Athens, N. M. 19355 (BA 214321); man holding out hare to a stele: Athens, N. M., 12750 (BA 209275); a youth with a kithara and a woman with a hare on either side on a stele: Paris, Louvre, CA612 (BA 215485); stele with a hare on top: Athens, N. M., A15041 (BA 24598); hare hunting around a stele on a white-ground lekythos: London, British Museum, D60 (BA 216378) and Bonn, Akademisches Kunstmuseum, 1011 (BA 216379), from the aptly named Thanatos Painter. See Barringer 2001: 97, 175–6.

175. E.g., on a rather touching red-figure alabastron, showing (A) a youth with a dead hare facing a young woman spinning and (B) a young man and woman embracing (eye contact, hands cupping the other's head): Athens, Ceramicus, 2713 (BA 352434, Para 331, Add 172).

176. E.g., Copenhagen, National Museum, CHR.VIII344 (BA 10754), where the hare seems ready to leap into the boy's arms; or a hare all by itself: Oxford, Ashmolean, 1951.109 (BA 21470). Others: Hoorn 1951: nos. 12 (BA 4913), 54 (BA 16175), 478, 722 (BA 16124), 728 (BA 10229), 964 (BA 10229); Hamilton 1992: 222. Even panthers are shown: Hoorn 1951: no. 216 (BA 16296), etc.

177. Under the handle in Bologna, Museo Civico Archeologico 365 (BA 204530); a heron, panther, and hare fill in spaces between women and erotes: New York, Metropolitan Museum, 17.230.42 (BA 230843).

178. Lear 2008: 36, correcting Koch-Harnack. E.g., Schnapp 1989: 76–77 (fig. 104, 105): London, British Museum B421 (BA 301203), London, British Museum B52 (1867.5–6.38 = BA 310458).

179. Barringer (2001: 179), however, is so fixed on hares as markers of pederastic courtship that she reads this into funeral steles, arbitrarily labeling figures, even single figures, as "*erastes*" and "*eromenos*," forgetting that steles were put up not by lovers but by family. The dangers of this type of assertion are shown by a damaged stele found in Porto Rafti and now in the museum in Brauron (BE 6), c. 400. Barringer (2001: 180–81) read the preserved bottom two-thirds of the three figures as: "An eromenos, characterized by his nudity, a hare, and two other male figures, faces the viewer. The hare, strigil, and aryballos signal the eromenos's desirability and youthful athleticism . . . Rather than a father and his two sons as suggested by Clairmont, the iconography indicates various areas of masculine life and contest: hunting, warfare, and pederasty." Though Barringer was informed that a piece in the Levy-White collection fitted the top of this stele (2001: 257n25), she did not see the significance. The top gives the names of the father, Menon, and the son, Kleobolos, in the standard fashion. Clairmont was right after all (1993, 3:75–76 no. 3.195 and 3.200). For an analysis of the top before the join, see Milleker in Von Bothmer 1990: 124–26, no. 97. For the join, see Despinis 1991–92 and Bergemann 1997: 159 no. 45. See Gill 2009 for the intellectual cost of this type of looting.

GROUP SEX

One other great conflict between the world represented on the vases and that found in the literary sources is "group" sex. On one hand, the literary record is quite clear that such things were not done by civilized people.[180] Plato uses it as an example of how circumstances alter cases: "And when it comes to sex, we would all contend that it's the sweetest thing, but if you're going to do it, you have to do it so that no one sees, since it's the most shameful thing to be seen."[181] Apollodorus charges the loathsome Phrynion with having "used her [the hetaira Neaera] shamelessly and outrageously, taking her with him to dinner whenever he drank, always partying with her, and openly having intercourse whenever and wherever he wished, making a display of his power over her to the onlookers."[182] It seems clear from these passages that public display was considered tasteless. Theophrastus in his *Character Sketches* hints at such bad behavior. He says of "The Obnoxious Man" (11.8): "He goes shopping for himself and hires flute-girls and shows what he's bought to everyone and invites them to share."[183] This is meant to be suggestive. And of the "The Tasteless Man" he writes (20.10): "When he invites people over for drinks, he says, 'A delight has been prepared for the guests,' and if they ask for it, he says, 'The slave will send for *her* from the pimp immediately, so that we may be played to by her and have a good time.'"[184]

On the other hand, the vases frequently depict various sexual acts that *seem* to occur in the same space, not only the handful of riotous vases, but the calmer scenes already discussed.[185] Dover early on warned against taking

---

180. Other discussions in ancient authors are more about sex in the open (generally among barbarians) and the proper behavior of wives specifically: *Dissoi Logoi* 2.4, Xenophon *Anabasis* 5.4.34. So Theopompus on the luxurious Etruscans: *FGrH* 115 F 204 (Athenaeus 12.517e–18b). But for a slave looking on, see Aristophanes *Frogs* 542–48. Literary descriptions of symposia are very decorous.

181. *Hippias Major* 299a (which I will take as genuine). The point is that Plato is not arguing about proper sexual activity; he is appealing to what everyone knows in order to prove his point.

182. [Dem.] 59.33.

183. 11.8: καὶ ὀψωνεῖν ἑαυτῷ καὶ αὐλητρίδα μισθοῦσθαι καὶ δεικνύειν δὲ τοῖς ἀπαντῶσι τὰ ὠψωνημένα καὶ παρακαλεῖν ἐπὶ ταῦτα. See Diggle 2004: 318: "He proposes to enliven the meal which he has bought for himself by hiring girl pipers, and then he has the bad taste to show the food to strangers in the street and invite them to share the meal (and by implication the girls)."

184. 20.10: ὅπως πάντες ὑπ' αὐτῆς αὐλώμεθα καὶ εὐφραινώμεθα. Diggle 2004: 403–4; he is probably right not to see an obscene sense in "pipe" (the same passive verb is at 19.9 with no dirty overtones).

185. On the images depicting sexual violence, see Kilmer 1990; Kilmer 1993: 104 and 214–15; Lewis (2002: 124–25) counts five instances: 51 (Nikosthenes), 74 (Pedieus Painter), 75 (Brygos), R530 (Foundry Painter, BA 275962: slipper), and 57 (Thalia), but the last is misread by Lewis, since the woman is using the slipper on the man. To these, we perhaps should add the unique scene of satyrs

the vases as visual records (1974: 206): "We must remember, however, that when vase-painters show what may seem to be two or more couples having intercourse in the same room or out of doors in close proximity, pictorial conventions play a part."

One important convention, too often ignored, is the role played by shape and place on the pottery: tondos in black-figure show couples, sometimes flanked by dancers or animals to fill the crescents, while tondos in red-figure almost always carry only individuals or couples. Cup rims and the shoulders or bellies of closed forms provide a longer pictorial space and are more likely (because more able) to carry what appears as uninterrupted space.

The problem is what indicates shared space in Attic art. Sutton investigated the matter more broadly and showed that even some of what we consider the most basic clues—overlap of figures and actions, for example—do not necessarily apply to Greek depictions of space. Using vases featuring the labors of Theseus, he concluded (1981: 20): "These scenes also indicate that incidental overlapping of unrelated figures cannot be used to argue that a scene's different episodes belong to the same time and space."

In fact, the majority of scenes lack any clear indicators of space at all. Lewis (2002: 120) rightly distinguishes two distinct types of scenes:

> The first comprises images of men and women engaged in sexual acts in vague or non-existent settings. These are found almost exclusively on cups, and are usually playful in tone: naked men and women roll about on wineskins and cushions, dance or copulate in sexualised play. . . . These scenes are found mainly in the work of the archaic pot-painters, and although their setting is clearly sympotic, with participants sometimes wearing wreaths, and with kraters, baskets and wineskins as "furniture," there is not the same sense of organisation as in scenes where diners recline. Here we are in what Lissarrague calls "l'espace du cratere"[186] where dance and play,

---

torturing a woman (African? A lamia?) by the creepy Beldam Painter (BA 352144, Athens, N. M. CC961). In 75, a man seems to be threatening the conjoined genitals of a man and woman with a lamp. Does this point in the direction of outrageous behavior or specifically male on female violence? Parisinou (2000: 25): "Without participating in the orgy, he attempts to touch with a burning lamp the bottom of a naked hetaira, who is busy making love with another bearded man, who lifts her in his arms." Frontisi-Ducroux (1996: 90) identifies him as a voyeur whose lamp is not threatening. Keuls (1985: 174–86) reads these scenes as abuse directed specifically at older, fatter prostitutes; so too Ferrari 2002: 163, 178; Sutton 2000: 194–9; Lear 2008: 119. See, however, the critique by Lewis 2002: 124–5, who also notes that the violent vases constitute only a tiny fraction of erotic images and seem confined to a handful of painters. See also Kurke 1999: 208–12. For an overview of the theme of violence in Greek vase painting, see Stähli 2005: 25–26.

186. Lissarrague 1987a: 23–48 = 1990a: Ch. 2 "Around the Crater."

including sexualised play, are part of the scheme of things. The playful aspects, including balancing acts with cups, and the lack of explicit setting should suggest that we are not meant to interpret these as scenes of reality: rather we are looking at a representation of the release of the symposium, a scenario in which inhibitions on behaviour are lifted.

The Tyrrhenian vases and most black-figure fall into this category. Even within this undifferentiated space, however, there is a natural tendency for the composition to break into individual couples. So for example, a black-figure kylix sitting on a phallic foot (**60**) has a continuous frieze showing twelve male–female couples having sex in a variety of positions. The space is filled with vine leaves at the top. There are no overt separations (pillar, vines, etc.) yet each couple stands in its own individual space. So, too, in the black-figure "orgy" vase, above (**26**, fig. 1.4).[187] Even on **61** it is difficult to say if the masturbating youths on either side of a central couple in rear-entry position are about to sodomize and irrumate them respectively, or are merely "interested spectators" (Stansbury-O'Donnell 2006: 16–17), or are just erotic flanking figures. Sutton's chronological change in black-figure is more a matter of differences in the placement of figures on different types of pottery by different potters. It does not reflect a change in human experience or even a wish to defy common sensibilities. Kilmer concludes about the features of black-figure (1993: 56–57):

> Most of the collections appear to serve almost as menus of erotic variation; none that I know demands to be interpreted as a group engaged in sexual acts in one place at one time. In the black-figure examples couples are most often physically separate one from another, which weakens any impression of unity of place and time; they are set up in a sort of parade order.

Lewis's second type (2002: 121) "is distinguished by a more complex setting, including dress and furniture—klinai, mattresses, cushions and chairs. Objects depicted in the background, such as baskets and aulos cases[,] sometimes make reference to sympotic settings, but other images show simple interiors, with stools and beds in the background." The setting of most of these "orgies" or "group sex" scenes seems to be vaguely sympotic (cups, couches, cushions), and this has had important consequences not only for how these vessels are read but for the way we envisage the symposium. Lewis notes (2002: 95–96):

---

187. E.g., Sutton 2009: no. 62, 66, 76–79, 85.

It is taken as axiomatic that aulos players in classical Athens were prostitutes; that they formed the lowest class of prostitutes, that they would play music early in the evening, then later have sex with the symposiasts, and that all auletrides were expected to offer oral sex to their patrons at the end of an evening.[188]

It is further assumed that the flute-players, hetairai, and the women, both clothed and naked, in sympotic scenes are all interchangeable.[189] Lewis notes the paucity of evidence for each of these assumptions.[190] Yet, that sex was an essential component, almost constitutive, of the symposium is a fairly widespread assumption.[191] Kurke (1997, 1999) has argued

---

188. Citing Stewart 1997: 165; Davidson 1997: 81–82; Landels 1999: 7. Davidson (2006: 39–40) has moderated his views (on this topic) somewhat: "Two conclusions seem certain: one, sexual opportunity was never casually and uncalculatingly assumed to be part of the bargain when you hired someone out to play aulos at a symposium: if they wanted sex too, they would have to pay extra; and two, a slave musician was never completely out of range . . . We may well have exaggerated the extent to which musicians, even aulos girls, were freely available, but their masters or mistresses were always probably open to bids"; this, too, is more speculative than factual. So Clarke 2010: 108–9 (2011: 172): "The images of heterosexual intercourse focus on the orgies with paid female sex-workers (hetairai) that constituted an entertainment of the all-male symposium . . . Visual representations change significantly in the early Hellenistic period. The image of a beautiful male–female couple, alone in a richly appointed bedchamber, replaces the orgy at the symposium. Scholars interpret this shift to one-on-one sexual representations as a reflection of the emphasis in Hellenistic society on the individual rather than the collective; the shift may also reflect the growth of the romance novel in this period." Clarke rightly warns: "Although black- and red-figure vase painting is the major source for study of ancient Greek sexual representation, it is not a straightforward record of sexual practices."

189. See Lewis 2002: 91–129, esp. 95–97; 111: "Just as in reality there was no method of distinguishing a prostitute from any other woman simply by looking, so there is no immediate way of telling the status of a woman on pottery"; Blazeby 2011 for detailed criticism.

190. Flute-players are frequently mentioned as entertainers, but not as sex workers; e.g., Pl. *Prot.* 347c, quoted and expanded by Athen. 3.97b, where they belong not to the symposia of the elite but to symposia "of people who are lower-class and unsophisticated" (φαύλων καὶ ἀγοραίων ἀνθρώπων), while in Pl. *Rep.* 373a hetairai belong to the banquets of the luxurious city (τρυφῶσαν πόλιν), and cf. 568e3, 573d3. However, see Metagenes 4 KA. Davidson (1997: 81n22) also cites Adespota 1025 KA (Satyrus's *Life of Euripides* = P. Oxy. 9 [1912] 1176, frg. 39, col. 5, 12–29): ἐν ταῖς [τριό]δοις σοι [προ]σγελῶ[σ'] αὐλητρίδες "At the street corners, flute girls smile at you" (it is not clear how or if the following lines are connected) and Theopompus 115 *FGrH* F 290 which mentions flute-girls in the Piraeus, both suggestive but not particularly clear evidence. We do have many scenes with naked women playing the aulos: Lewis 2002: 231n22, and many others.

191. E.g., Murray (1990: 7) in an influential formulation: "The *symposion* became in many respects a place apart from the normal rules of society, with its own strict code of honour in the *pistis* there created, and its own willingness to establish conventions fundamentally opposed to those within the *polis* as a whole. . . . The distinctive manipulation of Greek sexuality in the homosexual bonding of young males through *symposion* and *gymnasion* is one aspect of this self-conscious separation; another is the creation of a type of 'free love' associated with the *hetaira* and the other attendants or entertainers at the symposion; a third is the development of forms of ritual exhibitionism

that the institution of the symposium actually "invented" the category of hetaira.[192]

Sutton, who confines his article to "heterosexual" intercourse, sees a change over time (2009: 77) first in black-figure and then in red-figure:

> From the black-figure scenes it quickly became clear that lovemaking was introduced on Attic pottery as a public, group activity, and that scenes showing isolated couples appear rarely and late; moreover, the theme is widely distributed through Greek and Etruscan lands.[193]

Rather than a chronological development of subject matter, what we see are different schemes for placement. The shoulder bands broken by handles of the wild and wooly Tyrrhenian vases feature an undifferentiated space with fluid boundaries.[194] The vast majority of Sutton's sample are Little Master cups (2009: no. 19–59), which follow a simple linear layout. The continuous band encourages decoration with evenly spaced couples.[195] The progress that he sees towards couples in isolation is due rather to a change in the painted area. The new isolated couples are all in the tondos of cups.[196]

For red-figure, Sutton made a second claim (2009: 77):

> On red-figure pottery lovemaking is performed as often in groups as in private by isolated couples. This was surprising, since Herodotus and other

---

and violence in the komos at the end of the session." So, too, Pellizer in the same collection (1990: 181), who notes that "the few sources in our possession are often also rather late (from the fourth century BC onwards for the most part)" but adduces the "vase painting on this theme" as proof that "in many cases" a symposium would end with sex. "The least that one can say is that in these gatherings there could occur (and perhaps fairly frequently) activities which might cause a modest classical scholar to blush."

192. Cf. Lewis 2002: 101. On the false distinction of hetaira from mere prostitute, see Glazebrook and Henry 2011: 3–5; Glazebrook 2011: 34.

193. For isolated couples: Sutton 2009: no. 76–79, 92, 93. See also Paleothodoros 2012: 24.

194. Sutton 2009: 78, no. 1–14: "Tyrrhenian lovemaking is kinetic and sociable, performed in public by standing pairs without the aid of furniture, with or without clothing. Merry dancers passing among the lovers and on the back of many vessels create a sense of wild abandon and friendly group spirit. The painters' avoidance of strict symmetry contributes to a relaxed atmosphere and a sense of disorder."

195. Lewis 2002: 117: "the most striking feature is the lack of context"; Sutton 2009: 79: "The Little Masters are generally strict formalists who create an orderly, abstract world that completely lacks the social immediacy of the Tyrrhenians. Their lovers exist in a decorative world of visually discrete elements, either a single figure or a couple, that line up in a single plane without significant overlap."

196. Sutton 2009: 77, 77–78, 82, 88, no. 76–79.

authors regard public sex as alien to Greek practice and akin to bestial behavior.

Lewis, too, sees a chronological development (2002: 117):

> On the latest black-figure the subject becomes less popular, while in red-figure the scenes become more varied, both more detailed and explicit, and also more decorous: we now find sex in sympotic scenarios, usually more clearly delineated, and a move from group sex to individual couples, though this is gradual.

Both these claims seem mostly incorrect.

The first problem is what counts as group sex. Kilmer pointed out the problems (1993: 55–56):

> This is a difficult category to deal with. There are relatively few cases in which some variant of it is certainly occurring, but many in which it may be implied. . . . The question of the apparent orgy scenes is considerably more difficult. R156*, R192*, R223*, R490* (B), R518† and R697* [**73, 57, 51, 66, 74, 72,** respectively] all contain scenes in which many individuals are directly involved in sexual acts, others taking part in more or less active spectator roles. The question naturally arises whether these are intended as all happening in one place at one time, or whether some other interpretation is more likely.

His answer was (1993: 56):

> It is safe to conclude that, where two or more men have a single woman as the focus of their sexual actions or obvious intentions, there is group sex. Where we find several couples engaged as couples in sexual activity within a single spatial framework the problem is much more complex. Juxtapositions in pictorial space are not necessarily meant to portray either juxtaposition in real space or contemporaneity.

In short a threesome must necessarily be shared space, but other examples are less certain.[197] However, even what constitutes a triad of actors or "obvious intensions," or who counts as a "spectator," is not always clear.

---

197. Kilmer 1993: 112 (on **66**): "Although the two couples overlap physically, the conventions of this art do not allow us to infer that they are in the same place at the same time. They overlap; they do not show any signs of interacting."

Kilmer is properly cautious and counts thirteen possible examples of group sex. Of these, seven are said to depict threesomes, one of which is fragmentary but likely, and another too fragmentary to be sure. Another vase should be added (**69**).[198] A further six he labels "orgies (?)," that is, with more figures than a threesome depicted.[199] However, any clear picture of "group sex" grows blurry on closer examination. The vases fall into four groups.

(a) In the non-"orgy" vases, we seem to have only one threesome with clear body contact (**62**), "imminent" at that, where two naked ithyphallic men carry a naked woman between them, her legs over the shoulders of the man at left. Bringing up the rear, at a slight distance, is a draped man playing the barbiton. Kilmer (1993: R898) captions this "Copulation à trois to lyre music." However, it is not clear that the musician is in the same pictorial space as the other figures. On the other side two naked ithyphallic men accost a naked woman who is holding a pair of *auloi*. Here all three are clearly in the same space.

(b) Instead, most of Kilmer's "threesomes" fall into a pattern of what we might call "quasi" or "imminent" threesomes. All are the work of just two artists, the Antiphon Painter and the Onesimos Painter, who show a recurrent pattern of a woman on her back or on all fours, flanked by a beardless youth and an older man or by two youths (**63–68**). Threesomes are always two men and one woman in Greek vase painting—an interesting difference from modern pornography—and are not mentioned in Greek literature.[200] All of these examples, where we can tell, contain places where the couples overlap (most often the legs and feet of one figure crossing over, behind or before another's) or seem to intrude into another's space.[201] But as Sutton pointed out, overlap is no certain guide. Only in **63–64** do the two men both touch the woman in the center, making it absolutely clear that they are in the same space. One of his cups (**65**) is a good example of the difficulties of reading each vase: (A) on the right,

---

198. R461 (**70**), R464 (**63**), R486 (**64**), R487 (**67**), [R488] (**68**), R489 (**65**), R898 (**62**). Add Kilmer's R249 (**69**).

199. See quote above. R156 (**73**), R192 (**57**), R223 (**51**), R490 (**66**), R518 (**74**), R697 ([**72**]). Of these I count only four as good evidence. [**73**] is too damaged and the degree of overlap is too unclear to label it an "orgy."

200. Two late epigrams refer to three men sharing one woman, one for each orifice: *AP* 5.49 (Gallus) and 11.328 (Nicarchus), but such a scene is more a poet's conceit than an indication of practice.

201. A mild example in Athens, Acropolis 1040 (R9*; ARV 18; Peschel 1987: no. 85; not in BA) a damaged red-figure plaque as a dedication, where two men back to back are having intercourse from behind with two women. The men's buttocks do not just touch but actually overlap.

an older, balding man, holding his penis, stands behind a woman in the position for intercourse from behind; in front of them on the left a youth plays auloi. The two sets seem unified by the bolster that lies between them, but otherwise share nothing. Kilmer lists the aulos-player as part of a standard composition (1993: 55): "a third person (almost invariably male, and usually adolescent) looks on, sometimes showing signs of wanting to take part." However, since the youth is not part of the action, Kilmer speculates that "the spectator is a youth playing a flute (potentially, though not necessarily, a servile role)." However, we hear nothing of male slave *auletes* playing at symposia.[202] The youth is far more likely to be a symposiast. Learning to play the aulos was part of mousike (education), and aristocrats such as Callias and Critias were accomplished players.[203]

The other side (B) shows another couple in intercourse from behind; in front of them a youth with a staff bends down, with one knee extended. Kilmer identifies him as "probably just a spectator" and the caption reads, "Youth prepares to copulate *a tergo* with bending young woman; a second youth looks on." But in fact the youth is looking down at the ground, as though he were climbing a hill. Here there is no overlap even of a bolster and the youth's walking stick seems to form a frame. How exactly he relates to the couple on the left is uncertain.

(c) However, in most of the non-orgy vases, the couples form discrete units and we may be misreading them to take them as "groups," that is, sharing visual space (**66, 69–72**). A more difficult example is another cup by the Antiphon Painter (**66**), which Kilmer labels as an "orgy." One side of the cup shows the Antiphon Painter's typical triangle: a bearded man lifts both the legs of a woman on the ground and holds a slipper behind his back. On the left, a youth, naked but for a chlamys around his shoulder, seems to be running. His arm extends into the space over the woman's head. Keuls reads this as "a man about to beat an undefending hetaera on the buttocks with a shoe; another man, who approaches from the left, seems to be protesting" (1985: 180). He is not erect, and Peschel (1987: 129) describes him as a grotesque dancing figure. Side B shows one youth having sex from behind with a woman. Next to them is a woman on the ground, supporting herself on her left arm. Her right hand is up and open, a sign of surrender. A youth stands over her, holding her shoulder. He, too, is holding a slipper behind his back. All four are naked. The two women's

---

202. There were slave auletes, just as there were slave just about everything else: Ar. *Thesm.* 1175, 1203; Andoc. 1.12

203. Ath. 4.184df, cf. 624b by contrast. Ar. *Pol.* 1341ab. Wilson 1999.

supporting arms cross. The scene is minimally indicated as sympotic by the hanging food basket on the wall between the two women's heads. This would seem to be shared space but there is no reaction between the two pairs.

A cup by Epeleios (**69**, fig. 1.11) is not listed by Kilmer as an "orgy" vase though it seems to fit the scenario. Kilmer describes it (1993: 35):

> A naked ithyphallic youth (1) with long slender sideburns bends forward. With his left hand he grasps the right ankle, and with his right the calf, of a young woman (2) who bends down to our right, left forearm on the floor, right hand just touching it. The woman is naked . . . Interpretation seems simple: this is preparation for standing *a tergo* copulation. The scene is complicated by the arrival of an extra youth (5) at the far right, beyond a couple copulating on a couch. Like the spare youths in some scenes by Onesimos and the Antiphon Painter, he may wish to supplant youth (1); or he may wish to follow either of the successful youths in copulation with one of the women. Whatever his imagined hopes or intentions, for the moment he is clearly a spectator.

This may be correct but his stance is that of a dancer. A further example of the difficulties of interpretation is **L**, which shows a pair of tender scenes on the shoulders of each side of a red-figure hydria: two couples, each made of a beardless youth plus a young woman. Despite the fact that the Dikaios Painter has represented the kline mattress as one unbroken surface, all four couples seem isolated, unaware of the other, each person making eye contact only with their partner.[204]

(d) The "orgy vases" (**51, 57, 73, 74**) have received a great deal of press, so much that Lewis (2002: 124, 235n106) refused to illustrate them further.[205] She is right to note that they are "hardly numerous" and "statistically . . . not very significant," but we must not be misled into thinking that we have a cross-sample. The four cups are from four different painters (Nikosthenes, Thalia, Pedieus, Brygos) and may represent more that just one-offs.[206] The vases do seem to cluster around 500 BCE.[207] One of the

---

204. La Genière 2009: 341 claims this and other vases were painted "for" Vulci and reflect Etruscan banquets where men dined with women.

205. Though it is odd not to find this cup discussed in Keuls 1985. See n. 181 above for Lewis's list.

206. Contra Lewis 2002: 124.

207. **51**, Nikosthenes P., c. 520–510; **57**, Thalia P., c. 510; **74**, Pedieus P, c. 510; **75**, Brygos P., is later, c. 490–480.

FIGURE 1.11. Cat. 69. Malibu, Getty 82.AE.27. Epeleios Painter, c. 510. Man lifts woman's leg (in preparation for intercourse from behind?). Youth reclining on couch having intercourse with woman on top facing back. Left: Ithyphallic youth making uncertain gesture. The J. Paul Getty Museum, Villa Collection, Malibu, California, Gift of N. Bunker Hunt.

distinctive features of the Boston kantharos (51; fig. 1.8a and 1.8b) is the care the Nikosthenes Painter has taken to show the figures superimposed on each other receding into the depth of the visual plane. These scenes are clearly intended to denote shared space. It might be something of an argument from silence, but can we then be certain in the absence of such indicators that the space is meant to read as common?

The exterior of the name vase of the Thalia Painter (57) shows a kōmos of seventeen naked figures: six young men (one improper, displayed), two bearded man, and nine women. The men, where we can tell, are erect. "The figures range from a couple engaged in wild dance, to a hetaira leading a young man off by his penis, to a bearded man pursuing a running hetaira with an aulos-case suspended from his erect penis, to a couple standing in the far corner copulating" (Kurke 1997: 133 = 1999: 202). Above some of the women are the names Smik<r>a, Korone, and Thalia. The setting is sympotic, with lamp stands, cups, ladles, and both men and women in elaborate snoods and headpieces. Though there is minimal overlap, the unity of decoration implies a shared space. The tondo (fig. 1.12) is harder to read, and not just because it is damaged. In the center, an entwined couple. He is grasping the edges of the kline as he penetrates the woman lying under him, who, contrary to what might be assumed, is plying the sandal on the upraised buttocks of her bearded partner. Behind them, on a bolster, is a masturbating youth. The Thalia Painter has been careful to show the woman's leg wrapping around the man's and the youth's legs disappearing behind the couple's. Beneath them is a woman with her eyes languorously shut, also masturbating, the only depiction I know of a woman using her hand rather than a dildo or other objects. She is placed below the kline and above the top of a footstool. Is she meant to be actually under the kline or is she nearer the viewer? It is clear that we are looking at a unified space, since the lines of a tall lamp stand run up the entire tondo behind all four figures. The youth is almost certainly placed as an onlooker; the woman, almost certainly not.

There is a further interesting feature found in the cups by the Pedieus Painter (73, fig. 1.13a, 1.13b, 1.13c) and the Brygos Painter (74). These two cups, with disturbing scenes of sexual violence on the outside, reveal two calm, even tender scenes of a clothed man and woman on the tondo, a fact often hidden by the choice of illustrations.[208] Kilmer labels the tondo of 73, "Youth embraces lyre-playing woman. Prelude to A, B?," that is, to the forced fellatio and beatings with a slipper; so too the tondo of 74 is

---

208. Rightly noted by Lewis 2002: 124.

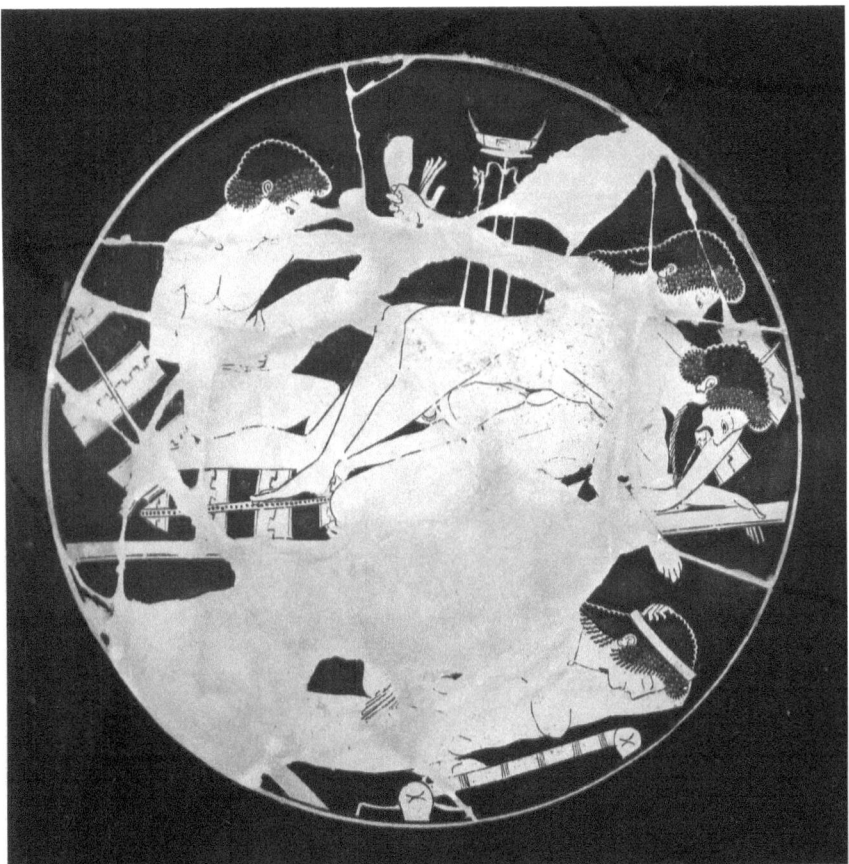

FIGURE 1.12. Cat. 57. Berlin, Antikensammlung, 3251. On couch, youth masturbates; bearded man has intercourse with woman who is holding a slipper above his buttocks. Below the couch, a woman masturbates. bpk, Berlin / Art Resource, New York.

captioned as "Man with flute-girl: prelude to A, B? Cf. R156*" (= 73). But a contrast is equally likely, and far from being a prelude, such scenes of a woman, often with a lyre (73) or a pair of auloi (74) escorting a drunken man are better read as part of the kōmos, the drunken and sometimes rowdy walk back from the symposium. One could drink deep and see revealed at the bottom of these two cups not the external excess but *calme, luxe, et volupté*.[209]

---

209. Compare the name vase of the Kiss Painter (Berlin F2269, R303*, BA 201624*): komos outside, tender kiss between youth and girl inside.

FIGURE 1.13A. Cat. 73. Paris, Musée du Louvre, G13. Pedieus P., c. 510. Side A. Two threesomes of a man irrumating a woman while another enters her from behind. Traces of another couple. Photo: commons.wikimedia.org

FIGURE 1.13B. Side B. Intercourse from behind; bearded man striding behind them. Ithyphallic youth with lamp stand holds his arm. Youth irrrumates woman. Photo: commons.wikimedia.org

FIGURE 1.13C. Tondo of the above. Youth with kylix and walking stick embraces woman with lyre. Photo: Les freres Chuzeville. © RMN-Grantl Palais / Art Resource, New York.

Are we then looking at what actually happened despite the decorum of the texts, at comic exaggeration, or at a pictorial convention?[210] In some cases perhaps the first, in more cases probably the second, in most cases merely the third. It seems that much of what appears to us as group sex was not intended to be read as such. In these cases perhaps, the texts and the pictures are not at such variance as we have thought.

---

210. Dover 1974: 206; Sutton 2000: 183–84.

FELLATIO

The literary and popular written sources make numerous boasts, claims, and threats of men using other men's mouths for their pleasure,[211] but there does not seem to be any surviving depiction of human males fellating other males,[212] though there are several of women fellating men.[213]

CUNNILINGUS

Nor despite the attacks on men as cunt-lickers are there any images.[214] Three scenes have been claimed.[215] The exterior of the Thalia Painter's cup (**57**) shows "a naked woman cavorting over a collapsing youth so that his face is within a few inches of her vulva, [but this] hardly qualifies as cunnilinctus."[216] A pelike from Tarquinia (**58**) shows a man with an erection

---

211. Aristyllus (Ar. *Eq.* 647–48; and his anus gapes, too: *Wealth* 314) and Cleisthenes (*Frogs* 423), a frequent butt; Agathon (*Thes.* 49), The Sausage-Seller (*Eq.* 167), and all the leaders of Athens (*Ach.* 79). For other examples in comedy, cf. Alexis 244 KA, Strattis 41 KA. Timaeus ap. Polybius 12.13.1–2. Graffiti: Attica. c. 323 BCE, Ziebarth 1934: 1024 (no. 1.B.16–20). Gager 1992: 145–47 (no. 56) with improved readings by David Jordan. One can see the difficulties with such sentences as "Literary evidence gives us reason to believe that by the fourth century fellation was thought to be a common (though not an approved) way for homosexual love to be expressed [citing Dover 1978: 99, which does not support this point]. The negative evidence of vase-painting suggests that it was not approved for the visual arts. It may also suggest that during the period in question it was not approved in real life; but that is an extension from the available evidence" (Kilmer 1993: 71). First, not "love," but sex. Second, "approved" by whom, for what? The man having his penis sucked completely approved of having his penis sucked. He may not have approved of the person sucking him.

212. Dover 1989: 99: "Homosexual fellation seems, so far as vase-painting is concerned, peculiar to satyrs (B271*, R1127*)"; Kilmer 1993: 70, 114–17. All this could be changed, however, by a single new find. See Kilmer 1993: 213–14 on the absence of certain types of images.

213. E.g., **26, 51, 74, 75**. Sutton (2009) lists two: no. 83 (BA 19757) and 84 (**26**). Kilmer 1993: 71–72 for a list of four in RF: R156* (**73**), R223* (**51**), R518* (**74**), R1188*. Kilmer claims three others as "Imminent": R47*, R464*, R490* (the last I do not see how).

214. E.g., Ar. *Knights* 1282–9 (see Henderson 1991: 185), Galen 12.249 K. For graffiti: Preisigke et al. 1915–93: 1, 288 (no. 4130); Bernand 1972: 52–3 (no. 23).

215. Evidence reviewed by Dover 1989: 101–2, Kilmer 1993: 71.

216. Dover 1989: 101–2. Taken as cunnilingus by Brendel 1970: 23, Reinsberg 1989: 117, Hupperts 2000: 203. Kurke (1997: 133 = 1999: 203–4): "If this is indeed what the vase depicts (and there is some dispute on the matter), it is the only representation of cunnilingus in all of Greek art." It would be quite easy to show cunnilingus unambiguously, but the painters chose not to. See below for further description.

looking up a woman's skirt.²¹⁷ A wild black-figure cup (**59**) shows improbably acrobatic male–female intercourse not cunnilingus.²¹⁸

BEGINNINGS AND ENDS

Our final problem, and perhaps most troubling for any straightforward interpretation of Greek visual culture, is that no one has a good explanation for either the sudden beginning of erotic images in black-figure (c. 560 BCE) nor of their even more surprising cessation in red-figure (c. 460 BCE).²¹⁹ We do not believe that the Athenians suddenly gave up sex (or alternatively that the Etruscans suddenly ceased to like porn). Are we dealing with a change in ethics, or esthetics, or sensibility? Hubbard and others have blamed the rise of democracy (2003: 115):

> The evidence is far more substantial for the fifth century and later, when one can note a progressive diminution in the status of pederasty at Athens, apparently in conjunction with the growth and radicalization of the democracy. . . . Art historians have noted that scenes of uninhibited pederastic courtship and sex are common on Athenian vases until about 460 . . . , parallel to the celebration of pederastic love in the lyric poets; afterward, however, such representations (and, indeed, even explicit heterosexual scenes) virtually disappear in favor of much more coded arrangements . . . This movement away from a libertine and hedonistic artistic style toward more prudish and "family-oriented" modalities seems to parallel the sexual conservatism and enforcement of moral norms evident in comedy and oratory of the late fifth and early fourth centuries, which, as we have seen, appeal emphatically to popular tastes and democratic values.

---

217. Tentatively suggested as cunnilingus by Sutton 1981: 120. See Kilmer 1993: 131–42.
218. Kilmer 1993: 71n14: "The man stands; the woman is doing a hand-stand, head and forearms on the ground, thighs on the man's shoulders so that her vulva ought to be right at his face. His penis, however, rises up to touch her abdomen near the hip joint: his intention may be to lower her on to his penis, rather than to stay in this position and continue the entertainment that way." Sutton 2009: 78–79: this and 59 "are the most convincing hint of cunnilingus on Attic pottery, and are far from certain." Note that BA 12960 attaches CAVI notes 3521 to this record that belong to BA 9023168.
219. Dover 1989: 152–53, Kilmer 1993: 2. The visual evidence dribbles away even as the literary evidence comes in floods.

The scare-quotes around "family-oriented" do little to diminish the anachronisms, and the idea of Aristophanes as an enforcer of "sexual conservatism" is itself very funny.[220] Lewis points out the obvious flaw in this argument (2002: 112):

> There is a clear development of the motif over time, and this reveals the danger of trying to read pots as a close reflection of society, since depictions of symposia become sexualised in early red-figure, then more decorous again in the fourth century, a change which cannot be reflecting reality in Athens since the fourth century was the age of the great courtesans.

Whitley (2001: 363) argues that it is not the society as a whole but the symposium that became more "democratic" at roughly the same time:

> By 450 BC the symposium had clearly ceased to be an exclusively aristocratic affair. Indeed, the popularity of andrones in most houses in both Athens and the Piraeus indicates clearly that this custom had "trickled down" to the citizen population at large. The sympsion had been democratised, and, as the fifth century wore on, the images on symposium pots changed too. Scenes with satyrs and Dionysos, and of aristocratic gatherings with fairly explicit sexual overtones, diminish in number, though myths remain as popular as ever.

Here I would simply dispute the idea that either the symposium or pederasty had ever been exclusively "aristocratic" (see above).

These readings are too simplistic. Erotic imagery had various tides and eddies. As Palaeothodoros points out (2012: 24):

> Scenes of intercourse in licentious public revels appear in the second quarter of the sixth century, and decline rapidly after 550 BC, only to be

---

220. See also Hubbard 2000, 2006. 2014: 129: "Pederasty was mainly an element of elite habitus in Athens, and the rising political dominance of what one might call the 'middle class' within Athenian democracy led to a privileging of middle-class taste—as reflected in the anti-elite posture of comedy, the simplified diction of Euripidean tragedy, and the marginalization of explicit sexuality in art." Describing Euripides' style as "simplified" is as curious as attributing it to the rise of democracy. Hubbard 2014: 138–39: "That [man–boy pederasty] ceased to be so represented in vase-painting of the later fifth century suggests that it was no longer so welcome in the family home of that period. As the market for painted wares broadened, pederastic enthusiasts had to collect antique vessels, purchase silver, or make do with modern, mass-marketed PG-13 works, in which the homoeroticism was at best coded and ambiguous." Closeted gay porn, it seems. Rich elite "pederastic enthusiasts" seem to have trouble commissioning vessels for their private homes. See also Shapiro 1981a: 141–43 and 2000a: 21. For criticism, see Lear 2014: 122.

replaced by orgies taking place in the context of the symposion; single couples engaging in sexual intercourse are often depicted from 520 to 470 BC, but are rarely shown afterwards; homosexual courtship scenes start around 560 and continue till the later part of the archaic period, but tend to disappear altogether after 470 BC; erotic pursuits appear near 500 and cease after the 430s; heterosexual courtship scenes have their prime in the late archaic period, and are replaced after the middle of the fifth century by images with clear nuptial overtones; female nudes are popular from 520 to 460, and again during the 4th century, but in the latter period, they clearly refer to goddesses and to anonymous brides.

The erotic scenes peter out around the same time that a number of different scene types disappear and others flourish. So Himmelmann (1994: 23–48) notes the decline in all types of scenes of daily life. At roughly the same time scenes of work, manufacture, and even symposium also start to fade in number.[221] Yet, at the same time, interior scenes of women start to proliferate. Sutton (1992: 33), Boardman (1989: 219), and Burn (1987: 84–85) speculate on changes in the status of or attitude to women. Bažant (1987) looked again to democratic reform which somehow promoted "interiority." There is a contemporaneous change not just in subjects but in the shapes of pots "away from the cups and large kraters [mixing-bowls]" to smaller shapes: lekythoi, and so forth.[222] Certain shapes may be less suitable for erotic art. Any monocausal connection has its difficulties (Lewis 2002: 131–32). Have painters simply exhausted the artistic possibilities of a genre and find that they have nothing further to say even about sex?

CONCLUSIONS

There are two things I would like us to take from this chapter. One: We need to be wary of *the* definite article, and the indefinite as well. We think we have something called *"the* up-and-down gesture." We think it has *a* single particular meaning. Thus the painter called the Affecter has played a lurking role in a number of books and articles as the mysterious artist who upsets all the rules.[223]

---

221. Similar appearances and disappearances of topics are common in vase painting: Fountain House scenes, for example, flourish only between 520 and 480. See Ferrari 2002: 1–7, 2003: 44–50; Lewis 2002: 1–4.
222. Lewis 2002: 132.
223. Beginning with a postscript palinode by Halperin in *100 Years of Homosexuality* (1990: 225).

So this (**N**, fig. 1.14a) has been claimed as an example of role reversal: a youth making *the* "up-and-down gesture" to a bearded adult. Hupperts, among others, attached great significance to these figures (1988: 261):

> The man and the boy on the right of fig. 4 [**N**] are *obviously* [my italics] involved in a seducing situation. Recognizable are the up and down position and the shielding hand. It is striking that the conventional roles have been reversed. The boy, normally playing the passive part in the ritual, is here the one who stands in the up and down position: he is apparently the one who takes the initiative. If we take this picture seriously, it is really shocking, not so much by the behavior of the boy as by the role the man is performing. The paintings of the Affecter are in an other [*sic*] way surprising. The attributes of the men on fig. 5 [**O**] remind us immediately of the conventional paederastic pictures. The gifts, the garland and the hare, belong to the traditional lovegifts. But in this painting also the iconological rules are broken. The men of the left pair stroke each other's beard. Does the painter indicate that the roles in this relation are equal?[224]

There is only one problem with this reading: to the left of the supposed couple, there is a man making the same "up and down gesture" to Dionysus's backside.[225] On the other side (fig. 1.14b) we see the same arrangement but the figures stand slightly further apart. Here it becomes clear that their hands are not chucking or even pointing at each other's chins, that the bearded man is not "shielding" his flaccid penis from the unwanted attentions of a beardless youth. On both sides, the three human figures stand frozen in the semaphore signal for the letter X.

Hubbard also presses a second amphora by the Affecter (**O**) as evidence of "Age-Equal Adult Interactions," where "Bearded Men Court Each Other."[226] His reading of the figures is tendentious:

---

224. Hupperts created his own δ-schema unique to this artist, 2000: 117–18, 132–37 *et passim*, catalogue zk30, zk51–96. See also Fisher 2001: 33.

225. Cf. the posture at London, British Museum B149 (BA 301348); Mommsen 1975, no. 59.

226. Hubbard 2003b. Hubbard (2014: 144) is more confident: "Another category of adult–adult contact is what we find in the work of one particular Athenian black figure painter known as 'the Affecter.' Here we do not see wild parties, but a series of bearded men courting each other with exactly the same gestures and gifts that we find in the more common scenes of pederastic courtship [**O**] . . . It surely must indicate, like the Tyrrhenian ware, that there actually were some adult men, whether in Attica or Italy, who preferred other men rather than adolescent boys. The Affecter himself may have shared this preference, or he may have produced work to please one or more patrons who liked adult partners. Queer as they might be in the Athenian context, such men surely existed and were the focus of at least one Athenian painter's study." The rhetoric is interesting: homosexuals (as we define them) must have existed in the ancient world and someone must have

FIGURE 1.14A. Cat. N. New York, Metropolitan Museum of Art 18.145.15. Affecter, c. 540–520. Dionysus with kantharos. Bearded man behind. Youth and man in front supposedly making *the* "up and down gesture." © The Metropolitan Museum of Art. Image source: Art Resource, New York.

FIGURE 1.14B. Side B. Same composition. Youth and man further apart.

On the left, the god Dionysus, accompanied by a fawn, offers a wine-cup to Icarius, whom he has taught the art of winemaking. In the center, two bearded men touch each others' chins (a typical courtship gesture): the fully naked and slightly shorter man holds a crown (a typical love gift). On the right, another bearded man offers a hare as a gift to his bearded partner. As in other work by this painter, we see evidence of homosexual contact among fully mature men. Are we to understand the relationship of Dionysus and Icarius as a romantic one, in light of the other couples?

The answer to this rhetorical question is, No. In fact, the men are not touching each other's chins, nor is that "a typical courtship gesture,"[227] nor are crowns a "typical love gift."[228] The man under the handle is not "offering" a hare; he is holding one. Lear asks the proper question (2008: 69): "But are these courting couples? All four figures' gestures resemble up-and-down gestures, but none of them clearly aim at the opposite figure's genitals—surely a *sine qua non* for down-gestures." Rather, what a complete survey of the Affecter shows is that what some have identified as the "up and down" gesture is in fact simply a stylistic convention, the Affecter's way of filling up space, sometimes in motifs of pederastic courtship, more often not.[229] Nearly every single figure on his pots stands sideways with his arms out in a K. As the Affecter's deepest student, Mommsen said (1975: 56): "The composition of many scenes is determined by no intellectually comprehensible content."

Kilmer (1997: 42–43) also thinks that a single painting topples everything:

> Illustrations [already a question-begging label] on pottery by the black-figure artist known as the Affecter show a quite different scenario, with men of similar ages or youths of similar ages carrying out the same sorts of courtship and sexual culmination as we already know in the more familiar youth-meets-boy, man-meets-youth age formats. This on its own is sufficient to call the traditional view into doubt.

---

painted them. The repeated "surely" is a sign of desperation. See also Sourvinou-Inwood 2003: 113, 137n233.

227. It is found, for example, on many grave monuments between husbands and wives, parents and children. See Baggio 2004: 95–99 for erotic significance (and etymological fancies).

228. Crowns mark gymnasium scenes, symposia, funerals, etc.

229. Rightly Lear 2008: 71: "Thus it is possible (to put the matter bluntly) that his revision of age conventions had no meaning; he may have used motifs from pederastic scenes for aesthetic rather than symbolic reasons." Or rather, that what looks like "revision of age conventions" is nothing of the sort.

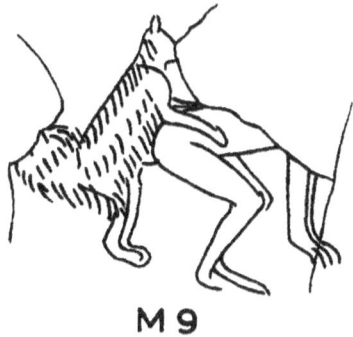

FIGURE 1.15. Athens, Agora P 27698. Second quarter fifth cent. Graffito (added before firing) on black-glazed stand of a dog sodomizing a man. Image courtesy of American School in Athens.

In fact there are no examples of "sexual culmination" in the Affecter.[230] We have to ask, why? Why should a single image (misunderstood) on a pot call into doubt everything that everybody said? It is easy to see the fallacy of this sort of (frequently deployed) argument. Let me risk a generalization: Greek men did not allow themselves to be sodomized by dogs, or to be more cautious: Greek men did not *normally* allow themselves to be sodomized by dogs or *publicly disapproved* of being sodomized by dogs. If I confront this statement with Agora P 27698 (fig. 1.15), an image of a man being sodomized by a dog, accompanied by the love name NIK[ΚΑΛΟ[Σ, this on its own is not sufficient to call the traditional view into doubt.[231]

These simplistic readings are rightly challenged by Shapiro (2000a: 20–21):

> But artistic context is also crucial. Poses and gestures that are intentionally erotic for one painter may not be for another. Thus, for example, an eccentric black-figure painter nicknamed the Affecter often pairs two men

---

230. The claim that the Affecter Painter shows sexual activity is incorrect, and the sources cited by Hupperts (1988: 260–62) do not say so. See Mommsen 1975, 56–60; Golden 1991: 333: "The depictions are decorous—there are no shockers."

231. Lang 1974: 12, fig. 30; Lang 1976: 13, 94, no. C 15, M 9, pl. 4, 61. Half of hemispherical black-glazed stand, incised before glazing and firing. Second quarter fifth cent. http://www.agathe.gr/id/agora/object/p%2027698.

conversing animatedly, their hands somewhat recalling Beazley's "up and down" position [**M, N**] . . . An animal that in other contexts would be a love gift, such as a live hare, may be exchanged, yet the fact that both men are bearded rules out a pederastic encounter. Rather, these encounters take place in the presence of the god Dionysos, far removed from the world of courtship in the gymnasium. It is obvious to anyone who has spent time in the Mediterranean that these men are doing nothing more than speaking with their hands (cf. Beazley, *ABV* 238).

I would argue that even labeling the stance as "talking with one hands" is overreading: this is simply the primary way that the Affecter fills up space.[232]

The second lesson of a survey of the differences between description and depiction is to question the very idea of a separate area of "the erotic" or "the pornographic." As Lewis notes (2002: 116; cf. 9): "A fundamental difficulty is the consideration of a category of art called 'erotica,' because this implies material produced for a specific purpose." Clarke (2010: 170–72) traces the history of the idea and concludes: "As is clear from our brief overview of essentialist scholarship on images of sexual activity, the separation of 'obscene' objects from their archaeological contexts in secret museums, as well as the practices surrounding their publication, created the categories of 'erotica' and 'pornography.'"

What I think we are looking at in most of these objects is not our narrow concept of "sex," but a wider concept of "The Good Things in Life." A couplet attributed to both Solon and Theognis put it best (Solon 23; Theognidea 1253–54):

ὄλβιος, ὧι παῖδές τε φίλοι καὶ μώνυχες ἵπποι
καὶ κύνες ἀγρευταὶ καὶ ξένος ἀλλοδαπός.

Happy the man who has dear boys and single-hoofed horses, and hunting dogs and a friend in a foreign land.[233]

---

232. The problems of interpreting gestures can be shown by a black-figure amphora (Providence 13.1479, BA 301624), which Lear says (2008: 29) "again presents an up-and-down scene, although the up-gesture takes an unusual form: the *erastes* seems to be patting the *eromenos*' head—or stroking his hair—rather than chucking his chin." That is, neither of the two elements of *the* up-and-down gesture is here. Lear continues: "The down-gesture has not yet reached its goal." That is because there is a miniaturized stag in the way. Lear gives this as an example of "the variation that can exist within a scene-type, even as to its most fundamental elements." But if a scene-type differs even in its most fundamental elements, how are we to be secure in recognizing it as a scene-type?

233. For the erotic nature of these two lines, cf. the version in Theognis 1253–54 where they are repeated with additions. See Linforth (1919) 176–77; Noussia-Fantuzzi 2010: 343–45.

The reason that sex is shown so often in the context of the symposium is not because that is where sex happened most often, but because Dionysus and Aphrodite are among the chief pleasures of life. Again, Solon (26):

ἔργα δὲ Κυπρογενοῦς νῦν μοι φίλα καὶ Διονύσου
καὶ Μουσέων, ἃ τίθησ' ἀνδράσιν εὐφροσύνας,

Now the works of Cyprus-born Aphrodite and Dionysus and the Muses are dear to me, the things that constitute happiness for men.

The "orgies" among the vines (**26**, fig. 1.2) are showing us not how or where the Greek had sex but what the Greeks thought about sex. We are used to looking at symposia and identifying the women there as hetairai.[234] It might be equally true that the women are there to mark the scene as a symposium.

Boys are shown with hares and rooster, not because these were the "love gifts" one would give to seduce a boy, but quite the opposite; they stand for a love uncorrupted by money or wealth. Sex is shown in the gymnasium, not because that is where one could go to pick up boys and then bang them (decorously) by the racetrack turning post, but because athletic victory, bodies in their perfect bloom, and love are the greatest things the gods offer us, as Pindar showed so often.

Exemplifying this conclusion are two intact tomb assemblages. The first contained a well-known and well-published askos from a tomb in the Kerameikos (**P**). The flat oil-jar shows two male–female couples on either side of the handle. One couple is having sex face-to-face; they make eye contact and the woman's hand cups the back of the man's head. The other couple are having sex with the man behind, his hands on the woman's breasts while the woman crouches and supports herself on a bolster. They have been variously interpreted. Hoffmann's structuralist reading (1977: 4) claimed anal penetration for the rear-entry couple, and that "the culturally approved or 'honorable' position of heterosexual intercourse was, therefore, rear-entry. The front facing position was held in low esteem, since it was considered undignified and 'effeminate.'"[235] Keuls drew the opposite conclusion: (1985: 176–79): "The one in the lower scene is young and trim: he is making love

---

234. Lewis 2002: 101–12 on the dangers of too ready an identification. Blazeby 2011 for a thorough re-examination.

235. Citing Aristophanes *Knights* 1284ff., *Peace* 885, *Wasps* 1280 for the first point, none of which support his position; and citing Bornemann 1975: 234 (non vidi) for the second, along with "the development of sadomasochistic tendencies in Greek culture."

to her from the front, in the 'missionary' position. The prostitute in the upper scene is older; her stomach sags, and she looks toothless. Her customer is penetrating her from behind, anally. The implication is clear: frontal copulation is the more refined method, reserved for desirable women, whereas sex from behind is less considerate and probably degrading." Close examination does not support Keul's description. There is no evidence in the literary sources that sexual positions were valorized in this way.

These irreconcilable readings operated free from context before the groundbreaking studies of Paleothodoros (2012) and Dilpa and Paleothodoros (2012). The askos was found in situ in a grave that is almost certainly that of a young Athenian wife, who was buried with her wedding vase (*lebes gamikos*), which shows a woman with a mirror being adorned by two other women (possibly her slaves), and a Nike bearing a wedding torch. The *lebes* formed part of the bridal gifts (that is, an unmarried girl would not have possessed one).[236] They have been found in domestic contexts and in funerary contexts, where they are only associated with female burials.[237]

---

236. Oakley and Sinos 1992: 6; Rehm 1994: 32: "In whatever way the vessel was used during the ritual, it seems to have been given as a wedding gift afterward, judging from the visual evidence. The painted iconography of *lebetes gamikoi* is almost exclusively nuptial." Paleothodoros 2012: 28 rightly identifies her as a married woman, while Dipla and Paleothodoros (2012: 220), if I am reading them correctly, assume that the tomb was of an unmarried girl: "[The ceramics] all allude to the expected accomplishments of a girl, which were never fulfilled because of her sudden, premature death." So too Kunze-Götte, Tancke, and Vierneisel. 1999: 132: "Das Nebeneinander des Hochzeitsgefäßes, des Askos mit erotischen Szenen sowie der Figur eines Kleinkindes zeigt Wünsche und Gedanken, welche die Hinterbliebenen einem wohl unverheiratet verstorbenen Mädchen ins Grab nachsandten." I believe that they are probably incorrect to assume that death pre-empted a wedding. It was more the function of the *loutophoros* to mark those who would never know the pleasures of marriage. Sgourou (1994: 28): "It [is] significant to note that in the few cases when [*lebetes gamikoi*] . . . were found in graves . . . they were never associated with *loutrophoroi*. The two vases had different functions when transposed into the funerary realm: the *loutrophoros* as marker of graves of people who died unwed, the [*lebetes gamikoi*] as grave offering especially prized during the life of the deceased and accompanying her at her final resting place. Since the [*lebes gamikos*] appears to be a vase associated exclusively with the female, it would be logical to assume that it stood as the symbol of a truly accomplished life which, for the Athenian woman was the wedding and the procreation of legitimate children." But as with all things Greek the rule is not hard or fast (see Grossman 2001: 77, 79n12; 2013: 25 for a few counterexamples of lekythoi for the married). A similar assemblage of *lebes* and *askos*, along with earrings and necklace, were found in a grave with a skeleton that the excavators labeled "di bambina." This might be a possible counterexample, if we knew what age range counted as "bambina": c. 340; Rhodes, Ialysos, grave CLVII; Rhodes 6677, type 2); see Iacopi 1929: 159–60, fig. 152. Sgourou 1994: 28, 228, 332–33 (UR80).

237. No skeletal remains were recorded, but the conclusion that the owner was female is sound. Oakley and Sinos 1992: 6; Sgourou 1995: 28; Sgourou 1997: 72; Paleothodoros 2012: 28: "Whenever the sex of a deceased buried with a nuptial bowl is determined, it is always female."

The grave also contained a terracotta figurine of a kneeling boy. The meaning is fairly clear (Dipla and Paleothodoros 2012: 220): "Taken together, the nuptial bowl (a shape always connected with brides: Sgourou 1997:72), the askos, and the statuette, point to female sexuality blossoming in the context of wedding, and having the creation of male offspring as its ultimate goal."

The second example is one of the more interesting finds of recent years, discovered in situ in a child's grave in the Ceramicus, circa 490 (**Q**).[238] The child was probably a girl, since the grave goods included two pyxides and the lid of a lekanis.[239] Her grave also contained sixty-nine knucklebones (the dice of antiquity); terra-cotta figures of a shepherd with his sheep, a man with two horses, also two birds, and a dog. There were also eight small black-figure lekythoi, four mythological, two Dionysiac, one sympotic.[240] The eighth shows nine male–female couples. Two central couches each support three couples making love: one with the man kneeling between the woman's legs, one with the woman straddling the man, and one with couple standing. The order is repeated on the second couch. Before the couches are tables loaded with food. Past a column on the left is a couple wrapped up and sitting on the floor, then two more couples similarly wrapped. Glazebrook describes them closely (2011: 36): "These last three couples do not appear to be engaged in sexual activity but rather converse or watch the couples on the couches. Despite the proximity of the figures in each group, there is no interaction between couples. In contrast to the typical symposium scene in which the common community of the participants is emphasized through the figures' participation in games, music, and physical or visual contact, each couple on the couch is focused on itself, suggesting a context other than the symposium." Grapevines fill every area.

Like the Dionysiac or symposiac vases, this little jar is not there as pornography, not even as erotica, but as an object symbolizing the good things of life, now never to be known by it young inhabitant.

---

238. Athens, National Museum, A15418, tomb 1010: Glazebrook 2011: 38 (fig. 2.2), unconvincingly identified as a brothel scene by Kavvadias 2000: 24; 2009: 215. La Genière 2009: 343: "Comment peut-on expliquer la présence de cette image dans la tombe d'un très jeune enfant, encore occupé par des astragales et des petits animaux? Le jeu des hypothèses est ouvert."

239. Roberts 1978: 178: "Pyxides are only connected with the graves of women." See Alexandridou 2011: 26 (lekanis) and 31 (pyxis); Dipla and Paleothodoros 2012: 214, 218, 219, 226. When skeletal remains can be sexed, they are always female (Sgourou 1994: 226 [R69], 228 [UR80]).

240. Type of Athens 581. Theseus vs. the Bull of Marathon (twice), Herakles vs. the Nemean Lion, Athena vs. Engelados. Dionysus with two women, Dionysus with Maenads and an ithyphallic mule. Symposiast with a kantharos reclining on couch with a naked woman.

We need to practice more of the *ars nesciendi*. We have to end with questions. Are certain sexual scenes meant to be normal or outrageous, exciting, amusing, satiric, cautionary, or apotropaic? Who are the consumers? What are the social function of the vases? Do different painters paint different worlds? Can we continue to read the iconography as confidently as we have?

CATALOG

Vases are cited by collection, vase type, painter (if attributed), approximate date, and find spot (FS), if known. Next, the numbers from the Beazley Archive (BA): http://www.beazley.ox.ac.uk/index.htm (an asterisk * indicates the vase is illustrated on the site), with references to Beazley's publications:

ABV = Beazley 1956; ARV = Beazley 1963; Para = Beazley 1971; Add = Carpenter 1989. *LIMC* = *Lexicon Iconographicum Mythologiae Classicae*. Zürich: Artemis Verlag, 1981–99.

Numbers from Dover's list in *Greek Homosexuality* follow: B and R for black-figure and red-figure, the system used by Kilmer (1993) for red-figure (an asterisk * indicates the vase is illustrated in Dover). Other catalogs are DeVries's numbers (from the Appendix to Lear 2008) and from Hupperts 2000. Square brackets [ ] mark damaged or "imminent" scenes. The usual abbreviations for illustrations: A and B: front and back.

Every effort has been made to trace copyright holders and to obtain their permission for the use of copyright material. The author apologizes for any errors or omissions in the above list and would be grateful for notification of any corrections that should be incorporated in future reprints or editions of this book.

The current chaos for licencing images makes it impossible to provide readers with illustrations for many of these vases. All the more reason to thank, for their enlightened policies, the British Museum, the American School of Classical Studies, the State Hermitage Museum (Dr. Anastasia Miklyaeva), and the Soprintendenza per i Beni Archeologici del Piemonte e del Museo Antichità Egizie (Dr. Patrizia Petitti), who kindly provided images free of charge. Funds to purchase other images were provided by the Semple Fund of the University of Cincinnati.

Some illustrations not included in this article may be found at http://classics.uc.edu/~parker/GreekErotica.htm

I. Black-Figure Vases Representing Interfemoral Intercourse

1. Univ. of Mississippi Museum 1977.3.72. BF tripod pyxis. Unattributed. c. 550. FS: "Said to have been found at Athens," Robinson 1956: 2.

   BA 7285. DeVries 2.106. Hupperts z194.

   Illustrations: Koch-Harnack 1983: fig. 96. Koch-Harnack 1989: 118, fig. 3; Rabinowitz 2002: 132, fig. 5.14a–c. Robinson 1956: pl.1., fig. 5–7. Shapiro 1981b: 159, no. 62; Skinner 2005: 89, fig. 3.6.

   http://www.laits.utexas.edu/ancienthomosexuality/imageindex.php?cat_id=17&topic_id=192 and topic_id=162.

[2]. Copenhagen, National Museum, 13966. BF Little Master lip cup. Epitimos P. (Heesen), Lydos (Beazley and Friis Johansen), Epitimos potter, c. 550–545. Damaged.

   BA 350369*, Para 48, Add 33. Dover B458. DeVries 2.3. Hupperts z10.

   Illustrations: *CVA, Copenhagen, National Museum* 8, 327, Pls. 324.1b; Friis Johansen 1960: 131, fig. 2; Heesen 2009: no. 235, pl. 68c. Lear 2008: 197, no. 2.3; Tiverios 1978, pinax 64.

3. Princeton, University Art Museum, 86.53. BF lekythos. Taleides P., c. 550–540.

   BA 350510*, Para 73, 12bis. Dover B114*, DeVries 2.20. Hupperts z23.

   Illustrations: "Acquisitions of the Art Museum 1986," 44; Dierichs 1993: Abb. 173; Lear 2014: 108, fig, 7.4; Theodorou 1991: 22.

4. Rome, Villa Giulia M556. BF lekythos. Taleides P., c. 550–525.

   BA 301130*, ABV 175.11, Beazley 1947/1989: 8 α 16, 20 γ 4. DeVries 2.19.

5. Florence, Museo Archeologico Etrusco (no number), ex Vagnonville. Taleides P., c. 550–525. FS: Etruria, Chiusi.

   BA 9023168, Beazley 1947/1989: 19 γ 2, DeVries 2.87. Hupperts z222.

   Illustrations: Malagardis 2009: 102, fig. 6–7 (color).; Iozzo 2006: 240, pl. X.6.

[6]. Berlin F1773 (lost). BF Little Master lip cup. P. of the Boston Polyphemos, c. 550–525. FS: Etruria. Damaged.

   BA 302570*, ABV 198.1, Para 80, Add 53, Beazley 1947/1989: 19 γ 3. Dover B130. Hupperts z25.

   Illustrations: Friis Johansen 1960: 135, fig. 14; Smith 2010 : 325, pl. 20b.

[7]. Athens, National Museum, Acropolis Collection 2242. BF fragment. Unattributed, c. 550–525. FS: Athens, Acropolis. Damaged

BA 32302, Beazley 1947/1989: 20 y 6. DeVries 2.88. Hupperts z266.

Illustrations: Graef and Langlotz 1925: I, fasc. 4, pl. 95; Vorberg 1965: 452.

[8]. Paris, Louvre, F85bis (CP55). BF cup fragment. Unattributed, c. 550–525. FS: Etruria. Damaged.

BA 7479*, Beazley 1947/1989: 21 y 9. Dover B482. DeVries 2.91. Hupperts z252.

Illustrations: *CVA Paris, Louvre* 8, III. H.e.62, pl. 79.6 (511); Koch-Harnack 198: 83, Abb. 18; Lear 2008: fig. 2.5; Schnapp 1979: 54, fig. 16; Schnapp 1989: 80, fig. 109; Schnapp 1997: 254, no. 192.

http://www.photo.rmn.fr/c/htm/Search_New.aspx; in "Inventory number," search "F85bis."

9. Once Rome, Hartwig collection. BF Little master band cup, c. 550–525. Unattributed. FS: Satumia

BA 30281, Beazley 1947/1989: 20 y 12. DeVries 2.94. Hupperts z220.

Illustrations; Vorberg 1965: 46 (drawing).

10. London, British Museum, 1865.11–18.39 (W39). BF amphora B. Painter of Berlin 1686, c. 550–540. FS: Etruria, Vulci.

BA 320395*, ABV 297.16, Para 128, Beazley 1947/1989: 19 y 1. Dover B250*. DeVries 2.59.

Illustrations: Boardman 1975: 79; Calame 1992: 74, pl. II; DeVries 1997: 23, fig. 2.8; Dierichs 1993: Abb. 172; Dierichs 2008: Abb. 72; Lear 2008: 66, fig. 2.1; Meyer 1993: Abb. 2; Oakley 2013: 148, ch. 6, fig. 13–15; Reinsberg 1989: 201, fig.110; Schnapp 1997: 252, no. 184; Sergent 1986: pl. 6; Shapiro 1989: pl. 55d; Shapiro 1992: 56–57, fig. 3.1; Vout 2013: 29, fig. 23.

http://www.laits.utexas.edu/ancienthomosexuality/imageindex.php?cat_id=17&topic_id=193

http://www.britishmuseum.org/research/search_the_collection_database/search_object_details.aspx?objectid=398881&partid=1

11. Bochum, Kunstsammlungen der Ruhr-Universität, S 1024. BF Little Master cup. Epitimos P. (Kunisch), c. 545–540 (Heesen).

BA 3878. DeVries 2.112. Hupperts z218.

Illustrations: Brijder 2000: *CVA, Deutschland 79: Bochum: Kunstsammlungen der Ruhr-Universität*, pl. 52 (4064), no. 2, pl. 54 (4065), 1–2; Heesen 2009, no. 239, pl. 70; Lear 2008: 204, no. 2.112; Kunisch 1972: 72–73, no. 68; Kunisch 1996: 102–6, color img. I; Hupperts 2000: ill. 12; Schnapp 1997: 254, no. 193.

12. Rome, Villa Giulia, 36061. BF skyphos. Amasis P. c. 540. FS: Etruria, Vulci.

    BA 24890.

    Illustrations: Davidson 2007: 478, fig. 53; Malagardis and Iozzo 1995: pl. 53; Morandi 1975.

13. Aegina, Archaeological Museum, 14701. BF tripod pyxis (nonsympotic). Amasis P. c. 540. FS: Aegina, Sanctuary of Aphaia.

    BA 14701. DeVries: 2.12.

    Illustrations: Ohly-Durnm 1985, pl. 4 (A, B, C). Shapiro 1989: pl. 42C, 68A. Shapiro 1997: 45, pl. 8. Davidson 2007: 489, fig. 56. Lear 2008: 183–84, fig. 7.3. Brinkmann 1994: 99.

14. New York private collection. BF neck amphora. Botkin class, workshop of the Phrynos Painter, c. 540 (Cahn). BA 14. DeVries 2.16. Hupperts z174.

    Illustrations: Mommsen 2009: 45–46, pls. 2.4, 3.4 (B, UH); Munzen und Medaillen, A. G., Basel, Sale Catalogue 51 (14–15.3.1975), pl. 23, no.123 (A, B, S, under handle); Sotheby's, catalogue 13–14.7.1981, 108–9, no. 244 (color of A and B); Schnapp 1997: 251, no.183 (A, B): [very poor picture].

15. San Antonio Museum of Art 86.134.44. BF amphora. P. of Berlin 1686, c. 540.

    BA 7277; Hupperts z100.

    Illustrations: Hupperts 2000: 397. ill. 43; Shapiro, Picón, and Scott 1995: nr. 43.

16. Hamburg, Museum für Kunst und Gewerbe, no number (once Helgoland, ex coll. Kropatscheck). BF Little Master band cup. Hermogenes P., c. 545–540 (Heesen).

    BA 6408 and 44981. DeVries 2.13. Hupperts z247. Sutton 2009: 87, no. 40.

    Illustrations: Dierichs 1988: 44, Abb. 64; Dierichs 1993: 54, Abb. 89; Heesen 2009: 275 no. 148, pl. 46b; Hornbostel 1980: 84–85, no. 53; Reichardt 2009, 1: 238.

17. London market. BF lekythos. Unattributed. c. 540.

    BA: not listed. Hupperts z184

    Illustrations: Christie's London, cat. 23 Sept. 1998, lot nr. 177.

18. St. Petersburg, Hermitage, O.1912.272. BF Lekythos. P. of the Carlsruhe Skyphos, c. 540–530. FS: Olbia, grave 64.

    BA 306382, ABV 626 (bottom of page), Beazley 1947/1989: 20 y 5. DeVries 2.73. Hupperts z160.

    Illustrations: Pharmakowsky 1913: 205, fig. 51; Hupperts 2000: ill. 58; Skudnova 1988: 120, no. 182; Trofimova 2007: 100, fig. 20a (color).

19. Private coll. Hamburg. BF kylix. Stroibos P. (Heesen); near Hermogenes P. (Hornbostel), c. 540–530

    BA: not listed. DeVries 2.109. Hupperts z204.

    Illustrations: Hornbostel 1986: 48–49, no. 11.

[20.] Toulouse, Musée St. Raymond 26088 (olim 349). BF cup. FP (Flower Palmette) Class, c. 530. "Imminent": youth facing r. bearded man crouched in the position for interfemoral but feet and bodies are still far apart.

    BA 350784*, Para 81.16, 82.3.

    Illustrations: Ugaglia 1993: 75–76, no. 63.

[21.] Paris, Stavros S. Niarchos, A036. BF Nikosthenic neck amphora. Painter N. Nikosthenes potter, c. 530–520. FS: Etruria, Cerveteri. "Imminent": beardless youth (l.) with arms around neck of bearded man (r.) who has the bent knees and posture of getting ready for interfemoral (might read affection/enthusiasm in the youth's embrace)

    BA 201942 and 302825, ABV 225.6 and 7; Para 105; ARV 122.1

    Illustrations: Marangou 1995: 70–73 no. 9 (color), but no good picture of the couple. *Munzen und Medaillen A. G. Auktion XVIII Kunstwerke der Anitke* 29.11.1958. pp. 30–31, no. 92, pl. 29 [the year in the Beazley database "1942" is incorrect].

22. London, market. BF amphora B. Euphiletos P. c. 530–520.

    BA 9040*. Hupperts z110.

    Illustrations: Sotheby's catalogue 11–12.7.1983, 97, no. 315 (color).

23. Sèvres, Musée Céramique 6405. BF amphora. Near the Euphiletos P. c. 550–525.

    BA 10478*, Beazley 1947/1989: 20 y 8. Dover B486*. DeVries 2.90.

    Illustrations: CVA Sèvres, *Musée Céramique*, 33, pl. 15.4 and 7 (544).

24. Syracuse, Museo Arch. Regionale Paolo Orsi, 9762 [not 9763 in DeVries]. BF amphora. Unattributed, c. 530–520 (Hupperts). FS: Sicily, Megara Hyblaea.

    BA 14208*. DeVries 3.47. Hupperts z175 (see also Hupperts 1988: 260).

    Illustrations: CVA, Syracuse, Museo Archeologico Nazionale 1, III. H.4, tav. 4 (pl. 809), no. 4.1–2; Hupperts 2000: ill. 40.

25. Cambridge, Trinity College T2. BF amphora. Unattributed. c. 530–510 (Nicholls 1970)

    BA: 2889, Beazley 1947/1989: 20 y 7. DeVries 2.89. Hupperts Z165 (y).

    Illustrations: none of the relevant side.

26. Berlin, Antikensammlung F1798 (lost at end of WWII). BF Little Master band cup. Unattributed. c. 530. FS: Vulci.

    BA 11037, Beazley 1947/1989: 20 y 13. Dover B634*. DeVries 2.95. Hupperts z241.

    Illustrations: Calame 1992, 73, pl. I; Lear 2008: 111, fig. 3.4; Lücken 1923: pls. 37; Poliakoff 1982: pl. 15; Reinsberg 1989: 109, fig. 57; Stewart 1997: 161, fig. 100.

[27]. Kurashiki, Ninagawa Museum, 27. BF kylix. Krokotos-group, c. 520. "Imminent": Bearded man bent in usual position for interfemoral but not yet, facing left; no penis visible.

    BA 302651*, ABV 207, Para 98. DeVries 3.24. Hupperts z45

    Illustrations: Hupperts 2000: ill. 56; Jouanna and Villard 2002: pl. 2; Martens 1992: 225–26, fig. 101–3.

[28]. Oxford, Ashmolean G 1112 (on long-term loan to the British Museum). BF cup fragment. Unattributed. "Later part of the sixth century"—Beazley. FS: Egypt, Naucratis.

    BA no number. Beazley 1947/1989: 21 y 14. DeVries 3.43. Hupperts z262.

    Illustrations: Photo kindly supplied by Marianne Bergeron of the Naucratis Project.

29. Eleusis Museum, no number. BF lekythos. Unattributed. Date uncertain. FS: Eleusis.

    BA no number. DeVries 2.103 (autopsy); Schauenburg 1965: 850n1; Kanta 1979: 128.

    Illustrations: non vidi.

30. Lausanne, Musée Olympique, no number. BF neck amphora. Unattributed. c. 510 (Dozio)

    BA 9024527

    Illustrations: Dozio 2009: 111, no. 57.

31. Rome, Museo Nazionale Etrusco di Villa Giulia, 1392 [**NB** Beazley 1947/1989: 20 gives the number as "1932"; so, following him, Dover and DeVries.]. BF lekythos. Near the Cock Class, c. 510–490. FS: Falerii Veteres (Civita Castellana), Necropoli di Celle, Tomba LXXV.

    BA 13077, Beazley 1947/1989: 20 y 5bis. Dover B534. DeVries 3.42. Hupperts z186.

    Illustrations: *CVA Rome, Museo Nazionale di Villa Giulia 3* (ITALY 3), III. H e Tav. 50 (pl. 134), no. 13.

32. Milan: private collection. BF Amphora B. Edinburgh Painter, c. 500.

    BA 360885, Para 2219. DeVries 3.32 (from photograph).

    Illustrations: non vidi.

33. "Princeton, Spitzer collection"—DeVries [prob. ex Collection of Mrs. Lyman Spitzer, Jr.] BF neck amphora. Unattributed. DeVries catalog implies a date c. 530–500.

    BA no number. DeVries 3.49: "B: man and boy in *diamerion* intercourse. To l., two dancing males with leftmost figure touching the buttocks of the other; to r., two further dancing males."

    Illustrations: non vidi.

34. New York market. BF lekythos (red background). Gela P., c. 510–490.

    BA 41361. DeVries 4.45. Hupperts z117.

    Illustrations: Royal-Athena Galleries New York, catalog. Eisenberg, J., *One Thousand Years of Ancient Greek Vases*, No. 66. Art of the Ancient World, Volume 6. Part 1, Nov. 1990, p. 14, lot nr. 41 (color). Hupperts 2000: ill. 47.

35. Kanellopoulos Museum, no number [not in catalog]. BF lekythos. Gela P., c. 510–490? FS: Athens (Hupperts).

    BA 340826, Para 216. DeVries 4.2. Hupperts z116.

    Illustrations: non vidi.

[36]. Athens Agora Museum AP 733. BF cup fragment. Unattributed, c. 500. FS: Athens, Agora, north slope. Damaged.

    BA no number, Beazley 1947/1989: 21 γ 10. DeVries 2.92. Hupperts z254.

    Illustrations: Pease 1935: 262, no. 103, fig. 25 (text at 267–68). Possibly from same workshop as the following (Pease 1935: 268).

    http://ascsa.net/id/agora/object/p%208890

[37]. Athens, Acropolis 1761. BF lip cup fragment. BF lip cup fragment. Unattributed, c. 500. FS: Athens, Acropolis. Damaged.

    BA no number, Beazley 1947/1989: 21 γ 11. DeVries 2.93. Hupperts z255.

    Illustrations: Graef and Langlotz 1925: pl. 86.

[38]. Eleusis, Archaeological Museum, no number. BF plate (phiale) fragment. P. of Anavyssos, c. 500–490 (Callipolitis-Feytmans 1974: 389). FS: Eleusis. Damaged.

    BA 8662. Hupperts z199.

    Illustrations: Callipolitis-Feytmans 1974: 252–53, no. 33, pl. 80.66.

II. Red-Figure Vases Representing Interfemoral Intercourse

[39]. Athens, Agora Museum P 7901. RF cup fragment. Euphronios (manner of), 510–500. FS: Athens, Agora: locus E 14:5, well, c. 520–490. Damaged: 2 fr. only intertwined feet and gym-kit above.

BA 200101*, ARV 20.1559; Beazley 1947: 24 γ 15. Dover R31. DeVries 3.84.

Illustrations: Kilmer 1993: R31; Moore 1997: 340, no. 1556, pls. 146–47; Thompson 1958: 157, pl. 45c.

http://ascsa.net/id/agora/object/p%207901

[40]. Athens, Agora P 7690 + P 8890 (joining fragments). RF cup fragments. Unattributed, style recalling Boston MFA 10.193 (Athenodotos cup) and early Douris (Beazley 1947/1989: 24), c. 500.

BA 43790, Beazley 1947/1989: 24 γ 16. Dover R1123

Illustrations: Cohen 2006: 49, fig. 7 (color); Davidson 2007: 510. fig. 58; Kilmer 1993: R1123; Moore 2007: 319, no. 1410, pl. 131;

http://ascsa.net/id/agora/object/p%207690

http://ascsa.net/id/agora/object/p%208890

[41]. Athens, Ceramicus, no number. Proto-Panaitian cup, c. 500. FS: Athens, Ceramicus: Isolated find from the Sacred Way. Damaged: bearded man and youth in posture for interfemoral. A: woman bending over youth, holding his penis, perhaps in preparation for fellatio.

BA 275913, Para 358, Add 214. DeVries 4.93.

Illustrations: Frel 1984: 59, pl. 9.8–9.

42. Munich, Antikensammlungen 2631. RF cup fragments. Douris, c. 500–490 (bare decoration, "Transitional II"). "Imminent": bearded man with erection in crouched posture with youth.

BA 205269*, ARV 443.224, Add 240, Beazley 1947: 25 γ 17. Dover R573*. DeVries 4.136.

Illustrations: Buitron-Oliver 1995: pl. 52, no. 79; Kilmer 1997: 39, pl. 2; Lear 2008: 110, fig. 3.3; Vorberg 1965: 461.

43. Mykonos, Archaeological Museum 966. Triptolemos P., 485–470 (B: kōmos by Flying-angle Painter). FS: Delos, Rheneia.

BA 203813* (drawing), ARV 280.18, 362.21, Add 208, Beazley 1947/1989: 25 γ 18. Dover R502*. DeVries 4.102.

Illustrations: Kilmer 1993: R502; Kilmer 1997: 43, pl. 6; Koch-Harnack 1983: 78, Abb. 15; Reinsberg 1989: 175, Abb. 96.

44. London market. RF pelike. Eucharides P., c. 480–470.

BA 13607. Dover R371*. DeVries 4.178.

Illustrations: Davdison 2007: 436–37, fig. 49; Dierichs 1988: 65, Abb. 108; Frontisi-Ducroux 1996: 92, fig. 39 (incorrect ARV listing); Keuls 1985: 295, fig. 264, 265; Kilmer 1993: R371; Münzen und Medaillen 1977: 19, 53, lot 50, fig. 50; Peschel 1987: taf. 144; Reinsberg 1989: 195, fig. 109; Robertson 1986: 82, fig. 3; Sotheby's, catalogue 7.7.1994, 25, no. 340 (color). See also Becker 1977: 1, 33–34, no. 107a.

45. Oxford Ashmolean 1967.304. RF cup. Brygos P., c. 470. FS: Vulci. "Imminent": bearded man with erection in crouched posture with boy.

    BA 204034*, ARV 378.137, Para 366, Add 226. Dover R520*. DeVries 4.108.

    Illustrations: Boardman 1975: fig.260; Dierichs 1988: 63, Abb. 105; Johns 1982: 98, fig. 81; Keuls 1985: 284, fig. 254; Kilmer 1993: R520; Kilmer 2002: 130, fig. 6; Lear, 2008: 56, fig. 1.13; Matthews 1994: 212, fig. 31.1 (drawing); Neer 2010: 52, fig. 33; Neer 2012: 209, fig. 8.18 (color); Reinsberg 1989: 166, fig. 89; Shapiro 1981a: pl. 25.6; Topper 2012: 74, fig. 28; Vanhove 1992: 238, no. 102; Vattuone 2004: fig. 3; Vout 2013: 32, fig. 25.

    http://www.laits.utexas.edu/ancienthomosexuality/imageindex.php?cat_id=17&topic_id=198

46. London, British Museum, F65 (1772.320.154). RF bell krater. Dinos P., c. 420. FS: Capua. "Imminent": youth preparing to climb onto lap of a youth sitting in a chair.

    BA 215288* (drawing), ARV 1154.35, Add 336. Dover R954*. DeVries 6.23.

    Illustrations: Boardman 1989: 95–96, fig. 182; Davidson 2007: 345, fig. 33; Hoepfner and Schwandner 1994: 316, fig. 301; Hupperts 2000: 197, no. R322, ill. 6; Johns 1982: 24, fig. 9; Kilmer 1993: 23–25, R954; Lear 2008: 175–78, fig. 6.1; Reinsberg 1989: 210, fig. 119; Schauenburg 1972: 6, pl. 8.2; Skinner 2005: 96, fig. 3.13; Vout 2103: 2–3, 30–31, fig. 24.

    http://www.britishmuseum.org/research/search_the_collection_database/search_object_details.aspx?objectid=461071&partid=1

    http://www.perseus.tufts.edu/hopper/artifact;jsessionid=E408654E8ACCD3E2A01DAF2769A1C37F?name=London+F+65&object=Vase

    http://www.laits.utexas.edu/ancienthomosexuality/imageindex.php?cat_id=17&topic_id=200 [also ibid. id=22].

III. Black-Figure Vases Showing Anal Intercourse, Male on Male

47. Orvieto, Coll. Faina 41 (2664). BF Tyrrhenian amphora. Guglielmi P. (also called Komos P., Von Bothmer), c. 560–540 (560–50, middle period, Kluiver). FS: Orvieto?

    BA 310099* and 211957; ABV 102.100, 684; Para 38; Add 27. DeVries 1.12. Hupperts zk10.

    Illustrations: Kilmer 1997: 44–45, plate 7; Kluiver 2003: 166, no. 208, fig. 108; Lear 2008: 125–26, fig. 3.14; Sutton 2000: 186; fig. 7.1; Wójcik 1989: fig. 1.1–4.

    Additional references: Hupperts 1988: 263; Skinner 1995: 90.

48. Montpellier, Musée Languedocien 149bis. Tyrrhenian amphora. Guglielmi P., c. 560–550, Early period, Kluiver). FS: Vulci.

BA 310101*, ABV 102.102, Add 27. DeVries 1.14. Hupperts zk12. Kluiver 2003: 166, no. 202

Illustrations: Hubbard 2003: fig. 5a; Laurens 1984: 45–49, no. 2, pl. II–IV; Lear 2008: 125–26, 128, fig. 3.15.

http://www.laits.utexas.edu/ancienthomosexuality/imageindex.php?cat_id=17&topic_id=189, also id=190, 91, (id= 37, 38, 69, 70, 71, 195)

49. Riehen, Switzerland, collection Heinz Hoek. BF skyphos. Unattributed, Hermogenes potter, c. 555–535.

BA 350489*, Para 68.87, Add 47.

Illustrations: Dierichs 1988: 44, fig. 65; Dierichs 1993: 53–54, fig. 91a; Dierichs 2008: 54, abb. 41a & b (mistakenly described as heterosexual); Hornbostel 1980: 85, no. 53; Sutton 2000: 189, fig. 7.3–4.

IV. Black-Figure Vases with "Imminent" Anal Intercourse

50. Kurashiki, Ninagawa Museum 22 (museum closed in 2000). BF Tyrrhenian amphora. Timiades P., c. 570–560.

BA 7283. Hupperts zk23.

Illustrations: Hupperts 2000: 113, ill. 45 (Hoofdstuk 4, pl. 27); Simon 1982: 48–49, no. 22; Smith 2010: 43, 60, 316, pl. 13B–C.

V. Red-Figure Vases with "Imminent" Anal Intercourse

51. Boston, Museum of Fine Arts 95.61. RF kantharos. Nikosthenes Painter, Nikosthenes as potter, c. 520–510. FS: Etruria, Vulci.

BA 201063, ARV 132, Add 177. Dover R223*. Hupperts RS4

Illustrations: Boardman 1975: fig. 99; Boardman and LaRocca 1978: 86; *Eros grec* 1989: 21; Hupperts 2000: ill. 78; Johns 1982: 120, fig. 97; Kilmer 1993: R223; La Genière 2009: 339, fig. 2; Lear 2008: 119–20, fig. 3.10; Peschel 1987: pl. 38–39; Rabinowitz 2002: 142–45, fig. 5.23; Reinsberg 1989: 100, fig. 49A–C (drawing); Vermeule 1969: pl. 9.1–3.

http://www.mfa.org/collections/object/high-handled-drinking-cup-kantharos-with-erotic-scenes-153641

52. Hamburg, Museum fur Kunst und Gewerbe, 1981.173. RF oinochoe (Beazley type 7). Triptolemos P., c. 460. The "Erymedon Vase."

BA 1107. Dover R1155*. DeVries 5.141.

Illustrations: Cohen 2000: 88, fig. 3.6–7; Davidson 1997: 166, pl. 11; Francis 1990: 39, fig. 12; Frontisi-Ducroux 1995: 118, pl. 83; Hölscher 1989: 19, fig. 12ab; Hornbostel 1977: 317–18, no. 271; La Rocca 1994: 37, fig. 34–35; Keuls 1985: 292, fig. 261; Kilmer 1993: R1155; Kilmer 2002: 136, fig. 10; Lear 2008: 111–13, fig. 3.5A–B; Miller 1997: 13, pl. 1–2; Miller 2010; Pinney 1984: pl. 8 C–D; Reinsberg 1989: 177, fig. 98A–B; Schauenburg 1975: 103 (dr. of inscription), pl. 25.1–3; Smith 1999: pl. 8A–B; Wannagat 2001: 52, Abb. 2.

VI. "Courting" Vases Mentioned in the Text

53. Paris, Musee du Louvre, A479. BF Skyphos. Amasis, c. 540 (middle period). FS: Camiros, Rhodes.

BA 310509*, ABV 156.80, 688; Para. 65, 90. Dover B84. DeVries 2.11.

Illustrations: Barringer 2001: 79–80, fig. 40–41; Bažant 1985: 2, pl. 17.27; *CVA Paris, Musée du Louvre 9*, III. H. E.83, III. H. E.84, pl. 92.1–9 (633); Denoyelle 1994: 76–77, no. 33; Lissarrague 2001: 50–51, fig. 35–36; Lear 2008: 132, fig. 3.17; Malagardis and Iozzo 1995: 193, pl. 49b; Schnapp 1997: 249, no. 178; Stewart 1987: 38, fig 15. Von Bothmer 1985: 200–203, no. 54 (with bibliography).

http://www.photo.rmn.fr/c/htm/Search_New.aspx; in "Inventory number," search "A479."

http://www.laits.utexas.edu/ancienthomosexuality/imageindex.php?cat_id=7&topic_id=96, 97; female figures not shown.

54. Vienna, Kunsthistorisches Museum 3737. RF column krater. Harrow P, c. 500–475.

BA 202658*. Dover R406*. DeVries 4.77.

Illustrations: *CVA, Vienna, Kunsthistorisches Museum 2*, 25–26, pl. 87.1–2. Kaempf-Dimitriadou 1979: pl. 5.1–2; Lear 2008: 149, fig. 4.9; Schefold 1981: 249, fig. 349–50.

55. Paris, Louvre G121. RF cup. Douris, c. 490–485 (Middle period: Buitron-Oliver).

BA 205123*, ARV 434.78, Add 238. DeVries 4.127. Buitron-Oliver 1995: 26, no. 125. Douris painted a duplicate of this: Buitron-Oliver 1995: no. 126.

Illustrations: Buitron-Oliver 1995: pl. 76–77; Lear 2008: 33, fig. 0.5; Reinsberg 186, fig. 104.

http://www.photo.rmn.fr/c/htm/Search_New.aspx; in "Inventory number," search "G121."

http://commons.wikimedia.org/wiki/File:Pederastic_courtship_Louvre_G121.jpg

56. Louvre G122, plus another fragment, Tübingen E 20 fr. RF cup. Douris, c. 510–409 (early period: Buitron-Oliver). FS: Taranto?

BA 205054*, ARV 428.10 + ARV 428.6, Add 235. Buitron-Oliver 1995: no. 22 + no. 18.

Illustrations: Buitron-Oliver 1995: pl. 12.18, 13. Williams 1996: 242, 244, fig. 9, 11.

VII. Vases Claimed to Show Cunnilingus

57. Berlin, Antikensammlung, 3251 plus fragments from Florence, Museo Archeologico Etrusco, 1B49, 1B58, 6B24. Thalia P., c. 510. FS: Vulci.

BA 200964*, ARF 113.7, 1592, 1626; Para 332; Add 173. Dover R192*.

Illustrations: Boardman and LaRocca 1978: 90–91; Boardman 1975: fig. 112; *CVA Berlin, Antiquarium 2*: 13–16, fig. 2, pls. 56.4, 57.1–2, 58.1–4, 59.1–4 (985, 986, 987, 988); *CVA Berlin, Antiquarium 3*: 19, 20, pls. 122.1.5, 134.2 (1051, 1063); *CVA Firenze, Regio Museo Archeologico 1*: Iii.I.4, Iii.I.8, pl. 1.49, 1.58, 6.24 (376, 381); Dierichs 2008: 87, fig. 65; Heilmeyer 1988: 116, no. 4 (part); Johns 1982: 140, fig. 117; Kilmer 1993: R192; Kurke 1997: 134–37, fig. 1–2 and Kurke 1999: 202–4, fig. 1–3; Peschel 1987: pl. 29; Reinsberg 1989): 96, 103, 116, fig. 42, 52, 63A–B; Schäfer 1997: pl. 32.3; Shapiro 1983: pl. 63A (part of rim); Stewart 1997: 166–67; Seki 1981: 57, fig. 6; Torelli 2009: 184, fig. 13; Topper 2012: 110, fig. 40.

58. Tarquinia, Museo Nazionale Tarquiniese, 2076. RF pelike. Nikoxenos P., c. 510–500.

BA 202076*, ARV 224.7, Add 198. Dover R361. FS: Tarquinia.

Illustrations: Boardman and LaRocca 1978: 106–7; *CVA Tarquinia, Museo Nazionale 1*, III. I.7, pl. 12.2–3 (1164); Dierichs 1997: 115, Abb. 124; Dierichs 2008 : 88, Abb. 66A–B (color); Frontisi-Ducroux 1996: 93, fig. 40; Keuls 1985: 159, fig. 131 and 178, fig. 159; Kilmer 1993: R361; Reinsberg 1989: 129, fig. 73A–B.

59. Florence, Museo Archeologico Etrusco, V34. BF Siana lip cup. Unattributed, c. 560–550 (Iozzo).

BA 12960.

Illustrations: Iozzo 2006: 128–29, Tav.IX.1–4 (color; no description); Koch-Harnack 1983: 202–5, fig. 100–101 (no text); Sutton 2009: 78–79, no. 15, fig. 2a–b; Vorberg 1965: 582–85, A–D.

VIII. Selected Examples of "Group" Sex in Black-Figure

6, 47, 48, 50, 59 above; Q below.

60. Paris, Louvre F130bis plus frag. Basel, Cahn HC 986 (Kreuzer 1992: 96–98, no. 102). BF cup. Circle of the Andokides Group (Bloesch). c. 510.

    BA 12213*.

    Illustrations: Bloesch 1940: 16 no. 13; *CVA Paris, Musée du Louvre 10*, III. H. E.97, pl. 109.5.8–11 (744); Marcadé 1962: 84–85, 102; Pottier 1897–1922: pl. 74; Sutton 2009: 84, 89, no. 82, fig. 9.

    http://www.photo.rmn.fr/c/htm/Search_New.aspx; in "Inventory number," search "F130bis."

61. Malibu, J. Paul Getty Museum, 80.AE.99.2. BF Little master band cup fragments. Elbows Out P.? (Haldenstein 1982), c. 530?

    BA 28752*.

    Illustrations: Sutton 2009: 80, no. 32, fig. 4c (BA no. is incorrect); Heesen 2009: 107n639, 146n869, 198n1232.

IX. "Group" Sex in Red-Figure

A. THREESOMES

62. Paris, Louvre, CP9682 (CP274). RF stamnos. Polygnotos attrib. Beazley. 475–425.

    BA 213398, ARV 1029.16, Add 317. Dover R898.

    Illustrations: Boardman, 1989: 62, fig. 3; Kilmer 1993: R898 ; Matheson 1995: 57, pl. 43; Peschel 1987: pl. 247–48; Reinsberg 1989: 134, fig. 78.

    http://www.photo.rmn.fr/c/htm/Search_New.aspx; in "Inventory number," search "CP9682."

B. QUASI OR "IMMINENT" THREESOMES (SAME SCHEMA OF WOMAN ON BACK ON OR ALL FOURS FLANKED BY YOUTH AND OLDER MAN) A FAV. OF THE ANTIPHON P.

63. Basel, Antikenmuseum und Sammlung Ludwig, BS440. RF cup. Onesimos, c. 490 (CVA).

    BA 203338*, ARV 326.86bis, 1706, Para 359, Add 216. Dover R464.

    Illustrations: Boardman 1975: fig. 233; *CVA Basel, Antikenmuseum und Sammlung Ludwig 2*, 27–28, Beilage 3.2, pl. 10.2, 11.1–2, 34.2.6, 38.12 (266, 267, 290, 294); Keuls 1985: 184, fig. 165; Kilmer 1993: R464; Sparkes 1996: 106, fig. IV.10; Vierneisel and Kaeser 1990: 230, fig. 37.3.

64. Orvieto, Museo Civico, 585. RF cup. Antiphon P., c. 490–475. FS: Orvieto.

    BA 203485*, ARV 339.51, Add 218. Dover R486.

    Illustrations: *CVA, Umbria, Musei Comunali 1*, III. I. C.III. I. D.9, III. I. C. III. I. D.10, pl. 6.1–3 (763); Kilmer 1993: R486 (drawing); Peschel 1987: pl. 99–100; Tamassia 1974: 150, fig. 4.

65. Florence, Museo Archeologico Etrusco, no number. RF cup. Antiphon P., c. 490–480.

    BA 203488*, ARV 339.54. Kilmer R489 [not "R490" as BA]

    Illustrations: Kilmer R489; Peschel 1987: pl. 97–98.

66. Once Munich, Collection Arndt, now lost. Antiphon P., c. 470.

    BA 203489*, ARV 339.55, Add 218. Dover R490.

    Illustrations: Boardman 1975: fig. 241; Brulé 2003: 102; Dierichs 1988: 54, fig. 85; Keuls 1985: 183, fig. 164; Peschel 1987: 128–29, Abb. 95–96 (A, drawing of B); Torelli 2009: 185, fig. 14 (drawing).

C. OTHER POSSIBLE BUT DAMAGED (FIT THE SCHEMA ABOVE)

[67.] Vienna, Kunsthistorisches Museum, 107B. RF cup, fragment. Antiphon P., c. 480. FS: Adria.

    Young woman bent over pillow. Her hands seem to touch the feet of a (young?) man in front of her, but he is not erect.

    BA 203486*, ARV 339.52, Add 218. Kilmer R487.

    Illustrations: *CVA, Wien, Kunsthistorisches Museum 1*: 13, pl. 7.2–3; Tamassia 1974: 151, fig. 7; Wiel-Marin 2005: 340, no. 1279.

[68]. Paris, Musee du Louvre, CP11355. RF cup fragments. Antiphon P., c. 490.

    BA 203487*, ARV 339.53. Kilmer R488.

    Illustrations: Kilmer 1993: R488: "Youth with wineskin and cup; head of a woman in position for copulation *a tergo*—see R489*" Peschel 1987: 132, pl. 102.

D. MULTIPLE COUPLES

69. Malibu (CA), The J. Paul Getty Museum, 82.AE.27. RF cup. Epeleios P, c. 510.

    BA 275067, ARV 1629.32bis.

    Illustrations: Kilmer 1993: 35, 42, R249.

70. Malibu (CA), The J. Paul Getty Museum, 86.AE.284 plus Paris, Louvre C 11337. RF cup fragments. Onesimos, c. 490–480 (later middle phase, Williams)

    BA 203337*, ARV 326.87, Para 360.74bis, Add 216. Dover R461*.

    Illustrations: *CVA Malibu, J. Paul Getty Museum 8*: 29–30, fig. 12, pl. 415.1–2, 416.3 (1692, 1693); Dierichs 1989: 54, Abb. 3; Dierichs 2008: 80, fig. 60; Kilmer 1993: R461; Peschel 1987: 132, pl. 101; Williams 1991: 46, fig. 6.

    http://www.perseus.tufts.edu/hopper/image?img=Perseus:image:1990.05.0294

71. Oxford, Ashmolean, 1984.131–32. RF pinax. Paseas, c. 500–470 Dierichs (6th–5th cent. Vickers). 3 couples on three couches.

    BA 41348.

    Illustrations: Dierichs 1989; Griefenhagen 1976: 44, pl. 12 (color); Kilmer 1993: R260; Robertson 1992: 51, fig. 38; Vickers 1992: 246, no. 12, pl. VII d.

[72]. Damaged. 3 couples. Degree of overlap unclear. Kilmer counts as "orgy."

    Athens, M. Vlasto, no number. RF dinos fragments. Pan P., c. 450 (late manner: Follmann).

    BA 206303*, ARV 552.28, Para 387, Add 257. Kilmer R697.

    Illustrations: Boardman 1975: 193, fig. 346; Follmann 1968: pl. 3, 11.5; Kilmer 1993: R697 (drawing); Peschel 1987: pl. 177.

E. "ORGIES"

51. Nikosthenes.

57. Thalia P. above under cunnilingus. Central couple with two masturbating. Onlookers?

73. Paris, Musée du Louvre, G13. RF cup. Pedieus P., c. 510.

    BA 200694*, ARV 1578.16, 86.A, Add 170. Dover R156.

    Illustrations: Bažant 1985: pl. 22.36; Boardman 1975: fig. 92; *CVA Paris, Musée du Louvre 19*, 44–45, pl. 68.1–2, 69.1–3 (1273, 1274); Corner 2014: 202, fig. 12.2; Dalby 1996: 19, fig. 3; Dierichs 1988: 52, fig. 80; Dierichs 2008: 71, 82–83, fig. 52, 62A–B; *Eros grec* 1989: 125–27; Frontisi-Ducroux 1995): pl. 59; Guerrieri 2007: 40–41; Humphreys 1995: 109, fig. 10; Johns 1982: 6 & 129, fig. 107; Johnson and Ryan 2005: 125, fig. 7; Keuls 1985: 184, fig. 166; Kilmer 1993: R156; Kilmer 2002: 125, fig. 1; Korshak 1984: 93–95, pl. 3, fig. 3; Korshak 1987: 95, fig. 22; Kurke 1997: fig. 5–7; La Genière 2009: 339, fig. 1; Marcadé 1962: 138–39; Peschel 1987: pl. 37, 40; Pfisterer-Haas 1989: 197, fig. 68–69; Reinsberg 1989: 94, 101, fig. 36, 50a–c; Schäfer 1997: pl. 33.3; Stewart 1997: 9, fig. 5; Sutton 2000: 196, fig. 7.7; Topper 2012: 111, fig. 41.

http://www.photo.rmn.fr/cf/htm/Search_New.aspx; in "Inventory number," search "G13."

http://commons.wikimedia.org/wiki/File:Erotic_scenes_Louvre_G13_n1.jpg , also _n2.jpg, _n3.jpg, _n4.jpg.

http://commons.wikimedia.org/wiki/File:Drunken_banqueter_Louvre_G13.jpg

74. Florence, Museo Archeologico Etrusco, 3921. RF cup. Brygos P. attrib. Beazley, Brygos potter, c. 490–480.

BA 203929*, ARV 372.31, 398; Add 225. Dover R518.

Illustrations: Boardman and LaRocca 1978: 97–99 (A); Dierichs 1988: fig. 51; Dierichs 1993: 80, Abb. 148a–c; Dierichs 2008: 84–85, fig. 63a–c; Esposito and De Tommaso 1993: 58, fig. 85; Frontisi-Ducroux 1996: 91, fig. 38; Goff 2004: 155, fig. 2; Johns 1982: 112, 130–31, fig. 93 and 108; Keuls 1985: 185, fig. 167–70; Kilmer 1993: R518; Mulas 1978: 47–49; Parisinou 2000: 25–26, fig. 3; Peschel 1987: pl. 84, 131; Pfisterer-Haas 1989: 198, fig. 70–71; Reinsberg 1989: 102, fig. 51a–c; Schäfer 1997: pl. 24.2; Sutton 1992: 13, fig. 1.3; Sutton 2002: 127, fig. 3–4; Torelli 2009: 185, fig. 15; Vorberg 1965:187–88; Vout 2013: 191, fig. 157; Wegner 1973: pl. 4–5, 37a; Wrenhaven 2009: 377, fig. 5.

X. Other Vases for Comparison

A. New York, Collection of Shelby White and Leon Levy 737 (not included in the catalog of Von Bothmer 1990). BF kalpis. Unattributed, c. 510 (Sutton).

BA: no number. DeVries 2.100.

Illustrations: Lear 2008: 116–18, fig. 3.8; Shapiro 2000a: 18–19; Sutton 2000: 187, fig. 7.2.

http://www.laits.utexas.edu/ancienthomosexuality/imageindex.php?cat_id=17&topic_id=195

B. Boston Museum of Fine Arts 1970.233, Douris, c. 480–470.

BA 205288*, ARV 444.241, Add 240. Dover R577*.

Illustrations: Peschel 1987: pl. 180; Dierichs 1988: 58, fig. 94; Sutton 1992: 12, fig. 1.2; Kilmer 1993: 39, 58 (color); Buitron-Oliver 1995: Pl. III, no. 233; Stewart 1997: 163, fig. 104; Skinner 2005: 102, fig. 3.1.6; Glazebrook and Henry 2011: 116, fig. 5.3; Neer 2012: 209, fig. 8.17.

C. Turin, Museo di Antichità 4117. RF cup. Exterior unattributed, c. 500 (see Immerwahr 2008: no. 2809). Orig. attributed to the manner of the Epeleios Painter (ARV 150.35) but withdrawn in ARV 1628; "the inside recalls the Epeleios Painter, but the outside does not."

BA 201359*, ARV 150.35, 1628, Para 336, Add 179. Dover R243*. DeVries 3.77.

Illustrations: Hubbard 2003: fig. 15; Kilmer 1993: 25–26, 60, 61, 73, no. R243. Lear 2008: 117–19, fig. 3.9; Pantò 2011: 31–32, 45.

http://www.laits.utexas.edu/ancienthomosexuality/imageindex.php?cat_id=1&topic_id=1

D. Boston, Museum of Fine Arts 65.873. RF kylix fragments. Onesimos, c. 500–475.

BA 275918, Para 360.74 *quater* [BMFA number miscited], Add 216. Dover R463. DeVries 4.95.

Illustrations: Boardman 1975: fig. 226); Deacy and Pierce 1997: 133, fig. 9; Kilmer 1993: 184–86, color pl. 3; Kilmer 2002: 132–34, fig. 9; Lear 2008: 184, fig. 7.2.

E. Tarquinia, Museo Nazionale Tarquiniese, no number. RF kylix. Triptolemos P., c. 490–480.

BA 203885*. Dover R506.

Illustrations: Boardman and LaRocca 1978: 114; Brulé 2003: 114; Dietrich 1988: 40, fig. 57;

F. Tarquinia, Museo Nazionale Tarquiniese, no number. RF kylix. Triptolemos P., c. 490–480.

BA 203886*, ARV 367.94, Add 223. Dover R507.

CVA Tarquinia, Museo Nazionale 1, III. I.7, pl. 11.1 (1163); Dierichs 1988: 39, fig. 55; 2008: 77, fig. 56; Keuls 1985: 170, fig. 145; Kilmer 1993: R507; Peschel 1987: pl. 90; Poliakoff 1982: pl. 13a.

G. Pulsano, Dr. Guarini 154. RF lekythos. Triptolemos P., c. 480.

BA 15469.

Illustrations: Boardman and LaRocca 1978: 115; Boardman 1975: fig. 302; Dierichs 1993: 75, fig. 135; Fedele 1984: 48, no. 154, pl. 49.4; Mannino 2006: 125, no. 192, fig. 136.

H. London, British Museum, E440. RF stamnos. FS: Siren P., c 480 (Shapiro).

BA 202628*; ARV 289.1, 1642; Para 355, Add 218.

Illustrations: Boardman 1975: fig. 184; *CVA London, British Museum 3*, III.Ic.8, pl. 20.1A–D (185); Koch-Harnack 1983: 226, fig. 111; Lear 2008: 152, fig. 4.12; *LIMC* 5, pl. 299, Himeros 1; Pellegrini 2009: pl. 13; Reeder 1995: 417, fig. 137; Smet 1982: 119–20, fig. 6.

I. Athens, National Museum, 1357 (CC1158). RF cup. Unattributed, c. 500 (Barringer: Brygos, c. 490)

BA 9534*.

Illustrations: Barringer 2001: 77, fig. 36. *CVA, Athens, Musée National 1*, III. I. C.3–III. I. C.4, pl. 3.1.3 (25); Durand, Frontisi-Ducroux, Lissarrague 1989: 129, fig. 176; Kaltsas 2006: 190, fig. 84; Koch-Harnack 1983: 88, fig. 22; Lear 2008: 34, fig. 0.6; Ober and Hedrick 1993: 39, fig. 1.4; Settis 1996, 2.1: 821, fig. 35; Topper 2012: 138, fig. 56.

http://www.agathe.gr/id/agora/image/2004.02.0064

J. Munich, Antikensammlungen 2656 (J603) plus 8956A. RF cup. Makron, c. 490–480 (Hauptwerk I—Kunisch).

BA 204869; ARV 471.186, 1607, 1566; Add 246.

Illustrations: *CVA, Munich, Antikensammlungen 16*, 72–75, fig. 32–34, pls. 50.1–6, 51.1–5 (4715, 4716); Kunisch 1997: no. 144, Lear 2008: 35–36, fig. 0.7.

K. Berlin, Antikensammlung, F2292. RF cup. Makron, c. 480 (Hauptwerk II—Kunisch)

BA 204878*; ARV 471.195, 482, 1701.

Illustrations: *CVA, Berlin, Antiquarium 2*, 35, pl. 90.1–4 (1019); Heilmeyer 1988: 112, no. 3; Kunisch 1997: no. 386, fig.17C, 21, pl. 51; Lear 2008: 36, fig. 0.8: Reden 1995: 199, pl. 4 a.

L. Brussels, Musees Royaux R351. RF Hydria. Dikaios, c. 510–500. FS: Etruria, Vulci.

BA 200192*; ARV 31.7. Dover R62.

Illustrations: Aloni 1980: 36, pl. 1B; Boardman 1975: fig. 46; *CVA, Bruxelles, Musées royaux d'art et d'histoire (Cinquantenaire) 2*: 9, pl. 16.3A.3B (069); Dierichs 1988: 53, Abb. 84; Dierichs 1997: 118, Abb. 131; Dierichs 2008: 72–73, Abb. 53a–c; *Eros grec* 1989: 28; Johns 1982: 114–15, pl. 31; Kilmer 1993: R62; La Genière 2009: 341, fig. 5; Lissarrague 1992: 218, fig. 53; Peschel 1987: Abb. 2; Reinsberg 1989: 99, Abb. 48; Smet 1982: 259, no. 172.

M. Berlin, Antikensammlung, F2414. RF oinoche. Shuvalov P., c. 430–420.

BA 216500*; ARV 1208.41, 1704; Para 463; Add 346. Dover R970*.

Illustrations: Blanckenhagen 1976: 11b; Boardman 1989: fig. 224; Boardman and La Rocca 1978: 124–25; Brendel 1970: fig. 25–26; *CVA, Berlin, Antiquarium 3*: 27, pl. 145.2, 146.1–2 (1074–75); Dierichs 1988: 61, fig. 100; Dierichs 2008: 79, Abb. 59; Heilmeyer 1988: 154, no. 10; Keuls 1985: 190, fig. 173; Kilmer 1982: pl. 2a; Kilmer 1993: 45, 52, 153–54, 163–64, 189–91, R970; Lezzi-Hafter 1976: fig. 111a, c, d; Mulas 1978: 56; Peschel 1987: Abb. 249; Reinsberg 1989: 133, fig. 77; Robertson 1992: 229, fig. 233; Scholl 2007: 76; Simon 1981: 144, Abb. 211; Stewart 1997: 163, pl. 2B, fig. 103; Valavanis 1996: 81.

http://www.photo.rmn.fr/c/htm/Search_New.aspx; in "Inventory number," search "F2414."

http://en.wikipedia.org/wiki/Oinochoe_by_the_Shuvalov_Painter_(Berlin_F2414)

XI. Vases by the Affecter Mentioned in the Text

N. New York, Metropolitan Museum of Art 18.145.15. BF amphora, Affecter, c. 540–520.

BA 301383*; ABV 247.90, 69, 715; Para 111; Add. 64. Dover B194. DeVries 2.55. Hupperts z92.

Illustrations: *CVA, New York, Metropolitan Museum of Art 3*: 20, pl. 54.1–2 (556); Hupperts 1988: 261, fig.4; Hupperts 2000: ill. 33; Isler-Kerényi 2007: ill. 2; Lear 2008: 68–71, fig. 2.2.; Mommsen 1975, no. 71: Shapiro 2000a: 19–20, fig. 8–9.

O. London, British Museum 1836.2-24.46 (B153). BF amphora. Affecter, c. 540–20.

BA 301333*, ABV 243.45, Add 62. DeVries 2.49. Hupperts z82.

Illustrations: Barringer 2001: 90–91, fig. 51; Hubbard 2014: 145, fig. 8.8; Hupperts 1988: 262, fig. 5; Hupperts 2000: ill.37; Kilmer 1997: 46, fig. 9; Lear 2008: 68–71, fig. 2.3; Mommsen 1975: no. 107; Schnapp 1997: 250, no. 179.

http://www.laits.utexas.edu/ancienthomosexuality/imageindex.php?topic_id=43&pc=1

http://www.britishmuseum.org/research/search_the_collection_database/search_object_details.aspx?objectid=399362&partid=1

XII. Erotic Vases from Known Attic Gravesites

P. Athens, Kerameikos 1063. RF askos, c. 440.

BA 6022.

Illustrations: Dierichs 1988: 62, fig. 101; 2008: 81, fig. 61a–b; Dipla and Paleothodoros 2012: 221, fig. 13; *Eros grec* 1989: 121; Hoffmann 1977: pl. 5.5–6; Keuls 1985: 178, fig. 160; Kilmer 1993: R1184; Kunze-Götte, Tancke, and Vierneisel. 1999: 131–32 (tomb 499), fig. 30, pl. 89.4; La Genière 2009: 342, fig. 7; Paleothodoros 2012: 28, fig. 6; Reinsberg 1989: 139, fig. 80; Stampolidis and Tasoulas 2009: 220, no. 185.

Part of a grave assemblage (tomb 499; NNr53 = WP 7 außen) with a *lebes gamikos* by the Painter of London E 489 (BA 9023003, Kerameikos 1060; Illustrations: Dipla and Paleothodoros 2012: 221, fig. 14; Kunze-Götte, Tancke and Vierneisel 1999: pl. 89.1.1, 89.2.1; Paleothodoros 2012: 29, fig. 7–9), an undecorated biconical cup (1062), a lamp (1061), and a terracotta figurine (1064) of a kneeling boy.

Q. Athens, Kerameikos 15418, BF lekythos, Diosphos workshop, c. 490 (Kavvadias).

BA: no number.

Found in situ in Kerameikos tomb 1010, that of a child, possibly female.

Illustrations: Dipla and Palaeothodoros 2013: 222, 223 fig. 15; Glazebrook 2011: 38 (fig. 2.2) and cover; Kavvadias 2009; La Genière 2009: 343–44 (fig. 9–11).

APPENDIX: VASES SAID TO SHOW "IMMINENT" OR "PREPARATION FOR" MALE ON MALE ANAL INTERCOURSE

In black-figure:

1) Heidelberg, Ruprecht-Karls-Universitat 67.4

    BA 310100*, ABV 102.101. Dover B53*. DeVries 1.13.

    On the far right an ithyphallic man approaches the back of a youth. DeVries 1.13: "preparation for kiss and anal sex." He may wish for anal intercourse, but this is not a depiction or it or even preparation for it, at least on the part of both partners. Lear (2008: 124): "The youth is a little farther away from his lover than the women and seems to be making a dance step or running—although like them, he is preparing to kiss his lover." I do not see how he can do both.

2) Berlin, Antikensammlung, 3267

    BA 300833*, ABV 90.6 (top), Para 33, Add 24. DeVries 1.6.

    DeVries: "Around rim, orgiastic scene (w/ anal, fellatio)" However, for the male figures at roughly 1 o'clock on the rim, the legs are beside each other, and the lower figure is just further recessed in the picture. The scene of "fellatio" clearly is not.

In red-figure:

3) Bochum, Ruhr Universität, Kunstsammlungen S507 by Makron

    BA 275245. DeVries 4.159. Lear 2008: fig. 2.11.

    Lear (2008: 84): "The right-hand couple, on the other hand, is in a highly unusual position: the *erastes* (whose penis is not visible, due to damage) is moving toward the *eromenos*, who has drawn up his cloak and bent over, offering him his bare buttocks." Lear calls this a "scene of anal intercourse (or the preparations for it).... Yet its [anal intercourse's] direct representation is rare, occurring among extant vases only in this scene and on vase 3.8 [the Levy-White vase]." Reinsberg (1989: 210) interprets the figure in the same way. This reading is incorrect: the leftmost figure is not bent over at the waist and the knees as one finds in the actual scenes of anal intercourse with either men or women. Nor are his legs bent together as in such scenes; one is more advanced. This is not a youth offering his posterior; it is a youth pulling off his clothes (cf. Makron, Paris, Louvre G158 and Louvre CP10918 for the stance). The older man may have a surprise in mind, but it does not constitute anal intercourse.

4) Toledo, OH 1964.126.

    BA 275906*, Para 370.12bis.

    Keuls (1985: 71): "an infibulated youth playing the guitar and being accosted sexually from the rear by a mature man. The aggressor's walking stick carries the symbolic phallic charge here." Lear (2008: 115) reads it as a "hint" of anal sex to come: "The *erastes* is in the almost seated intercrural posture of vase 1.13 [R520 = DeVries 4.108]. There is, however, a signal difference in this case: this *erastes* approaches the *eromenos* from the rear. Although his penis is not visible, his outstretched leg and cane both function as stand-ins for it; they are lifted up and cut across the *eromenos'* buttocks at a markedly phallic angle." Not on DeVries's list, since he not did consider it a case. The man is not in the position for interfemoral intercourse; he is dancing (note the right leg stuck straight out). See above for Turin, Museo di Antichità 4117.

5) Rome, Vilia Giulia 50384.

BA 201725*. Dover R322*.

Koch-Harnack 1983: 72 (fig. 8) argues that the youth being offered a hare is making an obscene gesture (forefinger to thumb forming a ring) that indicates his readiness for anal intercourse. Kilmer (1993: p. 22 of plates, R322) thought the boy was holding a flower. Rather, Greifenhagen 1976: 44 "Mit rhetorischen Geste" (citing Neumann 1965: 12); Dover 1989: 92: "a boy, speaking to a youth, holds finger and thumb together in an argumentative gesture."

BIBLIOGRAPHY

Acocella, Joan. 2006. "The Girls Next Door: Life in the Centerfold." *New Yorker*, March 20, 144–48.

"Acquisitions of the Art Museum 1986." 1987. *Record of the Art Museum, Princeton University* 46.1: 18–52.

Alexandridou, Alexandra-Fani. 2011. *The Early Black-Figured Pottery of Attika in Context (c. 630–570 BCE)*. Leiden and Boston.

Andrews, Edna. 1990. *Markedness Theory: The Union of Asymmetry and Semiosis in Language*. Durham, NC.

Avagianou, Aphrodite. 1991. *Sacred Marriage in the Rituals of Greek Religion*. Bern and New York.

Avramidou, Amalia. 2006. "Attic Vases in Etruria: Another View on the Divine Banquet Cup by the Codrus Painter." *American Journal of Archaeology* 110: 565–79.

Baggio, Monica. 2004. *I gesti della seduzione: Tracce di comunicazione non-verbale nella ceramica greca tra VI e IV secolo a.C.* Rome.

Bain, David. 1991. "Six Greek Verbs of Sexual Congress (βινῶ, κινῶ, πυγίζω, ληκῶ, οἴφω, λαικάζω)." *Classical Quarterly* 41: 51–77.

Barringer, J. M. 2001. *The Hunt in Ancient Greece*. Baltimore.

Bartol, Krystyna. 1999. "Between Loyalty and Treachery: P. Oxy. 2327 fr. 1 + 2(a) col. I = Simonides 21 West^2—Some Reconsiderations." *Zeitschrift für Papyrologie und Epigraphik* 126: 26–28.

Bažant, Jan. 1985. *Les citoyens sur les vases Athéniens du 6e au 4e siècle av. J.-C.* Prague.

———. 1987. "Les vases athéniens et les réformes démocratiques," in Claude Bérard, Christiane Bron, and Alessandra Pomari (eds.), *Images et société en Grèce ancienne. L'iconographie comme méthode d'analyse (Actes du Colloque international, Lausanne 8–11 février 1984; Université de Lausanne, 1987)*, 33–40. Lausanne.

Beard, Mary. 1991. "Adopting an Approach II," in Tom Rasmussen and Nigel Spivey (eds.), *Looking at Greek Vases*, 12–35. Cambridge.

Beazley, J. D. 1947/1989. *Some Attic Vases in the Cyprus Museum.* (Originally *Proceedings of the British Academy* 33 [1948] 7–31. As a separate offprint, London: G. Cumberledge, 1947. Reprinted edition by Donna C. Kurtz. Oxford: Oxford University Committee for Archaeology, 1989.)

Beazley, J. D. 1951. *The Development of Attic Black-Figure.* Berkeley.

———. 1956. *Attic Black-Figure Vase-Painters.* Oxford.

———. 1963. *Attic Red-Figure Vase-Painters.* 2nd ed. Oxford.

———. 1966. "Un realista greco." In *Adunanze straordinarie per il conferimento dei premi della Fondazione A. Feltrinelli,* 53–60. Rome.

———. 1971. *Paralipomena: Additions to Attic Black-Figure Vase-Painters and to Attic Red-Figure Vase-Painters.* 2nd ed. Oxford.

Becker, Regina-Maria. 1977. *Formen attischer Peliken: von der Pionier-Gruppe bis zum Beginn der Frühklassik.* Thesis: Tübingen.

Beltrami, Arnaldo, ed. 1897. *Esiodo: Le opere e i giorni.* Messina.

Bérard, Claude and Jean-Louis Durand. 1989. "Entering the Imagery," in *A City of Images: Iconography and Society in Ancient Greece,* trans. Deborah Lyons, 22–37. Princeton.

Berg, Steven. 2010. *Eros and the Intoxications of Enlightenment: On Plato's Symposium.* Albany.

Bergemann, Johannes. 1997. *Demos und Thanatos: Untersuchungen zum Wertsystem der Polis im Spiegel der attischen Grabreliefs des 4. Jahrhunderts V. Chr. und zur Funktion der gleichzeitigen Grabbauten.* Munich.

Bernand, André. 1972. *De Koptos à Kosseir.* Leiden.

Blanckenhagen, Peter Heinrich von. 1976. "Puerilia," in Larissa Bonfante and Helga von Heintze (eds.), *In Memoriam Otto J. Brendel: Essays in Archaeology and the Humanities,* 37–41. Mainz.

Blazeby, Clare Kelly. 2011. "Woman + Wine = Prostitute in Classical Athens?" in Madeleine M. Henry and Allison Glazebrook (eds.), *Greek Prostitutes in the Ancient Mediterranean, 800 BCE–200 CE,* 86–105. Madison.

Bloesch, Hansjörg. 1940. *Formen attischer Schalen von Exekias bis zum Ende des strengen Stils.* Bern-Bümpliz.

Boardman, John. 1975. *Athenian Red Figure Vases: The Archaic Period: A Handbook.* London.

———. 1989. *Athenian Red Figure Vases: The Classical Period: A Handbook.* London.

———. 1991. "Sixth-Century Potters and Painters," in Tom Rasmussen and Nigel Spivey (eds.), *Looking at Greek Vases,* 79–102. Cambridge.

———. 1996. Review of Michael J. Vickers and David Gill, *Artful Crafts: Ancient Greek Silverware and Pottery. Classical Review* 46: 123–26.

———. 2001. *The History of Greek Vases: Potters, Painters, and Pictures.* New York.

———. 2004. Review of Richard T. Neer, *Style and Politics in Athenian Vase-Painting: The Craft of Democracy, ca. 530–470 BCE. Common Knowledge* 10: 353.

Boardman, John and Eugenio La Rocca. 1978. *Eros in Greece.* New York.

Bonfante, Larissa. 1996. *Etruscan Sexuality and Funerary Art.* Cambridge.

———. 2013. "Mothers and Children," in Jean MacIntosh Turfa (ed.), *The Etruscan World,* 426–46. Abingdon.

Bremer, J. M., A. Maria van Erp Taalman Kip, and S. R. Slings. 1987. *Some Recently Found Greek Poems: Text and Commentary*, Mnemosyne Supplementum 99. Leiden and New York.

Bremmer, J. N. 1990. "Adolescents, *Symposion*, and Pederasty," in O. Murray (ed.), *Sympotica: A Symposium on the Symposion*, 135–48. Oxford.

Brendel, Otto J. 1970. "The Scope and Temperament of Erotic Art in the Greco-Roman World," in Theodore Bowie and Cornelia V. Christenson (eds.), *Studies in Erotic Art*, 3–107. New York.

Brinkmann, Vinzenz. 1994. *Beobachtungen zum formalen Aufbau und zum Sinngehalt der Friese des Siphnierschatzhauses*. Ennepetal.

Brommer, Frank. 1984. "Themenwahl aus örtlichen Gründen," in *Ancient Greek and Related Pottery: Proceedings of the International Symposion in Amsterdam 12–15 April 1984*, 178–84. Amsterdam.

Brulé, Pierre. 2003. *Women of Ancient Greece*. Trans. Antonia Nevill. Edinburgh.

Buitron-Oliver, Diana. 1995. *Douris: A Master-Painter of Athenian Red-Figure Vases*. Forschungen zur antiken Keramik. II Reihe, Kerameus Bd. 9. Mainz am Rhein.

Burn, Lucilla. 1987. *The Meidias Painter*. Oxford.

Burnett, Anne Pippin. 1983. *Three Archaic Poets: Archilochus, Alcaeus, Sappho*. Cambridge, MA.

Callipolitis-Feytmans, Denise. 1974. *Les Plats Attiques à Figures Noires*. École française d'Athènes. Travaux et mémoires fasc. 19. Paris.

Cantarella, Eva. 1992. *Bisexuality in the Ancient World*. Trans. Cormac Ó Cuilleanáin. 2nd ed. with new preface, 2002. New Haven.

Carpenter, T. H. 1989. *Beazley Addenda: Additional References to ABV. ARV2 & Paralipomena*. 2nd ed. Oxford.

Cartledge, Paul A. 1983. "'Trade and Politics' Revisited: Archaic Greece," in P. Garnsey, K. Hopkins, and C. R. Whittaker (eds.), *Trade in the Ancient Economy*, 1–15. Berkeley.

Clairmont, Christoph W. 1993. *Classical Attic Tombstones*. 7 vols. Kilchberg.

Clarke, John R. 2010. "Erotica," in *The Oxford Encyclopedia of Ancient Greece and Rome*, 1: 108–10. New York.

———. 2011. "Erotica: Visual Representation of Greek and Roman Sexual Culture," in Mark Golden and Peter Toohey (eds.), *A Cultural History of Sexuality*. Vol. 1, *A Cultural History of Sexuality in the Classical World*, 169–90. Oxford and New York.

Cohen, Beth. 1997. "Red-Figure Vases Take Wing," in John H. Oakley, William D. E. Coulson, and Olga Palagia (eds.), *Athenian Potters and Painters: The Conference Proceedings*, 141–55. Oxford.

Cohen, Beth (ed.). 2000. *Not the Classical Ideal: Athens and the Construction of the Other in Greek Art*. Leiden and Boston.

Cohen, David. 1987. "Law, Society and Homosexuality in Classical Athens." *Past and Present* 117: 3–21.

———. 1991. *Law, Sexuality, and Society: The Enforcement of Morals in Classical Athens*. Cambridge.

Conze, Alexander. 1893–1922. *Die Attischen Grabreliefs*. 4 vols in 6. Berlin.

Corner, Sean. 2010. "Transcendent Drinking: The Symposium at Sea Reconsidered." *Classical Quarterly*, 60.2: 352–80.

———. 2014. "Sumposion," in Hubbard, Thomas K. (ed.), *A Companion to Greek and Roman Sexualities*, 199–213. Malden, MA.

Csapo, Eric. 1993. "Deep Ambivalence: Notes on a Greek Cockfight (Part I)." *Phoenix* 47: 1–28.

Dalby, Andrew. 1996. *Siren Feasts: A History of Food and Gastronomy in Greece*. London and New York.

Davidson, James. 1997. *Courtesans and Fishcakes: The Consuming Passions of Classical Athens.* London.

———. 2001. "Dover, Foucault and Greek Homosexuality: Penetration and the Truth of Sex." *Past and Present* 170: 3–51.

———. 2006. "Making a Spectacle of Her(self): The Greek Courtesan and the Art of the Present," in Martha Feldman and Bonnie Gordon (eds.), *The Courtesan's Arts: Cross-Cultural Perspectives*, 29–51. Oxford.

———. 2007. *The Greeks and Greek Love: A Radical Reappraisal of Homosexuality in Ancient Greece*. London. The subtitle is also given as: A Bold New Exploration of the Ancient World.

Deacy, Susan and Karen F. Pierce (eds.). 2002. *Rape in Antiquity*. London.

Degani, E. 1974. "Il nuovo Archiloco." *Atene e Roma* 19: 113–28.

———. 1975. "Πάρεξ το θεῖον χρῆμα nel nuovo Archiloco di Colonia." *Quaderni Urbinati di Cultura Classica* 20: 229.

Denoyelle, Martine. 1994. *Chefs-d'oeuvre de la céramique grecque dans les collections du Louvre*. Paris.

Despinis, G. 1991–2. "Ἐπιτύμβια στήλη ἀπό το Πόρτο Ράφτη: ἀποκατάσταση και σχόλια." Εγνατία 3: 7–27.

DeVries, Keith. 1997. "The 'Frigid *Eromenoi*' and Their Wooers Revisited: A Closer Look at Greek Homosexuality in Vase Painting," in Martin Duberman (ed.), *Queer Representations: Reading Lives, Reading Cultures*, 14–24. New York.

Dierichs, Angelika. 1988. "Erotik in der Kunst Griechenlands." *Antike Welt*, Sondernummer 2.

———. 1989. "Liebesszenen auf einem Pinax." *Antike Welt* 20, Heft 2: 49–54.

———. 1993. *Erotik in der Kunst Griechenlands*. Mainz am Rhein.

———. 1997. *Erotik in der römischen Kunst*. Sonderhefte der *Antiken Welt*. Mainz.

———. 2008. *Erotik in der Kunst Griechenlands*. Mainz.

Dietrich, Nikolaus. 2010. *Figur ohne Raum? Bäume und Felsen in der attischen Vasenmalerei des 6. und 5. Jahrhunderts v.Chr.* Image & Context v. 7. Berlin and New York.

Diggle, James. 2004. *Theophrastus: Characters*. Cambridge.

Dillon, Matthew. 2002. *Girls and Women in Classical Greek Religion*. London and New York.

Dipla, Anthi and Dimitris Paleothodoros. 2012. "Selected for the Dead: Erotic Themes on Grave Vases from Attic Cemeteries," in Ing-Marie Back Danielsson, Fredrik Fahlander, and Ylva Sjöstrand (eds.), *Encountering Imagery: Materialities, Perceptions, Relations*. Stockholm Studies in Archaeology 57: 209–33.

Dover. Kenneth J. 1964. "Eros and Nomos: (Plato, Symposium 182a–185c)." *Bulletin of the Institute of Classical Studies* 11: 31–42.

———. 1973. "Classical Greek Attitudes to Sexual Behaviour." *Arethusa* 6: 59–73. Repr. in *Women in the Ancient World: The Arethusa Papers*, ed. John Peradotto and J. P. Sullivan, 143–57. Albany, 1984; repr. in *Sex and Difference in Ancient Greece and Rome*, ed. Mark Golden and Peter Toohey. Edinburgh, 2003.

———. 1974. *Greek Popular Morality in the Time of Plato and Aristotle*. Oxford.

———. 1989 [1978]. *Greek Homosexuality.* Cambridge, MA. [A postscript added in 1989 but text of 1978 unaltered.]

Dunbar, Nan (ed.). 1995. *Aristophanes: Birds.* Oxford.

Durand, Jean-Louis, Françoise Frontisi-Ducroux, and François Lissarrague. 1989. "Wine: Human and Divine," in Claude Bérard et al. (eds.), *A City of Images: Iconography and Society in Ancient Greece,* 121–30. Princeton. Orig. *La cité des images.* Paris, 1984.

Eder, Walter. 1998. "Aristocrats and the Coming of Athenian Democracy," in Ian Morris and Kurt Raaflaub (eds.), *Democracy 2500? Questions and Challenges,* 105–40. Dubuque.

Eros grec: amour des dieux et des hommes: [exposition] Galeries nationales du Grand Palais, 6 novembre 1989–5 février 1990, Athènes, 5 mars–5 mai 1990. Athens.

Ehrenberg, Victor. 1962. *The People of Aristophanes. A Sociology of Old Attic Comedy.* 3rd rev. ed. New York.

Esposito, Anna Maria and Giandomenico De Tommaso. 1993. *Vasi attici. Museo archeologico di Firenze. Antiquarium.* Florence.

Ferrari, Gloria. 2002. *Figures of Speech: Men and Maidens in Ancient Greece.* Chicago.

———. 2003. "Myth and Genre on Athenian Vases." *Classical Antiquity* 22: 37–54.

Fisher, N. R. E. 2000. "Symposiasts, Fish-Eaters and Flatterers: Social Mobility and Moral Concerns," in F. D. Harvey and J. Wilkins (eds.), *The Rivals of Aristophanes: Studies in Athenian Old Comedy,* 355–96. London.

———. 2001. *Aeschines: Against Timarchos.* Oxford.

Follmann-Schulz, Anna-Barbara. 1968. *Der Pan-Maler.* Bonn.

Foucault, Michel. 1985 [1984]. *The History of Sexuality.* Vol. 2, *The Use of Pleasure.* Trans. Robert Hurley. New York.

———. 1986 [1984]. *The History of Sexuality.* Vol. 3, *The Care of the Self.* Trans. Robert Hurley. New York.

Francis, E. D. 1990. *Image and Idea in Fifth Century Greece: Art and Literature After the Persian Wars.* Ed. Michael Vickers. London and New York.

Frel, Jiří. 1984. "A View into Phintias' Private Life," in Arthur Houghton et al. (eds.), *Festschrift für Leo Mildenberg: Numismatik, Kunstgeschichte, Archäologie = Studies in Honor of Leo Mildenberg: Numismatics, Art History, Archaeology,* 57–60. Wetteren, Belgium.

Freyer-Schauenburg, Brigitte. 1974. *Samos Bd. 11: Bildwerke der archaischen Zeit und des strengen Stils.* Bonn.

Friis Johansen, Knud. 1960. "Eine attische Trinkschale." *Acta Archaeologica* 31: 129–45.

Frontisi-Ducroux, Françoise. 1995. *Du masque au visage: Aspects de l'identité en Grèce ancienne.* Paris.

———. 1996. "Eros, Desire, and the Gaze," in Natalie Boymel Kampen with Bettina Bergmann (eds.), *Sexuality in Ancient Art: Near East, Egypt, Greece, and Italy,* 81–100. Cambridge.

Gager, John G. 1992. *Curse Tablets and Binding Spells from the Ancient World.* New York.

Gauthier, Philippe and Miltiadēs V. Hatzopoulos. 1993. *La loi gymnasiarchique de Beroia.* Athens and Paris.

Gentili, Bruno. 1988. *Poetry and Its Public in Ancient Greece.* Trans. A. Thomas Cole. Baltimore.

Gill, David W. J. 1994. "Positivism, Pots and Long-distance Trade," in Ian Morris (ed.), *Classical Greece: Ancient Histories and Modern Archaeologies,* 99–107. Cambridge.

———. 2009. "Looting Matters for Classical Antiquities: Contemporary Issues in Archaeological Ethics." *Present Pasts* 1: 14. http://dx.doi.org/10.5334/pp.14.

Giuliano, Antonio. 1969. "Osservazioni sulle pitture della 'Tomba dei tori' a Tarquinia." *Studi Etruschi* 37: 3–26; repr. in *Scritti minori,* 69–94. Rome.

Glazebrook, Allison. 2011. "Porneion: Prostitution in Athenian Civic Space," in Allison Glazebrook and Madeleine Henry (eds.), *Greek Prostitutes in the Ancient Mediterranean, 800 BCE–200 CE,* 34–59. Madison.

Glazebrook, Allison and Madeleine Mary Henry (eds.). 2011. *Greek Prostitutes in the Ancient Mediterranean, 800 BCE–200 CE.* Madison.

Goff, Barbara E. 2004. *Citizen Bacchae: Women's Ritual Practice in Ancient Greece.* Berkeley.

Golden, Mark. 1984. "Slavery and Homosexuality at Athens," *Phoenix* 38: 308–24.

———. 1991. "Thirteen Years of Homosexuality (and Other Recent Work on Sex, Gender and the Body in Ancient Greece)." *Echos du monde classique / Classical Views* 10: 327–40.

Goldhill, Simon. 1995. *Foucault's Virginity: Ancient Erotic Fiction and the History of Sexuality.* Cambridge.

———. 2011. *Victorian Culture and Classical Antiquity: Art, Opera, Fiction, and the Proclamation of Modernity.* Martin Classical Lectures. Princeton.

Gow, Andrew Sydenham Farrar and Denys Lionel Page (eds.). 1965. *The Greek Anthology: Hellenistic Epigrams.* Cambridge.

Greifenhagen, A. 1976. "Fragmente eines rotfig-urigen Pinax," in Larissa Bonfante and Helga von Heintze (eds.), *In Memoriam Otto J. Brendel: Essays in Archaeology and the Humanities,* 43–48. Mainz.

Grossman, Janet Burnett. 2001. *Greek Funerary Sculpture: Catalogue of the Collections at the Getty Villa.* Malibu.

———. 2013. *Funerary Sculpture. The Athenian Agora, 35.* Princeton, NJ.

Guerrieri, Marta Chiara. 2007. *Eros.* Milano.

Haldenstein, Joan Tarlow. 1982. "Little Master Cups, Studies in 6th Century Attic Black-Figure Vase Painting." PhD diss., University of Cincinnati.

Halperin, David M. 1986. "Plato and Erotic Reciprocity." *Classical Antiquity* 5: 60–80.

———. 1990. *One Hundred Years of Homosexuality: And Other Essays on Greek Love.* New York.

———. 1997. "Questions of Evidence: Commentary on Koehl, DeVries, and Williams," in M. Duberman (ed.), *Queer Representations: Reading Lives, Reading Cultures: A Center for Lesbian and Gay Studies Book,* 39–56. New York.

———. 2002. *How to Do the History of Homosexuality.* Chicago.

Hamilton, Richard. 1992. *Choes and Anthesteria: Athenian Iconography and Ritual.* Ann Arbor.

Hammer, Dean. 2004. "Ideology, the Symposium, and Archaic Politics." *American Journal of Philology* 125: 479–512.

Hastrup, Helene Blinkenberg. 1999. "La clientèle étrusque de vases attiques a-t-elle acheté des vases ou des images?" in M.-C. Villanueva-Puig et al. (eds.), *Céramique et peinture grecques: Modes d'emploi,* 439–44. Paris.

Heilmeyer, Wolf-Dieter. 1988. *Antikenmuseum Berlin: Die Ausgestellten Werke.* Berlin.

Henderson, Jeffrey. 1991. *The Maculate Muse: Obscene Language in Attic Comedy.* 2nd ed. New York.

Himmelmann, Nikolaus. 1994. *Realistische Themen in der griechischen Kunst der archaischen und klassischen Zeit.* Berlin and New York.

Hobden, Fiona. 2009. "The Politics of the *Sumposion*," in George Boys-Stones, Barbara Graziosi, and Phiroze Vasunia (eds.), *The Oxford Handbook of Hellenic Studies*, 271–80. Oxford.

———. 2013. *The Symposion in Ancient Greek Society and Thought.* Cambridge.

Hoepfner, Wolfram and Ernst-Ludwig Schwandner. 1994. *Haus und Stadt im klassischen Griechenland*, 2nd ed. Munich.

Hoffmann, Herbert. 1977. *Sexual and Asexual Pursuit: A Structuralist Approach to Greek Vase Painting.* London.

Hölscher, Tonio. 1989. *Die unheimliche Klassik der Griechen.* Bamberg.

Hoorn, Gerard van. 1951. *Choes and Anthesteria.* Leiden.

Hornbostel, Wilhelm. 1977. *Kunst der Antike: Schätze aus norddeutschem Privatbesitz: [Ausstellungsdauer 21. Januar–6. März 1977: Katalog].* Mainz.

———. 1980. *Aus Gräbern und Heiligtümern: Die Antikensammlung Walter Kropatscheck: [Ausstellungsdauer, 11. Juli–14. September 1980].* Mainz am Rhein.

———. 1986. *Aus der Glanzzeit Athens: Meisterwerke griechischer Vasenkunst in Privatbesitz.* Hamburg.

Hubbard, Thomas K. 1998. "Popular Perceptions of Elite Homosexuality in Classical Athens." *Arion* 6: 48–78.

———. 2000. "Pederasty and Democracy: The Marginalization of a Social Practice," in Thomas K. Hubbard (ed.), *Greek Love Reconsidered*, 1–11. NAMBLA Topics 9. New York.

———, (ed.). 2003a. *Homosexuality in Greece and Rome: A Sourcebook of Basic Documents.* Berkeley.

———. 2003b. Website with additional materials for Hubbard 2003a. http://www.laits.utexas.edu/ancienthomosexuality/index.php

———. 2006. "History's First Child Molester: Euripides' *Chrysippus* and the Marginalization of Pederasty in Athenian Democratic Discourse," in J. Davidson, F. Muecke, and P. Wilson (eds.), *Greek Drama III: Essays in Memory of Kevin Lee*, 223–44. BICS Supplement 87. London.

———. 2010. "Sexual Consent and the Adolescent Male, or What Can We Learn from the Greeks?" *Thymos: Journal of Boyhood Studies* 4: 126–48.

———. 2014. "Peer Homosexuality," in Thomas K. Hubbard (ed.), *A Companion to Greek and Roman Sexualities*, 128–49. Malden, MA.

Humphreys, Sally. 1995. "Women's Stories," in Ellen D. Reede (ed.), *Pandora, Women in Classical Greece*, 102–10. Baltimore.

Hupperts, Charles A. M. 1988. "Greek Love: Homosexuality or Pederasty? Greek Love in Black-Figure Vase Painting," in J. Christiansen et al. (eds.), *Proceedings of the 3rd Symposium on Ancient Greek and Related Pottery*, 255–68. Copenhagen.

———. 2000. *Eros Dikaios: De praktijk en de verbeelding van homoseksualiteit bij de Grieken.* 3 vols. Amsterdam.

Iacopi, Giulio. 1929. *Clara Rhodos. Studi e materiali pubblicati a cura dell' Istituto Storico-Archeologico di Rodi.* Vol. 3, *Scavi nella necropoli di Jalisso, 1924–1928.* Rhodes.

Immerwahr, Henry R. 2008. *Corpus of Attic Vase Inscriptions.* http://www.lib.unc.edu/dc/attic/ (online, searchable), http://www.unc.edu/~hri/Inscriptions.pdf (printed document).

Iozzo, M. 2006. "Osservazioni sulle più antiche importazioni di ceramica greca a Chiusi e nel suo territorio (circa 650/620–550/520)," in J. de La Genière (ed.), *Les clients de la céramique grecque,* 107–32. Paris.

Isler-Kerényi, Cornelia. 2007. *Dionysos in Archaic Greece: An Understanding through Images.* Leiden and Boston.

Johns, Catherine. 1982. *Sex or Symbol: Erotic Images of Greece and Rome.* Austin.

Jones, J. E. et al. 1962. "The Dema House in Attica." *Annual of the British School at Athens* 57: 75–114.

———. 1973. "An Attic Country House Below the Cave of Pan at Vari." *Annual of the British School at Athens* 68: 355–452.

Johnson, Marguerite and Terry Ryan (eds.). 2005. *Sexuality in Greek and Roman Society and Literature: A Sourcebook.* London and New York.

Jouanna, Jacques and Laurence Villard (eds.). 2002. *Vin et santé en Grèce ancienne: actes du colloque organisé à l'Université de Rouen et à Paris (Université de Paris IV Sorbonne et ENS) par l'UPRESA 8062 du CNRS et l'URLLCA de l'Université de Rouen, 28–30 septembre 1998.* Paris.

Kaempf-Dimitriadou, Sophia. 1979. *Die Liebe der Götter in der attischen Kunst des 5. Jahrhunderts v. Chr.* Bern.

Kaltsas, Nikos E., ed. 2006. *Athens–Sparta.* New York.

Karakasi, Katerina. 2003. *Archaic Korai.* Los Angeles.

Kavvadias, G. 2000. "Black-Figure *Lekythos* (Secondary Type)," in L. Parlama and N. Stampolidis (eds.), *Athens, the City Beneath the City: Antiquities from the Metropolitan Railway Excavations,* 298–99. New York and London.

———. 2009. "Attic Black-Figure *Lekythos* of a Secondary Type, 500–475 BC," in Nikolaos Chr. Stampolidis and Giorgos Tasoulas (eds.), *Eros: From Hesiod's Theogony to Late Antiquity,* 215. Athens.

Καββαδίας [Kαββαδίας], P. 1890–92. Γλυπτά του Εθνικού Μουσείου. Athens.

Keuls. Eva C. 1985. *The Reign of the Phallus: Sexual Politics in Ancient Athens.* New York.

Kilmer, Martin F. 1982. "Genital Phobia and Depilation." *Journal of Hellenic Studies* 102: 104–12.

———. 1990. "Sexual Violence: Archaic Athens and the Recent Past," in E. M. Craik (ed.), *Owls to Athens: Essays on Classical Subjects Presented to Sir Kenneth Dover,* 261–80. Oxford.

———. 1993. *Greek Erotica on Attic Red-Figure Vases.* London.

———. 1997. "Painters and Pederasts: Ancient Art, Sexuality, and Social History," in Mark Golden and Peter Toohey (eds.), *Inventing Ancient Culture: Historicism, Periodization, and the Ancient World,* 36–49. London.

———. 2002. "Rape in Early Red-Figure Pottery: Violence and Threat in Homo-erotic and Hetero-erotic Contexts," in Susan Deacy and Karen F. Pierce (eds.), *Rape in Antiquity,* 123–41. London.

Kluiver, Jeroen L. 1996. "The Five Later 'Tyrrhenian' Painters." *BABESCH—Bulletin Antieke Beschaving* 71: 1–58.

———. 2003. *The Tyrrhenian Group of Black-Figure Vases: From the Athenian Kerameikos to the Tombs of South Etruria.* Amsterdam.

Koch-Harnack, Gundel. 1983. *Knabenliebe und Tiergeschenke: ihre Bedeutung im paderastischen Erziehungssystem Athens.* Berlin.

Korshak, Yvonne. 1984. "Frontal Faces in Attic Vase Painting of the Archaic Period." *Ancient World* 10: 89–109.

———. 1987. *Frontal Faces in Attic Vase Painting of the Archaic Period.* Chicago.

Kreuzer, Bettina. 1992. *Frühe Zeichner, 1500–500 vor Chr.: ägyptische, griechische, und etruskische Vasenfragmente der Sammlung H. A. Cahn, Basel.* Freiburg im Breisgau.

Kunisch, Norbert. 1972. *Antiken der Sammlung Julius C. und Margot Funcke.* Bochum.

———. 1996. *Erläuterungen zur griechischen Vasenmalerei: 50 Hauptwerk der Sammlung antiker Vasen in der Ruhr-Universität Bochum.* Köln.

———. 1997. *Makron.* Forschungen zur antiken Keramik. II Reihe, Kerameus Bd.10. Mainz.

Kunze-Götte, Erika, Karin Tancke, and Klaus Vierneisel. 1999. *Kerameikos: Ergebnisse der Ausgrabungen VII.2, Die Nekropole von der Mitte des 6 bis zum Ende des 5 Jahrhunderts. Die Beigaben.* Munich.

Kurke, Leslie. 1997. "Inventing the Hetaira: Sex, Politics, and Discursive Conflict in Archaic Greece." *Classical Antiquity* 16: 106–50.

———. 1999. *Coins, Bodies, Games, and Gold: The Politics of Meaning in Archaic Greece.* Princeton.

La Genière, Juliette de. 2006. "Clients, potiers et peintres," in J. de La Genière (ed.), *Les clients de la céramique grecque,* 9–15. Paris.

———. 2009. "Les amateurs des scenes érotiques de l'archaïsme recent," in A. Tsingarida (ed.), *Shapes and Uses of Greek Vases, 7th–4th centuries BC* (Études d'archéologie 3), 337–46. Brussels.

La Rocca, Eugenio. 1994. "Ferocia barbarica. La rappresentazione dei vinti tra Medio Oriente e Roma." *Jahrbuch des Deutschen Archaologischen Instituts* 109: 1–40.

Lambourne, Lionel. 2005. *Japonisme: Cultural Crossings between Japan and the West.* London and New York.

Landels, John G. 1999. *Music in Ancient Greece and Rome.* London and New York.

Lang, Mabel L. 1974. *Graffiti in the Athenian Agora.* Princeton.

———. 1976. *Graffiti and Dipinti.* The Athenian Agora 21. Princeton.

Laurens, Annie France. 1984. *Catalogue des collections. 2. Céramique attique et apparentée. Société archéologique de Montpellier.* Montpellier.

Lazarides, Dēmētrios I. 1969. Νεάπολις, Χριστούπολις, Καβάλα. Οδηγός Μουσείου Καβάλας. Athens.

Lear, Andrew. 2014. "Ancient Pederasty: An Introduction," in Thomas K. Hubbard (ed.), *A Companion to Greek and Roman Sexualities,* 102–27. Malden, MA.

Lear, Andrew with Eva Cantarella. 2008. *Images of Ancient Greek Pederasty: Boys Were Their Gods.* London and New York.

Lee, Mireille M. 2003. Review of Sian Lewis, *The Athenian Woman: An Iconographic Handbook. Bryn Mawr Classical Review* 2003.09.28. http://ccat.sas.upenn.edu/bmcr/2003/2003-09-28.html.

Lewis, Sian. 1997. "Shifting Images: Athenian Women in Etruria," in T. Cornell and K. Lomas (eds.), *Gender and Ethnicity in Ancient Italy*, 141–54. London.

———. 2002. *The Athenian Woman: An Iconographic Handbook.* London and New York.

———. 2003. "Representation and Reception: Athenian Pottery in its Italian Context," in J. Wilkins and E. Herring (eds.), *Inhabiting Symbols: Symbol and Image in the Ancient Mediterranean*, 175–92. London.

Lezzi-Hafter, Adrienne. 1976. *Der Schuwalow-Maler: Eine Kannenwerkstatt der Parthenonzeit.* Forschungen Zur Antiken Keramik: Reihe 2, Kerameus 2. Mainz.

Linforth, I. M. 1919. *Solon the Athenian.* Berkeley.

Lissarrague, François. 1987a. *Un flot d'images: une esthétique du banquet grec.* Paris.

———. 1987b. "Voyages d'images: iconographie et aires culturelles." *Revue des études anciennes* 89: 261–70.

———. 1990a. "Around the Krater: An Aspect of Banquet Imagery," in Oswyn Murray (ed.), *Sympotica: A Symposium on the Symposion*, 196–209. Oxford.

———. 1990b. "The Sexual Life of Satyrs," in David M. Halperin, John J. Winkler, and Froma Zeitlin (eds.), *Before Sexuality: The Construction of Erotic Experience in the Ancient Greek World*, 53–81. Princeton.

———. 1992. "Figures of Women," in Pauline Schmitt Pantel (ed.), *A History of Women in the West.* Vol. 1, *From Ancient Goddesses to Christian Saints*, trans. Arthur Goldhammer, 139–229. Cambridge, MA.

———. 2001. *Greek Vases: The Athenians and Their Images*, trans. Kim Allen. New York.

Lissarrague, François and Alain Schnapp. 1981. "Imagerie des Grecs ou Grèce des imagiers?" *Le temps de la réflexion* 2: 275–97.

Lombardo, Mario. 1985. "Nuovi documenti su Pisticci in età arcaica: Il graffito." *Parola del passato* 40: 294–307.

Lücken, Gottfried von. 1923. *Greek Vase-Paintings. Peintures de vases grecques.* The Hague.

Ludwig, Paul W. 2002. *Eros and Polis: Desire and Community in Greek Political Theory.* Cambridge and New York.

Lynch, Kathleen. 2007. "More Thoughts on the Space of the Symposium," in R. Westgate, N. Fisher, and J. Whitley (eds.), *Building Communities: House, Settlement and Society in the Aegean and Beyond*, 243–49. Athens.

———. 2009. "Erotic Images on Attic Pottery: Markets and Meanings," in J. Oakley and O. Palagia (eds.), *Athenian Potters and Painters*, vol. 2: 159–65. Oxford.

———. 2011. *The Symposium in Context: Pottery from a Late Archaic House Near the Athenian Agora.* Princeton.

Malagardis, Nassi. 2009. "Coupes à lucarne à figures noires: une création attique. Un étrange attelage au service d'Héracles sur une coupe à lucarne de Sellada, Théra," in Eric M. Moormann, and Vladimir V. Stissi (eds.), *Shapes and Images: Studies on Attic Black Figure and Related Topics in Honour of Herman A. G. Brijder*, 99–118. Leuven.

Malagardis, Nassi and Mario Iozzo. 1995. "Amasis et les autres—Nuovi documenti del Pittore di Amasis." *Ephemeris Archaiologike* 134: 185–208.

Marangou, Lila. 1995. *Ancient Greek Art from the Collection of Stavros S. Niarchos.* Athens.

Marcadé, Jean. 1962. *Eros Kalos: Essay on Erotic Elements in Greek Art.* Geneva and New York.

Marcovitch, Miroslav. 1975. "A New Poem of Archilochus: P. Colon. inv. 7511." *Greek, Roman, and Byzantine Studies* 16: 5–14.

Martens, Didier. 1992. *Une esthétique de la transgression: Le vase grec de la fin de l'époque géométrique au début de l'époque classique.* Bruxelles.

Matheson, Susan B. 1995. *Polygnotos and Vase Painting in Classical Athens.* Madison.

Matthews, Keith. 1994. "An Archaeology of Homosexuality? Perspectives from the Classical World," in Sally Cottam et al. (eds.), *TRAC 94: Proceedings of the Fourth Annual Theoretical Roman Archaeology Conference, Held at the Department of Archaeology, University of Durham, 19th & 20th March, 1994.* Oxford.

Maxwell-Stuart, P. G. 1972. "Strato and the Musa Puerilis." *Hermes* 100: 215–40.

Mayer-Emmerling, Stamatia. 1982. "Erzählende Darstellungen Auf 'Tyrrhenischen' Vasen." Diss. Frankfurt am Main.

Mead, Margaret. 1950. *Male and Female: A Study of the Sexes in a Changing World.* London.

Mehren, M. von. 2001. "Two Groups of Attic Amphorae as Export Ware for Etruria—The So-called Tyrrhenian Group and Nikosthenic Amphorae," in Charlotte Scheffer (ed.), *Ceramics in Context: Proceedings of the Internordic Colloquium on Ancient Pottery, Held at Stockholm, 13–15 June 1997,* 45–53. Stockholm.

Miller, Margaret Christina. 1997. *Athens and Persia in the Fifth Century BC: A Study in Cultural Receptivity.* Cambridge and New York.

———. 2010. "I Am Eurymedon: Tensions and Ambiguities in Athenian War Imagery," in David M. Pritchard (ed.), *War, Democracy and Culture in Classical Athens,* 304–38. Cambridge.

Milne, Marjorie J. and Dietrich von Bothmer. 1953. "ΚΑΤΑΠΥΓΩΝ, ΚΑΤΑΠΥΓΑΙΝΑ." *Hesperia* 22: 215–24.

Mommsen, Heide. 1975. *Der Affecter.* Mainz.

———. 2009. "Die Botkin-Klasse," in Athéna Tsingarida (ed.), *Shapes and Uses of Greek Vases (7th–4th Centuries BC): Proceedings of the Symposium Held at the Université Libre De Bruxelles, 27–29 April 2006,* 31–46. Bruxelles.

Moore, Mary B. 1997. *Attic Red-Figured and White-Ground Pottery.* The Athenian Agora 30. Princeton.

Morandi, Adriana Emiliozzi. 1975. *Nuove scoperte e scquisizioni dell'Etruria meridionale,* Rome.

Mulas, Antonia. 1978. *Eros in Antiquity.* New York.

Münzen und Medaillen, A. G., Basel. 1975. *Kunstwerke der Antike. Sale Catalogue* 51 (14–15.3.1975).

———. 1977. *Antike Vasen: Bücher über Archäologie. Sonderliste R,* December 1977.

Murray, Oswyn. 1983a. "The Greek Symposion in History," in Emilio Gabba (ed.), *Tria Corda: Scritti in onore di Arnaldo Momigliano,* 257–72. Como.

———. 1983b. "The *Symposion* as Social Organisation," in R. Hagg (ed.), *The Greek Renaissance of the Eighth Century BC: Tradition and Innovation. (Proceedings of the Second International Symposium at the Swedish Institute in Athens),* 195–99. Stockholm.

———. 1990. "Sympotic History," in Oswyn Murray (ed.), *Sympotica: A Symposium on the Symposion,* 3–13. Oxford.

Neer, Richard T. 2002. *Style and Politics in Athenian Vase-Painting: The Craft of Democracy, ca. 530–460 BCE.* Cambridge.

———. 2010. *The Emergence of the Classical Style in Greek Sculpture*. Chicago.

———. 2012. *Art and Archaeology of the Greek World. A New History, c.2500–c.150 BC*. London.

Neils, Jenifer and John H. Oakley (eds.). 2003. *Coming of Age in Ancient Greece: Images of Childhood from the Classical Past*. New Haven.

Nicholls, R. V. 1970–1971. "The Trinity College Collection and Other Recent Loans at the Fitzwilliam Museum." *Archaeological Reports* 17: 77–85.

Noussia Fantuzzi, Maria. 2010. *Solon the Athenian, the Poetic Fragments*. Leiden and Boston.

Oakley, John H. 2003. Review of Richard T. Neer, *Style and Politics in Athenian Vase-Painting. American Journal of Archaeology* 107: 509–10.

———. 2009. "Greek Vase Painting: State of the Discipline." *American Journal of Archaeology* 113: 599–627.

———. 2013. *The Greek Vase: Art of the Storyteller*. Los Angeles and London.

Oakley, John H. and and Rebecca H. Sinos. 1993. *The Wedding in Ancient Athens*. Madison.

Ober, Josiah. 1989. *Mass and Elite in Democratic Athens: Rhetoric, Ideology, and the Power of the People*. Princeton.

Ober, Josiah and Charles W. Hedrick (eds.). 1993. *The Birth of Democracy: An Exhibition Celebrating the 2,500th Anniversary of Democracy at the National Archives, Washington, DC, June 15, 1993–January 2, 1994*. Athens.

Ohly-Durnm, Martha. 1985. "Tipod-pyxis from the Sanctuary of Aphaia on Aegina," in Dietrich von Bothmer (ed.), *The Amasis Painter and His World*, 236–38. Malibu.

Oleson, John Peter. 1975. "Greek Myth and Etruscan Imagery in the Tomb of the Bulls at Tarquinia." *American Journal of Archaeology* 79: 189–200.

Osborne, Robin. 2001. "Why Did Athenian Pots Appeal to the Etruscans?" *World Archaeology* 33: 277–95.

Paleothodoros, Dimitris. 2012. "Sex and the Athenian Woman: A Contextual Analysis of Erotic Vase-Paintings from Attic Graves of the 5th century BC," in Dimitris Paleothodoros (ed.), *The Contexts of Painted Pottery in the Ancient Mediterranean World (Seventh–Fourth Centuries BCE)*, 21–39. Oxford.

Parisinou, Eva. 2000. "'Lighting' the World of Women: Lamps and Torches in the Hands of Women in the Late Archaic and Classical Periods," *Greece and Rome* 47: 19–43.

Parker, Holt N. 2011. "Sex, Popular Beliefs, and Culture," in Peter Toohey and Mark Golden (eds.), *A Cultural History of Sexuality in the Classical World*, 125–44. Oxford.

Pease, Mary Zelia. 1935. "The Pottery from the North Slope of the Acropolis." *Hesperia* 4: 214–302.

Pellizer, Enzio. 1990. "Outlines of a Morphology of Sympotic Entertainment," in Oswyn Murray (ed.), *Sympotica: A Symposium on the Symposion*, 177–84. Oxford.

Pellegrini, Elisa. 2009. *Eros nella Grecia arcaica e classica, iconografia e iconologia*. Rome.

Perreault, Jacques-Yves. 1986. "Céramique et échanges : les importations attiques au Proche-Orient du VIe au milieu du Ve av. J.-C.—Les données archéologiques." *Bulletin de correspondance hellénique* 110: 145–75.

Peschel, Ingeborg. 1987. *Die Hetäre bei Symposion und Komos in der attisch-rotfigurigen Vasenmalerei des 6.–4. Jahrh. v. Chr*. Frankfurt am Main and New York.

Pfisterer-Haas, Susanne. 1989. *Darstellungen alter Frauen in der griechischen Kunst*. Frankfurt am Main.

Pharmakowsky, B. V. 1913. "Funde in Südrussland im Jahre 1912." *Jahrbuch des Deutschen Archäologischen Instituts: Archäologischer Anzeiger* 28: 178–234.

Pickard-Cambridge, Arthur Wallace. 1988. *The Dramatic Festivals of Athens*. Reissued with suppl. and corrections. Oxford.

Pitzulo, Carrie. 2011. *Bachelors and Bunnies: The Sexual Politics of Playboy*. Chicago.

Poliakoff, Michael. 1982. *Studies in the Terminology of the Greek Combat Sports*. Königstein.

Pottier, Edmond. 1897–1922. *Vases antiques du Louvre*. 3 vols in 2. Paris.

Preisigke, Friedrich et al. (eds.). 1915–93. *Sammelbuch griechischer Urkunden aus Ägypten*. 27 vols. Strassburg.

Pütz, Babette. 2003. *The Symposium and Komos in Aristophanes*. Stuttgart.

Rabinowitz, Nancy Sorkin. 2002. "Excavating Women's Homoeroticism in Ancient Greece," in Nancy Sorkin Rabinowitz and Lisa Auanger (eds.), *Among Women: From the Homosocial to the Homoerotic in the Ancient World*, 106–66. Austin.

Rasmussen, Bodil Bundgaard. 2008. "Special Vases in Etruria: First- or Secondhand?" in Kenneth Lapatin (ed.), *Papers on Special Techniques in Athenian Vases*, 215–24. Los Angeles.

———. 2013. "The Imagery of Tomb Objects (Local and Imported) and Its Funerary Relevance," in Jean MacIntosh Turfa (ed.), *The Etruscan World*, 672–80. Abingdon.

Reden, Sitta von. 1995. *Exchange in Ancient Greece*. London.

Reeder, Ellen D. 1995. *Pandora: Women in Classical Greece*. Baltimore and Princeton.

Reichardt, Bettina. 2009. "Anasyrma und Liebeswerbung—Ein attisch schwarzfiguriger Skyphos vom Taxiarchis-Hügel in Didyma," in Ralph Einicke (ed.), *Zurück zum Gegenstand: Festschrift für Andreas E. Furtwängler*, 2 vols, 1: 235–43. Langenweissbach.

Reinsberg, Carola. 1989. *Ehe, Hetärentum und Knabenliebe im antiken Griechenland*. Munich.

Reusser, Christoph. 2002. *Vasen für Etrurien: Verbreitung und Funktionen attischer Keramik im Etrurien des 6. und 5. Jahrhunderts vor Christus*. Zurich.

Richlin, Amy. 1992. *The Garden of Priapus: Sexuality and Aggression in Roman Humor*. Rev. ed. New York.

Roberts, Sally Rutherfurd. 1978. *The Attic Pyxis*. Chicago.

Robertson, Martin. 1986. "Two Pelikai by the Pan Painter," in *Greek Vases in the J. Paul Getty Museum* 3: 71–90.

———. 1992. *The Art of Vase-Painting in Classical Athens*. Cambridge.

Robinson, David M. 1956. "Unpublished Greek Vases in the Robinson Collection." *American Journal of Archaeology* 60: 1–25.

Schäfer, Alfred. 1997. *Unterhaltung beim griechischen Symposion: Darbietungen, Spiele und Wettkämpfe von Homerischer bis in spätklassische Zeit*. Mainz.

Schauenburg, Konrad. 1965. "*Erastes* und *Eromenos* auf einer Schale des Sokles." *Jahrbuch des Deutschen Archäologischen Instituts: Archäologischer Anzeiger* 80: 849–67.

———. 1972. "Frauen im Fenster." *Deutsches Archäologisches Institut. Abteilung Rom. Römische Mitteilungen* 79: 1–15.

———. 1975. "ΕΥΡΥΜΕΔΩΝ ΕΙΜΙ." *Mitteilungen des Deutschen Archäologischen Instituts, Athenische Abteilung* 90: 97–121.

Schefold, Karl. 1981. *Die Göttersage in der klassischen und hellenistischen Kunst*. Munich.

Schmitt-Pantel, Pauline and Françoise Thélamon. 1983. "Image et histoire. Illustration ou document?" in *Image et céramique grecque Actes du Colloque de Rouen 25–26 novembre 1982*, 9–20. Rouen.

Schnapp, Alain. 1979. "Pratiche e immagini di caccia nella Grecia antica." *Dialoghi di Archeologia* n.s. 1: 36–59.

———. 1989. "Eros the Hunter," in Claude Bérard et al. (eds.), *A City of Images: Iconography and Society in Ancient Greece*, trans. D. Lyons, 71–87. Princeton. Orig. *La cité des images*. Paris, 1984.

———. 1997. *Le Chasseur et la cité: Chasse et érotique en Grèce ancienne*. Paris.

Schneider, K. 1912. "Hahnenkämpfe." *Realencyclopädie der classischen Altertumswissenschaft* 7: 2210–15.

Scholl, Andreas and Gertrud Platz-Horster (eds.). 2007. *Die Antikensammlung: Altes Museum, Pergamonmuseum / Antikensammlung Staatliche Museen zu Berlin* 3, vollständig überarbeitete und erw. Aufl. Mainz.

Schulze, Wilhelm. 1934. *Kleine Schriften*. Göttingen.

Seki, Tabashi. 1981. "Eine neue Schale mit Bogenschützen." *Archäologischer Anzeiger* 1981: 44–64.

Settis, Salvatore (ed.). 1996. *I Greci: Storia, Cultura, Arte, Società*. 4 vols. in 6. Turin.

Sgourou, Marina. 1994. "Attic Lebetes Gamikoi." PhD thesis, University of Cincinnati.

———. 1997. "Lebetes Gamikoi," in J. H. Oakley, W. D. E. Coulson, and O. Palagia (eds.), *Athenian Potters and Painters: The Conference Proceedings*, 71–83. Oxford.

Shapiro, H. A. 1981a. "Courtship Scenes in Attic Vase-Painting." *American Journal of Archaeology* 85:133–43.

———. 1981b. *Art, Myth, and Culture: Greek Vases from Southern Collections*. New Orleans.

———. 1983. "Epilykos Kalos." *Hesperia* 52: 305–10.

———. 1989. *Art and Cult under the Tyrants in Athens*. Mainz.

———. 1992. "Eros in Love: Pederasty and Pornography in Greece," in Amy Richlin (ed.), *Pornography and Representation in Greece and Rome*, 53–72. New York.

———. 1997. "Painters and Pederasts: Ancient Art, Sexuality, and Social History," in Mark Golden and Peter Toohey (eds.), *Inventing Ancient Culture: Historicism, Periodization, and the Ancient World*, 36–49. London.

———. 2000a. "Leagros and Euphronios: Painting Pederasty in Athens," in Thomas K. Hubbard (ed.), *Greek Love Reconsidered*, 12–32. New York.

———. 2000b. "Modest Athletes and Liberated Women: Etruscans on Attic Black-Figure Vases," in Beth Cohen (ed.), *Not the Classical Ideal: Athens and the Construction of the Other in Greek Art*, 315–37. Leiden.

Shapiro, H. A., Carlos A. Picón, and Gerry D. Scott, III (eds.). 1995. *Greek Vases in the San Antonio Museum of Art*. San Antonio, TX.

Skudnova, V. M. (Varvara Mikhailovna). 1988. *Arkhaicheskii nekropol Olvii: publikatsiia odnoi kollektsii*. Leningrad.

Simon, Erika. 1981. *Die griechischen Vasen*. 2. durchges. Munich.

———. 1982. *The Kurashiki Ninagawa Museum: Greek, Etruscan and Roman antiquities*. Mainz.

———. 1983. *Festivals of Attica: An Archaeological Commentary*. Madison.

Smet, Robert de. 1982. *Hommes et dieux de la Grèce antique: Europalia 82, Hellas-Grèce: [exposition], 1er octobre–2 décembre 1982, Palais des Beaux-Arts, Bruxelles.* Bruxelles.

Smith, Amy C. 1999. "Eurymedon and the Evolution of Political Personifications in the Early Classical Period." *Journal of Hellenic Studies* 119: 128–41.

Smith, Tyler Jo. 2010. *Komast Dancers in Archaic Greek Art.* Oxford and New York.

Snodgrass, Anthony M. 1980. *Archaic Greece: The Age of Experiment.* Berkeley.

Sotheby's (Firm). 1994. *Greek Vases from the Momirovic Collection.* Sale LN4401. July 7, 1994. London.

Sourvinou-Inwood, Christiane. 2003. *Tragedy and Athenian Religion.* Lanham, MD.

Sparkes, Brian A. 1996. *The Red and the Black: Studies in Greek Pottery.* London.

Spivey, Nigel. 1991. "Greek Vases in Etruria," in Tom Rasmussen and Nigel Spivey (eds.), *Looking at Greek Vases,* 131–50. Cambridge.

———. 1997. *Etruscan Art.* London: Thames and Hudson.

Stackelberg, Otto Magnus. 1837. *Die Graeber der Hellenen.* Berlin.

Stähli, A. 2005. "Die Rhetorik der Gewalt in Bildern des archaischen und klassischen Griechenland," in Günter Fischer and Susanne Moraw (eds.), *Die andere Seite der Klassik: Gewalt im 5. und 4. Jahrhundert v. Chr.,* 19–44. Stuttgart.

Stampolidis, Nikolaos and Giorgos Tasoulas (eds.). 2009. *Eros: From Hesiod's Theogony to Late Antiquity.* Athens.

Stansbury-O'Donnell, Mark. 2006. *Vase Painting, Gender, and Social Identity in Archaic Athens.* New York.

Steiner, Ann. 2002. "Private and Public: Links Between *Symposion* and *Syssition* in Fifth-Century Athens." *Classical Antiquity* 21: 347–90.

———. 2007. *Reading Greek Vases.* Cambridge.

Stein-Holkeskamp, Elke. 1992. "Lebensstil als Selbstdarstellung: Aristokraten beim Symposion," in Irma Wehgartner (ed.), *Euphronios und seine Zeit,* 39–48. Berlin.

Stewart, Andrew. 1987. "Narrative, Genre, and Realism in the Work of the Amasis Painter," in Marion True (ed.), *Papers on the Amasis Painter and His World,* 29–41. Malibu.

———. 1997. *Art, Desire, and the Body in Ancient Greece.* Cambridge.

Stissi, Vladimir. 1999. "Production, Circulation, and Consumption of Archaic Greek Pottery (Sixth and Early Fifth Centuries BC)." in Jan Paul Crielaard, Vladimir Stissi, and Gert Jan van Wijngaarden (eds.), *The Complex Past of Pottery: Production, Circulation and Consumption of Mycenaean and Greek Pottery (Sixteenth to Early Fifth Centuries BC),* 83–113. Amsterdam.

Sutton, Robert F. Jr. 1981. *The Interaction Between Men and Women Portrayed on Attic Red-Figure Pottery.* PhD thesis, University of North Carolina at Chapel Hill.

———. 1985. Review of *Knabenliebe und Tiergeschenke,* by Gundel Koch-Harnack. *American Journal of Archaeology* 89: 183–84.

———. 1992. "Pornography and Persuasion on Attic Pottery," in Amy Richlin (ed.), *Pornography and Representation in Greece and Rome,* 1–33. New York.

———. 2000. "The Good, the Base, and the Ugly: The Drunken Orgy in Attic Vase Painting and the Athenian Self," in Beth Cohen (ed.), *Not the Classical Ideal: Athens and the Construction of the Other in Greek Art,* 180–202. Leiden, Boston and Cologne.

———. 2009. "Lovemaking on Attic Black-Figure Pottery: Corpus with Some Conclusions," in Stefan Schmidt and J. Oakley (eds.), *Hermeneutik der Bilder: Beiträge zur Ikonogra-*

phie und Interpretation griechischer Vasenmalerei, Beiheft of the *Corpus Vasorum Antiquorum Deutschland* 4, 77–91. Munich.

Tamassia, Anna Maria. 1974. "Frammento inedito del Pittore di Antiphon." *Bollettino d'Arte* 59: 147–51.

Tarán, Sonya Lida. 1985. "ΕΙΣΙ ΤΡΙΧΕΣ: An Erotic Motif in the Greek Anthology." *Journal of Hellenic Studies* 105: 90–107.

Theodorou, Jerry. 1991. "Ancient Art at Princeton." *Minerva* (London) 2.3: 22–24.

Thompson, Homer A. 1958. "Activities in the Athenian Agora: 1957." *Hesperia* 27: 145–60.

Thornton, Bruce S. 1997. *Eros: The Myth of Ancient Greek Sexuality.* Boulder.

Todd, Stephen. 1990. "*Lady Chatterley's Lover* and the Attic Orators: The Social Composition of the Athenian Jury." *Journal of Hellenic Studies* 110: 146–73.

Topper, Kathryn. 2009. "Primitive Life and the Construction of the Sympotic Past in Athenian Vase Painting." *American Journal of Archaeology* 113: 3–26.

———. 2012. *The Imagery of the Athenian Symposium.* New York.

Torelli, Mario. 2009. "Status femminile e calzature, con appendice di Massimo Cultraro, I vasi a forma di scarpa nella produzione attica di età Geometrica: una nota." *Ostraka* 18: 175–92; repr. in Filippo Giudice and Rosalba Panvini (eds.), *Il greco, il barbaro e la ceramica attica: immaginario del diverso, processi di scambio e autorappresentazione degli indigeni,* vol. 1: 1–19. Roma.

Trofimova, Anna A. (ed.). 2007. *Greeks on the Black Sea: Ancient Art from the Hermitage.* Los Angeles.

Ugaglia, Evelyne. 1993. *L'art grec au Musée Saint-Raymond: Catalogue raisonné d'une partie pe la collection.* [Toulouse]: Le Musée.

Ulieriu-Rostás, Theodor E. 2013. "Music and Socio-Cultural Identity in Attic Vase Painting." *Music in Art* 38: 9–26.

Valavanis, Panos. 1996. *Drinking Vessels = Chaire kai Piei.* Athens.

Van Sickle, John. 1975a. "Archilochus: A New Fragment of an Epode." *Classical Journal* 71: 1–15.

———. 1975b. "The New Erotic Fragment of Archilochus." *Quaderni Urbinati di Cultura Classica* 20: 123–56.

Vanhove, Doris (ed.). 1992. *Le sport dans la Grèce antique: du jeu à la compétition.* Bruxelles.

Vermeule, Emily. 1969. "Some Erotica in Boston." *Antike Kunst* 12: 9–15.

Vickers, Michael J. 1983. "Les vases peints: image ou mirage," in *Image et céramique grecque Actes du Colloque de Rouen 25–26 novembre 1982,* 29–42. Rouen.

———. 1985. "Artful Crafts: The Influence of Metal Work on Athenian Painted Pottery." *Journal of Hellenic Studies* 105: 108–28.

———. 1992. "Museum Supplement: Recent Acquisitions of Greek and Etruscan Antiquities by the Ashmolean Museum, Oxford 1981–90." *Journal of Hellenic Studies* 112: 246–48.

Vickers, Michael J. and David Gill. 1994. *Artful Crafts: Ancient Greek Silverware and Pottery.* Oxford.

Vierneisel, Klaus and Berthold Helmut Kaeser. 1992. *Kunst der Schale, Kultur des Trinkens* 2, berichtigte Aufl. München.

Vlastos, Gregory. 1987. "Socratic Irony." *Classical Quarterly* 37: 79–96.

Von Bothmer, Dietrich. 1951. "Attic Black-Figured Pelikai." *The Journal of Hellenic Studies* 71: 40–47.

———. 1985. *The Amasis Painter and His World: Vase-Painting in Sixth-Century BC, Athens.* Malibu.

———. 1990. *Glories of the Past: Ancient Art from the Shelby White and Leon Levy Collection.* New York.

———. 1995. Review of Martin F. Kilmer, *Greek Erotica on Attic Red-Figure Vases. Classical Journal* 91: 82–86.

Vorberg, Gaston. 1965. *Glossarium Eroticum.* Hanau. Reprint, orig. Stuttgart, 1928–32.

Vout, Caroline. 2013. *Sex on Show: Seeing the Erotic in Greece and Rome.* Berkeley: University of California Press.

Wannagat, Detlev. 2001. "Eurymedon eimi—Zeichen von ethnischer, sozialer und psychischer Differenz in der Vasenmalerei des 5. Jahrhunderts v. Chr." in R. von den Hoff and S. Schmidt (eds.), *Konstruktionen von Wirklichkeit: Bilder im Griechenland des 5. und 4. Jahrhunderts v. Chr.,* 51–71. Stuttgart.

Wegner, Max. 1973. *Brygosmaler.* Berlin.

Węcowski, Marek. 2014. *The Rise of the Greek Aristocratic Banquet.* 1st ed. Oxford: Oxford University Press.

West, M. L. 1993. "Simonides redivivus." *Zeitschrift für Papyrologie und Epigraphik* 98: 1–14.

———, (ed.). 1978. *Hesiod: Works and Days.* Oxford.

Whitley, James. 2001. *The Archaeology of Ancient Greece.* Cambridge.

Wiel-Marin, Federica. 2005. *La ceramica Attica a figure rosse di Adria: La Famiglia Bocchi e L'archeologia.* Padova.

Wilkins, John. 2000. *The Boastful Chef: The Discourse of Food in Ancient Greek Comedy.* Oxford.

Wilkins, John and Shaun Hill. 2006. *Food in the Ancient World.* Malden, MA and Oxford.

Willi, Andreas. 2003. *The Languages of Aristophanes: Aspects of Linguistic Variation in Classical Attic Greek.* Oxford.

Williams, Dyfri. 1991. "Onesimos and the Getty Iliupersis." *Greek Vases in the J. Paul Getty Museum* 5: 41–64.

———. 1996. "Refiguring Attic Red-Figure: A Review Article." *Revue archéologique* 1996: 227–52.

Wilson, Peter. 1999. "The Aulos in Athens," in S. Goldhill and R. Osborne (eds.), *Performance Culture and Athenian Democracy,* 58–95. Cambridge.

Wit, Johannes de. 1929. "Die Vorritzungen der etruskischen Grabmalerei." *Jahrbuch des deutschen archäologischen Instituts* 44: 38–42.

Wohl, Victoria. 2002. *Love Among the Ruins: The Erotics of Democracy in Classical Athens.* Princeton.

Wójcik, Maria Rita. 1989. *Museo Claudio Faina di Orvieto: Ceramica attica a figure nere.* Perugia.

Wrenhaven, Kelly L. 2009. "The Identity of the 'Wool-Workers' in the Attic Manumissions." *Hesperia* 78: 367–86.

Yates, Velvet Lenore. 2005. "Anterastai: Competition in Eros and Politics in Classical Athens." *Arethusa* 38: 33–47.

Ziebarth, Erich. 1934. "Neue Verfluchungstafeln aus Attika. Boiotien und Euboia." Preussische [Deutsche] Akademie der Wissenschaften. *Sitzungsberichte* 1934: 1022–50.

CHAPTER TWO

Lesbians Are Not From Lesbos

KATE GILHULY

*I*n May of 2008, the BBC reported that campaigners from the island of Lesvos had mounted an (ultimately unsuccessful) attempt to stop gay rights organizations from employing the name "Lesbian," claiming that the use of the word to denote sexual orientation violated their human rights. In a subsequent interview, lesbian women countered that the name was given to them, not taken, in the first place (Brabant 2008).

How does a place get a reputation? As David Harvey writes, places "are an intense focus of discursive identity, filled with symbolic and representational meaning" (1996: 316). In this essay, I want to examine the evolution of the discursive identity of Lesbos, how being a lesbian came to be first and foremost associated with female homosexuality, nearly obscuring in most parts of the world the base meaning of the word—to be an inhabitant of the East Greek island, Lesbos.

If there is a history of sexuality, then there is also a geography of sexuality. For, as Adrienne Rich reminds us, "a place on the map is also a place in history." It seems that classicists should have a pressing interest in interrogating the notion of place, since our field is in part defined by it. For those also interested in the history of sexuality, it seems even more important to consider geography, since Athenian sexual practices have been so privileged in the construction of Foucault's argument—applied so effectively to the field by Winkler and Halperin—that sex is culturally constructed and historically contingent.

Anyone who has ever been anywhere knows that places are complicated. Even the smallest town on a distant island will reveal diversity, peculiarity, and surprises to the attentive visitor. This complexity is related to our perception of the openness of place—an openness revealed in the way spatial metaphors are used to convey the possibility of numerous combinations of meaning, or open-ended interpretations, such as "field of signification," or the concept of a "horizon of expectations," which refers to the cultural expectations, textual conventions, and ideology that readers and authors share. These fields and horizons are subject to change over time, so that successive generations see new things in texts (Jauss 1982). The following argument examines the associations and projections in the ancient world that laid the ground for the identification of a place, Lesbos, with female homosexuality.

While there is a sense of permeability to place, each place is also distinctive, and people are wont to articulate and share these distinctions. Places, it seems, can be put into words, and thus given identities. In contrast to the porous quality of place, however, language has a way of fixing boundaries, containing meaning. Often, the intricate knot of meaning that a place has gets condensed and communicated through a concise tag. The Athenians, especially the comic poets, were especially prone to speaking through geography, and by way of them, though not necessarily directly, we can speak of Spartan accommodations, Corinthian leather, Sybaritic pleasures, and Lesbian women. Encoded in each one of these characterizations is a range of significations, a collocation of perceptions that could be understood as just an image, or perhaps a brand, or even slander of the various coordinates that give a place an identity.[1]

An unexamined modern conception is that the association of Lesbos with female homosexuality is linked to the poetry of Sappho, which describes erotic scenarios between women.[2] While Sappho's poetry is not unrelated to the reputation of Lesbos, the dynamic between poetry and sexuality needs to be examined more closely. Although Sappho's poetry was well known throughout antiquity, her sexual orientation is not explicitly defined until centuries after her death, and when Lesbos is directly associated with women who love other women in Lucian's *Dialogues of the Courtesans,* Sappho is not explicitly named. Furthermore, there is a significant

---

1. For a discussion of Corinth and its association with prostitution, see Gilhuly 2014; on Corinth and sacred prostitution, see Budin 2008 and Beard and Henderson 1997.

2. See Brabant 2008 for the articulation of this idea.

gap bridged by associating one person's birthplace and her sexual orientation, and a still more significant gap between every single person from all the cities and villages on the island of Lesbos and a collective sexual orientation.

In what follows, I suggest that a complex, centuries-long collocation of cultural conceptions about the culture of Lesbos, combined with Athenian comic practice, the representation of the courtesan, and the reception of Sappho, eventually paved the way for the strong association of Lesbos with an image of alternative feminine sexuality. Although the figure of the courtesan is not necessarily integral to any aspect of this web of meaning, the plasticity of this figure, her relevance to issues of sexuality, and her suitability to represent women doing unwifely things draw her into this set of associations, where, as I shall argue, she becomes the *sine qua non* for the articulation of female homosexuality.

In his important book on the early reception of Sappho, Dimitrios Yatromanolakis considers the transmission of Sappho's image and her poetry; he introduces the notion of interdiscursivity, which he describes as "a textural [sic] interplay among habitually or intentionally enacted systems of signification from various domains of experience and expression." This cultural transmission occurs through "metonymic webs of signification," that is, the image of Sappho in his work, or here the idea of "Lesbians," is projected through a range of discourses and cultural tropes that transform the meaning of the subject (Yatromanolakis 2007: 23). I have found these notions helpful for conceptualizing the inevitably nonlinear trajectory and evolution of the associations pertaining to the people of Lesbos in antiquity. Yatromanolakis makes suggestive observations about the relationship between Sappho's image and its interaction with stereotypes about sexuality, Lesbos, and its musical culture; however, this essay has a different emphasis and argument: I consider an arc of literary interplay that demonstrates how, in the case of lesbian sexuality, discourse constructs sexual identity.[3] Furthermore, I emphasize the role of the reception of Lesbos, suggesting that Athenian discourses surrounding New Music and its personification on the comic stage played a pivotal role in evolving perceptions about Lesbos and its association with sexuality.[4]

---

3. In this sense, my essay might be thought of as an exploration of the after-effects of Worman's contribution to this volume, where she argues that erotic slurs do not reflect sexual practice but are used in the manipulation of power dynamics. In my essay, I do not think of literature as reflecting erotic practice, but rather I am interested in the way that discourse is involved in creating (perhaps articulating) sexual identity.

4. While Yatromanolakis 2007 considers the history of the reputation of East Greek music,

IMAGES OF LESBOS: EROTICS AND GENDER

As early as Homer, when Lesbos is mentioned in the catalog of gifts that Agamemnon wants to give Achilles to persuade him back into the fray of battle, the way the island and its inhabitants are evoked is significant. Agamemnon says:

δώσω δ'ἑπτὰ γυναῖκας ἀμύμονα ἔργα ἰδυίας
Λεσβίδας, ἃς ὅτε Λέσβον ἐϋκτιμένην ἕλεν αὐτὸς
ἐξελόμην, αἳ κάλλει ἐνίκων φῦλα γυναικῶν.

And I will give seven women from Lesbos, knowing blameless works, whom, when (Achilles) himself took well-built Lesbos, I myself chose, who surpassed the tribes of women in beauty.
(*Iliad* 9.128–30)[5]

In the first place, Lesbos is represented by its women. They are distinguished by their beauty and their skill at women's work, that is, weaving and other domestic labor. The reason that Agamemnon has these women to offer is because his forces overcame Lesbos in war. Here Lesbos is introduced as gendered and subjugated to the Greek army. At the same time it is described as well built; it is a worthy prize. The erotic aura of Lesbos, and its association with the feminine, is replicated throughout the ancient reception of Lesbos, and emphatically so through the lens of Athenian democracy.

The erotic identity of Lesbos was galvanized to a great extent in the crucible of Athenian comic representational practices involving places, prostitutes, and the personification of style. Making a verb out of a place name and imbuing it with derogatory and sexually explicit meaning was a familiar ploy in Athenian comedy. This tactic is important for the evolution of the meaning "lesbian" because it attributes a shared sexual identity to other communities, as well as to people from Lesbos. Thus *korinthiazomai* means to traffic in prostitutes, *phoenikizein* means to perform cunnilingus,[6] *sybarizein* is to be a voluptuary. Eustathius (a Greek bishop and scholar who lived circa 1115–95 CE) comments on a passage in the *Iliad*:

---

he only passingly considers New Music, and does not explore the implications of the comic muse as courtesan in relation to the reception of Sappho.

5. The list is repeated at *Il.* 9.270–72.
6. See Henderson 1991: 186; Morales 2004: 48–50 on the connotations of Phoenicia and words linked to it. Lucian *Pseudol.* 28 links *lesbiazein* and *phoinikizein* as outrageous insults.

περὶ τοῦ ... λεσβιάζειν ... γράφουσιν οἱ παλαιοὶ καὶ ταῦτα. εἰσὶ βλα-
σφημίαι καὶ ἀπὸ ἐθνῶν καὶ πόλεων καὶ δήμων πολλαὶ ῥηματικῶς
πεποιημέναι· ἐθνῶν μὲν οἷον κιλικίζειν καὶ αἰγυπτιάζειν τὸ πονηρεύε-
σθαι καὶ κρητίζειν τὸ [ψ?] φεύδεσθαι ... ἐκ πόλεων δὲ οἷον λεσβιάζειν
τὸ αἰσχροποιεῖν.

Concerning "to act like a Lesbian" the ancients write also the following things: many slanders have been created through verbs from peoples and cities and demes. For instance, from peoples, to act like a Cilician or an Egyptian means to be a rascal and to act like a Cretan means to lie ... from cities for example, to act like a lesbian means to do shameful things.[7]

As Jocelyn notes, many verbs of this type could denote a constellation of inclinations, thus to act like a Spartan meant to be a pederast, break promises, *and* love money. He notes, however, that "the ancient grammarians attribute no characteristic vice to the whole population of Lesbos except the practice of fellation" (1980: 32).[8]

Despite the help of ancient commentators like Eustathius, it is not entirely certain what sexual act *lesbiazein* implies. LSJ defines *lesbiazein* and *lesbizein* succinctly as "to do like the lesbian women, LAT. *fellare*." Jocelyn also argues for *fellatio,* noting that in a fragment of Pherecrates, the quote from Homer above is parodied, and women from Lesbos are jokingly assimilated to *laikastriai*, a word he has argued persuasively means mouthing of the penis:[9]

δώσει δέ σοι γυναῖκας ἑπτὰ Λεσβίδας.
καλόν γε δῶρον, ἔπτ᾽ ἔχειν λαικαστρίας

He will give to you seven Lesbian women
A fine gift, to have seven *Laikastriai*.[10]

While I follow Jocelyn in his assessment of the meaning of *laikastria,* I think it is important to note here that the evocation of the Homeric passage might at the same time recall the original passage, which described the

---

7. P.741.19–24 of the text printed in Rome, 1542 (Vol. 2) See also Suetonius Περὶ Βλασφη-μιῶν καὶ πόθεν ἑκάστη preserved in cod. Paris. Bibl. Nat. suppl. Gr. 1164.
8. See also Henderson 1991: 183–84.
9. Pherecrates produced comedies in Athens between the 440s and 420s BCE; nineteen titles and 300 fragments survive (K-A 7.102–220).
10. Pherecrates 149 K-A (cited in scholium on *Frogs* 1308).

women as skilled in blameless works, or weaving—that is, a *manual* occupation. In the *Iliad*, the women are eroticized because of their beauty, but considered superior as "gifts" because of their sexual allure and productive capacity. Perhaps then *lesbiazein* may imply manual stimulation in addition to oral stimulation of the penis and thus mean something similar to *laikazein*, but not exactly the same thing.

There has been speculation that this Pherecrates fragment linking Lesbians to *laikastriai* plays on the lambda with which both words begin. This same association is articulated in a suggestive passage from Aristophanes' *Assemblywomen*, where an old hag tells a young woman that you put the "L back in Lesbian":[11]

ἤδη τὸν ἀπ' Ἰωνίας
τρόπον τάλαινα κνησιᾷς
δοκεῖς δέ μοι καὶ λάβδα κατὰ τοὺς Λεσβίους.

Already poor girl, you want to itch
In the Ionian mode
In fact, you seem to me to be the L, Lesbian-style.
(Aristophanes *Ekkl.* 918–20)

Musurus (a Greek scholar who lived in Italy c. 1470–1570) comments: λάβδα·λαιχάζουσιν οἱ Λέσβιοι ἀπὸ τοῦ πρώτου στοχείου ("L: the lesbians fellate from the first letter"). While the meaning of this explanatory note is not crystal clear, Jocelyn 1980 suggests that Aristophanes' point is to elicit the act *laikazein* without actually having the old woman utter the obscenity. While some scholars think the Λ refers to the shape of legs in a sexual position,[12] others suggest that the letter is emphasized to create the onomatopoetic suggestion of lapping (Henderson 1991: 183–84). The context of Aristophanes' reference to Lesbians is intriguing, since it is preceded by his reference to the Ionian itch (κνησιᾷς). The desiderative κνησιάω also appears at Plato *Gorgias* 494c–e, when Socrates pushes Callicles to consider the culmination of scratching freely when one itches—becoming a *kinaidos*! It is likely that in Aristophanes, as in Plato, the term indicates inappropriate sexual initiative, or prodigious sexual desire.

While it seems likely that *lesbiazein* includes an oral component, Dover cautions that to assume *lesbiazein* referred exclusively to fellation is not

---

11. Adapted from Henderson's translation.
12. Yatromanolakis 2007: 187 and n. 97 explains the sexual implication of lambda to originate from the leg position that the uppercase letter suggests: "Λ." See also Jocelyn 1980: 43–44.

clear from the evidence; he says "'Lesbian women' could connote sexual initiative and shamelessness" (1978: 182). Indeed the use of the word *lesbiazein* in Aristophanes' *Frogs*, which I will consider in a moment, would support a definition along the lines of "polymorphously perverse," but, I think, with a strong suggestion of orality. In any case, whatever the sexual innuendo referred to exactly, it involved a sex act shared between men and women and was derogatory only to the person performing the act.

But *lesbiazein* DOES have another meaning, not included in the dictionary, which is rarely mentioned in discussions about sexuality.[13] However, this usage is not controversial for anyone who is familiar with the contexts in which *lesbiazein* and *lesbizein* occur: it denotes making music in a Lesbian style—referring to a fifth-century perception of East Greek music as voluptuous, suggesting the Aeolic style of Terpander, Alcaeus, and Sappho, or some combination thereof.

While the original works of these poets were admired, in the second half of the fifth century the appropriation of Eastern-style music by dramatic poets for Athenian audiences became associated with a popular hybrid style of innovative, professionalized music known as "New Music." The discourse around the New Music was politicized, explicitly in Plato's famous description of the degradation of music in the *Laws*:

> But later on, with the progress of time, there arose as leaders of unmusical illegality poets who, though by nature poetical, were ignorant of what was just and lawful in music; and they, being frenzied and unduly possessed by a spirit of pleasure, mixed dirges with hymns and paeans with dithyrambs, and imitated flute-tunes with harp-tunes, and blended every kind of music with every other; and thus, through their folly, they unwittingly bore false witness against music, as a thing without any standard of correctness, of which the best criterion is the pleasure of the auditor, be he a good man or a bad. By compositions of such a character, set to similar words, they bred in the populace a spirit of lawlessness in regard to music, and the effrontery of supposing themselves capable of passing judgment on it. Hence the theater-goers became noisy instead of silent, as though they knew the difference between good and bad music, and in place of an aristocracy in music there sprang up a kind of base theatrocracy. (Pl. *Laws* 700a–701a, trans. Bury)

Although it seems unlikely that innovations in dramatic music were politically motivated, Plato's description makes clear that these developments

---

13. Henderson 1991 notes the musical sense of the word in *Frogs*, but not in *Wasps*.

could be described in political rhetoric. Plato constructs an opposition between lawful standardized conventional music and a contemporary style that mingled genres and evoked nothing but pleasure. As Csapo notes regarding the elite reception of this new wave of music, "The critical assault took a pattern familiar to fifth century ideological debate, tainting the New Music as effeminate, barbarous and self-indulgent" (2004: 246). Indeed, the gendering of musical style has been traced back to Damon of Oa, who, in the 440s BCE, classified notes as "female" or "male" according to their effect on the listener's ethos.[14] In the *Republic*, Plato genders musical modes, strongly linking Lydian styles to the feminine:

> λέγε μοι: σὺ γὰρ μουσικός.
> μειξολυδιστί, ἔφη, καὶ συντονολυδιστὶ καὶ τοιαῦταί τινες.
> οὐκοῦν αὗται, ἦν δ' ἐγώ, ἀφαιρετέαι; ἄχρηστοι γὰρ καὶ γυναιξὶν ἃς
>   δεῖ ἐπιεικεῖς εἶναι, μὴ ὅτι ἀνδράσι.
> πάνυ γε.
> ἀλλὰ μὴν μέθη γε φύλαξιν ἀπρεπέστατον καὶ μαλακία καὶ ἀργία.
> πῶς γὰρ οὔ;
> τίνες οὖν μαλακαί τε καὶ συμποτικαὶ τῶν ἁρμονιῶν;
> ἰαστί, ἦ δ' ὅς, καὶ λυδιστὶ αὖ τινες χαλαραὶ καλοῦνται. ταύταις οὖν, ὦ
>   φίλε, ἐπὶ πολεμικῶν ἀνδρῶν ἔσθ' ὅτι χρήσῃ; οὐδαμῶς, ἔφη.

"Tell me, for you are a musician." "The mixed Lydian," he said, "and the tense or higher Lydian, and similar modes." "These, then," said I, "we must do away with. For they are useless even to women who are to make the best of themselves, let alone to men." "Assuredly." "But again, drunkenness is a thing most unbefitting guardians, and so is softness and sloth." "Yes." "What, then, are the soft and convivial modes?" "There are certain Ionian and also Lydian modes that are called lax." "Will you make any use of them for warriors?" "None at all," he said.
(Pl. *Rep.* 398e–99a, trans. Paul Shorey)

Furthermore, as Mariella De Simone has argued, a schematic opposition coalesced around Aeolic and Doric music that served as a paradigm for making ethical distinctions between New Music and tradition (2008: 489–90).

From this fifth-century Athenian perspective, playing Aeolic music simultaneously evoked a positive image of Lesbian lyric poets and the

---

14. Wallace 1991: 48–49; Csapo 2004: 230.

propensity of Athenian dramatists like Euripides and Timotheus to incorporate complex eastern music in the alleged mash-up of genres that was called New Music. Furthermore, by considering *lesbiazein* from the vantage of musical criticism, we can deduce that Lesbos was gendered as feminine in part as a result of a fifth-century Athenian rhetorical strategy, following the lead of Damon of Oa, who used gendered terms to describe the ethics of musical style.

In the two Aristophanic plays where a verb derived from Lesbos is used, *Wasps* and *Frogs*, the primary issue at hand is clearly music, specifically the cultural associations of the New Music. *Wasps* dramatizes the efforts of a young sophisticate, Bdelycleon, to lure his father Philocleon away from his addiction to judging court cases in the assembly by exposing him to the finer things in life, especially contemporary sympotic practice. He instructs his father in the proper way to dress, walk, sit, talk, and sing at a symposium. While Philocleon feigns interest in his education, he mocks the pretensions of the elite. In the course of this education, the competition of musical styles, old and new, is elaborated in both content and meter.[15]

Bdelycleon tries to teach Philocleon how to sing skolia while an imaginary *auletris* accompanies them:

αὐλητρὶς ἐνεφύσησεν. Οἱ δὲ συμπόται
εἰσίν Θέωρος, Αἰσχίνης, Φᾶνος, Κλέων,
ξένος τις ἕτερος πρὸς κεφαλῆς Ἀκέστορος.
τούτοις ξυνὼν τὰ σκόλι' ὅπως δέξει καλῶς.

The flute-girl has started playing. Your drinking companions are Theorus, Aeschines, Phanus, Cleon, and a second foreigner placed above Acestor. With them for company, be sure and take up the party songs well.
(Ar. *Wasps* 1219–22)

The father and son then trade skolia back and forth. One commentator notes that these skolia (*Wasps* 1240ff.) are adapted from Alcaeus and Sappho (Van Der Valk 1974). Bdelycleon sings a skolion adapted from Alcaeus—"you man, who desires great power, you'll ruin the city yet, she is close to the turn of the scale" (fr. 249 L-P). This skolion is written in Aeolic meter, and Bdelycleon ends with the Kleitagora song, a drinking song named after a woman poet. It was famous in antiquity but little is

---

15. On metrical style, see Parker 1997: 214–61.

now known about it. In antiquity Kleitagora was thought to be Thracian or Spartan, but Hesychius records that she was from Lesbos.

After Bdelycleon has taught his father the ways of the symposium, the two go off to put the teaching into practice and the next scene depicts Philocleon's bad sympotic behavior. At the symposium, Philocleon is rude, drunk, and disorderly. He then stumbles home, and hits everyone he encounters, including Bdelycleon. He is accompanied by an *auletris* named Dardanis, whom he has stolen from the party.

Philocleon tells Dardanis that he has rescued her so that she won't have to λεσβιεῖν τοὺς ξυμπότας, "lesbian the symposiasts." Recalling the musical exchanges between Bdelycleon and Philocleon, and the prominence of Aeolic music in the father's sympotic education, there is clearly a double entendre in this statement. Philocleon's words have both a musical and a sexual meaning (Henry 2007):

ὁρᾷς ἐγώ σ᾽ ὡς δεξιῶς ὑφειλόμην
μέλλουσαν ἤδη λεσβιεῖν τοὺς ξυμπότας·
ὧν οὕνεκ᾽ ἀπόδος τῷ πέει τῳδὶ χάριν.
ἀλλ᾽ οὐκ ἀποδώσεις οὐδ᾽ ἐφιαλεῖς οἶδ᾽ ὅτι,
ἀλλ᾽ ἐξαπατήσεις κἀγχανεῖ τούτῳ μέγα·
πολλοῖς γὰρ ἤδη χἀτέροις αὕτ᾽ ἠργάσω.

Do you see how cleverly I snuck you out
just as you were going to *lesbiein* the symposiasts?
For the sake of these things then pay back gratitude to this here penis.
But you will not pay back and you will not get busy, I know that.
But you will deceive, and you will gape wide at this.
For you have already done these same things to many others.
(Ar. *Wasps* 1345–50)

With this context in mind, we can see that Philocleon's joke, that Dardanis won't have "to lesbian" the symposiasts, means both that she won't have to entertain them sexually OR play accompaniment to Aeolic music.

The relationship between *lesbiazein* and song is most clearly marked in Aristophanes' *Frogs* when Aeschylus condemns Euripides' musical inspiration:

AESCHYLUS: οὗτος δ᾽ ἀπὸ πάντων μὲν φέρει πορνῳδίων
σκολίων Μελήτου, Καρικῶν αὐλημάτων,

θρήνων, χορειῶν, τάχα δὲ δηλωθήσεται.
ἐνεγκάτω τις τὸ λύριον, καίτοι τί δεῖ
λύρας ἐπὶ τούτων; ποῦ 'στιν ἡ τοῖς ὀστράκοις
αὕτη κροτοῦσα; δεῦρο Μοῦσ' Εὐριπίδου,
πρὸς ἥνπερ ἐπιτήδεια ταῦτ ᾄδειν μέλη.

DIONYSUS: αὕτη ποθ'ἡ Μοῦσ' οὐκ ἐλεσβίαζεν; οὔ;[16]

AESCHYLUS: This one takes from every thing—prostitute songs, from the drinking songs of Meletus, from Carian flute songs, dirges and dance songs. This will be made clear immediately—someone bring me a lyre. But why is there need of a lyre for these? Where is the lady clacking with the castanets? Come here muse of Euripides, to whom these songs are suitable/adapted to sing.

DIONYSUS: But this muse did not play the lesbian part? No?

(Ar. *Frogs* 1301–8)

Clearly the primary significance of ἐλεσβίαζεν in this passage is musical, and the sexual connotation is secondary. Aeschylus derides Euripides' music because he is inspired by multiple sources that are trivial, erotic, sympotic, emotional, and pathetic.

The notion that a pastiche of styles is decadent is consonant with Plato's criticism of contemporary music in the *Laws*. The description of this musical hodgepodge is then embodied somehow in Euripides' muse, who arrives onstage playing castanets, ready to sing.[17] Castanets were known for their use in orgiastic ritual and in what Dover refers to as "down-market" music in general. It seems possible that the muse is dressed in such a way as to represent an unappealing mélange of exotic musical styles, and the joke depends on understanding the evolving connotation of Lesbian music, that it was once highly esteemed, but in the hands of New Musicians had been appropriated as part of a new style that was innovative, iconoclastic, and lacking in the cultural prestige that previously had been attributed to the poets of Lesbos. The transformation of the implications of style can be easily understood by juxtaposing the tradition surrounding the saying "second only to the Lesbian poet," which the Suda records was

---

16. For this punctuation, I am following DeSimone 2008: 483, who interprets the line as a question after the ancient scholiasts (and some ms support) who write: αὕτη ποθ' ἡ Μοῦσα] ἐν ἐρωτήσει λέγει.

17. Dover 1997: 212 suggests that the muse's use of castanets is a mocking reference to Euripides' *Hypsipyle*, in which Hypsipyle entertains the baby Opheltes by playing castanets.

said proverbially of people who come off second best, with the degraded image of Lesbian musicality that seems to be represented by Euripides' muse.[18]

The exact nature of the decline that is supposed to be depicted here is, however, not clear. Because of the unusual repeated negative in the interrogative οὐκ ἐλεσβίαζεν; οὔ; and because we have no way of knowing how Euripides' muse appeared—both old hag and young hottie have been suggested—it is somewhat difficult to interpret the musical meaning of the geographical slur. De Simone has recently noted that the lines following the introduction of the muse, which are a pastiche of quotes from Euripides' plays followed by dialogue, are written in an Aeolic rhythm (2008: 488). Euripides is being ridiculed for the way he adapts lesbian lyric, incorporating it into his Attic drama. Perhaps we could even understand the unusual repetition of οὐ in a question as a comic means to evoke the oral sexuality implied by *lesbiazein*. The red-figure kalathos that pictures Alcaeus playing his barbiton with the letters ooooo emanating from his mouth suggestively comes to mind.[19] In combination with the *Wasps* passage, the use of λεσβιάζειν suggests that the idea of Lesbian sexuality comes from Athens and is the by-product of a critical discourse about music. This idea is not, however, one that maps onto modern conceptions of "Lesbian" sexuality.

COURTESANS, MUSIC, AND GEOGRAPHY

The *Frogs* passage depicts the comic embodiment of New Music in the figure of a culturally debased woman whose relationship to the musical tradition is emblematized by the use and abuse of the Lesbian poetic tradition. As Hall characterizes the muse, she is the "personification of a qualitative aesthetic evaluation" (2001: 409). Euripides' muse signifies nostalgia and loss for traditional music, and stylistic propriety, much in the same way that *Mousike* in Pherecrates' *Cheiron* does.[20] In the fragment that preserves this depiction, Justice is asking Music how she has gotten into such bad shape.

---

18. Edmonds 1922, s.v. "Terpandros."

19. Alcaeus and Sappho (each with a barbitos, a kind of lyre), Attic red-figure kalathos, c. 470 BC, Staatliche Antikensammlungen (Inv. 2416).

20. The courtesan is a figure of nostalgia and decay in a variety of contexts—thus she is deployed by Machon and others cited in Athenaeus, Lucian, and Alciphron to recall and emphasize the loss of the classical period. Similarly, the courtesan represents the degradation of rhetorical style, e.g., in Lucian's *Praeceptor Rhetorum* 13, *Bis Accusatus* 31. See also McClure on nostalgia and courtesans 2003: 27–58.

She describes her relationships with Melanippides, a virtuoso dithyrambic poet who made changes to the lyre, with Phrynis, a kitharode from Mytilene, and with Kinesias, an Athenian dithyrambic poet. As in the case of Euripides' muse, Mousike is embodied as a sexualized and abused woman: she has been lowered, bent, and loosened. The fragment culminates in a description of Timotheos, who surpasses all of her exploiters in evil:

> Μο. ὁ δὲ Τιμόθεός μ', ὦ φιλτάτη, κατορώρυχεν
> καὶ διακέκναιχ' ᾄσχιστα.
>   Δι. ποῖος οὑτοσί
> ὁ Τιμόθεος;
>
> Μο.   Μιλήσιός τις πυρρίας·
> κακά μοι παρέσχεν οἷς ἅπαντας οὓς λέγω
> παρελήλυθ', ἀγαγὼν ἐκτραπέλους μυρμηκιὰς
> ἐξαρμονίους, ὑπερβολαίους τ' ἀνοσίους
> καὶ νιγλάρους, ὥσπερ τε τὰς ῥαφάνους ὅλην
> καμπῶν με κατεμέστωσε. . . .
> κἂν ἐντύχῃ πού μοι βαδιζούσῃ μόνῃ,
> ἀπέδυσε κἀνέλυσε χορδαῖς ἕνδεκα.

MUSIC: Now Timotheos, my dear friend, has buried me
    And worn me out most shamefully.
JUSTICE: Who is this Timotheos?
MUSIC: A red headed Milesian: he has
    done evils to me, by which he outstripped everyone
    whom I mention by drawing devious anthills
    all outside the modes and notes that are excessive, unhealthy, and
    trilling. And has stuffed me full of wiggles like a cabbage with worms
    . . . and if he happens upon me walking alone, he undresses me
    and loosens me up with his eleven notes.
(Pherecrates 145)

Here, the sexual abuse Mousike has suffered doubles as a pejorative depiction of musical innovation. She enumerates the names and deeds of her successive abusers, whose violations are increasingly serious. Her list culminates with the most serious offenders, to whom she attributes a place of origin, identifying Kinesias as an Athenian and Timotheos as a Milesian. In this depiction, Music has been sexually mistreated by the onslaught of Athenian and East Greek musical innovators.

Some scholars have argued that Mousike is a courtesan,[21] while others caution that her status is more ambiguously represented. Henderson says there is "deliberate ambiguity in the portrayal of her sexual status," and also that she resembles a *hetaira* in many respects.[22] As I have argued elsewhere, I think the contours of the *hetaira* could be legible to the audience in ambiguous portrayals of women, without the need for the character to be perfectly delineated as this type (Gilhuly 2009: 140–79). Mousike talks about multiple sex partners in suggestive language, and being assaulted when she was out *alone* at night. Her presentation in this fragment strongly evokes the image of the courtesan, despite any residual ambiguity.

Pherecrates' fragment brings together the thematics of courtesan, music, and geography. Pherecrates implies, as does the *Frogs* depiction of Euripides' muse, that the intersection of Athenian drama and East Greek music are responsible for the degradation of music.[23] We have seen that the term λεσβιάζειν was used on the comic stage to epitomize a trend in Athenian popular musical culture that appropriated aspects of East Greek musical style. A secondary meaning of this comic term implies a kind of sex performed by a woman on a man. Lesbianism as sexuality was invented on the Athenian comic stage to describe an Athenian style of music. Lesbianism therefore comes from Athens. In the case of the *Frogs* passage, the personification of musical style as sexual decline focalizes the comic brand of lesbian sexuality, whatever it may refer to exactly, on an individual female body suggestively marked as a courtesan type.

The association of the courtesan with *lesbiazein* is an important strand of the discursive web in which we see shifting combinations of Lesbos, Sappho, the courtesan, and muse. The link between Sappho and the muses, or the notion of Sappho as muse, probably was derived from the prominence of the Muses in her poetry (e.g., fr. 150). Thus the *Palatine Anthology* records that Antipater of Sidon refers to her as "a mortal muse" (7.14), and Plato is credited with calling her the tenth muse (7.17).[24] The figure of Sappho as muse encapsulates the same ambiguity between admiration and contempt for Aeolic music that I noted in the case of Aristophanes' depiction of the Lesbian muse. For Sappho as muse is also susceptible to

---

21. Lloyd-Jones 1981: 25; Dobrov and Urios-Parisi 1995.

22. Henderson 2000: 143. He also notes that Pherecrates is credited with inventing the hetaira-comedy (138).

23. The depiction of Agathon in *Thesmophoriazousai* also dovetails with the Pherecrates fragment in its characterization of trilling, sharing in some of the representational strategies and associations that the *Frogs* passage and Pherecrates' fragment deploy to mock the pretensions of Attic dramatists in their appropriation of Eastern style.

24. For a similar sentiment, see also *Anth. Pal.* 7.17.

representation as a courtesan. Indeed, in the fragmentary evidence for the ancient reception of Sappho, there is also a persistent association between the courtesan and the image of Sappho.[25]

METALITERARY HETEROEROTICS

I turn now to the ancient historical and literary reception of Sappho herself. In this section I shall be arguing that homoerotics were rarely associated with her persona; it is impossible to know whether this aspect of her poetry was ignored, overlooked, or suppressed. In discourse, she was represented in an emphatically heteroerotic metaliterary mode. That is to say, the process through which Sappho was integrated into masculine literary discourse persistently imagined her in a heteroerotic context.

Since it belongs to the public realm, Sappho's image is stalked by the figure of the courtesan.[26] Sappho first enters the historical record along with, or rather, in opposition to, the earliest attested use of the word *hetaira* in ancient Greek literature. The *hetaira* Rhodopis is introduced by Herodotus as a fellow slave of Aesop (described as a prose writer, *logopoios*). In his description of Rhodopis, Herodotus mentions that she was freed in Egypt for a high price by Sappho's brother, Charaxos. In distinction from Aesop, Sappho is identified as a *mousopoios*. After debunking the idea that Rhodopis could afford to leave behind a pyramid and then demonstrating the actual extent of her wealth through a description of her dedication of spits at Delphi, he launches into a narrative about her reputation:

---

25. Yatromanolakis (2007) has discussed extensively the Athenian reception of Sappho and her songs with their references to music playing, instruments and song, *hetairai* and *hetairoi*, drinking vessels and other accoutrements of the symposium. He considers the valence of these images through the rubric of fifth-century Athenian sympotic discourse. He argues that the "receptorial dynamics" projected one image among others of Sappho "that ranged from the *hetaira* schema to more pederastic and even female homoerotic contexts" (Yatromanolakis 2007: 278). In his treatment of the Bochum vase, he argues that the figures and inscriptions assimilate Sappho to a pederastic model. While it should be noted that the depiction of one sexual orientation should not be thought to preclude another in antiquity, my argument is concerned with Sappho's representation *in literary discourse*. If Yatromanolakis correctly interprets the Bochum vase (2007: 88–110), then it seems all the more significant to note that we do not find Sappho discussed in terms of pederasty in her literary reception. Surely it is possible that things were painted on pots that were not said out loud or written down. For instance, consider the vases Peschel identifies as "reine Hetärensymposia," or "*hetaira* only symposia" (1987: 70–74, 110–12). Consider also the name piece of the Thalia painter, with Kurke's discussion (1999: 201–6).

26. Raymond 2001: 65–66 also discusses the association between Sappho and the *hetaira*.

> For some reason, the courtesans in Naukratis are particularly beguiling. Not only was there the one we have been talking about, who became so famous (κλεινή) that all Greeks are familiar with the name of Rhodopis, but there was also another one later, called Archidice, who became the subject of a popular Greek song (ἀοίδιμος), although she is less notorious (περιλεσχήνευτος) than Rhodopis. After he bought Rhodopis' freedom, Charaxus returned to Mytilene, where Sappho railed violently against him (κατεκερτόμησέ) in her poetry (ἐν μέλει). That is all I have to say about Rhodopis. (Herodotus 2.135, trans. Waterfield, adapted)

As many scholars have noted, this passage evokes a range of literary genres that serve as vehicles for the courtesan's fame, juxtaposing high and low culture. Aesop the slave is invoked as a prose writer in contrast to Sappho the music maker. Archedice was ἀοίδιμος, the subject of song, a term with an epic pedigree, famous from a single use in Homer's *Iliad*, when Helen tells Hector that Zeus gave them an evil doom, so they would be subjects of song for people to come, ἀοίδιμοι ἐσσομένοισι (6.357–58). περιλεσχήνευτος occurs only here in antiquity.[27] The range of genres alluded to in this passage, soaring from high to low in terms of level of decorum, culminates in a stylistic clash when Herodotus notes that Sappho mocked her brother in lyric, presumably for his devotion to this beautiful *hetaira*.[28] As Kurke points out, κατεκερτομεῖν, "to rail violently," is a manner of speech appropriate to iambic poetry, ill-suited to lyric, and characterizes Sappho as a "fishwife" (1999: 226n11).

Herodotus's description is important for this argument in the way that it depicts the dynamic of the relationship between Sappho and the courtesan. Here we see the generic range and effect of the courtesan—she is linked to slave stories through her association with Aesop, as well as lyric poetry, but at the same time she has a destabilizing effect on genre, provoking the mocking lyric. Sappho is introduced in the historical record in opposition to the courtesan—she looks down on her brother's entanglement with Rhodopis, but at the same time she is pulled into her orbit, for Herodotus depicts the generic havoc illustrated in the description of Rhodopis as contaminating the image of Sappho, for it is in relationship to Rhodopis that Sappho suffers genre confusion. By railing like a fishwife,

---

27. Its social valence is the subject of debate. See Kurke 1999: 225, vs. Yatromanolakis 2007: 322–25.

28. Kurke describes "mocking in lyric" as violating the terms of Greek poetic decorum, "nearly an oxymoron" (1999: 225).

Sappho degrades herself and contaminates her own lyric, "and is perhaps no better than the object of her vilification" (Kurke 1999: 226).

Another element of Herodotus's narrative that will be repeated in later reception is the way that Sappho is evoked through metaliterary play. The literary context in Herodotus's narrative is distinctively heteroerotic. It is first established through the representation of the famous courtesan, much discussed in men's circles. These men's circles are given social parameters through marked literary terms—the courtesans they talk about are described with adjectives appropriate to epic: κλεινή and ἀοίδιμος—and Sappho's image emerges in this context. In Herodotus, the love evoked is Charaxos's immoderate devotion to a courtesan. The characterization of Sappho as a sister does nothing to perturb this vantage point, and indeed obliquely situates her identity in a matrix of heterosexuality. We encounter her in the role of sister, policing her brother's sexual relations, with an eye to the prosperity of the οἶκος, promulgated through heterosexual marriage.[29]

Sappho is absorbed into the masculine literary canon through the matrix of masculine desire, in Herodotus as condemning her brother's sexual exploits, and in comedy often as the embodied object of male desire. On the comic stage, I shall argue, the combination of metapoetics and the strong association of the feminine with the body produce representations of Sappho as an embodied, public, fetishized object of masculine desire. In order to be included among the ranks of other poets, to be known by many male poets, Sappho is produced as a promiscuous heterosexual, or courtesan type. Furthermore, the incongruous biography that results from a reading of her poetry together with the heteroerotic prism through which she is incorporated into literary culture produces the need for the invention of another Sappho to explain the dissonance, one who, because of her public exposure and devotion to love, is (surprise!) also a courtesan.[30]

Athenaeus preserves an excerpt from Hermesianax's elegies (330 BCE) that describe poets in love with their subjects. In these elegies, Homer's wasting love of Penelope is attested, and Hesiod's passion for "Eoie" is recorded (clearly named after his mostly lost poem *Eoeae*). Hermesianax mentions that Alcaeus and Anacreon loved Sappho.[31] This is the context

---

29. See "The Brothers Poem," Obbink 2014.

30. For a similar interpretation see Most 1996, who also suggests a similar "splitting" of the Sapphic tradition into multiple Sapphos in order to make sense of the different erotic subjects.

31. Alcaeus's love for Sappho is also represented on pots. For a discussion and images see Yatromanolakis 2007: 73–81.

where we find Anacreon 358 PMG preserved, a poem that depicts a game of love that mediates, I suggest, between the Homeric image of Lesbian women considered above, and that projected in Aeolic lyric. Just before the poem is quoted, Athenaeus says: Χαμαιλέων δ'ἐν τῷ περὶ Σαπφοῦς καὶ λέγειν τινάς φησιν εἰς αὐτὴν πεποιῆσθαι ὑπὸ Ἀνακρέοντος τάδε ("Yet Chamaileon, in his book on Sappho, says that some say that the following verses were made by Anacreon for her," 13.599c). Generally this phrase is taken to mean that the words were spoken *to* Sappho. Athenaeus brings up the issue, criticizing Hermesianax for thinking that Sappho and Anacreon lived at the same time, and Chamaileon next records "Sappho's" response. It seems odd, however, to construe εἰς αὐτὴν πεποιῆσθαι ὑπὸ Ἀνακρέοντος τάδε as "these verses were addressed by Anacreon to her," rather than made for her, in the sense of "in regard to her."

The fragment itself echoes the conceptualization of Lesbos we saw in the *Iliad* as well built and home to beautiful women:

σφαίρῃ δηὖτέ με πορφυρῇ
βάλλων χρυσοκόμης Ἔρως
νήνι ποικιλοσαμβάλῳ
συμπαίζειν προκαλεῖται·
ἡ δ'ἐστὶν γὰρ ἀπ' εὐτίκτου
Λέσβου, τὴν μὲν ἐμὴν κόμην,
λευκὴ γάρ, καταμέμφεται,
πρὸς δ' ἄλλην τινὰ χάσκει.

Once again, golden-haired Eros hits me
with a purple ball, and challenges me to
play with a girl with intricately wrought sandals.
But she, for she is from well-built Lesbos,
Finds fault with my hair, because it is white,
and she gapes at some other.
(Anacr. 358 PMG / Gentili 13)

The significant detail that the girl is from Lesbos, combined with the enigmatic ending of this poem, has provoked a great deal of speculation. Are we meant to understand that the girl from Lesbos gapes at another woman, or some other hair, since the closest feminine singular antecedent for ἄλλην τινὰ is κόμη? Because the girl is from Lesbos, she has been thought by modern commentators to be homosexual, and therefore the hair she gapes at belongs to a woman, or if the reader wants the object of her gape to be male, the hair could be pubic. Many aspects of interpretations of this fragment are inherently speculative or doubtful. Even if we knew that Greek audiences recognized Sappho as homosexual, which we do not, there are other significant conceptual leaps involved in the search for early traces of Lesbian sexuality, most importantly that when Anacreon wrote this poem, it was thought that everyone from Lesbos shared Sappho's erotic proclivities.[32] Those who argue that the hair the girl gapes at is pubic suggest the girl is hoping for the chance to perform fellatio—an attribution to a woman of erotic agency and desire that is unparalleled through the classical period.[33]

As some have noted, the language in the poem evokes Sappho's diction and imagery. While the colors of gold and purple are too pervasive to be closely associated with anyone in particular, certainly they are part of Sappho's palette. Anacreon's use of δηὖτε is shared by Sappho: "No one who reads Greek lyric poetry can fail to be struck by the frequency with which this adverb is used. The poets of love prefer it to any other designation of time."[34] The ποικιλο- prefix is reminiscent of Sappho 1.1, and the Aeolic- σαμβάλῳ resonates with the language and imagery of fancy footwear found several times in the fragments of Sappho.[35] Anacreon's erotic triangle explicating his unrequited love echoes the dynamics of the erotic triangle represented in Sappho 31.

Ilja Pfeijffer has explored the Homeric resonance, not only in the mention of well-built Lesbos (ἡ δ'ἐστὶν γὰρ ἀπ'εὐτίκτου Λέσβου), which recalls *Il.* 9.129–30 (quoted above), but also in the conceit of playing ball, which calls to mind Odysseus's encounter with Nausicaa. Pfeijffer sees Anacreon's poem as alluding to the Homeric scene but with gender inversion of the lover and beloved. In Homer, Odysseus encounters girls playing ball, but here the man, Odysseus, refuses the woman Nausicaa in favor of Penelope, whereas in Anacreon's poem the Lesbian girl who gapes at some other (πρὸς δ'ἄλλην τινὰ χάσκει) rejects the presumably male speaker.[36]

Through these allusions, we might see Anacreon's poem, and his lyric "I," as mediating Homeric and Sapphic erotics. At first we encounter Homer's Lesbos, with beautiful and elegant women, fleshed out by the allusion

---

32. Bowra 1961: 284–86; Campbell 1967: 320–21; Easterling 1997: 318–37; Gerber 1970: 229–30; Kirkwood 1974: 166–67; Marzullo 1965: 157–58; West 1970: 209.

33. Gentili 1973; Giangrande 1973; Komornicka 1976. Pfeijffer 2000 notes that the most relevant passage would be Ar. *Eccl.* 920, which describes, she argues, a woman desiring to have cunnilingus performed on herself

34. Carson 1998: 118. See also Nagy 1996: 99–102; Yatromanolakis 2007: 217n238.

35. Sappho 110.2, 39.1–2, 123.

36. Pfeijffer 2000. She reads ἄλλην τινὰ as referring to another woman.

to Nausicaa and her maids. As the finely wrought poem progresses, it seems we are being conditioned by the Lesbian reference to read the poem with Sappho in mind, and then we are presented with the possibility that ἄλλην τινά, although grammatically parallel to "hair," is open-ended enough to suggest a female object of the girl's desire.

My purpose here is not to determine Anacreon's conception of Lesbian or Sappho's sexuality, but to notice the effect of the emphatically heteroerotic metapoetic elements of the poem as well as the context in which it was preserved. Thus we note not only the desire of the (presumably male) speaker for the girl from Lesbos, but also Chamaileon's report that "some say" that Sappho, whatever her own desire may have been, was conceived of as the object of the poet's heterosexual desire, who apparently did not reciprocate the poetic ego's love. Both Chamaileon and Athenaeus equate the "I" with the poet. Indeed, Athenaeus concludes this section on Sappho and the poets who love her with the remark that καὶ γάρ Δίφιλος ὁ κωμῳδιοποιὸς πεποίηκεν ἐν Σαπφοῖ δράματι Σαπφοῦς ἐραστὰς Ἀρχίλοχον καὶ Ἱππώνακτα ("For in fact Diphilus the comic poet, in his play *Sappho*, made Archilochus and Hipponax the *erastai* of Sappho!" Ath. 13.599d).

These metaliterary depictions of Sappho, which are thought to belong mostly to the comic stage, have contributed significantly to a facet of Sappho's reputation in antiquity, "the reputation of one who exemplified insatiable heterosexual promiscuity, as instanced in her sexual relations with poets like Archilochus, Hipponax and Anacreon."[37] This heterosexual image is magnified by the narrative of her unrequited love for Phaon.[38] Her longing for this ferryman drove her to leap from the cliffs of Leucas (an Ionian island near the western coast of the Greek mainland) to free herself from her unrequited passion. In a passage on Leucas, Strabo quotes Menander:

οὗ δὴ λέγεται πρώτη Σαπφώ,

---

37. Most 1996: 14. He also notes that the biographical data that she was married to a man named Kerkulas, from the Island of Andros ("Tail of Man"), is also probably derived from the comic stage. On Kerkulas see also Parker 1996: 146, who translates his name as Dick Allcock from the isle of MAN. Recently, however, Yatromanolakis 2007: 299 has questioned this view, analyzing the comic fragments available to us, pointing out that nowhere is there any evidence that Sappho was depicted as promiscuous at all.

38. We know of five plays entitled *Sappho*, written by Ameipsias, Amphis, Diphilus, Ephippus, and Timocles. Comedies entitled *Phaon* may have also dealt with Sappho; these were written by Plato Comicus, and Antiphanes, as well as those called *The Leucadian*, titles attributed to Menander, Diphilus, Alexis, Antiphanes, and Amphis. See Campbell 2002: 27.

ὥς φησίν ὁ Μένανδρος,
τὸν ὑπέρκομπον θρῶσα Φάων·
οἰστρῶτι πόθῳ ῥίψαι πέτρας
ἀπὸ τηλεφανοῦς ἅλμα κατ' εὐχὴν
σήν, δέσποτ' ἄναξ.

Where it is said that Sappho
first, as Menander says,
hunting after the super-haughty Phaon,
in her goading desire
threw herself from the
far-seen rock, calling upon you in prayer,
o lord master.
(Strabo 10.2.9)

In apparent reference to the image of Sappho as unrequited in her love for a man, perhaps to eliminate its incongruity with the love Sappho depicts in her own poetry, the Suda records the history of another Sappho: a lyre player, who leapt from the cliff of Leucates to her death, out of love for Phaon (Sud. Σ 108). Aelian also mentions the other Sappho: ἑταίρα οὐ ποιήτρια ("hetaira, not poet" Ael. *V. H.* 12.19).[39] The second Sappho crystallizes the tensions in the poet's reputation. As a woman in the public domain, associated with erotic discourse, ancient scholars reflexively imagine her in a heterosexual matrix. Apparently, the sexual politics of reading in the ancient world could not fully support the representation of a female poet as a subject position.[40] Because Sappho had such a strong association with the theme of desire, the courtesan became her surrogate. As a result, Sappho's afterlife is haunted by the figure of the *hetaira*.

The most extensive depiction we have of Sappho in a comedy is Antiphanes fragment 194, which depicts Sappho riddling:

---

39. See Most 1996: 15.
40. The fact that we have record of a number of female poets, including Erinna, Anyte, Nossis, Moero, and Corinna, but such scant and inconsistent depictions of their lives and public personae, underscores my point that woman as poet was a subject position scarcely articulated in the ancient Greek literary record. For instance, ancient sources tell us that Korinna was born in May and that she was Pindar's teacher. Pausanius and Aelian say she competed with Pindar. Pausanias explains her victory as due to her dialect, or her beauty (9.22.3). According to other writers, she lived in the fifth or fourth century (we now think she lived around 200 BCE). Erinna was a contemporary of Sappho who was a native of Rhodes, or Telos or Tenos. For a discussion of the idea of a "woman's tradition," see Bowman 2004 with extensive bibliography on the poetry and reception of these poets.

Sappho: ἔστι φύσις θήλεια βρέφη σώιζουσ' ὑπὸ κόλποις
αὑτῆς, ὄντα δ'ἄφωνα βοὴν ἵστησι γεγωνὸν
καὶ διὰ πόντιον οἶδμα καὶ ἠπείρου διὰ πάσης
οἷς ἐθέλει θνητῶν, τοῖς δ'οὐδὲ παροῦσιν ἀκούειν
ἔξεστιν· κωφὴν δ'ἀκοῆς αἴσθησιν ἔχουσιν.

Sappho: There is a female nature protecting unborn children in her folds;
although voiceless, they emit a great shout,
across the swelling sea, and throughout
every land to whomever of mortals they wish;
even for those not present it is possible to hear them.
And they have a dull perception of hearing.

Sappho's male interlocutor suggests that the answer to her riddle is a city, ἡ πολίς, and the babies are orators. Sappho then replies that "the female nature" is in fact a letter:

Sappho: θήλεια μέν νυν ἐστὶ φύσις ἐπιστολή
βρέφη δ'ἐν αὐτῆι περιφέρει τὰ γράμματα·
ἄφωνα δ'ὄντα <ταῦτα> τοῖς πόρρω λαλεῖ
οἷς βούλεθ'· ἕτερος δ' ἂν τύχηι τις πλησίον
ἑστὼς ἀναγιγνώσκοντος οὐκ ἀκούσεται

Sappho: The female nature is a message,
and the babies she carries around on her are letters;
these have no voice, yet they speak to those far off
to whomever they wish, and if someone happens to be
standing near the one reading, he will not hear.
(Antiphanes 194.17–21 K-A)

Clearly the riddle is rooted emphatically in femininity. The gender of ἐπιστολή is materialized as a woman's body in its reproductive capacity—figured as a vessel for offspring. Writing and the dissemination of language are mapped onto the maternal female body, and authorship is figured through the image of feminine heterosexual reproduction.

The gender dynamics of the exchange between Sappho and her male interlocutor, whom she addresses as *pater*, are complex and intriguing—the male interlocutor's response, solving the riddle with the *polis*, nurturing orators as babies, speaking before a voiceless and deaf *demos*, translates the fertile female into the emphatically masculine domain of political discourse (Yatromanolakis 2007: 304–5). Sappho's response—that the interlocutor is wrong and that the body is a message—gives her the opportunity to reconstitute literature as feminine at the same time that she retains control of the discourse. This exchange dramatizes female "double-consciousness," the paradigm Winkler invoked to understand Sappho's lyric and its relationship to Homeric poetry (1990: 162–87). He suggested that Sappho constitutes the erotic and feminine space of her poetry both as opposed to and as in dialogue with the dominant poetic discourse that knew only the subjects of military heroics and other masculine pursuits. Here Sappho's riddle is susceptible to a masculine interpretation, but the authoritative understanding insists on the possibility of a feminine literary discourse.

There is a counterintuitive element to this riddle, insofar as it suggests that a mother is composed of her children, rather than the other way around. Perhaps we might see this as a literalization of the dynamics of reception that preserve the figure of Sappho. As Prins notes, "the body of the text is made to speak in place of the author, according to the logic by which Sappho comes to be read as the personification of her own texts" (1996: 48).[41] Sappho's poetry is scrutinized for what it might contain of her material reality, especially her sexuality. The existence of poetry spoken from a feminine perspective seems to demand the production of a body.

There is another intriguing twist that we might consider in terms of this fragment—riddling speech has a strong association with the courtesan, and it has been obliquely suggested that thus Antiphanes' Sappho was associated with the *hetaira*.[42] If this is the case, we can observe the representational contortions dictated by the conventions of comedy in order to represent an authoritative female speaker, the result of which is Sappho as mother and courtesan, and poetry as body.[43] All of these strands emphasize the notion of woman as body. Significantly, all of these bodies belong distinctly to a field of heteroerotics.

---

41. While this attribution is not explicitly made here, among females, courtesans are strongly associated with riddling speech.

42. For a collection of Courtesan's witty sayings, see Machon's *Chreiai* quoted at Athenaeus *Deipnosophistai* 13.577d–83d. See Kurke 2002: 20–65; McClure 2003: 79–105; Yatromanolakis 2007: 301–12.

43. As I have argued elsewhere, the contours of the courtesan can be detected elsewhere in comic depiction of authoritative women, especially in Aristophanes' *Lysistrata*. There is a precedent for the representation of the mother of a courtesan (Xen. *Mem.* Theodote). The identity of the courtesan is generally not combined with maternity. See Gilhuly 2009: 1–28.

ROMAN SAPPHO

In Latin literature we encounter similar as well as newly emergent strategies for incorporating Sappho into the literary canon. It should be noted here that Rome would have inherited Sappho in part through Hellenistic scholars who included her in the list of nine lyric poets. In Catullus's lyric, Sappho is called to mind as poetic predecessor in Catullus's use of meter, image, and provider of source material. At the same time, she is evoked by the very name of Catullus's poetic love object, Lesbia, or woman from Lesbos. Through these evocations, Catullus intimately explores the issues proposed by the figuration of Sappho as muse—poetic inspiration in a female body—but here from a Roman perspective. In her suggestive analysis of Catullus 51, the famous translation of Sappho 31, Elizabeth Young emphasizes the pivotal role played by the name Lesbia in the poem. It allows Catullus to circumvent the problems of female homosexuality and authorship. By inserting Lesbia as the name of his version's beloved, "Catullus usurps Sappho's authorial position and inserts himself as the poem's new speaker." He resolves the problem of "a maternal poetic inheritance . . . by transforming its most formidable matriarch into the object of desire rather than a producer of speech."[44] Here Catullus enacts the same heterosexual erotics of reception that we have seen in the Greek context. Young also notes that Lesbia is identified through geography, and this has a contemporary Roman significance. For Lesbos came under Roman power in 79 BCE. She concludes that the jealous and unrequited love that Catullus explores between the poetic I and Lesbia is an exploration of the conflicts of Roman cultural imperialism.

While Lesbia may be a means for Catullus to dominate and control the problems posed by Sappho as poetic source, the power dynamics in his relationship to Lesbia are nothing if not ambiguous. His naming of Lesbia also acknowledges his reliance on Sappho as poetic inspiration. That is to say, he positions himself in relationship to her as both female love object and (silenced) poet. It is as though he exposes the reconfiguration of Sappho from poet to love object as a type of erotic dominance akin to imperialism. As a by-product of this imperialist discourse, Sappho is identified by her geography.[45] This seamless identification of poet and place is found

---

44. Young (forthcoming).

45. The identification between poet and place is also found in Ovid *Tr.* 3.7.20. For the identification of Lesbos with its poetic culture, see Horace *Carm.* 1.32.5; 4.6.35; 1.1.34; Ovid *F.* 2.82 *H.* 15.82.

elsewhere in Roman poetry, and the evocation of Lesbos for its musical reputation is also common.

In *Epistles* 1.19, Horace refers to Sappho in a way that completely diverges from literary precedent, both Greek and Roman, but in a way that is illustrative. As he ruminates on his own poetic identity he situates himself in relationship to Greek predecessors Archilochus, Alcaeus, and Sappho. He writes: *temperat Archilochi Musam pede mascula Sappho, temperat Alcaeus* ("manly Sappho moderates with her foot the muse of Archilochus, Alcaeus moderates it . . ." 1.19.28–29). Because he evokes Sappho primarily as a poetic predecessor, Horace refers to her as manly, with the intriguing adjective *mascula*. As Anastasia Peponi asks, "How else could the woman poet appear in this fantasy of mutually exchangeable roles with a Roman poet, if not as masculinized?"[46] She also allows that there may be an allusion to Sappho's homosexuality in that she is said to moderate not Archilochus, but rather his muse.[47] The problem with Sappho as a poet is that she is not a man. Poets are men and women are bodies that become visible through the lens of male heterosexual desire. It seems significant in this regard that Sappho is described through a poetic bodily metaphor she moderates with her foot, *pede*. For Horace to evoke Sappho primarily as a poet, she must become *mascula*. Furthermore, Horace's unqualified recognition of Sappho as poet is inextricably related to the submerged allusion to Sappho's homosexuality, if we interpret her moderating the muse in a sexual way. At any rate, the idea that we imagine Sappho erotically involved with a muse nevertheless insists on her identity as poetic.

While I think that any notable gesture toward Sappho's sexuality here is subtle, nevertheless Horace's description of Sappho does take an important step in terms of representing female homosexuality—for in Rome, when female homosexuals are depicted, they are shown as masculine women linked to a Greek past (Hallett 1989). By describing Sappho with the intriguing term *mascula* Horace forges a strong link between Sappho and the Roman discourse of female homosexuality.

Ovid's representation of Sappho in *Heroides* 15 takes a by now familiar and yet innovative approach. He provides a narrative that rationalizes many of the contradictions presented by a consideration of Sappho's poetry, wherein the poetic ego clearly desires women, and her reception, which persistently depicts her through the lens of male heterosexual desire. He

---

46. Peponi 2002: 41. See also Barchiesi 2000: 168–70 and further bibliography in Peponi.
47. Peponi 2002: 41n39. See Sappho fr. 150V.

depicts Sappho as she pines for Phaon, incidentally providing a rationale for her homoerotic poetry:

> Lesbides aequoreae, nupturaque nuptaque proles,
> Lesbides Aeolia nomina dicta lyra
> Lesbides, infamem quae me fecistis amatae,
> Desinite ad citharas turba venire meas.
> Abstulit omne Phaon, quod vobis ante placebat
> Me miseram, dixi quam modo paene "meus!"
> Efficite ut redeat . . .

> Lesbian women born of the sea, women about to marry and already married, names spoken by my Aeolian lyre. Lesbian women, you, beloved, have made me infamous, stop coming in a crowd to my lyre. Phaon has taken away all that pleased you before. I am miserable! How nearly I came to calling him mine. Accomplish his return!
> (Ov. *Her.* 15.199–205)

Ovid's version (if this text is correctly assigned to him) acknowledges Sappho as a lover of women at the same time that she denies it in favor of heterosexual desire. The emphatic repetition of *lesbides* draws crowds of women from Lesbos into the conceptual sphere of Sapphic homoerotic desire, although still asserting their role in the heterosexual framework of marriage, *nupturaque nuptaque*. The masses of women, their lack of specificity, stand in stark contrast to her one new love, Phaon, and their importance is diminished by their number (Lindheim 2003: 157).

In Sappho's letter to Phaon, Ovid refers to a wide array of associations with Sappho in her poetry and reception. "Sappho" refers to her lovers, Anactoria and Atthis among others, her daughter, father, and brother, recalling her criticism of him for spending time with unsuitable women. She talks about her past sexual encounters with Phaon and her own prowess very explicitly, in a way that would seem more appropriate to a courtesan. She even recounts her experience of a wet dream when she imagines herself having sex with Phaon (15.125–35)!

Most describes Ovid's strategy of narrativizing all the seemingly incoherent elements of Sappho's story, and its subsequent enduring appeal: "a richly detailed literary image could be obtained not by skeptically rejecting many of the traditional reports but by uncritically accepting as many of them as possible," proving "that such an image could become quite lively and appealing" (1996: 18). In a more critical reading of this text, Sara Lindheim sees Ovid reshaping Sappho through intertextual dialogue with Middle Comedy and Sappho's own poetry, producing a Sappho that is an exact replica of the other abandoned heroines in the *Heroides*, effacing what is distinctive about Sappho's poetry, the multiplicity of women presented there (Lindheim 2003: 176). As Ovid transfigures Sappho, it is her dying wish to be the object of male desire.

These representations and allusions to Sappho in Roman literature seem to work within the same constrictions as the earlier Greek images of Sappho did: there is the tendency to veer away from a straightforward depiction of woman as poet, and both Catullus and Ovid reconfigure her as the object of male desire. Horace's strategy also addresses the problem of woman as poet in a new way, by depicting Sappho as masculine.

All three of these Roman authors share self-consciousness about the use of Sappho. Catullus elicits Sappho both as poet and as love object, and thus draws attention to the dynamics that transform her from poet to beloved. Horace, in his innovative description of Sappho as masculine, reveals the problem of Sappho as poet and the anxiety inherent in a male poet's identification with her. Ovid embraces her identity as homosexual even as he denies it; he asserts its insignificance in comparison to her pathetic and unrequited hope to be an object of male heterosexual desire. In this way, he draws attention to the incoherence of Sappho's image even as he normalizes it. All three of these Roman poets expose the receptorial dynamics they are engaging with, in a playful way. The distance they have from Sappho's context, and perhaps her canonization as a lyric poet, gives them more room for analysis of her figure, which in turn allows new possibilities for her representation. Now Sappho can be masculine, she can be homosexual, she can be a poet. While all of these traits suggest interesting possibilities for Sappho as visible subject, she nevertheless remains an object.

THE COURTESAN'S CONTRIBUTION TO LESBIAN SEXUALITY

Thus far, we have seen the way the courtesan threads her way through the afterlife of Sappho, in later representations of her on the comic stage, in poetry and prose and in ancient scholarship, trying to integrate the various strands of her story. The courtesan in Aristophanes' *Frogs* embodied the musical style and sex act that imbued Lesbos with meaning that far exceeded its geographical coordinates. The courtesan, then, is the common denominator between representations of Sappho and the notion of a common lesbian sexuality, albeit one that is heterosexual.

In the realm of representation, as in the real world, the courtesan can go where a respectable woman could not. As Henderson writes (2001: 140):

> The legacy of the *hetaira*-comedy was its creation of women who, because of their non-citizen status, could safely be portrayed as both objects and subjects of erotic desire; who could be shown interacting with men, or even dominating them; who could exemplify the negative "iambic" traits of bibulousness, gluttony, masturbation, drug use (especially aphrodisiacs), preoccupation with fine clothes and jewelry, skill at depilation and in the use of sex-toys, greed, and disruptive effects on males.

I want to push Henderson's argument further, suggesting that the flexibility accorded to representations of the *hetaira* was essential to the invention of female homosexuality. As I shall argue in this final section, certain attributes of the *hetaira,* especially the possibility of depicting her subjective perspective and agency with regard to sexuality, made her very appealing to writers of a much later period, the Second Sophistic, and it is as a result of the literary concerns and investments of that age that the courtesan together with the idea of Lesbos—Sappho implicitly associated—are involved in the articulation of a female homosexual subject position.

The authors of the Second Sophistic had a penchant for bringing high culture and low culture into dialogue. Because the courtesan could be both the object and subject of erotic desire, and be shown interacting with men, in some cases, she served to mediate between the realms of masculinity and femininity, and, as I will argue, this is crucial to imagining the female homosexual. At home at the symposium, she also had a strong association with poetry and philosophy. From the analysis above, we have seen how the image of Sappho resonates with many aspects of the courtesan— as a woman trafficking in a man's literary world, she pushed the bounds of gender norms and she always had a strong association with erotic discourse. If we think of her poetry and image together, they combine subjectively articulated sexuality with erotic objectification and strong literary identification.

The first explicit articulation of a sexual orientation associated with Lesbos is found in Lucian's *Dialogues of the Courtesans.* These dialogues are one set among others in a genre that Lucian claims to have invented, the comic dialogue—the result of conjoining elements from comedy and philosophy that do not form a harmonious union.⁴⁸ As I have argued elsewhere, in the *Dialogues of the Courtesans* Lucian channels the elite masculine form of philosophical dialogue through the marginalized and eroticized female figure of the courtesan.⁴⁹ This new genre constitutes a kind of social vertigo in which topics familiar from the classical Greek canon are channeled through unlikely subjects.⁵⁰ By mining inherited literary elements, and conjoining them in this unlikely manner, Lucian innovates through an interplay of familiarity and alienation.

In *Dialogues of the Courtesans* 5, Lucian depicts a conversation between two *hetairai*: Klonarion interrogates her friend Leaina in response to rumors that she has taken up with a rich woman from Lesbos. Leaina responds that her new friend is δεινῶς ἀνδρική ("terribly manly," *DMeretr.* 5.1), and Klonarion responds:

οὐ μανθάνω ὅ τι καὶ λέγεις, εἰ μή τις ἑταιρίστρια τυγχάνει οὖσα· τοιαύτας γάρ ἐν Λέσβῳ λέγουσι γυναικᾶς ἀρρενωπούς, ὑπ' ἀνδρῶν μὲν οὐκ ἐθελούσας αὐτὸ πάσχειν, γυναιξὶ δὲ αὐτὰς πλησιαζούσας ὥσπερ ἄνδρας.

I do not understand what you are saying, unless she happens to be some kind of *hetairistria*. For they say that on Lesbos there are man-faced women, they don't like to take it from men, but they get close to women as though they are men.
(Lucian, *DMeretr.* 5.2)

The noun *hetairistria* is found elsewhere in classical Greek only in Aristophanes' speech in Plato's *Symposium*. When he is describing the origin of love, Aristophanes unforgettably imagines that people once were big round balls that were sundered in punishment for their hubris against Olympus. He identifies three types of balls, one all male, one all female, and one androgynous. He says: "As many women as have been cut from the

---

48. Lucian makes various programmatic statements about his literary innovations in *Prometheus Es*: "And in fact we dared to bring these elements thus disposed toward each other together and to harmonize them, even though they were not entirely ready to be persuaded, nor did they readily put up with the union" (*Prom. Es* 6).

49. A scholiast suggested that Lucian's courtesans come from Menander: "One must know that all these *hetairai* have been the subjects of comedy for all the comic poets, but especially for Menander, from whom, in fact, all the material for the Lucian in the present work is provided in abundance." Rabe 1906: 275. For more on Lucian's invented genre see Gilhuly 2004, 2007.

50. *The Dialogues of the Gods*, for instance, works the other way around, where august figures discuss mundane topics.

female (sphere), these pay no attention to men, but rather are attracted to women and *hetairistriai* come from this breed" (Pl. *Symp.* 191e5). Halperin has suggested that Lucian's use of the term is a deliberate gloss on this passage.[51] Yatromanolakis suggests also that through a contamination of homophones, the word *hetairistria* that Plato puts in the mouth of Aristophanes in the *Symposium* to describe "women who love women" would have been metonymically associated with the *hetaira*. Lucian is surely playing with the homophonic association when he has *hetairai* discussing, even giving definition to, the rarely mentioned word *hetairistria*.[52]

Because Klonarion cannot understand how women can actually have sex with each other, she prods Leaina for details. Leaina tells her that as she was making out with Megilla and her friend Demonassa, Megilla took off her wig, and identified herself as Megillos—the name of the Spartan interlocutor in Plato's *Laws*. Demonassa's name is the feminization of Demonax, a contemporary philosopher from Cyprus about whom Lucian wrote, calling him most similar to Socrates (*Dem.* 5). Yatromanolakis notes that her name also recalls Sappho's Arkheanassa. Finally at the end of the dialogue when Leaina admits that she let Megilla do what she wanted, she shuts down her friend's request for specifics with another reference to Plato's *Symposium*, by telling her: μή ἀνακρίνε ἀκριβῶς, αἰσχρὰ γὰρ· ὥστε μὰ τὴν οὐρανίαν οὐκ ἂν εἴποιμι ("Don't inquire too closely, for these things are shameful; so by heavenly [Aphrodite], I won't say," *DMeretr.* 5.3). The reference here to Ourania recalls Pausanius's description of Eros in Plato's *Symposium* 180e–d.

This accumulation of clear allusions to the masculine domain of philosophy, and the *Symposium* in particular, suggests that we read this dialogue in light of the pederastic practices of Greek philosophers. For the *Symposium* provides the clearest articulation of the relationship of pederasty to philosophy.[53] The dialogue also brings Sappho to mind, through the detail that Megilla is from Lesbos, along with the Sapphic sounding Demonassa, and the longstanding linking of Sappho to the *hetaira*. While Megilla and Demonassa are not *hetairai,* they are drawn into association with courtesans since they become known to us through the conversation of Leaina and Klonarion. As was the vogue in the Second Sophistic, the courtesan becomes a mouthpiece for the expression of nostalgia for the Greek cultural past (McClure 2006: 6–9). Indeed, Lucian uses this figure in a way similar

---

51. This is the only surviving record of this word in a nongrammatical context. See Halperin 1990a: 180n2, 2002: 248–49.

52. Dover 1978: 172, 20–21.

53. For a reading along these lines see Gilhuly 2006.

to Alkiphron and Athenaeus to articulate a longing for and fetishization of classical Greek philosophy and rhetoric during the Roman Empire. All of these authors enlist the lineaments of the courtesan's subjectivity—her ability to mediate between masculine and feminine gender roles, her inherent inauthenticity, her eroticization—to express the dynamics of longing for a bygone cultural moment. It is in this context of gender transposition, poetic and philosophical allusion, that Lucian animates the *hetairistria,* exploring the contours of a subject position that was rarely mentioned in the classical period and thus advertising the absent presence of the Greek past.[54] As Sandra Boehringer suggests in this volume, and as I have argued earlier, the "lesbian" in this text is an illusion created from Lucian's metadiscursivity.[55] In much the same way as the attribution of a corporate sexuality to Lesbos was almost a by-product of a self-critical Athenian musical discourse, so here we see that the *hetairistria* comes into view as Lucian's subversive and playful embodiment of the nostalgic longing for Greek culture under the Roman Empire.

Like Euripides' Lesbian muse, like Sappho's promiscuous heterosexuality, like the courtesan-other who haunts the reception of Sappho, Lucian's man-faced women who don't like to take it from men, but prefer women, are constructed through allusion and genre play; they are the product of literary discourse. The last hundred years of scholarship on Sappho have demonstrated that the way the poet's sexuality informed her poetry can never be known. What I have tried to show in this essay is that we are asking the wrong question: rather than trying to excavate what reality literary images of Lesbos and Sappho may or may not refer to, we should explore the reality that representations create. Sappho's poetry, the evolving significance of its context and reception, has shaped her sexuality. The discursive identity of Lesbos, the meaning of this place, was created on the comic stage. The trajectory of Lesbos, from Sappho to Lucian, exemplifies the way that discourse creates sexuality and not the other way around. Lesbians do not come from Lesbos. They come from Athens and from Rome. Lesbians come from literature.

---

54. Dover 1979: 173 attributes the absence of the female homosexual on the comic stage to male anxiety. Plato alludes to female homosexuality when he articulates the notion that homosexuality of any sort is against nature in *Laws* 636b.

55. Perhaps Longus's *Daphnis and Chloe* participates in a related construct of Lesbos, which combines the motifs of heterosexual initiation with a courtesan-figure in a tale set on Lesbos that is saturated with allusions to Sappho's poetry. I hope to consider the role of Lesbos in this text in the near future.

BIBLIOGRAPHY

Adams, J. N. 1982. *The Latin Sexual Vocabulary.* Baltimore.

Barchiesi, Alessandro. 2000. "Rituals in Ink: Horace on Greek Lyric Tradition," in Mary Depew and Dirk Obbink (eds.), *Matrices of Genre: Authors, Canons, and Society,* 47–70. Cambridge, MA.

Beard, Mary and John Henderson. 1997. "With This Body I Thee Worship: Sacred Prostitution in Antiquity." *Gender and History* 9.3: 480–503.

Bowra, Cecil Maurice 1961. *Greek Lyric Poetry.* Oxford.

Brabant, Malcolm. May 1, 2008. BBC News, Athens. "Lesbos Islanders Dispute Gay Name" http://news.bbc.co.uk/2/hi/7376919.stm.

Branham, R. Bracht. 1989. *Unruly Eloquence: Lucian and the Comedy of Traditions.* Cambridge, MA.

Budin, Stephanie. 2008. *The Myth of Sacred Prostitution in Antiquity.* New York.

Campbell, David A. 1967. *Greek Lyric Poetry.* London.

Carson, Anne. 1996. *Eros the Bittersweet: An Essay.* Princeton.

Csapo, Eric. 2004. "The Politics of the New Music," in P. Murray and P. Wilson (eds.), *Music and the Muses: The Culture of Mousike in the Classical Athenian City,* 207–48. Oxford.

Depew, Mary and Dirk Obbink (eds.). 2000. *Matrices of Genre: Authors, Canons, and Society.* Cambridge, MA.

De Simone, Mariella. 2008. "The 'Lesbian' Muse in Tragedy: Euripides Μελοποιος in Aristoph. *RA* 1301–28." *Classical Quarterly* 58: 479–90.

Dobrov, Gregory and Eduardo Urios-Aparisi. 1995. "The Maculate Music: Gender, Genre and the Chiron of Pherekrates," in G. Dobrov (ed.), *Beyond Aristophanes: Transition and Diversity in Greek Comedy,* 139–74. Atlanta.

Dover, Kenneth J. 1978. *Greek Homosexuality.* Cambridge, MA.

———. 1980. *Plato: Symposium.* New York.

Easterling, Pat. 1977. "Literary Tradition and the Transformation of Cupid." *Didaskalos* 5: 247–55.

Edmonds, John Maxwell. 1922. *Lyra Graeca* vol. 1. Loeb vol. 28. Cambridge, MA.

Gentili, Bruno. 1973. "La Ragazza di Lesbo." *Quaderni Urbinati di Cultura Classica* 16: 124–28.

Gerber, D. E. 1970. *Euterpe.* Amsterdam.

Giangrande, G. 1973. "Anacreon and the Lesbian Girl." *Quaderni Urbinati di Cultura Classica* 16: 129–33.

Gilhuly, Kate. 2006. "The Phallic Lesbian: Philosophy, Comedy and Social Inversion in Lucian's *Dialogues of the Courtesans,*" in Christopher A. Faraone and Laura McClure (eds.), *Prostitutes and Courtesans in the Ancient World,* 274–94. Madison.

———. 2007. "Bronze for Gold: Subjectivity in Lucian's *Dialogues of the Courtesans.*" *American Journal of Philology* 128: 59–94.

———. 2009. *The Feminine Matrix of Sex and Gender in Classical Athens.* New York.

———. 2014. "Corinth, Courtesans, and the Politics of Place," in Kate Gilhuly and Nancy Worman (eds.), *Space, Place, and Landscape in Ancient Greek Literature and Culture,* 171–99. New York.

Greene, Ellen (ed.). 1996. *Re-reading Sappho: Reception and Transmission*. Berkeley.

Hall, Edith. 2001. "Female Figures and Metapoetry in Old Comedy," in D. Harvey and J. Wilkins (eds.), *The Rivals of Aristophanes*, 407–18. London.

Hallett, Judith. 1989. "Female Homoeroticism and the Denial of Roman Reality in Latin Literature." *Yale Journal of Criticism* 3.1: 209–27.

Harvey, David. 1996. *Justice, Nature and the Geography of Difference*. Malden, MA.

Henderson, Jeffrey. 1991. *The Maculate Muse: Obscene Language in Attic Comedy*. New York.

———. 2001. "Pherekrates and the Women of Old Comedy," in D. Harvey and J. Wilkins (eds.), *The Rivals of Aristophanes*, 135–50. London.

Henry, W. B. 2007. "Pindaric Accompaniments," in P. J. Finglass, C. Collard, and N. J. Richardson (eds.), *Hesperos: Studies in Ancient Greek Poetry Presented to M. L. West on His Seventieth Birthday*, 126–32. New York.

Jauss, Hans Robert. 1982. *Toward an Aesthetic of Reception*. Trans. Timothy Bahti. Minneapolis.

Jocelyn, H. D. 1980. "A Greek Indecency and Its Students: λαικαζειν." *Proceedings of the Cambridge Philological Society* n.s. 26: 12–66.

Kirkwood, G. M. 1974. *Early Greek Monody*. Ithaca.

Komornicka, Anna M. 1976. "A la suite de la lecture 'La Ragazza di Lesbo.'" *Quaderni Urbinati di Cultura Classica* 21: 37–41.

Kurke, Leslie. 1999. *Coins, Bodies, Games, and Gold: The Politics of Meaning in Archaic Greece*. Princeton.

Lindheim, Sara. 2003. *Mail and Female: Epistolary Narrative and Desire in Ovid's Heroides*. Madison.

Marzullo, B. 1965. *Frammenti della Lirica Greca*. Firenze.

McClure, Laura. 2006. *Courtesans at Table: Gender and Greek Literary Culture in Athenaeus*. New York and London.

Most, Glenn. 1996. "Reflecting Sappho," in E. Greene (ed.), *Re-reading Sappho: Reception and Transmission*, 11–35. Berkeley.

Murray, Penelope and Peter Wilson. 2004. *Music and the Muses: The Culture of Mousike in the Classical Athenian City*. Oxford.

Nagy, Gregory. 1996. *Poetry as Performance: Homer and Beyond*. Cambridge.

Obbink, Dirk. Feb 5, 2014. "New Poems by Sappho." *Times Literary Supplement*. http://www.the-tls.co.uk/tls/public/article1371516.ece.

Parker, L. P. E. 1997. *The Songs of Aristophanes*. Oxford.

Peponi, Anastasia. 2002. "Fantasizing Lyric: Horace Epistles 1.19," in M. Paschalis (ed.), *Horace and Greek Lyric Poetry*, 19–46. Rhethymno.

Peschel, Ingeborg. 1987. *Die Hetäre bei Symposion und Komos in der attisch-rotfigurigen Vasenmalerei des 6.-4. Jahrh. v. Chr.* Frankfurt and New York.

Pfeijffer, Ilja Leonard. 2000. "Playing Ball with Homer: An Interpretation of Anacreon 358 PMG." *Mnemosyne* 53: 164–84.

Prins, Yopie. 1996. "Sappho's Afterlife in Translation," in E. Greene (ed.), *Re-reading Sappho: Reception and Transmission*, 36–67. Berkeley.

Rabe, Hugo. 1906. *Scholia in Lucianum*. Leipzig.

Raymond, Janice. 2001. *A Passion for Friends: Toward a Philosophy of Female Affection.* Melbourne.

Van der Valk, Marchinus. 1974. "On the Composition of Attic Skolia." *Hermes* 102: 1–20.

Wallace, Robert W. 2004. "Damon of Oa: A Music Theorist Ostracized?" in P. Murray and P. Wilson (eds.), *Music and the Muses: The Culture of Mousike in the Classical Athenian City,* 249–68. Oxford.

West, Martin L. 1970. "Melica." *Classical Quarterly* 20: 209.

Winkler, John J. 1990. *The Constraints of Desire: The Anthropology of Sex and Desire in Ancient Greece.* New York.

Yatromanolakis, Dimitrios. 2007. *Sappho in the Making: The Early Reception.* Hellenic Studies 28. Washington, DC.

Young, Elizabeth Marie. Forthcoming. *Translation as Muse: Poetic Translation in Catullus's Rome.* Chicago.

CHAPTER THREE

Pederasty and the Popular Audience[1]

JULIA SHAPIRO

The theory that forensic oratory and comedy illustrate popular contempt for pederasty at Athens, whereas the homoerotics espoused by Plato were confined to elites, has been an influential one.[2] However, recent scholarship has argued against this division of attitudes towards homoerotic relationships along class lines.[3] Scholars are right to see tensions in the sources: the Athenian moral evaluation of pederasty, let alone homoeroticism in general, is complex.[4] While many texts—notably the philosophical works of Plato and Xenophon—speak of male pederastic relationships in glowing terms, these same behaviors appear to come in for abuse and serious disparagement in Greek comedy and oratory.[5] In this chapter I shall attempt to reconcile this seeming

---

1. I would like to thank Sara Forsdyke, David Halperin, Ruby Blondell, Kirk Ormand, and Andrew Lear for their help, insight, and suggestions on this project. All errors are strictly my own.

2. Henderson 1975: 216–17; Hubbard 1998–99; Sissa 1999; Todd 2007: 344; Dover 1978: 149–51.

3. Wohl 2002: 3–29; Davidson 2007: 484–86; Parker 2011: 129–30.

4. Mendelsohn 1996: 1–2, 9; Carnes 2004: 1–10.

5. My focus here is the moral evaluation of formal pederastic courtship. No Classical text suggests that the bare fact of sexual contact with youths, without benefit of a "proper" pederastic relationship, was morally improving for either party; hence the morality of pederasty defined strictly as sex between men and youths is not under debate.

divergence in the Athenian moral reception of pederasty by demonstrating that genres labeled popular and elite, respectively, share criteria by which they morally evaluate a pederastic relationship. The apparent disparity emerges because the abuse in comedy and oratory focuses on homoerotic behavior that goes beyond socially sanctioned forms. When oratorical sources focus on good pederastic conduct, they echo the discourse of philosophical sources. Moreover, orators use good pederastic conduct to portray a man as decent and humane, and mistreatment of the *eromenos* to illustrate an unfeeling and cruel nature, a *topos* which demonstrates that the speaker expects the common audience of jurors to respect and approve of pederastic relationships.

Much of the praise of homoerotic relationships is found in texts written for elite audiences by authors such as Plato, Xenophon, and the author of the pseudo-Demosthenic *Erotikos Logos*. The "legitimate eros" portrayed by the philosophers is that of an *erastes* who is in love with his *eromenos* for his soul, and not solely for his body.[6] His beloved is persuaded to accept this love out of affection and friendship, not for the sake of profit or social advancement.[7] Comedy and oratory, in contrast, which are directed at a popular audience, contain numerous *ad hominem* attacks directed at elite citizens' homoerotic activities (Hubbard 1999). Dover, Henderson, and, most recently, Hubbard, resolve the difficulties inherent in identifying a single Greek opinion on homoerotics by suggesting a discrepancy between approved sexual behavior in texts aimed at popular audiences and those aimed at aristocratic ones. According to this analysis, conflicting evidence on the moral evaluation of pederasty reflects a difference between the poorer classes and the aristocratic men of Athens regarding what sexual practices were acceptable: the lower classes view pederasty as morally wrong, and characteristic of a corrupt aristocracy.

"Proper" pederastic courtship was expensive and time-consuming, which limited active participation to men with sufficient wealth and leisure. The social spaces in which Plato and Xenophon depict it (the gymnasium, the symposium) imply education and leisure.[8] The usual love-offerings required more of the same, for example composing poetry or speeches of praise to the beloved, and wealth, too, since gifts, such as

---

6. Pl. *Symp.* 182e, 183d–e; Xen. *Symp.* 8.17–27, cf. also 8.6–7.

7. Wohl 2002: 4–5; Dover 1978: 44–49; Aeschines 1.132, 2.166; Phdr. 255A–265D; Pl. *Symp.* 181d, 184a–b; Xen. *Symp.* 8.19–24.

8. Gymnasium: Pl. *Phaedr.* 255b-c, *Symp.* 217c; Fisher 2002: 94–95; see also Theogn. 1335–36. Symposium: Xen. *Symp.* 1.2–10.

fighting-cocks or quail, were costly.⁹ However, the desire to participate need not be limited to those who can afford to do so.¹⁰ One popular source condemns excessive spending on youths, but so does an elite source, albeit more gently. Isaeus's speech *On the Estate of Aristarchus,* aimed at a popular audience, treats large expenditures on *paidika* as frivolous and reprehensible. The speaker claims his cousin has wasted his estate on boys, and contrasts his own respectable use of funds to dower his sisters (Isae. 10.25). Xenophon, writing for an elite audience, is more sympathetic to the outlay of large sums towards *paidika,* but still expresses concern about the cost. In the *Oeconomicus,* Xenophon's Socrates lists *paidika* as one of Critoboulos's allegedly ruinous expenses, which also include horse-raising and miscellaneous liturgies. The passage casts him as a wealthy man pursuing the traditional, expensive habits of the Athenian aristocrat, some of them civic necessities and others relatively respectable indulgences (Xen. *Oec.* 2.7). Xenophon takes a decidedly more tolerant tone than Isaeus 10, but both sources reflect concern over such expenditures. Whether an Athenian could afford formal pederastic courtship was not the primary determining factor in his moral judgment of pederasty.

Historians have increasingly challenged the theory that the popular audience felt contempt for the homoerotic practices of their "betters." Though wealthier men would have more opportunities for engaging in this practice, such tastes were not confined to the elite. Rather, Athenians generally assumed that any adult male would see a beautiful youth as sexually desirable.¹¹ As Stuart and Wohl have suggested, those who lacked access to the social environment of pederastic practice nevertheless could share in approbation of *dikaios eros,* and aspire to it,¹² participating in formal pederastic courtship ideologically, if not literally.¹³ These scholars do not suggest that pederasty lacked class inflection, but argue, rather, that Athenians associated pederastic courtship with social elevation. They suggest that the sources treat the sentiments involved in legitimate pederasty as signs of an educated and refined sensibility (an inner quality that need not correspond to an individual's economic circumstances) instead of counting pederasty the sole province of the aristocrat. In other words, Athenians of all classes saw pederasty as "classy."

---

9. Speeches and Poetry: Pl. *Lys.* 204d, *Phaedr.* 227c; Dem. 61.1–3; Dover 1978: 57. Expense: Xen. *Oec.* 2.7; Isae. 10.25; Dover 1978: 92.

10. Dover 1978: 150.

11. Halperin 1990: 93–94; Parker 2011: 129–30.

12. Naturally, there were sexual outlets, such as prostitutes, for those who did not have the leisure time, money, and education to woo an elite *eromenos* (Halperin 1990: 90–94).

13. Stewart 1997: 63–85; Wohl 2002: 3–10.

This is corroborated by the fact that texts directed at popular as well as elite audiences appropriate legitimate pederasty and its symbolic capital for whatever audience the author aims to flatter. To be sure, texts generated for and by wealthier and better educated Athenians do sometimes suggest that poorer Athenians did not share but rather disapproved of the erotic preferences that fired the aristocracy. For example, Plato's Socrates in the *Phaedrus* suggests that a well-bred man of sensitive nature would naturally assume that a conversation about the evils of lovers for beloveds was between low-class people who were unacquainted with the best sort of love.[14] But such statements need not be taken entirely at face value; they can plausibly be explained as an effort to reserve for the elite the common cultural approbation bestowed upon legitimate *eros*.[15]

A forensic text aimed at a popular audience of jurors arrogates proper pederasty to the *demos* in a discursive strategy similar to that of Plato's Socrates in *Phaedrus* when he treats it as the exclusive province of the elite. In Aeschines's *Against Timarchus,* in order to alienate his allegedly prostituted opponent from all decency, Aeschines arrogates legitimate *eros* to his own cause. In doing so, he accuses his opponents of being aristocratic snobs, and claims the decorous pursuit of youths for all free men as a means of shaping the virtue of the young citizen (Aeschin. 1.132–41). Aeschines thus appropriates the symbolic capital of proper pederasty for himself and the nonelite jurors, implying that, as Parker puts it, "pederasty is democratic" (2011: 130). Texts implying that pederastic *eros* was the sole province of the elite are, by contrast, contending for exclusive rights to a set of ideals actually held in common by all Athenians.

Fisher has argued, moreover, that leisure for and access to the social world of pederastic courtship, the symposium and the gymnasium, increased dramatically during the fourth century, suggesting expanded participation in both the practices and the values of these traditional provinces of the elite (1998, 2000). These traditional spaces of pederastic courtship, although hitherto identified as elite, may thus have offered broader access and appeal than used to be recognized. If poorer Athenians both thought pederastic desire a natural impulse for adult males and approved of the *mores* of good pederasty, it becomes harder to say where the limits of participation may have fallen, and what forms that participation may have taken. Given an appetite for legitimate *eros,* poorer Athenians might have adjusted the practice of formal pederastic courtship to their own means and education.

---

14. Pl. *Phaedr.* 243c; cf. Pind. fr. 123.1–10.

15. I borrow the phrase "legitimate *eros*" from Dover (who takes it from Aeschin. 1.136) and use it to refer to appropriate pederastic courtship (Dover 1978: 42–43).

The narrative of the Athenian tyrant-slayers Harmodius and Aristogeiton was a vehicle for the ideology of *dikaios eros*, through which popular and elite audiences demonstrated similar values regarding pederasty, despite unequal access to the costly and time-consuming components of courtship. Both Plato's *Symposium* and Aeschines 1 (*Against Timarchus*) present the *eros* of the culture heroes as (in Wohl's phrase) "socially productive" (Wohl 2002: 4–5). For Pausanias in Plato's *Symposium*, the tyrannicides' steadfast love forged the affections and mind-set that induced them to destroy the tyranny (Pl. *Symp.* 182BC). Aeschines likewise uses the lovers as exemplars of the moral benefits of proper *eros* (1.139–41). The public, democratic mythology of the tyrannicides was also reflected in the visual arts. As Stewart points out, Kritias's over-life-size statue of Harmodius and Aristogeiton in the Agora depicted a beardless Harmodius beside a mature Aristogeiton, making visible their age difference and their eligibility for erotic partnership; by admiring the beautiful and loyal Harmodius, the viewer is invited to identify with Aristogeiton, and to share vicariously in his *eros*; at the same time, the lovers' shared slaying of Hipparchos politicizes their action, demonstrating that their *eros* is, as Plato's Pausanias put it, the foundation of their act of freeing Athens from tyranny and thus the foundation of democracy.[16] The Athenians collectively shared this narrative, regardless of whether each had personal access to the social environs and the wealth necessary for the practice of formal pederasty.

If this line of thinking is correct, however, we are still left with a problem: why do popular genres—comedy and oratory—often ridicule homoerotic behavior, and what does this form of humor signify? The answer, I will suggest, is that popular forms of entertainment do not criticize pederasty *per se*, but rather a particular set of potential misbehaviors within a broadly accepted set of practices. Yet the line between good and bad behavior remained a gray and shifting boundary, due to conflicts inherent in Athenian thought about pederastic relationships. Athenians were ready to see the emotional aspects of *eros* as aiding in the formation of the democratic citizen psyche. But they found it difficult not to conceive of physical gratification—an expected part of such relationships—as a *quid pro quo*, making the entire relationship potentially exploitative and shameful on both sides. This ideological tension colors even the most positive

---

16. Stewart 1997: 70–73. On the role of the Tyrannicides in democratic ideology, see Ober 2003: 215–26 and Raaflaub 2003: 83–89. Apart from Aeschines and Plato, the only other author to describe the tyrannicides' pederastic relationship is Thucydides, who discredits Harmodius's and Aristogeiton's political motive and suggests instead that private sexual jealousy played a larger role (Thuc. 6.54–59). Ober 2003: 221 notes that depoliticization of the Tyrannicides' act was, according to the Aristotelian *Ath. Pol.* (18.5), a version of history espoused by critics of Athenian democracy.

moral evaluations of pederasty, and is also partly responsible for the aforementioned negative evaluations.

Nevertheless, I shall argue that texts aimed at the common Athenian as well as his wealthy or aristocratic counterparts treat pederastic courtship as a means of making a youth better, even if they are deeply ambivalent about how much physical contact could be part of such a relationship without tainting it. Proper pederastic behavior was a *topos* of Athenian popular—as well as aristocratic—moral discourse. Athenian anxieties over pederasty thus represent conflicting ideas within Athenian culture as a whole, not an ideological division along class lines. Comedy and oratory share similar anxieties about immoral erotic behavior, in the form of deceitful lovers and mercenary beloveds, with philosophical works written for educated and wealthy audiences.[17] As a result, in both comedy and oratory an Athenian's conduct in a pederastic relationship becomes a particularly sensitive index of morality.

I shall begin by outlining the problems involved in defining the "popular" audience, in particular the difficulties that arise when an audience of poorer Athenians apparently identifies with the ideology and rhetoric of elites. I then turn to comedy, in order to show that this genre, if more cynical about the existence of "good" pederasty, nevertheless maintains fundamentally the same moral map of erotics as philosophical and oratorical texts. In the final section, on oratory, I show how forensic speakers use proper pederastic conduct to characterize themselves as decent, humane men, while using their opponents' alleged treacherous and unfeeling erotic conduct as indicative of their moral depravity in other spheres as well.

THE POPULAR AUDIENCE

The discussion of "popular morality" in the study of Classical Athens is based on the classification of textual sources according to the audience for whom they were composed. The sources labeled "popular" are those composed for public delivery and designed to win the favor of a socially and economically diverse audience, as in the case of theater, or an audience of poorer citizens, in the case of the courts. These are distinguished from texts aimed at a coterie of readers essentially sympathetic to the author's elitist political perspective, including the historical works of Xenophon and

---

17. Pl. *Symp.* 181d, 184a–b; Xen. *Symp.* 8.19–24; Arist. *Eth. Nic.* 1164a2–8.

Thucydides as well as philosophical texts.[18] Thus classicists have historically defined as "popular" texts that are necessarily a negotiation between an elite producer (since the producers of comedy and oratory, poets and logographers, are themselves members of the elite in education and wealth) and their allegedly popular audience (Forsdyke 2012: 4–9). This phenomenon, combined with the tendency of these "popular" discourses to appropriate elite class narratives, has led some to suggest either that there are no genuinely popular sources extant for Classical Athens, or that there is no popular culture distinct from and independent of the culture of the aristocracy (e.g., Loraux 1986: 180–202). Recent scholarship has also nuanced the sometimes simplistic division between "popular" and "elite" discourses. Thus Forsdyke shows that no discourse is ever purely the narrative of a single class, but that each represents an interaction among class narratives.[19]

The origin of the class-division hypothesis lies in methodology. Dover's *Greek Popular Morality in the Time of Plato and Aristotle* begins with a full articulation of the differentiation between audiences of texts composed for public delivery versus private reading.[20] If we accept this division of genres and texts according to the social class and assumed politics of the intended audience, the case for a split between the sexual morals of the theater-goer and juryman and those of the philosopher appears a strong one.

There are difficulties with this approach, however. First, the category of "elite" is more porous than has sometimes been assumed. If we define "elite" purely in terms of wealth, it appears simple enough to divide the Athenian social world into distinct classes. The most significant economic division in the fourth century divided Athenians into two groups: liturgists and *eisphora*-payers, and those exempt from both forms of taxation.[21]

---

18. Dover 1974: 5–8; Hubbard 2003: 8–9.

19. Forsdyke 2012: 6–12. Having acknowledged the problems inherent in the division of Athenians and their writings into "popular" and "elite," I recognize and use these categories, seeing them as an imperfect but important tool for social historians.

20. Dover 1974: 5–33. Dover builds on Earp 1929: 11–17. Dover's classification system roughly corresponds to Pearson's, whose work divides texts into philosophical texts and all other sources (Pearson 1962: 1–7). While Pearson focuses on fifth-century Athens because he finds the evidence richest for that period and location, Dover chooses fourth-century Athens, and therefore engages more with oratory than his predecessor. Pearson prioritizes drama—especially tragedy, whence the bulk of his evidence is drawn—as a source because of its wide audience; his arguments for its usefulness as an index of Greek popular thought are echoed by Dover and later Ober, who crystallizes the division of discourses, and introduces the term "elite" to classify texts composed for reading, educated, and wealthier audiences, naming Thucydides and Plato as examples (Ober 1989: 43–52).

21. By 358 BCE, the richest 1,200 men (4 percent of the population of citizen males) paid the *eisphora*. In the fourth century, there were approximately 500 liturgies including trierarchies and festival liturgies combined, so at least 500 of these men and probably more were liturgists. The Solonian property classes and their corresponding military divisions were less meaningful in the fourth

The highest economic class, the liturgists, were liable to be called upon by the state to conduct liturgies, that is, to finance and organize state festival expenditures, or to command and pay for the upkeep of a ship of the fleet. The *eisphora* was a lesser financial burden, an annual tax imposed only on the rich, and even then adjusted according to an individual's net worth (Hansen 1991: 110–16). These wealthiest citizens (and metics) had the greatest access to the components of the Athenian "aristocratic lifestyle," which Ober describes as "athletic training and contests, hunting, horse-raising, involvement in homoerotic love affairs, and attendance at exclusive drinking parties (*symposia*)."[22] As this statement suggests, however, aristocratic ideology properly consists of markers of status, not merely economic requirements. Some of these status markers, such as noble birth, did not require financial outlay and could be appropriated by the democracy as a whole.[23] The markers and narratives of the elite lifestyle were not confined to the wealthy, but became a contested source of social credentials.[24] This problematizes the issue of deciding whether the values expressed in any discourse are "popular" or "elite."

Since the principal sources for a positive view of pederasty are Plato's and Xenophon's dialogues on *eros,* the audience for their works is also relevant. Douglas Kelly argues that the small, private groups of well-educated and wealthy men portrayed discussing philosophical topics in Plato and Xenophon are realistic: these are the sort of people by whom, and gatherings at which, such topics were read (usually aloud) and discussed.[25] But their audience may have been broader than is usually assumed. Evidence from Aeschines the Socratic (as distinct from the orator) and Antisthenes shows that philosophical dialogues on *eros* constituted a literary fashion.[26] The audience for philosophical works featuring morally improving pederasty was thus potentially as large as the reading public of Athens, which was defined more by education and interest than by economics.[27] A comic fragment from Alexis (fourth century BCE) suggests at the least

---

century, in the latter decades of which the state funded hoplite training for all (Dem. 21.151–54; Hansen 1991: 110–15).

22. Ober 1989: 250. See further Ober 1989: 248–92.

23. Ober 1989: 248–92, esp. 259–61; Loraux 1986: 174–220; see also Fisher 2002.

24. Loraux 1986: 180–202; Ober 1989: 248–92.

25. Kelly 1996: 151. For further exploration of the problems surrounding Plato's audience, see Blondell 2002: 25–26, 52.

26. Kahn 1994: 87–94, 103–6. Note that, unlike the aristocratic Plato, Aeschines Socraticus was an educated but poor man, who charged for lectures and practiced as a *logographos* to make ends meet (Kahn 1994: 87–89).

27. As Plato's Socrates notes, the books of Anaxagoras may be bought cheaply (a drachma at most) in the agora (Pl. *Apol.* 26d–e; W. Harris 1989: 85n92).

a loose cultural familiarity with such dialogues among Athenians. The play is entitled "Phaedrus," and seems to be a send-up of a philosophical dialogue on *eros*.[28] Of course, the comic audience would not necessarily need to have read Plato's *Phaedrus* or any other dialogue to find the play amusing. Still, the play's existence suggests broad familiarity with the phenomenon of philosophical literature on *eros* (Nails 2002: 249).

Plato and Xenophon set two of their principle dialogues on eros at that most aristocratic and homoerotic of venues, the symposium, but this too appears to have attracted the attention of less wealthy participants. *Kalos*-inscriptions have been found on cheap dinnerware used in the magistrates' dining hall. These remnants bear hand-inscribed (not, it seems, by the potter) *kalos*-inscriptions naming famous beauties similarly honored on red-figure ware of the same period. It is difficult to prove that the diners engaged in the same sort of pederastic practices found at symposia.[29] In her discussion of these inscriptions, Steiner can only speculate as to whether any youths were actually present at the magistrates' mess.[30] Nevertheless, even in this public context, the diners apparently engaged in pederastic discourses similar to those at a private symposium.

I turn now to the audiences of oratory. There was arguably no more "popular" audience at Athens than the mass juries of 501 to 2,501 citizens assigned to judge *graphai*, or public suits, and there is substantial reason to believe that many of these jurors were from the lower classes.[31] Lysias and Demosthenes both depict jurors as dependent on their 3-obol daily wage.[32] References in the Demosthenic corpus to jurors' financial status as *eisphora*-payers can be explained as flattery: jurors did not mind being

---

28. Alexis, *Phaedrus* fr. 247 *PCG* and Hubbard 2003: 114.

29. While Steiner emphasizes the public context of these practices hitherto identified as private and elite, she stops short of positing non-elite practitioners of pederasty. Instead, she identifies the diners who left the deposits as magistrates serving before the reforms of Ephialtes in 462 and 457/6: members of the top two property classes who were elected to their posts (and therefore more likely to be wealthy aristocrats). In reply to those who contest that the deposits are later, Steiner says of the archons chosen by lot who were not necessarily aristocratic, "the newcomers adapted 'up' to an elite standard rather than bringing down dining-room ambiance to less elite levels" (2002: 371, 373–77).

30. She offers the possible presence of young *grammateis* and *hypogrammateis* employed by the magistrates (2002: 358–61). Steiner tentatively identifies a bobbin found at the site as a gift from an *erastes* to an *eromenos;* this is again an intriguing suggestion, but cannot prove that the diners engaged in pederastic courtships at table, as in symposia (2002: 369–70).

31. Hansen 1991: 181–89. For the Aristophanic evidence see Todd 2007: 321–50; Hansen 1991 ibid; Ar. *Vesp.* 290–303; Isoc. 8.130 and 7.54.

32. Dem. 21.182; Lys. 27.1–2; Ober 1989: 143–44. Todd 2007: 335 suggests a jury composed of mainly peasant farmers, who identified with the interests and ideologies of gentleman farmers as well.

counted as more well-to-do than they actually were.³³ Indeed, this exemplifies a willingness to appropriate aspects of elite identity that can be detected elsewhere in oratory. For example, Demosthenes, speaking before a mass jury in 343 BCE, expects jurors to agree with his contempt for tradesmen (Dem. 19.237). Similarly, Demosthenes and Aeschines each rebuke the other for lacking elite education.³⁴ Whatever their actual class status, juries were clearly not above being persuaded to value the status markers of the aristocracy.

Aeschines provides much of the oratorical evidence for pederastic conduct as a measure of morality. His paean to proper homoerotics in *Against Timarchus* (132–59) has led some scholars to propose two audiences for the speech: Aeschines appeals to the populist audience with his lurid and condemnatory account of Timarchus's alleged sexual misadventures, while defending his own social credentials to the wealthier or more aristocratic listeners who approve of properly conducted pederasty. Hubbard suggests that Aeschines's praise of *dikaios eros* was not delivered before the popular audience of *dikastai* (jurors) but added post-delivery to bolster Aeschines's image with the elite readers of his published speeches.³⁵ However, the hypothesis that the jurors would not tolerate such praise of pederasty is the only evidence that prompts and supports this suggestion. Moreover, speeches in Demosthenes and Dinarchus seem to allude to the passages in which Aeschines praises legitimate pederasty, and may therefore corroborate the delivery of the speech in a form very much like the text we have.³⁶ Be that as it may, I shall offer an interpretation of the speech as it stands that takes its popular audience into account.

Aeschines appropriates proper pederastic sensibility for himself and the jurors in *Against Timarchus* in a way that is not simply or strictly elitist. For all the traditional elite values expressed therein, Aeschines frames his apology for proper pederasty as a defense of the refined values and elite credentials of himself and the jurors against the snobbery of his patron-

---

33. Dem. 22.50; Todd 2007: 341–43; Hansen 1991: 181–89.
34. Dem. 18.128, 265; Aeschin. 1.166, 2.113, 147; see Ober 1989: 177–87.
35. Hubbard 1999: 67–68; Sissa 1999: 156–59; *contra* Fisher 2001: 59–60.
36. Aeschin. 1.132ff., rebutting the accusation that Timarchus's unsavory sexual reputation arose from slander because of his beauty, is apparently referred to by Demosthenes (19.233). The scandal of Aristarchus son of Moschus, concerning which Aeschines (1.171, 2.166) portrays Demosthenes as a treacherous and cold *erastes*, is picked up by Dinarchus (1.30, 47). Admittedly, these passages do not echo Aeschines' sentiment about pederasty specifically, but answer or repeat the point made in the passage. It also remains possible that all such references to the passages are post-delivery themselves, and reply to an original post-delivery inclusion by Aeschines, but it is more likely that all parts of the exchange were taken from delivered speeches.

izing opponents. He starts by demonstrating a subtle understanding of the legitimate *eros* of Achilles and Patroclus, thus casting himself and the jurors as equally sophisticated and cultured in the ways of poetry and pederasty:

ἐπειδὴ δὲ Ἀχιλλέως καὶ Πατρόκλου μέμνησθε καὶ Ὁμήρου καὶ ἑτέρων ποιητῶν, ὡς τῶν μὲν δικαστῶν ἀνηκόων παιδείας ὄντων, ὑμεῖς δὲ εὐσχήμονές τινες [προσποιεῖσθε εἶναι] καὶ ὑπερφρονοῦντες ἱστορίᾳ τὸν δῆμον, ἵν' εἰδῆτε ὅτι καὶ ἡμεῖς τι ἤδη ἠκούσαμεν καὶ ἐμάθομεν, λέξομέν τι καὶ ἡμεῖς περὶ τούτων. (Aeschin. 1.141)

But since you make mention of Achilles and Patroclus and Homer and other poets, as if the jurors are ignorant of education/culture, and you are some elegant fellows who despise the people because of your knowledge, in order that you may know that we, too, already listened and learned something, I will say something about these matters, also.

Aeschines does not question the value of *paideia*, but democratizes it, making it a possession of the jurors who represent the *demos*.

He goes on to imply that the jurors are the educated and sophisticated equals of his snobbish and pretentious opponents because of their implied familiarity with the pederastic version of the myth:[37]

ἐκεῖνος γὰρ πολλαχοῦ μεμνημένος περὶ Πατρόκλου καὶ Ἀχιλλέως, τὸν μὲν ἔρωτα καὶ τὴν ἐπωνυμίαν αὐτῶν τῆς φιλίας ἀποκρύπτεται, ἡγούμενος τὰς τῆς εὐνοίας ὑπερβολὰς καταφανεῖς εἶναι τοῖς πεπαιδευμένοις τῶν ἀκροατῶν. (Aeschin. 1.142)

For that great poet, although he mentions Patroclus and Achilles many times, conceals their *eros* and the proper name of their affection, considering that the excesses of favor were manifestly evident to the educated among the hearers.

---

37. Homer was performed regularly at the Greater Panathenaia (Nagy 1999). Aeschines casts familiarity with Homeric poetry as the attainment of an educated man, but in doing so, he sets criteria for *paideia* which most citizens could meet, and thus further democratizes *paideia*. The jurors might also have been familiar with Aeschylos's *Myrmidons*. We do not know whether *Myrmidons* specifically was ever produced after its debut, but from 386 BCE on (based on evidence from inscriptions) an old tragedy was performed regularly at the City Dionysia in addition to the new ones, and if anyone was willing to produce a play of Aeschylus, he was given the slot to perform it (Pickard-Cambridge 1968: 72, 86, 99–100; Philostr. *Vit. Apoll.* vi. II, *Vit. Aesch.* 12).

He uses the story to provide an opportunity for the jurors and the *demos* as a whole to participate in the virtue-production and social credentials of legitimate *eros*, suggesting that they would have embraced ideologically a practice to which full access depended on wealth, leisure, and education.

The approach adopted by Aeschines in these passages in praise of proper pederasty is in keeping with the attitudes conveyed by his speeches as a whole. Aeschines's social background was modest for a *rhetor*, and justifying his elite political status is an integral part of his self-fashioning throughout his extant works (E. Harris 1995: 21–40). For this reason, he habitually appropriates traditional aristocratic sources of social credentials—*paideia*, poetry, gymnastics and the gymnastically developed body, as well as legitimate pederasty—for himself, his adherents, and the jurors,[38] while depicting his high-born and/or wealthier rivals as failures in these spheres of elite attainment.[39] This agenda increases the difficulty inherent in detecting distinctly "popular" or "elitist" sections in his speeches.

As a defense against a charge of attempted murder, Lysias 3 (*Against Simon*) was heard and judged by the Areopagus (Carey 1989: 109). Since I shall be discussing aspects of the speech in some detail, it is necessary to determine the popular credentials of the judges who heard that case. Up until the early fifth century, the Areopagus was a stronghold of oligarchical sentiment. During the early fifth century, moreover, the Areopagus was composed of ex-archons who had gained their posts by election, and the social composition and politics of the council favored the aristocracy. After the reforms of 458 the archons were chosen by lot, however, resulting inevitably in a shift in the makeup of the court. By the time Lysias 3 was delivered (no earlier than 394 BCE), the class composition of the Areopagites had become, according to Hansen, "a normal cross-section of the Athenian citizen male population over thirty" (1991: 289).[40] A speech addressed to such Areopagites should therefore be a credible source for Athenian popular morality.

Finally, the dramatic audience also has a claim to the title "popular," yet they too were willing to hear elitist narratives in addition to anti-elite invective. There is no known distinction between the audience for tragedies and that of comedies. The Theater of Dionysus seated as many as 14,000 people, the majority of whom were citizen males (Goldhill 1997: 57–60). There is reason to believe that the dramatic audience was, on average, better-off

---

38. For his adherents see Aeschin. 2. 147–51.
39. Aeschines' self-fashioning: Education: 1.141, 1.166–69, 2.153, 3.117, 3.130. Poetry: 1.141–52, 3.134–35. Gymnastics and the gymnastically honed body: 1.26, 2.147, 149, 151; 3.255. Pederasty: 1.136–67, 1.138–42, 1.158–59, 1.166–69, 2.166, 3.255.
40. See also n. 28 above.

than the jurors. The theater was unique among civic institutions in that there was a fee for admission, albeit a small one (2 obols). Sommerstein argues for a wealthier and more elite comic audience, especially before the institution of the *theorikon* stipend in the mid-fourth century.[41] Nevertheless, even in this period, the majority of the theater seats were filled with non-elites (Ober 1989: 128).

Producers and playwrights were competing to win at the Greater Dionysia, and the judges were believed to be influenced by the audience's reception of the play.[42] Yet this audience was not averse to legitimate pederasty in the right genre. Athenians watched a depiction of such a relationship between Achilles and Patroclus in Aeschylus's *Myrmidons;* it was probably sympathetic to the lovers, since Achilles and Patroclus are an exemplary couple for both Aeschines and Plato.[43] They also watched Euripides' *Chrysippus,* which told the story of a pederastic rape and the punishment of the rapist, Laius. This is certainly a negative depiction of pederastic desire.[44] However, the plot (as far as we know) showed poor pederastic behavior punished, and thus does not constitute a condemnation of correct pederastic behavior.[45]

In sum, the Athenian audiences regularly defined as "popular," the courts and the dramatic audience, may justifiably be considered to represent the prevailing moral opinions of the common (citizen) man at Athens. However, these same common citizens were apparently ready to hear themselves described using narratives traditionally identified as elite. This affinity suggests that the audiences addressed by Aeschines, Demosthenes, and Lysias, as well as the dramatists, would have embraced ideologically a practice that required significant financial and time commitments, as well as education, to carry out its rituals as we know them. Although the formal pederastic courtship described in Plato and Xenophon required wealth and leisure, poorer Athenians aspirationally participated in the ideological framework of *dikaios eros,* "legitimate eros."

---

41. This would place the comedies of Aristophanes and their mockery of homoerotics within the period when the comic audience was at its most exclusive. Cf. Hansen 1991: 98; Sommerstein 1997: 66.

42. Sommerstein 1997: 63, esp. n. 2; Pl. *Leg.* 659a–b; Ar. *Eq.* 546–50, Ar. *Av.* 445–46, Ar. *Eccl.* 1141–42.

43. For Achilles and Patroclus as a model couple: Aeschin. 1.133, 142–50; Pl. *Symp.* 179c–80b. On *Myrmidons* see also Hubbard 2006: 239.

44. Hubbard 2006: 223–31 sees this as a sign of changing attitudes towards homoeroticism in the late fifth century.

45. Hubbard 2006: 227, 238. Hubbard argues that Laius was not portrayed as wholly evil, even if his crime was abhorrent to the audience. At the same time, Laius was, according to a scholium to Eur. *Phoen.,* the world's first pederast, in which case he sets a grim moral precedent.

DIKAIOS EROS, FAITHLESS LOVERS, AND MERCENARY BELOVEDS: COMEDY

Aristophanic comedy presents sexual desire for youths as normal for adult males. Despite comic invective like that directed against one Misgolas's predilection for beautiful young cithara-players, other evidence suggests that such appetites were expected of any man, regardless of social class.[46] In Aristophanes' *Clouds,* for example, the pleasures that Wrong Argument promises Pheidippides include "youths, women, drinking games (*kottabos*), delicacies, big laughs" (Ar. *Nub.* 1073). In his menu of options, Wrong Argument lists youths on a par with women as pleasing objects for sexual consumption.[47] Right Argument, who would have the boy groomed as an object of sexual desire, cannot compete (Ar. *Nub.* 960–1025). Similarly, Philokleon, the elderly and decidedly unaristocratic juror in *Wasps,* considers it one of the many privileges of the jurors to ogle boys' genitals when they stand for examination at their *dokimasia.*[48] Such passages imply that the fundamental desire to take advantage of youths' sexual availability is shared by all males, regardless of class. Leaving aside the propriety of the characters' behavior, comic invective about homoerotics is not rooted in opprobrium for an adult male's sexual appetite for youths, like the appetite assumed in normative pederasty.

Comedy is the genre least delicate and respecting of "legitimate *eros,*" the most eager and willing to conflate it with its evil opposite.[49] Comedy expresses exaggerated doubts about the idea of anyone practicing correct pederasty, suspecting all alike of the coarsest motives.[50] Certain passages, in particular, have been interpreted as condemning components of proper pederasty in order to cater to the tastes of the popular audience. I shall

---

46. Hubbard 1999: 52, 71; Fisher 2002: 170–72; Dover 1978: 73–74; Alexis fr. 3 *PCG*; Antiphanes fr. 27.12–18 *PCG;* and Timocles fr. 32 *PCG*. Misgolas is named as the first lover of Timarchus in Aeschines' *Against Timarchus,* and Aeschines' description of him appears to draw on his reputation in comedy (Aeschin. 1.41–42).

47. Pheidippides has crafted an aristocratic *persona,* wearing his hair long, to match his expensive equestrian pursuits (Ar. *Nub.* 14–18). If one accepts a class division in Athenian sexual culture, one might explain that Wrong Argument offers a long-haired, horse-crazy lad love-objects to match his social aspirations. However, this joke more likely depends on the choice between the two Arguments being obvious for any youth looking to enjoy himself. It is easier to read the list of fun as costly things whose appeal is nevertheless broad.

48. Ar. *Vesp.* 578; Parker 2011: 129–30.

49. Hubbard 1999: 50–55 and 2003: 86–89; contra Dover 1978: 138. Hubbard's account is convincing and philologically thorough; I offer here a refinement to his picture of popular contempt for pederasty in comedy and oratory.

50. Comic exaggeration: Parker 2011: 129–30 and cf. Arist. *Poet.* 1448a.

argue, however, that this genre uses the same criteria for the moral evaluation of pederasty as the texts most hospitable to that practice; it does not find pederasty reprehensible in itself, or in every form.

Let us consider the aspects of pederasty that comedy does criticize. Comic and philosophical texts share the same suspicion of the lecherous *erastes*. The speaker in the following fragment of Amphis (from the fourth century BCE) is cynical about the existence of a good lover, one who actually loves the boy's character:

τί φής; σὺ ταυτὶ προσδοκᾷς πείσειν ἐμέ,
ὡς ἔστ' ἐραστής, ὅστις ὡραῖον φιλῶν
τρόπων ἐραστής ἐστι, τὴν ὄψιν παρείς;
ἄφρων γ' ἀληθῶς. οὔτε τοῦτο πείθομαι,
οὔθ' ὡς πένης ἄνθρωπος ἐνοχλῶν πολλάκις
τοῖς εὐποροῦσιν οὐ λαβεῖν τι βούλεται.
(Amphis fr. 15 *PCG*)

What are you saying? Do you really think that you will persuade me of
    this,
that there exists a lover, who, although he is fond of youthful beauty,
is a lover of [sc. boys'] characters and disregards appearance?
You are, indeed, truly witless. I am persuaded neither of this,
nor that a poor man, when he often makes a pest of himself to the rich,
doesn't want to get something.

This comic character's doubt that any *erastes* has the right motives has been interpreted as a reflection of the comic audience's general condemnation of all *erastai* (see Hubbard 1999: 50–55). However, the fragment uses the same moral distinctions as those found in philosophical condemnations of the bad lover, and assumes the same moral poles of reference as do texts for elite consumption. Amphis's speaker does not say that the lover of the boy's character would be morally reprehensible; he denies that there is genuinely such a one. Both Plato and Xenophon define the good *erastes* as one who loves the soul of the boy above his body, in contrast to the wicked *erastes* who prizes physical gratification alone.[51] The comic speaker exhibits a similar moral map.

Comic texts also echo philosophical anxieties about the mercenary *ero-*

---

51. Pl. *Symp*. 183e, cf. Xen. *Symp*. 8.23–28. Plato's Pausanias claims that it is praiseworthy to love καὶ μάλιστα τῶν γενναιοτάτων καὶ ἀρίστων, κἂν αἰσχίους ἄλλων ὦσι, "most of all those who are noblest and most virtuous, even if they are uglier than others" (Pl. *Symp*. 182d).

menos, who gratifies his lover for the sake of profit, as in this conversation between Carion and Chremylos in Aristophanes' *Wealth*:

ΧΡΗΜΥΛΟΣ: καὶ τάς γ' ἑταίρας φασὶ τὰς Κορινθίας,
ὅταν μὲν αὐτάς τις πένης πειρῶν τύχῃ,
οὐδὲ προσέχειν τὸν νοῦν, ἐὰν δὲ πλούσιος,
τὸν πρωκτὸν αὐτὰς εὐθὺς ὡς τοῦτον τρέπειν.
ΚΑΡΙΩΝ: καὶ τούς γε παῖδάς φασι ταὐτὸ τοῦτο δρᾶν,
οὐ τῶν ἐραστῶν ἀλλὰ τἀργυρίου χάριν.
ΧΡ: οὐ τούς γε χρηστούς, ἀλλὰ τοὺς πόρνους· ἐπεὶ
αἰτοῦσιν οὐκ ἀργύριον οἱ χρηστοί.
ΚΑ: τί δαί;
ΧΡ: ὁ μὲν ἵππον ἀγαθόν, ὁ δὲ κύνας θηρευτικάς.
ΚΑ: αἰσχυνόμενοι γὰρ ἀργύριον αἰτεῖν ἴσως
ὀνόματι περιπέττουσι τὴν μοχθηρίαν.
(Ar. *Plut.* 149–59)

CHREMYLOS: And they say the Corinthian hetairai, at any rate,
Whenever some poor man happens to come on to them,
they don't even pay attention, but if the man is rich,
right away they turn their butts toward him.
CARION: And in fact they say that boys do this same thing,
not for the sake of their lovers but for money.
CHR: Not the good boys, but the whores,
since the good boys don't ask for money.
CA: What then?
CHR: One asks for a good horse, another for hunting dogs, . . .
CA: Perhaps because they are ashamed to ask for money:
in name, they hide their wickedness.

This passage has been used to show that the comic audience would view elite *eromenoi* as the functional equivalent of prostitutes.[52] However, Carion's cynical response that all boys yield for the sake of gifts, just like courtesans, is not a condemnation of the "good boys," who "yield for the sake

---

52. Hubbard 1999: 51–53, 64; Dover 1978: 145–46. The designation "whore" does not here indicate literal prostitution, but is a slur against mercenary *eromenoi* (Fisher 2002: 56–57; cf. Aeschin. 1.74–76 in which Aeschines attempts to collapse the two uses). This passage in *Wealth* has also been interpreted as a debunking of aristocratic ideology. The characters are revealing elite gift-exchange as no different from or better than exchange of coin. (On gift-exchange in aristocratic ideology, see further Kurke 1999: 41–60, 178–99.)

of their lovers." As with Amphis's comic cynicism about the existence of the virtuous lover, it displays a comic skepticism about the possibility that such an *eromenos* exists. Carion's and Chremylos's exchange suggests that an *eromenos* accepting gifts in the context of formal courtship is (superficially) respectable, but vulnerable to the criticism of being a greedy—which is to say bad—*eromenos*. Aristophanes' moral distinctions between good and mercenary *eromenoi* are thus the same as those drawn by Plato and Xenophon.

In Aristophanes' *Birds,* the unaristocratic Euelpides envisions his ideal city as one in which fathers would willingly allow him sexual access to their sons.

> ὅπου ξυναντῶν μοι ταδί τις μέμψεται
> ὥσπερ ἀδικηθεὶς παιδὸς ὡραίου πατήρ·
> καλῶς γέ μου τὸν υἱόν, ὦ Στιλβωνίδη,
> εὑρὼν ἀπιόντ' ἀπὸ γυμνασίου λελουμένον
> οὐκ ἔκυσας, οὐ προσεῖπας, οὐ προσηγάγου,
> οὐκ ὠρχιπέδισας, ὢν ἐμοὶ πατρικὸς φίλος.
> (Ar. *Av.* 137–42)

> Where when some father of a youth in his bloom, when he meets me,
> reproaches me like a man wronged: "Oh, just charming, Stilbonides,
> how when you find my son, bathed and coming back from the gymnasium,
> you didn't kiss him, greet him, embrace him,
> grab his testicles—and you a friend of the family."[53]

Scholars have argued that this passage illustrates the popular audience's general hostility to pederasty, since it implies that the father would ordinarily keep Euelpides away from his son.[54] But the joke only requires that real-life fathers would be expected to discourage the kind of advances described, not all kinds of overtures from all *erastai*. If fathers guard male children from unsupervised sexual advances, this no more indicates general

---

53. Note that the character's name is Euelpides, not Stilbonides. The verb στίλβω means, "to glitter, gleam"; the name is unattested at Athens, although other names from the στιλβ- root are. The point of the name is most likely that in his fantasy, Euelpides is addressed with a name meaning he is sleek with oil, a gymnasticized and aristocratized desirable suitor. Euelpides imagines himself as receiving a social promotion in his ideal city, even if only in the eyes of this theoretical neighbor (Dunbar 1995: 178; see also Dover 1978: 136–37).

54. Hubbard 1999: 54–55. For the role of a boy's father as a guardian of his virtue from the wrong kind of pederastic attentions see Pl. *Symp.* 183cd; Xen. *Symp.* 8.10–11.

disapproval of pederasty and pederastic desires than fathers' guarding their daughters from similar advances shows broad condemnation of hetero-erotic behavior and proclivities.⁵⁵ The behavior Euelpides desires is obviously improper, exemplifying the "sexual opportunism" characteristic of the comic stage (Dover 1978: 139). As such it belongs to Euelpides' fantasy utopia, in which "bad" pederastic conduct will win him even more praise from the lad's father (and access to the lad himself) than appropriate pederasty could ever do.

As these passages illustrate, comic characters are as a rule not proper pederasts but sexual opportunists. An exception to this rule is found in the parabasis of *Wasps*, where the chorus claim that the poet never took advantage of the sexual perks his fame might afford:

ἀρθεὶς δὲ μέγας καὶ τιμηθεὶς ὡς οὐδεὶς πώποτ' ἐν ὑμῖν,
οὐκ †ἐκτελέσαιt φησὶν ἐπαρθείς, οὐδ' ὀγκῶσαι τὸ φρόνημα,
οὐδὲ παλαίστρας περικωμάζειν πειρῶν· οὐδ,' εἴ τις ἐραστὴς
κωμῳδεῖσθαι παιδίχ' ἑαυτοῦ μισῶν ἔσπευσε πρὸς αὐτόν,
οὐδενὶ πώποτέ φησι πιθέσθαι, γνώμην τιν' ἔχων ἐπιεικῆ,
ἵνα τὰς μούσας αἷσιν χρῆται μὴ παραγωγοὺς ἀποφήνῃ.
(Ar. *Vesp.*1023–28)

And he says that when he became famous and honored as no poet ever was among you, he did not end up conceited, nor did he puff up his pride,
nor did he go about the wrestling-grounds making sexual advances. And, if some
lover was after him to lampoon his boyfriend, out of spite after a lovers' quarrel,
he says he never ever obeyed any of them, because he has a certain fair-minded
understanding, in order that he not make the muses with whom he deals into procuresses.

Some have interpreted this passage as the poet's personal denial of any pederastic practice, because his audience looked down on this as an objectionable, elite custom.⁵⁶ A simpler interpretation would be that Aristophanes is

---

55. I thank Kirk Ormand for this excellent point.
56. Hubbard 1999: 50–55. For the suggestion that Aristophanes is contrasting his own behavior with that of his rival Eupolis in a running gag, see Davidson 2007: 471 and 580n11. See also Ar. *Pax* 762–64.

dissociating himself from conduct ill-befitting a good *erastes*, and aiding or abetting such conduct in another, because his audience will consider that decent, genteel behavior in pederasty is praiseworthy.

In this passage, Aristophanes denies two separate species of erotic misbehavior. First, he suggests that he refrained from cheap conquests over youths who are themselves morally suspect for hoping to capitalize on his fame. This accords with philosophical texts condemning both lovers who make promises of advancement in hopes of taking advantage sexually, and youths who are attracted by wealth or hope of advancement (e.g., Pl. *Symp.* 183e–84e).[57] But the word περικωμάζω suggests another possibility: the poet is denying that he has become a species of athletics-pest.[58] As we shall see, Aeschines in *Against Timarchus* claims that his opponents will accuse him of making a nuisance of himself at the gymnasium with boorish and coarse innuendo; the poet here distances himself from such behavior. Second, Aristophanes says that he has never selected his targets for invective at the behest of a spiteful lover.[59] The primary purpose of the passage is to assert that the poet's mockery is always genuine and deserved. It is a claim for the purity of Aristophanes' poetic motives. There is no sign that he is distancing himself from the spiteful lover's pederasty as such, as opposed to that lover's bile against his (former) beloved. This is consistent with Plato's and Xenophon's version of pederastic morality.

Comedy is also well known for its repeated condemnation of the *eromenos* who allows himself to be physically penetrated, particularly after he has attained adulthood—the very opposite of "proper" sexual behavior. The comic *topos* that all politicians are "wide-arsed" appears frequently.[60] For example, the Sausage-seller in Aristophanes' *Knights* suggests that the Cleon-figure Paphlagon was moved by fear to strike the buggered from the citizen lists, lest they become serious rivals as politicians.[61] The implication

---

57. For condemnation of the man who tempts *eromenoi* with advancement, see Demosthenes' specious offer of political preeminence to his would-be lover Aristarchus at Aeschin. 1.171–72.

58. The verb κωμάζω is used of people parading in festival processions, but can also mean to conduct oneself as in a *komos,* a disorderly revel (*LSJ*, s.v. κωμάζω; cf. Dem. 19.287. For the sense "disorderly revelry" see Isae. 3.14).

59. We have two examples of this kind of *ad hominem* comic mockery of youths. Aeschines recounts a comedy, apparently performed after Timarchus was an adult, in which there appeared, in Fisher's words, "big Timarchean whores" (Aeschin. 1.157; Fisher 2002: 57), and Eupolis produced a comedy entitled "Autolykos" in 421, featuring the young beloved of Kallias in Xen. *Symp.* with the nickname *Eutresios,* which appears to mean that he works well as a vagina (Eupolis fr. 56 and Dover 1978: 147).

60. For an alternate interpretation of comic abuse, see Worman, chapter 4, in this volume.

61. For politicians specifically as εὐρύπρωκτος, see Ar. *Nub.* 1088–94.

is that the shamelessness required for freely (and perhaps indiscriminately?) allowing oneself to be the object of penetration is excellent preparation for a politician's shameless pandering to the people.[62] It is not obvious from the *Knights* whether the fault of the successful politician is enjoying penetration or selling himself, but oratorical evidence suggests that the latter was the more frequent accusation.[63] As Halperin puts it, by yielding his bodily integrity for money, the prostitute "indicated by that gesture that his autonomy was for sale to whoever wished to buy it" (1990: 97). Such men are dangerous as politicians, because they have shown that their loyalties can be bought, and they cannot be trusted to speak only in the interests of the city.[64] The figure of the prostitute politician is a reverse image of the good *eromenos*: he is trained by men who make him worse for their own benefit, not by men who make him better out of affection.

If one assumes that pederasty is a practice confined to those in the elite social strata from which political leaders came, then the theme of the buggered and/or prostitute politician may seem to reflect the common man's resentful perspective on a pederastic practice confined to elites (Ober 1989: 112–18). Characterizing elites as immoral because of improper sexual behavior is indeed a theme of anti-aristocratic sentiment, in both comedy and oratory.[65] But condemnation of aristocrats for homoerotic misbehavior should not be assimilated to a blanket condemnation of all homoerotic (and specifically pederastic) behavior. Moreover, the scare-figure of the prostitute politician is hardly elite; it is his very lack of traditional aristocratic qualities that gives him the boldness and agora-savvy which allow him to beat out "better" men.[66] In comedy, it is whores of the lowest origin who are the most successful in wooing the *demos* (Ar. *Eq*. 735–40). This comic inversion of the political, tyrant-slaying *eros* of Harmodius and Aristogeiton, hymned by Aeschines and Plato's Pausanias, provides a complementary picture of reprehensible *eros* that helps to create and define the norms of praiseworthy *eros*.[67]

---

62. For this same *topos*, see Ar. *Eq*. 423–28, 876–80, 1241–45.

63. Aeschin. 1, Andoc. *De Myst*. 100, Dem. 22.57–58. There is no evidence for any legal procedure restricting the rights of men who engaged in sex as the penetrated party, unless they took money for doing so. The *dokimasia rhetoron*, such as that which Aeschines brought against Timarchus, would only apply to an alleged prostitute who later spoke in the assembly, and the punishment was *atimia* (see also Winkler 1990: 186–87).

64. See Worman, chapter 4, in this volume.

65. Cf. Dem. 54.17, and Comica Adesp. fr. 12K-A: οὐδεὶς κομήτης ὅστις οὐ ψηνίζεται, "There's no long-hair who isn't buggered" (see Dover 1978: 142; Hubbard 1999: 53).

66. Ar. *Eq*. 180–81; see also 735–40, and Worman, chapter 4, in this volume.

67. Aeschin. 1.132, 140; Pl. *Symp*. 182c–d.

EROTIC CONDUCT AS A MEASURE OF MORALITY IN ORATORY

Athenian oratory of the late fifth and early fourth centuries contains some of the sternest condemnations of homoerotic behavior. Moreover, these condemnations are often embedded in anti-elite invective against adult men who are engaging in pederastic relationships (or same-sex sex generally).[68] This combination makes oratory the strongest potential evidence for the hypothesis that popular audiences at Athens scorned the pederastic practice of aristocrats. I shall argue, however, that an alternative explanation is more plausible. The charge leveled by such invective is not that one's opponent practices legitimate pederasty, but that he does not: his actions discredit him because they depart from acceptable homoerotic behavior. As several passages from forensic oratory suggest, litigants expect the mass audiences of jurors to treat pederastic conduct as a measure of a man's moral character.

I begin with Aeschines' court battles with Demosthenes. When Aeschines brought a preemptory prosecution against Timarchus for allegedly speaking in front of the assembly after acting as a prostitute,[69] he contrasted his own legitimate erotic practice and the superior character it indicates with the indecent and hubristic sexual conduct and morals of his rival. In the course of this prosecution, Aeschines claims that his opponents will accuse him of improper erotic conduct, namely making a nuisance of himself at the gymnasium by writing lecherous, suggestive poetry to his many *eromenoi* and getting into fistfights (Aeschin. 1.135).[70] In response, he defends the propriety of his own behavior, and stakes his claim to the good moral character it indicates, in contrast to the alleged grotesque behavior and violence of his opponent:

ὁρίζομαι δ' εἶναι τὸ μὲν ἐρᾶν τῶν καλῶν καὶ σωφρόνων φιλανθρώ-
που πάθος καὶ εὐγνώμονος ψυχῆς, τὸ δὲ ἀσελγαίνειν ἀργυρίου τινὰ

---

68. Aeschin. 1.41–50, 64–71, 131; Dem. 54. 16–17; see Hubbard 1999: 59–69.

69. Aeschines capitalizes on the word *pornos,* which could be used as a literal term for a professional prostitute and a slur for a too-easy or mercenary *eromenos* (cf. Aeschin. 1.74–76).

70. It is not entirely clear what about Aeschines' behavior at the gymnasium is inappropriate. Since, immediately following this passage, he owns with pride to being frequently in love, and even getting into fistfights, there cannot be anything too deeply inexcusable in these practices *per se.* The only thing Aeschines denies is the lascivious character of some of his poetry to youths, which the defense has threatened to read aloud: he refuses the implication that he is the sort of lover who wants mere sex from his *eromenoi.* I suggest therefore that Aeschines' alleged gymnasium offenses consist of indiscriminate and coarsely sexual overtures, a crime consistent with overly suggestive poetry.

μισθούμενον ὑβριστοῦ καὶ ἀπαιδεύτου ἀνδρὸς ἔργον εἶναι. (Aeschin. 1.137)

I make the distinction that loving the beautiful and chaste is the condition of a humane and reasonable soul, but acting licentiously because one is hired for money is the deed of a violent and uncultured man.

In this passage, Aeschines annexes for himself legitimate *eros* and the superior moral character it shows, reversing the anticipated attack on his pederastic habits. He describes a contest between defense and prosecution for ownership of legitimate *eros*, with each side attempting to tar the erotic practice of the other.[71] This would not be an effective strategy for either litigant before a mass audience of relatively poor Athenians if they did not approve of proper pederasty, or thought of pederasty as inherently improper.[72]

A similar strategy is adopted by the speaker in Lysias 3 (*Against Simon*), who is defending himself in front of the Areopagus against a charge of attempted murder in a fight over a Plataean youth named Theodotus.[73] The speaker measures his own and his opponent Simon's conduct by the standards of proper pederasty, because he hopes that the jurors will be more sympathetic to him as an affectionate pederastic lover and consider a fight over a *paidika* something to be settled outside of court.[74] He claims the moral high ground by portraying himself as an affectionate *erastes*, while casting Simon as brutal to their common love interest.

Theodotus's precise status is hard to identify.[75] He is never explicitly called an *eromenos*, but he is not called a *pornos*, either.[76] It is possible that he is a slave, but the evidence here is unclear.[77] If he is a slave, then he is

---

71. Cf. Dem.19.233; Aeschin. 1.126, 132–34, 136.

72. For a discussion of the hypothesis that the pro-pederastic passages in the works of Aeschines are included for the elite, reading audience and separate from the delivered speeches, see above.

73. On the non-elite status of the Areopagites at this period, see above.

74. For the term *paidika* meaning *eromenos*, see Dover 1978: 16.

75. The speaker's reticence in identifying Theodotus's status is very different from Lysias 4, in which the speaker expresses outrage at being brought into such a serious lawsuit over his slave (Lys. 4.19). I thank Kirk Ormand for drawing my attention to the difficulties in identifying the status of Theodotus.

76. The closest the speaker comes to such pejorative language is when he indirectly refers to Theodotus as τὸν ἑταιρήσοντα, when speaking as if from Simon's perspective (Lys. 3.24). For the distinction between ἑταιρεῖν and πορνεύεσθαι, see Aeschin. 1.51; Carey 1989: 104.

77. The point hinges on whether or not he should be identified with a certain παιδίον or "child" to whom the speaker refers (τοῦτό ... τὸ παιδίον, Lys. 3.33), and who is liable to being made to give evidence under torture. Since we have not heard of any other young individual, it is

no proper *eromenos,* and probably a prostitute of some variety. Even if he is not a slave, however, the possibility that he is a citizen should not deter us from counting him a sex worker. There was no law preventing a male Athenian citizen from acting as a prostitute, though there were legal restrictions placed on him if he did.[78] There is thus nothing to prevent Theodotus from being both a free-born Athenian and a prostitute.[79] Granted, the speaker denies Simon's claim to have a contract with Theodotus. He does so, however, not by defending the youth's honor, but on the basis of Simon's finances (Lys. 3.22–25). In other words, he tacitly acknowledges that Theodotus's role is not that of a decent *eromenos.*

There is, then, no scenario on which Theodotus is an *eromenos* in a regular pederastic relationship. He is at best a lad who has gone to live with his lover (a scandalous arrangement for an *eromenos*) and at worst under contract as a prostitute of sorts.[80] Nevertheless, the speaker's picture of the relationship is painted over with the gloss of legitimate *eros.* Thus he claims that he himself attempted to gratify his love-object, while Simon treated the youth with *hubris* (Lys. 3.5):

ἡμεῖς γὰρ ἐπεθυμήσαμεν, ὦ βουλή, Θεοδότου, Πλαταικοῦ μειρακίου, καὶ ἐγὼ μὲν εὖ ποιῶν αὐτὸν ἠξίουν εἶναί μοι φίλον, οὗτος δὲ ὑβρίζων καὶ παρανομῶν ᾤετο ἀναγκάσειν αὐτὸν ποιεῖν ὅ τι βούλοιτο.

For we both desired, council, a Plataean youth, and I for my part by treating him well considered that I would make him a friend to me, but this man, by treating him with outrage and lawlessness, thought that he would compel him to do whatever he wanted.

---

natural to think that τοῦτο refers to Theodotus, and conclude, as Carey does, that he is present in the court. However, the demonstrative could also mean that the speaker is pointing to another person, a slave present in the court. Hubbard suggests that the παιδίον is not Theodotus, but another person who could also act as a witness (Hubbard 2003: 124n14). He points out other evidence against Theodotus's being a slave: the speaker seems to believe Theodotus legally competent to make a contract with Simon, and Theodotus is called Plataean (Lys. 3.5, 22–25). On Theodotus's contract, see Lys. 3.22–25; Carey 1989: 87, 102–3, 107n33. Plataeans who escaped the razing of their city by the Spartans in 427 BCE were granted Athenian citizenship; Carey supposes that Theodotus's father was a Plataean yet not in this category (1989: 87).

78. These amounted to exclusion from participation in the democracy, such as speaking in the assembly. See Aeschin. 1. 19–20, 26–32; Dem. 45.79, Dem. 22.30–31; Fisher 2001: 39–40; Halperin 1990: 90–91, 94–95, 98–99.

79. If Theodotus is truly a paid sex worker, no pimp is mentioned, nor is an owner (Carey 1989: 90).

80. On Theodotus's cohabitation with the speaker or Simon: Lysias 3.10, 24, and Aeschin. 1.51 for cohabitation as a feature of τὸν ἑταιρήσοντα (Lys. 3.24). On the impropriety of a youth living with his lover: Aeschin. 1.42, 75.

The speaker casts his own actions toward Theodotus in the guise of those of a proper pederastic lover,[81] and Simon as pressing a violent and unwelcome suit. When Simon and company attempt to snatch Theodotus from a fuller's shop where he has taken refuge from them, the speaker comes to his defense in a rescue that imitates the valor generated by legitimate *eros*.[82] There is no way to detect that Theodotus is a paid prostitute until approximately halfway into the speech (Lys. 3.22–24). It is only now, when the speaker is retelling his version of Simon's case, that he even mentions anything as sordid as a contract. The speaker's version of Simon's case is decidedly unromantic: he claims Simon will argue that he paid three hundred drachmas for Theodotus under contract, and that the speaker plotted and stole him away. These rhetorical maneuvers depend on the assumption that the audience of Areopagites would approve of the love of a good (pseudo-)*erastes* and not consider it to be exclusively the practice of an alien aristocratic culture.

The speaker further undermines Simon's claim to pederastic legitimacy by "demonstrating" that he cannot be in love: Simon's spiteful and calculating actions prove his lack of genuine *eros*, in contrast to the speaker's own *eros*, which is the mark of an honest and direct character:

> θαυμάζω δὲ μάλιστα τούτου τῆς διανοίας. οὐ γὰρ τοῦ αὐτοῦ μοι δοκεῖ εἶναι ἐρᾶν τε καὶ συκοφαντεῖν, ἀλλὰ τὸ μὲν τῶν εὐηθεστέρων, τὸ δὲ τῶν πανουργοτάτων. (Lys. 3.44)

> But I wonder most of all at the spirit of this man's action. Because being in love and bringing false charges do not seem to me to be characteristic of the same man, but the one seems characteristic of better-natured people, and the other of the most villainous men.

Because he is merely pretending his *eros* and is not genuinely a lover (like the speaker), Simon is the kind of "heartless" man who would bring a groundless prosecution.

In a different passage, the speaker argues that lovers, as open and genuine people, are inclined to seek justice immediately when they are wronged, but Simon bided his time until the speaker was especially vulnerable:[83]

---

81. Cf. Lys. 3.31. For εὖ ποιεῖν as the proper language of love, see Ar. *Eq.* 734.

82. Lys. 3.21–26, 3.17. The speaker's gallantry, however, fails him at section 13, in which he admits abandoning Theodotus to Simon's alleged predations.

83. Simon waited to prosecute until the speaker lost an *antidosis* (Lys. 3.20).

τὸ δὲ μέγιστον καὶ περιφανέστατον πάντων· ὁ γὰρ ἀδικηθεὶς καὶ ἐπιβουλευθεὶς ὑπ' ἐμοῦ, ὥς φησιν, οὐκ ἐτόλμησε τεττάρων ἐτῶν ἐπισκήψασθαι εἰς ὑμᾶς. καὶ οἱ μὲν ἄλλοι, ὅταν ἐρῶσι καὶ ἀποστερῶνται ὧν ἐπιθυμοῦσι καὶ συγκοπῶσιν, ὀργιζόμενοι παραχρῆμα τιμωρεῖσθαι ζητοῦσιν, οὗτος δὲ χρόνοις ὕστερον. (Lys. 3.39)

> But this is the greatest and clearest proof of all. For this man, after—as he says—being wronged and schemed against by me, over four years did not dare to denounce me before you. Other people, when they are in love and are deprived of what they desire and are beaten up, right away get angry and demand vengeance, but this man did so far later.

Again, the figure of the lover stands for the straightforward honesty which is absent from the dealings of Simon, the nonlover and hubristic suitor. The speaker makes a show of catching Simon out in a lie regarding his motives: if all happened as Simon claimed, and he had truly been struck by *eros*, he would not have waited four years to bring charges. He is, the speaker implies, no true *erastes*.

Despite this presentation as a high-minded lover, twice in the course of the speech the speaker admits to embarrassment at his own behavior. In both passages, the speaker is explaining why he did not undertake a prosecution against Simon, given that he now says he was the wronged party. In the first he says that he was embarrassed by the fervor of his desire and the behaviors it occasioned, especially in one of his age (Lys. 3.3–4). In the second, after a description of a nocturnal battle, the speaker claims that if he were to bring charges, he would lay himself open to resentment of his elite status (Lys. 3.9).

Hubbard suggests that the speaker anticipates such hostility because of the pederastic nature of his desires, with which none but the speaker's own class would sympathize.[84] As Parker points out, however, the terms in which the speaker confesses his embarrassment are hardly a condemnation of pederastic *eros* as such (2010: 129–30). The speaker presents such fights—fights over *paidika*, a normal part of pederastic courtship—as the sort of trivial affair in which apologies, not lawsuits, are called for (Lys. 3.40).[85] Brawls over youths and courtesans (female as well as male) were stuff for young bucks, and the speaker is apparently of mature years: this is

---

84. Hubbard 1999: 60. The speaker is a wealthy man, a liturgist, else he would not be involved in an *antidosis* (Lys. 3.20).

85. For embarrassment, see also Lys. 3.19. For hitting as a normal part of pederastic courtship, see Aeschin. 1.136 and Dover 1978: 54–57.

part of why he claims to prefer reticence.⁸⁶ His embarrassment is at his age-inappropriate behavior, not the gender of his love-object. His fear that he may look a fool (ἀνόητος) coincides with his concern. When he mentions class resentment, he does not suggest that it would be caused by his *eros* for the Plataian youth. A more plausible explanation is that it would be caused by the nocturnal brawl occasioned by his *eros*: the speaker fears being painted as a violent and hubristic member of the elite.⁸⁷ Such concerns would have nothing to do with the gender of his love-object.

Lysias's strategic use of legitimate *eros* in *Against Simon* may be elucidated by comparing the speech with Lysias 4 (*On a Wound by Premeditation*). The cases are similar—a wounding in a fight over a prostitute—but in the latter, the contested individual is female. In contrast to Lysias 3, this speaker distances himself from all desire, and portrays his opponent as crazed by love. His sober persona is well designed to make the charge that he struck his opponent with malice aforethought appear unlikely. His opponent, he claims, struck first, driven by his *eros*-sickness for the woman; the opponent has an erotic motive for initiating the fight in question but the speaker does not (Lys. 4.8).⁸⁸ *Eros* for a woman is characterized not as a feature of "better-natured people" but as a catalyst for violence. The speaker explicitly calls the woman a *pornē* and a slave, and implies that as such she is not worth fighting over (Lys. 4.19). The difference between the strategies of these two speakers underscores the ways in which the speaker of Lysias 3 recasts his dispute with Simon as if it had taken place in the context of legitimate pederastic courtship.

Aeschines similarly treats pederastic love as the sign of a humane man in his speeches against Demosthenes, and uses his opponent's allegedly cold and manipulative treatment of his *eromenos*, Aristarchus son of Moschus, to characterize Demosthenes as deceptive and vicious. When defending himself against Demosthenes' charge that he accepted bribes from Philip of Macedon, Aeschines used Demosthenes' scandalous treatment of his *eromenos* to characterize him as a natural-born traitor.⁸⁹

εἰσῆλθες εἰς εὐδαιμονοῦσαν οἰκίαν τὴν Ἀριστάρχου τοῦ Μόσχου. ταύτην ἀπώλεσας. προὔλαβες τρία τάλαντα παρ' Ἀριστάρχου φεύγοντος.

---

86. Cohen 1995: 119–42; cf. Dem. 54.14.
87. Like, for example, Konon and his sons in Demosthenes 54 (*Against Konon*). See also Lys. 3.9; Ober 1989: 208–12; Cohen 1995 119–42; Dem. 21, Dem. 54.13–14 (elite), 20 (violent).
88. Cf. Lys. 4.2, where the speaker claims the opponent has initiated an *antidosis* for the sake of getting exclusive ownership of her.
89. Cf. also Aeschin. 2.163–65: ὁμοσπόνδων καὶ συσσίτων κατήγορος, "accuser of libation-sharers and dining-fellows," and ἐκ φύσεως προδότην, "a traitor by nature."

τοῦτον τὰ τῆς φυγῆς ἐφόδια ἀπεστέρησας, οὐκ αἰσχυνθεὶς τὴν φήμην, ἣν προσεποιήσω, ζηλωτής εἶναι τῆς ἡλικίας τοῦ μειρακίου. οὐ γὰρ δὴ τῇ γε ἀληθείᾳ· οὐ γὰρ προσδέχεται δίκαιος ἔρως πονηρίαν. ταῦτ᾽ ἐστὶν προδότης καὶ τὰ τούτοις ὅμοια. (Aeschin. 2.166)

You came to the household of Aristarchus son of Moschus while it was flourishing; this household you destroyed. You took three talents in advance from Aristarchus when he went into exile. You robbed him of the provisions for his exile, not ashamed at the report, to which you laid claim, that you were an admirer of the young man's youthful bloom. But this is not really how it was. For legitimate love has nothing to do with wickedness. These and all similar acts characterize the traitor.

Aeschines here treats genuine *eros* as indicative of a humane nature.[90] He further suggests that Demosthenes should—and the jurors will—consider treachery against a onetime beloved as especially reprehensible, because Demosthenes breached the faith inherent in the bonds of legitimate love. Aeschines uses this scandal to portray Demosthenes as the sort of man who would bring a wrongful prosecution against a fellow ambassador.

Proper pederasty requires the right behavior from the *eromenos* as well as the *erastes*, and wrong behavior by an *eromenos* equally demonstrates a vicious and unfeeling character. Thus Aeschines at Aeschin. 1.137 (quoted above) juxtaposes his own conduct as an *erastes* with Timarchus's misconduct as an *eromenos*, and apparently considers the proper fulfillment of either role to be equally an index of decency and humanity. Similarly Demosthenes, as *logographos* for one Diodoros in a public prosecution of the *rhetor* Androtion in 355, uses Androtion's alleged conduct as a prostitute (in this case revealed as a slang term for an easy and mercenary *eromenos*) to characterize him as a man incapable by nature of mercy (cf. Dem. 22.29). Androtion has, according to Demosthenes, been too harsh in his *eisphora*-collecting measures, having the Eleven arrest men in their homes for their outstanding debt to the state (Dem. 22.52–53). He is so cruel as to distrain even on the property of people who do not owe money (Dem. 22.56–57).

---

90. Aeschines recounts also Demosthenes' other deviant relationships with *eromenoi*: see Aeschin. 2.149 (about one Cnosion), Aeschin. 3.162 (Aristion son of Aristoboulos) and 256, and Fisher 2002: 272–73, 315–20. Elsewhere Aeschines uses Demosthenes' relationship with Aristarchus son of Moschus to show Demosthenes as a perverted mentor and a dangerous sophist (Aeschin. 1.172–73). If we can believe Aeschines' report of Demosthenes' speech, then Demosthenes paid Aeschines back in kind; at 166–69 he depicts Demosthenes accusing him of improper flirtations with Alexander and responds that Demosthenes is boorish and ill-bred to suggest such a thing.

After Androtion supposedly seized the property of Sinope and Phanostrate (themselves allegedly *pornai*) who did not actually owe the *eisphora*, Demosthenes notes that some people may say that they deserved it nevertheless, because they were *pornai*. However, he declares that such a lack of pity is unseemly in a democracy and is in keeping with Androtion's violent nature, which is further revealed by his erotic failure:

> ἀλλ' οὐ ταῦτα λέγουσιν οἱ νόμοι, οὐδὲ τὰ τῆς πολιτείας ἔθη, ἃ φυλακτέον ὑμῖν· ἀλλ' ἔνεστ' ἔλεος, συγγνώμη, πάνθ' ἃ προσήκει τοῖς ἐλευθέροις. ὧν οὗτος ἁπάντων εἰκότως οὐ μετέχει τῇ φύσει οὐδὲ τῇ παιδείᾳ· πολλὰ γὰρ ὕβρισται καὶ προπεπηλάκισται συνὼν οὐκ ἀγαπῶσιν αὐτὸν ἀνθρώποις, ἀλλὰ δοῦναι μισθὸν δυναμένοις·
> (Dem. 22.57–58)

> But the laws do not say this, nor does the character of civic life, which you should guard. But in them are pity, pardon, all the things that properly belong to free men. In all of which this fellow, it stands to reason, has no share by nature or by education. For many times he has been treated with outrage and foul abuse, when he consorted not with fellows who had affection for him, but with those who could pay his wage.

Demosthenes suggests that a male who lies with men who do not care for him is a person without the mercy inherent in the spirit of free people in a democracy.[91] He implies that if Androtion had kept intimate company with men who held him in affection, this might have engendered *paideia* and the sentiments of a free man. Poor pederastic morality, this time by the *eromenos*, is an indicator of a violent and cruel nature and deficiency of culture and education.

CONCLUSION

I have endeavored to show that the genres of Athenian literature delivered before audiences of a broad spectrum of Athenians show the same moral indices for erotic morality as philosophical texts aimed at Athenians with wealth, leisure, and education. The evidence of the orators shows that pederasty is not free from class valence: not only was the practice of

---

91. A democratic jury would not necessarily be sympathetic with a man who pressured the rich to pay their *eisphora*-taxes. Cf. Forsdyke's discussion of the democratic value of *praotēs*, "mildness" (2005: 265–66).

formal pederastic courtship expensive, but the articulation and espousal of legitimate *eros* could be used as evidence of refinement and good character, traits associated with genteel upbringing. Yet the orators' strategies suggest that the popular audience of jurors wanted that proof of refinement for themselves, and shared the view that the absence of good pederastic morals was a sign of general moral depravity. Every passage discussed here can plausibly be interpreted as criticizing not pederasty *per se*, but pederasty performed badly, by one or other partner in the relationship. Anti-elite invective took the form not of repudiation of pederasty, but of accusations that aristocrats failed to live up to the rules of legitimate *eros*. The idea that legitimate *eros* is "classy" did not inspire class resentment among the popular audience, then, so much as social aspiration. Philosophical texts, comic texts, and oratory all agree in using the proper performance of pederasty as a trope signifying educated, humane behavior in which all citizens of the Athenian democracy might participate.

BIBLIOGRAPHY

Blondell, Ruby. 2002. *The Play of Character in Plato's Dialogues*. Cambridge.

Burke, Peter. 1992. *History and Social Theory*. Cambridge.

Carey, Christopher. 1989. *Lysias: Selected Speeches*. Cambridge.

———. 1994. "Comic Ridicule and Democracy," in Robin Osborne and Simon Hornblower (eds.), *Ritual, Finance, Politics: Athenian Democratic Accounts Presented to David Lewis*, 69–84. Oxford.

Carnes, Jeffrey S. 2004. "'Certain Intimate Conduct': Classics, Constructionism and the Courts," in *Gender and Diversity in Place: Proceedings of the Fourth Conference on Feminism and Classics*, http://www.stoa.org/diotima/essays/fc04.

Cohen, David. 1995. *Law, Violence and Community in Classical Athens*. Cambridge.

Davidson, James. 2007. *The Greeks and Greek Love: A Radical Reappraisal of Homosexuality in Ancient Greece*. London.

Dover, Kenneth J. 1974. *Greek Popular Morality in the Time of Plato and Aristotle*. Indianapolis.

———. 1978. *Greek Homosexuality*. Cambridge, MA.

Dunbar, Nan. 1995. *Aristophanes' Birds: Edited with Introduction and Commentary*. New York.

Earp, F. R. 1929. *The Way of the Greeks*. London.

Fisher, Nick. 1998. "Gymnasia and the Democratic Values of Leisure," in P. Cartledge, P. Millett, and S. von Reden (eds.), *Kosmos: Essays in Order, Conflict and Community in Classical Athens*, 84–104. Cambridge.

———. 2000. "Symposiasts, Fish-Eaters and Flatterers: Social Mobility and Moral Concerns in Old Comedy," in David Harvey and John Wilkins (eds.), *The Rivals of Aristophanes: Studies in Athenian Old Comedy*, 355–96. Swansea.

———. 2001. *Aeschines Against Timarchus: Translated with an Introduction and Commentary.* New York.

Forsdyke, Sara. 2005. *Exile, Ostracism, and Democracy: The Politics of Expulsion in Ancient Greece.* Princeton.

———. 2012. *Slaves Tell Tales: And Other Episodes in the Politics of Popular Culture in Ancient Greece.* Princeton.

Goldhill, Simon 1997. "The Audience of Athenian Tragedy," in P. E. Easterling (ed.), *The Cambridge Companion to Greek Tragedy*, 54–68. Cambridge.

Halperin, David M. 1990. *One Hundred Years of Homosexuality: And Other Essays on Greek Love.* New York.

Hansen, Mogens Herman. 1991. *The Athenian Democracy in the Age of Demosthenes: Structure, Principles, and Ideology.* Trans. J. A. Crook. Oxford.

Harris, Edward M. 1995. *Aeschines and Athenian Politics.* New York.

Harris, William V. 1989. *Ancient Literacy.* Cambridge, MA.

Henderson, Jeffrey. 1975. *The Maculate Muse: Obscene Language in Attic Comedy.* Oxford.

Hubbard, Thomas K. 1998. "Popular Perceptions of Elite Homosexuality in Classical Athens." *Arion* 6: 48–78.

———. 2006. "History's First Child Molester: Euripides' *Chrysippus* and the Marginalization of Pederasty in Athenian Democratic Discourse," in J. Davidson, F. Muecke, and P. Wilson (eds.), *Greek Drama III: Essays in Memory of Kevin Lee*, 223–44. BICS Supplement 87. London: Institute of Classical Studies.

———, (ed.). 2003. *Homosexuality in Greece and Rome: A Sourcebook of Basic Documents.* Berkeley.

Kahn, Charles H. 1994. "Aeschines on Socratic Eros," in Paul A. Vander Waerdt (ed.), *The Socratic Movement*, 87–106. Ithaca.

Kelly, Douglas. 1996. "Oral Xenophon," in Ian Worthington (ed.), *Voice into Text: Orality and Literacy in Ancient Greece*, 149–64. Leiden.

Kurke, Leslie. 1999. *Coins, Bodies, Games, and Gold: The Politics of Meaning in Archaic Greece.* Princeton.

Loraux, Nicole. 1986. *The Invention of Athens: The Funeral Oration in the Classical City.* Trans. Alan Sheridan. Cambridge, MA.

Mendelsohn, Daniel. 1996. "The Stand: Expert Witnesses and Ancient Mysteries in a Colorado Courtroom." *Lingua Franca*, September/October. http://linguafranca.mirror.theinfo.org/9609/stand.html.

Nagy, Gregory. 1999. "Homer and Plato at the Panathenaia: Synchronic and Diachronic Perspectives," in Thomas M. Falkner, Nancy Felson, and David Konstan (eds.), *Contextualizing Classics: Ideology, Performance, Dialogue*, 123–50. Oxford.

Nails, Deborah. 2002. *The People of Plato.* Indianapolis.

Ober, Josiah. 1989. *Mass and Elite in Democratic Athens: Rhetoric, Ideology and the Power of the People.* Princeton.

———. 2003. "Tyrant Killing as Therapeutic *Stasis*: A Political Debate," in Kathryn A. Morgan (ed.), *Popular Tyranny: Sovereignty and Its Discontents in Ancient Greece*, 215–50. Austin.

Parker, Holt. 2011. "Popular Culture," in Mark Golden and Peter Toohey (eds.), *A Cultural History of Sexuality I: Sexuality in the Classical World*, 125–44. Oxford.

Pearson, Lionel. 1962. *Popular Ethics in Ancient Greece.* Stanford.

Pickard-Cambridge, Sir Arthur. 1968. *The Dramatic Festivals of Athens.* Second edition, revised by J. Gould and D. M. Lewis with new supplement. Oxford.

Raaflaub, Kurt A. 2003. "Stick and Glue: The Function of Tyranny in Fifth-Century Athenian Democracy," in Kathryn A. Morgan (ed.), *Popular Tyranny: Sovereignty and Its Discontents in Ancient Greece,* 59–93. Austin.

Sissa, Giulia. 1999. "Sexual Bodybuilding : Aeschines Against Timarchus," in James I. Porter (ed.), *Constructions of the Classical Body,* 148–68. Ann Arbor.

Sommerstein, Alan H. 1997. "The Theatre Audience, the *Demos,* and the *Suppliants* of Aeschylus," in Christopher Pelling (ed.), *Greek Tragedy and the Historian,* 63–80. New York.

Steiner, Ann. 2002. "Private and Public: Links Between *Symposion* and *Syssition* in Fifth-Century Athens." *Classical Antiquity* 21: 347–90.

Stewart, Andrew. 1997. *Art, Desire and the Body in Ancient Greece.* Cambridge.

Tarrant, Harold. 1996. "Orality and Plato's Narrative Dialogues," in Ian Worthington (ed.), *Voice into Text: Orality and Literacy in Ancient Greece,* 129–48. Leiden.

Todd, Stephen. 2007. "*Lady Chatterley's Lover* and the Attic Orators: The Social Composition of the Athenian Jury," in Edwin Carawan (ed.), *Oxford Readings in Classical Studies: The Attic Orators,* 312–58. Oxford.

Winkler, John J. 1990. "Laying Down the Law: The Oversight of Men's Sexual Behavior in Classical Athens," in David M. Halperin, John J. Winkler, and Froma F. Zeitlin (eds.), *Before Sexuality: The Construction of the Erotic Experience in the Ancient Greek World,* 171–210. Princeton.

Wohl, Victoria. 2002. *Love Among the Ruins: The Erotics of Democracy in Classical Athens.* Princeton.

CHAPTER FOUR

What Is "Greek Sex" For?

NANCY WORMAN

This essay centers on what should be an uncontentious claim: literary depictions of classical Greek sexual practices—and, most relevant for the purposes of this volume, of homosexual practices—are largely metaphorical. In claiming this I do not mean to overlook the few trace references in erotic poetry and philosophical dialogue to body parts and what one might do with them.[1] Rather, since these are sparse and mostly only suggestive, my argument focuses on the more dominant literary sources, comedy and oratory, to which scholars have often turned for evidence of sexual attitudes and practices in classical Athens.[2] As part of the larger ancient discourse surrounding social behaviors and the appetites, these abusive depictions may indicate something about attitudes toward actual sexual practices in ancient Greece; but within the frame of literary (largely comic) representation they most clearly serve as vehicles, in the technical language of metaphor, for a more general and pervasive concern: the regulation of citizen behaviors.

This is a deflationary thesis, and it has certain sorry consequences. First, it means that comic/abusive sexual metaphors in fact target other

---

1. I thank Andrew Lear for helpful comments on delimiting genre parameters for this imagery.

2. Most influentially Dover 1978; Winkler 1990; Davidson 1997. Contrast especially Wohl 2002 and Gilhuly (ch. 2 in this volume).

208

behaviors, primarily those involved in public speaking (e.g., speaking style, deportment). Second, it questions the specificity of both the metaphors and their targeted behaviors in relation to real bodies and actual practices. In fact, following Roland Barthes we might recognize that literary figuration quite generally wreaks havoc on the body's integrity.[3] In Barthes' view, semiotic schemes often depend on the human form for their coherence; when a text does not preserve coherences perceived as natural (the most essential trope of which is this bodily integrity), the organizing principles that the body should provide the narrative give way to multiplying metonymies. Discrete entities (e.g., the unclean mouth, the "big decree"[4]) then come to stand in for concepts such as character and larger, unified notions of identity are reduced to their representative parts.[5] These parts are often rearranged and misaligned, so that characters emerge as grotesques or look to be one thing while being in fact another.

Third, my thesis expands upon the larger problem that David Halperin's critique of Foucault offered up to classical scholars, which is whether sexual practices were really that central to identity and self-presentation in classical Athens. Let me take this last point first. Sexual imagery carries a misleading amount of weight for modern readers, since we assume that it must be singularly revealing of the self. But, as Halperin points out, "The social body precedes the sexual body" (1990: 38). Further, ancient Greeks may have constituted the "sexual body" itself as an entity practically unrecognizable to modern moralizing views that condemn certain behaviors outright and condone others (cf. 68–69). Halperin also notices (65) that although Foucault regards sex as having to do with subjectivity, in the classical setting public modes of engagement and self-measuring, especially military and political agonism, were much more primary and dominant in determining strength of character and civic stature. It thus makes some sense that sexual imagery was reserved for the figurative realm and introduced into public discourse at an angle, as a means of inflecting widely witnessed public activities such as speaking in the courts and Assembly with suggestive behaviors largely reserved for the elite symposium and the bedroom.

The cautionary attitude that I am urging, then, entails less talk about "real" sex and more about a sexual semiotics forged of a fairly limited and

---

3. E.g., the blazon (Bakhtin 1984: 426–27); see further below.
4. The first image is from Aeschines (of Demosthenes, 2.23, 88); the second from Aristophanes' *Clouds* (*Nub.* 1019), where the phrase is a pointed euphemism for the overly active penis of the decadent citizen.
5. Cf., e.g., Barthes 1974: 214–15. On Aristophanes' figurative language in broader scope, see Taillardat 1962; Müller 1974; Wilkins 2000.

specialized set of figures and referents, the latter of which are not really sexual at all. But it also calls for a recommitment to the Foucauldian understanding of ancient sexual practices as part of a larger range of social behaviors. That is to say, my general argument is one for which Foucault (as well as Halperin and Winkler) should have or have had sympathy. The schematic regulation of behaviors and the appetites to which these metaphors gesture falls under what Foucault refers to as "a stylization of attitudes and an aesthetics of existence" (1985: 92). I am advocating a fuller understanding of the dynamics of figuration that underpin this crucial insight and a more rigorous commitment to its proper purview. Thus, somewhat ironically, my extrapolation of such historicist insights reveals that, much more than has been generally acknowledged, they severely limit both "attitudes" and "existence" as "stylization" and "aesthetics"—namely, as refractions of unrecoverable real-life practices. My approach is, then, only Foucauldian in this narrow and revisionist sense, in that it seeks to reorient the focus and redraw the boundaries for studying representations of ancient styles and behaviors.

MAKING METAPHORS WORK

As many scholars have noted, with varying degrees of consternation, metaphors confound the precise delineation of meaning. This is at least in part because figuration, particularly figuration that operates by combination and substitution (e.g., *iambeiophagos*, "iamb eater"; *stomatourgos*, "mouth worker"), imports into the given formulation another set of references that may be quite discrete—that is, not obviously related to the central realm that the imagery targets.[6] Aristotle focuses on the capacity of metaphor to do what its name suggests, to "carry over" (*metapherein*) or transfer one term to another setting in which it does not strictly belong (μεταφορὰ δέ ἐστιν ὀνόματος ἀλλοτρίου ἐπιφορά, "metaphor is the application of a term from another realm," *Po.* 1457b6–7).[7] This etymological precision has seemed to many modern scholars to be a less than satisfying account of the workings of metaphor, since they tend to view it as holding both the lit-

---

6. One of these examples is oratorical, the other comic (Dem. 18.139; Ar. *Ran.* 826 *et passim*).
7. Cf. Philod. *de Rhet.* 4 [= test. Theophr. 689A Fortenbaugh]: οἷαν προσήκει δή τιν' ἀλλοτρίαν, ὥσπερ οἰκίαν εἰσιοῦσαν; also Arist. *Rhet.* 1405a6–b11; Demetr. *de Eloc.* 78–80; Cic. *ad Familiares* 16.17.1 [= test. Theophr. 689B F]; Cic. *Orat.* 27.92. See Stanford 1936: 6–12. De Certeau (1984: 115) comments on the functional similarities of story patterns and *metaphorae* (i.e., public transportation) in modern Athens: "Narrative structures have the status of spatial syntaxes."

eral and figurative meanings in suspension.[8] While for Aristotle metaphor operates by means of the perception of likeness (τὸ γὰρ εὖ μεταφέρειν τὸ ὅμοιον θεωρεῖν ἐστιν, "for to make a metaphor well is to observe the similar," *Po.* 1459a7–8), modern scholars shift this capacity to metaphor itself, which creates the likeness and in so doing forges a new vocabulary where there previously was none.[9]

But Aristotle's emphasis on likeness should not be merely treated as insufficiently subtle or expressive of how metaphor operates more generally, since his characterizations of it were very influential on ancient thought about figuration and thus offer us a window on the effects aimed at by poets, orators, and later theorists who make striking use of and often also comment on innovative metaphors. Further, both Aristotle and Plato appreciate the significance of and problems inherent in the fact that the comprehension of likeness lies also at the heart of mimesis. It thus fundamentally underpins the intellectual endeavor as a whole, since analogical thinking is central not merely to artistic composition but to rational argument as well (cf. *Po.* 1451b4–7, *Rhet.* 1410b12). We might notice, by way of grasping the importance of this set of associations, that when Aristotle talks about language and style, he identifies metaphor as the most important category of usage because it signals the presence of a "natural" (i.e., creative) capability (. . . πολὺ δὲ μέγιστον τὸ μεταφορικὸν εἶναι. μόνον γὰρ τοῦτο οὔτε παρ' ἄλλου ἔστι λαβεῖν εὐφυΐας τε σημεῖόν ἐστι· "the greatest by far is the metaphoric; for this alone cannot be taken from another, and is a sign of inborn talent," *Po.* 1459a5–7).[10]

This creative capacity generates the powerful referential bridges forged between the players, postures, attitudes, or behaviors indicated by the vehicle (the metaphor part) and those targeted by that metaphor. In comic and oratorical settings, however, it can be unclear how specific the envisioning of likeness in fact is. For instance, in one of the early scenes of Aristophanes' *Thesmophoriazusae,* when Euripides' crude relative cries out that he will be a "Kleisthenes" (235) and a "piggy" (δελφάκιον γενήσομαι, 237) if he has his pubic hair singed off, the double joke of his transformed body

---

8. See, e.g., many of the articles in Sacks (ed.) 1978, in contrast to Ricoeur's; also Franke 2000; Boys-Stones (ed.) 2003. Moran 1989 rightly emphasizes the visualizing capacity of metaphor, as well as its ancient origins (89n3). Derrida 1982: 234–35 points out that the emphasis on resemblance has been quite sustained in western intellectual tradition.

9. Perhaps the most obvious (if not very interesting) example in the last twenty years is the explosion of computer and Internet vocabulary (e.g., mouse, web, stream).

10. For a fuller discussion of ancient theorizing about metaphor, see Worman forthcoming, ch. 1.

combines denigration of effeminate men, female genitalia, and pigs.[11] But does this mean that we know anything much about how old male Athenians treated piglets? The metaphors (including the use of a proper name as a metonymic gloss for a type) do appear to indicate negative attitudes toward the feminine, which is hardly surprising. The point here is that extrapolating from there to hypothesize about bodily care and/or sex acts involving women or animals, or even contemporaneous attitudes toward these, is difficult at best. Not to put too obscene a point on it, but when, for instance, we Americans call someone an "asshole," we do not normally envision anything involving actual practices, whether these are sexual or (more relevant to the American imaginary) bowel-related. In fact, although the term does seem to be used most often to target male behaviors, the extrapolation from body part to character type is so generalizing as to indicate almost nothing except, perhaps, a broadly negative attitude toward the anus and a tendency to associate it with men behaving badly (as opposed to, say, the crude terms for vagina that index female conduct). Although an ancient comic abusive term such as *katapugōn* ("ass-inclined"?) may well have retained some more visceral associations with the body part to which it draws attention, its usage in comedy covers quite wide-ranging notions of behavioral excess.

Other vehicles appear to refer to particular behaviors by predicating a condition of a body part, as is the case with *euruprōktos* ("gape-holed"), a favorite insult of Aristophanes.[12] In Aristophanes' comedies, this open-assed image highlights one of the two orifices that are central to the depiction of homosexual appetites in ancient reference. Much of comic discourse about the body effectively collapses it on its holes, forging patterns of succinct metonymies that focus on the male body and most commonly calibrate mouth and anus. This emphasis on holes means that certain bodily types and deportments become central vehicles for Athenian anxiety about citizen appetites: in essence, those marked as "open" and sometimes as feminized, ready for penetration at either end (Worman 2008).

This should sound familiar. But curiously, while these metaphors do point to oral and anal sex, they do not necessarily indicate passivity or feminization. Against Foucault's emphasis on the oppositions active/passive

---

11. Kleisthenes, a politician famed for his beardless, "softy" deportment, was a favorite comic target (e.g., Crat. fr. 195 K-A; Pherecr. fr. 135 K-A; Ar. *Acharn.* 117–19; *Nub.* 355; *Lysis.* 620–24, 1090–92; *Ran.* 422–24).

12. Unlike *katapugōn*, which turns up in graffiti, *euruprōktos* appears to be a comic, and maybe primarily Aristophanic term. (On *katapugōn*, see Lear and Cantarella 2008: 170–71, 247nn11–15; Steiner 2002: 358–60). On other sexual or "sexual" terms, see Gilhuly, ch. 2, in this volume.

and dominant/submissive (following Dover 1978), which both Halperin (e.g., 1990: 30) and Winkler (e.g., 1990: 70) accept as generally descriptive, this openness does not coincide with what it might seem naturally to suggest. As both Davidson and Wohl have recognized, metaphors that appear to indicate submissive roles in sex in fact may index a wider array of excesses; and these are not only more broadly construed than soft, passive, or vulnerable, they are not even all sexual, but can include appetites for drink and/or food as well.[13] Further complicating this picture is the fact that Attic comedy and oratory depict female appetites, especially those for sex, as rapacious and insatiable rather than passive. Instead, in comic discourse and in other settings that appropriate comic schemes, a focus on holes tends to point up a variety of behaviors that are deemed excessive. We are thus left with few distinct sexual references, little clear delineation of attitudes, and the possibility that even the vehicles themselves may not always be sexually indicative.

Despite all these difficulties, many readers of ancient comedy feel strongly that figurative distinctions ought to tell us something about attitudes toward different types of appetites, including sexual ones, if not about actual behaviors and practices. Thus it might seem, for instance, that when metaphors and metonymies index sexual activities involving penetration, these activities are framed as submissive and therefore made parallel to, say, flattery and groveling in the public arena. Some scholars have argued, however, that it is unclear whether metaphors that apparently refer to excessive inclinations for "Greek sex" really are that firmly distinguished in literary settings from other appetitive indulgences such as gourmandizing and heavy drinking.[14] And yet in the face of such ambiguities, even those like Davidson who argue for the indeterminacy of this vocabulary most often aim at reconstructing social practices.

METAPHOR AND THE PERFORMING BODY

The literary settings themselves quite obviously redouble this difficulty of extrapolating from metaphor to attitudes and practices. The conjunction on the comic stage of figuration and spectacle uniquely highlights the body as an unnatural object, something not only fenced around by social delimi-

---

13. Davidson 1997: 177–80; Wohl 2002: 12–20.
14. Again, see Henderson (1975) 1991; Davidson 1997; Wohl 2002. Contrast Worman 2008, ch. 2 and see further below. The present argument resituates some of the metaphors discussed in my book.

tations but also formed (or deformed) by language and marked by visible cues in performance.[15] While comic representation offers its audiences visibly distinct bodies and behaviors, these are so stylized and embellished as to confound clear expectations as to status and type. Attic comedy's primary performers sported protruding bellies, asses, and outsized phalluses on stage, sometimes also donning female bodily attributes, especially breasts.[16] In the spectacular jumble of parts that such performance throws up for viewing, figurative imagery that refers to excessive behaviors by exaggerated metonymies or the grotesque juxtaposition of these parts would have augmented and sometimes reconfigured the visibly outsized form in question.[17] In Aristophanes' *Knights,* for instance, the slave Demosthenes, an opponent of the obnoxious demagogue Paphlagon, gleefully envisions checking him out as if he were a pig at market. They would, Demosthenes says, "put a peg in his mouth butcher-wise, pull out his tongue, and manfully peer down his yawning throat, to assess the state of his . . . anus, whether it gapes open" (καὶ νὴ Δι' ἐμβαλόντες αὐ- / τῷ πάτταλον μαγειρικῶς / εἰς τὸ στόμ,' εἶτα δ' ἔνδοθεν / τὴν γλῶτταν ἐξείραντες αὐ- / τοῦ σκεψόμεσθ' εὖ κἀνδρικῶς / κεχηνότος / τὸν πρωκτόν, εἰ χαλαζᾷ [375–81; cf. Ar. *Thesm.* 222]). This rearrangement of the body by language renders Paphlagon's big-bellied, open-mouthed comic form as not only (potential) meat on the slab; it also aligns his gaping mouth with his flapping anus, offering up its matching holes as a measure of his character.[18]

While clearly operating in the realm of comic play, this targeting of certain parts as metonymies for excess (e.g., the open apertures used to signal general incontinence) nevertheless broadcasts attitudes that we must assume were generally recognizable and shared enough to make for laughs. Judith Butler, following the sociologist Pierre Bourdieu's groundbreaking work on bodily hexis,[19] has famously called attention to the body as a social construct crafted by means of performative articulations involv-

---

15. Regarding the effects of taboo on the body, see Douglas 1969: 4: "It is only by exaggerating the differences between within and without, above and below, male and female, with and against, that a semblance of order is created."

16. On the comic body, see Foley 2000.

17. For a discussion of the evidence from vase paintings and its relation to extant comedies, see Taplin 1993; Foley 2000.

18. For a powerful discussion of this imagery in relation to Athenian political attitudes, see Wohl 2002: ch. 2.

19. Bourdieu is expanding on Aristotle's use of the word, meaning naturalized habits, attitudes, and deportments (e.g., 1991: 81–88).

ing stylistic choices, especially dress, deportment, and language.[20] While Butler argues that all social interactions are constitutive in this way, for our purposes it is important to note that the spaces of public performance available for the lampooning of citizen behaviors were not restricted to the comic poets. Athenian orators also, and frequently with brutal wit, target opponents' physical deportments and behavioral foibles while highlighting their own chaste and self-contained bodily hexis. That said, the dramatic stage, with its costumes and explicit fictions, more overtly redoubles the sense of the body as amassed through signification. Indeed, since comedy dismantles and reassembles the body in grotesque permutations, it further disrupts notions of natural coherences and demarcations in relation to class, generation, and especially gender.[21] This means that when, for instance, a character is "pegged" as a pig open at both ends, his body effectively collapsed on its holes, his mockers may appear to assign him to a category that includes a "softy" like the tragic poet Agathon or louche writers and politicians more generally. And yet despite scholars' arguments that targeting the ass-end highlights very little beyond excess (Henderson [1975] 1991; Davidson 1997), Paphlagon is clearly not similar in type to Agathon, or even to his demagogic opponent in *Knights,* the sassy Sausage Seller. He is outsized, voracious, and loud, and his wide-open body broadcasts an all-consuming attitude toward the world.[22] His swaggering deportment straddles whole "territories," his body stretched from one obnoxious activity to another. He has one leg in Pylos and other in the Assembly; his anus is "in Chaos" (ὁ πρωκτός ἐστιν αὐτόχρημ' ἐν Χάοσιν [Chaonia]), his hands in Extortion (τὼ χεῖρ' ἐν Αἰτωλοῖς [Aetolia]), and his mind in Larceny (ὁ νοῦς δ' ἐν Κλωπιδῶν [Clopis, a little deme in northern Attica]) (78–79).

The figure of Agathon in *Thesmophoriazusae* shows a similar vulnerability at both ends, but the contrast between these two comic types is glaring and potentially offers us the strongest indication of the ways in which the contextualizations of metaphors can reveal how precisely they are turned. Early in the action Agathon's servant comes out of the poet's house and announces haughtily to Euripides and his relative that the younger poet is busy "twisting new ties of words" (κάμπτει δὲ νέας ἁψῖδας ἐπῶν), turning some and welding others (τὰ δὲ τορνεύει, τὰ δὲ κολλομελεῖ), as well

---

20. Cf. Butler's unwieldy expression: "fabrications manufactured and sustained through corporeal signs and other discursive means" (Butler 1990: 136). Cf. Bourdieu 1991.
21. Cf. Bourdieu 1991: 88 and further below.
22. Again, see Wohl 2002: ch. 2 on the imagery's political import.

as "rolling and casting" (γογγύλλει / καὶ χοανεύει) them. Although this vocabulary clearly glosses crafts such as boat-building and statue-making, the gleefully obscene relative caps the metaphors with a verb indicating oral or anal penetration (καὶ λαικάζει) (57).[23] He declares that he will "roll and twist" (συγγογγυλίσας καὶ συστρέψας) both the poet and his servant around and "cast in this here penis" (τουτὶ τὸ πέος χοανεῦσαι) (61–62).[24] That is to say, the relative transfers the images of twisting and rolling onto the poet himself, so that the scene confirms that how one talks can be forcibly read on the body, as the relative cashes out poetic style as physical inclination. Later, in response to Agathon's girlish trilling and feminine dress, the relative deems the poet both "gape-holed" (εὐρύπρωκτος) and "ass-inclined" (κατάπυγον) not merely in his words but also in his "experiences" (οὐ τοῖς λόγοισιν ἀλλὰ τοῖς παθήμασιν), (200–201).

How, then, ought those of us seeking a window on ancient homosexuality to approach the absurd body that the comic texts fabricate, a pointedly artificial deformation whose freewheeling, rebellious idiom belies its elite provenance and subtle literary tenor? Bourdieu, in exploring the many ways that social habituation shapes and controls the body, considers comic usage a rejection of the censorship that dominant discourses (e.g., educated, "polite," or official) impose on speakers and uses Bakhtinian imagery to characterize this outspokenness: "in reducing humanity to its common nature—belly, bum, bullocks, grub, guts, and shit—it tends to turn the social world upside-down, arse over head."[25] Bourdieu has some confidence in the power of this linguistic rebellion, referencing Bakhtin's work as evidence of the ties between festive talk and revolutionary crisis.[26] Both foster what he terms a "verbal explosion" of restrictions normally imposed, especially on subjugated groups, restrictions that enforce socially hierarchized

---

23. Jocelyn 1980 argues that λαικάζειν primarily denotes fellatio, and points briefly to the connections forged in comic depictions of demagogues between talking and fellating (26). Henderson [1975] 1991: 153 argues instead that λαικάζειν refers more generally to "whoring" and/or pederastic sex. The thrust of the joke could thus be that Agathon might perform fellatio (so Sommerstein) in a similarly fancy manner, or "roll and mold" a plug for his own anus (as per Barrett's rather overly imaginative translation [1964]). Cf. Dover 1978: 142. On the vocabulary of crafting, see Austin and Olson 2004 (*ad* 56).

24. The deictic τουτὶ points to the comic phallus that the relative is sporting; cf. Foley 2000.

25. Bourdieu 1991: 88. Cf. Robert Herrick's interplay of body parts and "vine," which engages a similarly insouciant dismantling: "Her Belly, Buttocks, and her Waste, / By my soft *Nerv'lits* were embraced" ("The Vine," 1648 [1963]: 26).

26. Contrast Bakhtin 1984: 426–27, who regards the disruptive force possible in elite venues such as Attic comedy as quite limited. Möllendorf 1995: 150–51 argues that for Bakhtin the equivalence between festival and literature is functional rather than causal (i.e., the one is not primary and the other only vital in proximity to it).

notions of sex, class, and generation. In Bourdieu's analysis, literature and social history both reveal how emblems of power identify authoritative speakers and inhibit the speech of those subordinated to (most often) him in social interactions.[27]

Ancient comedy is a paradox in this regard, since it both perpetuates dominant discourses and ridicules them in volatile ways. As a state festival it did not so much foster revolution as the reverse, combining communal insult (i.e., *iambos*) with revelry (*kōmos*) and transforming looser festive modes into an official ritual.[28] Yet insofar as comedy mocks and collapses both the body and social rituals, its aesthetic texture is indeed "explosive"—that is, obscene, irreverent, challenging of norms. It also bears traces of festive rituals not restricted to elites and targets a wide audience, while its literary character and its institutional function both importantly limit its political reach. In fact, it stages social practices in a ritualized setting as a means of civic regulation, targeting public figures in their political capacities in a ventriloquism of the common citizen. Ancient comedy thus introduced abusive talk into official contexts, rendering it at least somewhat accessible to other public settings, as the orators' techniques of character defamation reveal.[29]

Athenian orators made claims about their opponents that were openly slanderous or outrageously suggestive, deploying innuendo and hearsay strategically to set up accusations about transgressions of citizen norms. The orators treat bad behavior as visible, as witnessed in one's body and its disposition in revealing attitudes in notorious spaces around the city. While this notion of the proper citizen was itself a fantasy shaped by the normative rhetoric of dominant orators, these same orators depended on their audience's faith in this normative body for the impact of their insulting contrasts.[30] In saying this I am not suggesting that the orators' images share in the full, piquant range of comic abuse; this is clearly not the case, most obviously because an orator could not augment his talents for invective by using sexually explicit language. And yet some orators—the infamous enemies Demosthenes and Aeschines most especially—devised ways

---

27. E.g., Bourdieu's analysis of *skeptron* as conferring visible status in the *Iliad*, as does the judge's wig and robe in modern settings (1991: 109–13).

28. See Henderson 1990: 271–75. Carrière 1979 rightly emphasizes the political ambiguities of Aristophanic comedy; see also Rosen 1988; Bowie 1986; Konstan 1995; Heath 1997.

29. I do not mean to ignore the existing ritual settings in which abusive talk was central (e.g., the *aischrologia* of fertility rituals, which are neither public nor narrowly political; cf. O'Higgins 2003); my point concerns the incorporation of insult into heterogeneous literary and political settings (i.e., those that produce a dominant narrative of one form or another).

30. See further below on the case against Timarchus, for example.

to suggest things about each other's bodies and inclinations that verge on the grotesque and obscene.

In comedy and more reservedly in oratory, metaphors and metonymies engage playful but cautionary disintegrations of the body by activating at least two strategies that Barthes identifies: the laudatory or abusive blazon, with its enumeration of body parts; and the metonymic "falsehood," which indexes debasing categories such as the female or animal in the characterization of male behaviors.[31] A third figure employs the form of metaphor that Aristotle calls analogy (ἀνάλογον, *Po.* 1457b9), which involves the substitution of one metonymic item for another, such as calling a wine goblet the "shield of Dionysus."[32] Comic settings (including the satyr play) commonly activate this figure by drawing analogies between two sets of metonymies and then exchanging one part (often anatomical) for another.[33] A notorious moment in the long dispute between Demosthenes and Aeschines shows a similar inclination for this kind of suggestive trade-off. In their final confrontation (the dispute over the benefactor's crown, 330) Aeschines declares that Demosthenes is all tongue and no proof—a man "cobbled together out of words" (ἐξ ὀνομάτων συγκείμενος ἄνθρωπος).[34] Like an *aulos* robbed of its reed, if one were to take away Demosthenes' tongue, there would be nothing left (οὗ τὴν γλῶτταν ὥσπερ τῶν αὐλῶν ἐάν τις ἀφέλῃ, τὸ λοιπὸν οὐδέν ἐστιν, 3.229).[35] Aeschines' simile positions the instrument in a manner similar to his other cloaked references to Demosthenes' sexual inclinations, so that it hints at rude conflations of body parts like to those familiar from Attic comedy.[36]

---

31. The blazon involves the predication of an attribute or condition to (usually female) body parts, as in the Herrick quote above (n. 25); see Barthes 1974: 214–15 and Bakhtin 1984: 426–27.

32. Cf. Foley 1988 on Brechtian theater's politicization of the audience, insofar as these dismantling figurations disrupt emotional identification with characters and encourage critical understanding.

33. See further below.

34. Cf. Ps.-Demades *Dodek.* 51. Note that Aeschines dwells repeatedly on Demosthenes' purported cowardice in battle (3.159–61 *et passim*), as well as his various other weaknesses. Ober 1989: 283 has argued that Aeschines sought to present himself as a gentlemanly denizen of the gymnasium, in contrast to whom Demosthenes would appear not only feeble but also dishonorable. See also Fox 1994: 138–39; Golden 2000: 171–74.

35. The *aulos* was a narrow, tubular wind instrument fitted with a reed or "tongue" (*glōssa*) and played in pairs of pipes held on the face by straps; it was widely used at Athenian festivals (see Wilson 1999, 2000; Martin 2003).

36. Wilson 1999: 72. Cf. as well the figure of Procne in Aristophanes' *Birds*; from the reaction of Peisthetaerus and Euelpides, she would seem to be a hybrid character with a woman's body, a bird's head, and *auloi* (cf. Dunbar 1995 *ad loc.*). Her looks incite an urge to prod both her and her costume: not only does Euelpides want to "spread her legs" (διαμηρίζοιμ' ἂν αὐτήν, 669); he also envisions "peeling the shell [i.e., mask?] off her head like an egg" (ἀλλ' ὥσπερ ᾠὸν νὴ Δί' ἀπολέψαντα χρὴ / ἀπὸ τῆς κεφαλῆς τὸ λέμμα κᾆθ' οὕτω φιλεῖν, 673–74).

These orators were also fond of drawing analogies among dress, deportment, and speaking styles that suggest craven or prurient attitudes. Aechines depicts Demosthenes' colleague Timarchus as leaping half-naked about the *bema*, while Demosthenes himself is an effete presence, pirouetting around the platform and squeaking out strange locutions. They offer these lampooning images, whether expressed directly or not, as obvious deformations of restrained and authoritative dress and deportments: the closed cloak, the steady hand, the stately pace. I take up this oratorical imagery more fully below; but I should note here that in both oratory and comedy, such images ultimately are used to control and neutralize the ramifying, polymorphous body. In comedy most especially, the concertedly nonnaturalistic costume (including a body stocking with parts attached) and the "explosive" figuration amasses the grotesque body as an emblem that was effectively apotropaic. Thus when anatomical tropes drew joking, slanderous correlations between, say, the mouth and the anus, these were further arrayed in grotesque comparison with other parts held up for praise or abuse in contrasts instructive for citizen spectators.

Clouds offers a dizzying instance of how comic spectacle and figuration together may undo and yet reinforce social hierarchies. In the *agōn* the old-fashioned Stronger Argument celebrates the chaste youth of old with a loving blazon: in addition to other features this perfect young man had large buttocks, a physiognomy that ought to signal only athleticism and modest restraint. The Stronger Argument opposes the impressive ass of this earlier form to the flabby backsides of contemporaneous open-mouthed operators, those who have worn down their parts by seducing boys, women, and the body politic more generally. Thus one type of body emerges as a cluster of ludicrous metonymies, while the other only appears to resist mocking reconfiguration, since its celebration nonetheless reduces it to its parts. The upstanding youth's deportment and anatomy—from modest mouth to dewy balls—which should signal his physical integrity (*Nub.* 978–80), is undone by the dismantling operations of the blazon itself. And there is a further complication, since the comic body usually exhibited a big ass in addition to its other outsized features (e.g., mouth, belly, phallus).[37] In the comic environment even the celebrated body of the old-fashioned youth cannot escape being degraded by comic tropes and comic spectacle, since there the big ass may indicate either athleticism or lewdness, both of which may be exercised in the gymnasium.

---

37. As Foley (2000: 301) has noted; she thinks that Strepsiades, Socrates, and likely also the Arguments wore a version of the comic body. See also Revermann 2006: 153–59, who thinks it doubtful that many characters escaped what he terms "the ubiquitous pattern of comic ugliness" (159).

We can, however, recognize in this jumbling of anatomy that the openholed body generally receives the biggest share of mockery, followed by one with pliable parts (esp. the phallic and vigorously overused). In the section that follows I explore further how and to what extent context helps to refine and situate more specifically the bodily metaphors that comedy and oratory generate to target certain behaviors.

FROM BODIES TO BEHAVIORS?

As many scholars who drew upon the insights of Halperin and Winkler have noted, the classical Athenian body was measured in relation to citizen action (political, military, etc.), including the telegraphing of stature and status achieved by clothes and deportment mapped onto the social spaces of Athens. Thus, most famously, Aeschines' prosecution of Demosthenes' colleague Timarchus aims at depicting him as a reprobate with outsized appetites that even extend to prostituting himself, an activity that leads one to frequent certain districts. Such appetites can be read on his body: not only does he wrangle his way around the speaker's platform "half-naked" (i.e., with cloak thrown back) like a pancratist, the roughest kind of all-out fighter (ῥίψας θοἰμάτιον γυμνὸς ἐπαγκρατίαζεν); he also disposes his body basely and shamefully because of his crudity and drunkenness (κακῶς καὶ αἰσχρῶς διακείμενος τὸ σῶμα βδελυρίας καὶ ὑπὸ μέθης) (1.26; cf. 1.33, 60).[38] Aeschines deploys the moderate figure of Solon to set this vulgar display in relief. He claims that Solon would have regarded as ineffectual in Assembly any citizen who comported himself in so ludicrous a manner and shamefully used up his patrimony (παρὰ δὲ ἀνθρώπου βδελυροῦ καὶ καταγελάστως μὲν κεχρημένου τῷ ἑαυτοῦ σώματι, αἰσχρῶς δὲ τὴν πατρῴαν οὐσίαν κατεδηδοκότος, οὐδ' ἂν εὖ πάνυ λεχθῇ συνοίσειν ἡγήσατο, 1.31). Since Aeschines liked himself to enact this restrained deportment, his framing of his opponent would have been further offset in performance by his visibly austere carriage. In his speech on the embassy to Philip, Aeschines remarks that the elder statesman delivered speeches with even his hand inside his cloak (i.e., fully covered and with

---

38. Fisher 2001: 154 argues that the image of the pancratist suggests a no-holds-barred attack on one's opponent. Cf. Aristogeiton, who struck a man out of *bdeluria*, almost lost due to drunkenness, and bit off his nose in a fight (Ps.-Dem. 25.61). Tragedy and oratory both characterize clever, aggressive speakers as wranglers (e.g., Soph. *Phil.* 431; Eur. *Hec.* 132; Aesch. 1.26, 33; Dem. fr. 61); cf. also Pl. *Euthyd.* for parallels between physical wrangling and sophistic argument.

a minimum of gestures) (2.25), a pose that Demosthenes mocks when it is adopted by his opponent.[39]

Aeschines' depiction of Timarchus connects most obviously to comic portraits of public speakers whose profligate habits align them with prostitutes.[40] This type is familiar from Aristophanes' *Knights,* where the demagogue is a whorish reprobate whose visible behaviors broadcast his moral failings, because he is either loud and haranguing or a crafty panderer. Timarchus's obnoxiousness is similarly visible to the naked eye.[41] The focus on self-prostitution should mean that the practices it characterizes are primarily sexual, although the use of *bdeluria* in old comedy and Plato reveals that it embraces a much more inclusive set of behaviors, including speaking or argumentational styles.[42] Aeschines also situates Timarchus's immoderate attitudes toward food, drink, and money in relation to places in the city that one ought not to frequent, the mere mention of which inhibits effective public speaking. He claims that Timarchus's bad behavior has rendered him incapable of addressing his fellow citizens in the Assembly without risking derisive response. Thus his references to public works or certain events suggest double entendres: "When he mentioned 'the repair of walls' or 'tower' or 'someone taken off somewhere,' straight away you shouted and hooted and yourselves uttered the proper name of his acts, which you all knew" (εἰ γὰρ μνησθείη τειχῶν ἐπισκευῆς ἢ πύργου, ἢ ὡς ἀπήγετό ποί τις, εὐθὺς ἐβοᾶτε καὶ ἐγελᾶτε καὶ αὐτοὶ ἐλέγετε τὴν ἐπωνυμίαν τῶν ἔργων ὧν σύνιστε αὐτῷ, 1.80, cf. 1.84).[43] Even worse is any mention of Timarchus's oversight of the cisterns (τῶν λάκκων, 1.84), presumably because this recalls for the audience a common slur for rapacious citizens (*lakkoprōktos; lakatapugōn*).[44] For all their apparent rowdiness,

---

39. Dem. 19.251–53. Ancient writers depict Demosthenes as emphasizing deportment over all (Cic. *Orat.* 8.26–28), and as using theatrical gestures that some found a "vulgar, ill-bred, and effeminate imitation" (ταπεινὸν ἡγοῦντο σκαὶ ἀγεννὲς τὸ πλάσμα καὶ μαλακόν, Plut. *Dem.* 9.4). Plutarch also depicts Cleon as having a reputation as a mobile and gesticulating speaker (Plut. *Nic.* 8).

40. Cf. O'Sullivan 1992: 145. For more general remarks on this analogy, see Wohl 2002: 75–76, 86–90.

41. Fisher (2001: 155). Fisher argues that the *bdeluria* "covers more than sexual acts, and may include violence, and . . . perhaps excessive consumption of food and drink"; he notes how often *bdeluria* and its cognates occur in Aeschines' speech, indicating its centrality to his denigrating of Timarchus and those like him. Demosthenes uses *bdeluros* repeatedly to describe Meidias as violent and aggressive (Dem. 21). Cf. Aesch. 2.13–14, 109; 3.62. (2001: 155).

42. E.g., Ar. *Eq.* 198, 304–5; Pl. *Rep.* 338d3.

43. These areas were presumably on the outskirts of the city and thus typical venues for prostitutes; cf. Fisher 2001: 216.

44. Cf. *Ach.* 664; *Nub.* 1330; Eup. fr. 351. Henderson ([1975] 1991: 212, 214) points out that these

however, such insinuations do not aim at prosecuting Timarchus for prostituting himself; rather, Aeschines wants to persuade the audience that because of his excesses Timarchus should not be allowed even to *speak* in formal settings in which citizens exercise their rights (cf. Ar. *Eq.* 877–80).[45]

Similarly, in his speech on the embassy to Philip, Aeschines gives color to a picture of Demosthenes' oratorical skills by correlating sexual innuendoes with other slurs that lampoon his deportment on the *bēma* and his inclinations. In *Against Timarchus* he draws attention to Demosthenes' silken, luxurious clothes, which he claims are as soft as a woman's (1.131); here in similar fashion he emphasizes his "unmanly" qualities. One reference to Demosthenes being a *kinaidos* includes intimations about bodily "filth" ("not being clean in his body," μὴ καθαρεύοντα τῷ σώματι) that extends to his mouth ("where his voice comes from," ὅθεν τὴν φωνὴν ἀφίησιν) (2.88; cf. κιναιδίαν, 2.23).[46] The phrase suggests coyly that Demosthenes' organ may also have been used in other "unclean" ways, those particularly related to his putatively weak and submissive type.[47] It is just possible that Aeschines intimates this inclination earlier, when he depicts Demosthenes as a corrupt seller of his body's parts who nevertheless claims to "spit" (καταπτύει, 2.23) on bribes.[48] In addition, he repeatedly brings up Demosthenes' nickname Battalos as a joking proof of his character (cf. 1.126, 131, 164). Whether this nickname means "Chatterer" or "Bumsy," Aeschines links it to *kinaidia* as well as to the tricks and toadying of the agile speaker (κιναιδίαν Βάτταλος, cf. κιναίδους, 2.151, 1.181[49]).

---

terms, unlike *eurupr<U+014D>ktos*, do not seem to indicate effeminacy since they are appended to violent or appetitive characters (respectively, Cleon, Pheidippides, a wine guzzler).

45. Prostitution was not illegal, but exercising certain rights as a citizen while selling oneself sexually was; see Halperin 1990: 88–112.

46. Winkler 1990: 45–54 emphasizes the difficulty of translating this term; as he explains, it points to sexual deviance, especially of a passive nature. See also Davidson 1997: 167–82. Cf. Aeschines 1.126, 131, and the remarks of Dover 1978: 75 regarding "Battalos"; also Barthes 1974: 109–10 on lodging "sexual density" in the throat.

47. That the mouth may be worryingly versatile has its reflection in Roman oratorical invective; see Corbeill 1996: 97–127. For instance, in his speeches against Verres, Clodius, and Cloelius (*De domo sua*), Cicero draws connections between the visible mouth/tongue (*os, lingua*) of his opponent and its uses other than for speaking (e.g., cunnilingus, *Domo* 25). Cicero's attack on Anthony in the *Philippics* is even more extravagant in its depiction of the voracious, explosive mouth of his enemy (e.g., 2.63–68).

48. Both passages claim that Demosthenes' body either has "nothing unsellable" (οὐδὲν ἄπρατον, 23) or is unclean (μὴ καθαρεύοντα, 88), and both use essentially the same phrase to tie this to his mouth (ὅθεν τὴν φωνὴν προΐεται, 23; ὅθεν τὴν φωνὴν ἀφίησιν, 88). Cf. Dem. 18.196, where Aeschines is "one who must be spit upon" (κατάπτυστον).

49. Cf. Aeschin. 1.131: Βάταλος προσαγορεύεται ἐξ ἀνανδρίας καὶ κιναιδίας. In the dispute over the crown, Demosthenes responds to this insult by declaring that at least "Bumsy" behaved

These coy implications appear to echo an overt joke in Aristophanes' *Knights,* when the slave Demosthenes assures the Sausage Seller that upon assuming demagogic leadership he will not only rough up the council and generals but also have (oral?) sex in the Prytaneum (λαικάσει, 166–67), rather than eating and drinking there. Such mockery points directly to sexual practices, but it does so to emphasize ways of talking and engaging in other oral activities (e.g., communal dining) common among citizens of high standing. The Sausage Seller may be lowbrow (itself a slur on public speakers), but he has been well trained by his marketplace upbringing, a background that he tartly reduces to his habit of stealing meat by hiding it in his ass (ἀποκρυπτόμενος εἰς τὰ κοχώνα, 424) and lying about it.[50] His trick, he says, caused an orator to say that he would one day become a guardian of the people (τὸν δῆμον ἐπιτροπεύσει, 426); the chorus leader confirms that perjury, robbery, and "meat-packing" are sure signs of future leadership (ὁτιὴ 'πιώρκεις θ' ἡρπακὼς καὶ κρέας ὁ πρωκτὸς εἶχεν, 427–28).[51] Thus swearing falsely ('πιώρκεις) corresponds to offering up the ass to someone's "meat."[52] In his "messenger speech" about his behavior in the Assembly, the Sausage Seller also takes the fart of a "bugger" (ἐπέπαρδε καταπύγων ἀνήρ) as the good omen he needs for his entrance into politics. He knocks aside the barrier that keeps the public out of the council chamber by wagging his "asshole" (τῷ πρωκτῷ θενῶν / τὴν κιγκλίδ'), and shouts out, "yawning widely" (κἀναχανὼν μέγα) (638–42). Sashaying like a prostitute and gaping like a fatuous speechifier,[53] this comic demagogue gleefully inhabits a visible persona scorned by the orators for its shameful pliancy and marketability.

---

better than the bad actor (i.e., Aeschines), who cast himself as a dramatic hero (τινὰ τῶν ἀπὸ τῆς σκηνῆς) (18.180). Yunis (*ad* 18.180) argues that Demosthenes would only have referred openly to the nickname if it indicated a speech defect rather than passive sex, but this depends on assumptions about speakers' control of figurative meaning and presumes that sexual metaphors indicate actual sexual behaviors.

50. A scholiast on this line (Triclinii *ad* 428) offers two explanations for the force of the joke: the Sausage Seller either ate the meat afterward or was used as a "woman" in his youth. The first figure works by collapsing one body (anus to mouth) and two categories of activity (sex and eating); the other merges two bodies by matching holes (vagina and anus) and sexual categories (female and male).

51. Henderson [1975] 1991: 200–201 argues that κοχώνη refers to the perineum; like πρωκτός, it usually indexes anal intercourse. Cf. also Taillardat 1962: 70–71.

52. The Sausage Seller later equates hawking his wares with being raped as a boy (ἡλλαντοπώλουν καί τι καὶ βινεσκόμην, 1242); in passive forms, the verb βινεῖν seems to refer to pederastic sex, especially violent types (i.e., rape); cf. Henderson [1975] 1991: 152.

53. Cf. the council members themselves (καὶ πρὸς ἔμ' ἐκεχήνεσαν, 651) and Demos's gaping (755, 804, 1119); see further in Wohl 2002: 84–87.

Similarly, in *Clouds* Aristophanes predicates *euruprōktos* of those with preternaturally open mouths: poets and politicians who talk too much and who "prostitute" themselves in this special manner. The Weaker Argument, who represents the "new youth," a decadent, sophistic crowd, is both an overly fastidious chatterer (*stōmullos*) and a groveling buffoon (*bomolochos*). Meanwhile the Stronger Argument obviously lusts after his young charges and indulges in extravagant insults, wielding elaborate compounds like the blustering old Aeschylus in *Frogs*. While he claims that his traditional education will make the students visibly upright and firm (1012–14), his own style is flowery and dreamily homoerotic.[54] He offers a nostalgic, lascivious vision of the chaste young men of earlier times, when Athenians were educated properly in the ways of modesty and hardy living. These youths were never heard grumbling (παιδὸς φωνὴν γρύξαντος μηδέν' ἀκοῦσαι, 963); they marched to school in an orderly fashion, "naked" (γυμνούς, 965 [i.e., without their cloaks]), with their thighs apart (τὼ μηρὼ μὴ ξυνέχοντας [i.e., swaggering manfully?]), singing only martial hymns handed down from their elders (964–68). If anyone played the fool (βωμολοχεύσαιτ') or "twisted" (κάμψειεν) a tune, he would be beaten for having sullied the Muse (τυπτόμενος πολλὰς ὡς τὰς Μούσας ἀφανίζων) (972).

Further, a young man did not soften his voice for a lover (μαλακὴν φυρασάμενος τὴν φωνὴν πρὸς τὸν ἐραστήν), or lead him on with his eyes (προαγωγεύων τοῖν ὀφθαλμοῖν) (979–80). When dining he did not snatch up goodies before his elders (981–82), nor show too much fondness for fancy foods (ὀψοφαγεῖν), nor titter (κιχλίζειν), nor cross his legs (ἴσχειν τὼ πόδ' ἐναλλάξ) (983). Instead of chattering vulgarities in the agora (στωμύλλων κατὰ τὴν ἀγορὰν τριβολεκτράπελ'), young men spent their time in the gymnasium or on the paths of the Academy (1002–8).[55] The deportments that the Stronger Argument spurns assemble a feminized, pliable body that traipses around symposium, agora, and Assembly.[56] Of course, the Stronger Argument's fine superiority is given the lie when he is quickly persuaded that most of the educated elites are "wide-holed" (*euruproktoi*) and indulge in similar habits. Having recognized many of these softies in the audience, he exclaims, "O Bumsies (κινούμενοι), take my

---

54. As Dover remarks (*ad loc.*); contrast Papageorgiou 2004.

55. This parkland in Colonus on the banks of the Cephisus was famous for its beauty (see Eur. *Med.* 824–44; Soph. *OC* 668–93), which may have encouraged Plato and Aristotle to locate their schools there.

56. Cf. again Demosthenes "pirouetting" around the *bêma* (κύκλῳ περιδινῶν . . . ἐπὶ τοῦ βήματος, Aeschin. 3.167) during an Assembly speech on Macedonian policy.

cloak, damn it, so I can desert to your side" (ὡς ἐξαυτομολῶ πρὸς ὑμᾶς, 1102–4).

In Aristophanic abuse, this cozy little triangle of sex at the ass-end, talk, and the feminine takes as its most pointed targets poets such as Agathon and, to a lesser extent, Euripides. Recall that when Agathon emerges at the beginning of the *Thesmophoriazusae* draped in feminine style and trilling a maiden's song, Euripides' crude relative responds by calling him "ass-inclined" and "gape-holed" (ὦ κατάπυγον, εὐρύπρωκτος εἶ, 200). In *Frogs* a blustering Aeschylus lampoons Euripides in less explicit but similar terms, charging his talky, "mouth-working" style with emptying the wrestling rings and wearing out the asses of jabbering young men (στωμυλίαν ἐδίδαξας, / ἣ 'ξεκένωζεν τάς τε παλαίστρας καὶ τὰς πυγὰς ἐνέτριψεν / τῶν μειρακίων στωμυλλομένων, 1069–71). So too with the Sausage Seller in *Knights,* whose active ass-end in boyhood turns out to be a cheeky foreshadowing of the oratorical agility to come (*Eq.* 424–28). And of course, the most famous *euruprōktoi* of all are those politicians and poets in *Clouds,* who witness a face-off between the Weaker and Stronger Arguments that pits a more manly archaic style (of deportment, speaking, singing, and so on) against the prancing indulgences of the younger generation (*Nub.* 963–83).

What we can say, then, is that homosexual practices (however vaguely referred to) serve as the primary vehicles for mocking politicians' weaknesses for pandering to and manipulating the crowd. Add to this that the comic writers depict sex quite generally as a peculiarly feminine obsession, which should by association feminize male appetites for lots of it, perhaps particularly sex that takes the form of penetration. Thus when at the outset of *Lysistrata* the stringent protagonist asks her fellow Athenian women to "give up the cock" (ἀφέκτεα ... τοῦ πέους, 124) in order to end the war, they express horror and she roundly abuses them as "utterly sex mad" (again, lit. "utterly ass-inclined," παγκατάπυγον, 137). Fittingly, it is the stoic, muscular Spartan Lampito who declares that she will give it up (143), while the Athenians follow suit only reluctantly. In *Ecclesiazusae* the similarly stringent Praxagora draws equations among men who "are pounded the most" (πλεῖστα σποδοῦνται, 112), their oratorical abilities, and the chattering indulgences of Athenian women (112–20).

These intricate metaphorical schemes would seem more promising than those that target general excess, since they do offer a fairly distinct set of associations at one end of the appetitive spectrum. The problem is that almost all of the extant imagery like this is comic. Whatever insults the common idiom might have sustained in downtown Athens, the concretizing aesthetic unique to comedy cashes out, in obnoxiously explicit terms, associations that might otherwise remain only vaguely felt. Further, despite all this contextualizing and refining of what are otherwise metaphors too generalized to help in identifying specific targeted behaviors, we still cannot claim that they offer evidence of actual homosexual practices. Instead they call up, often in cloaked or ambiguous language, these practices as figures for public activities such as producing plays and speaking in the courts and Assembly (cf. Henderson 1991: 210). And while we might, again, recognize some generally denigrating attitudes in images that link penetration to feminized weakness or openness to insatiability, extrapolating from there to negative attitudes about homoerotic practices or perhaps even homosexual sex would be a mistake. As attested by Aeschines' own celebration of erotic attachments, which he elaborates upon in the same speech in which he thoroughly maligns Timarchus's tendencies, what dominant attitudes reject is less the homo- in homosexual than the sexual—especially when this suggests weakness or excess of some sort.

THUS in classical Athenian performative (i.e., dramatic and oratorical) settings, sex pretty much remains "sex," the figurative realm invoked to mock pandering, among other things, in male arenas such as the Assembly and the Prytaneum. And although more recent studies of such topics as "democratic *erōs*" (Wohl 2002; also Scholtz 2004) assume awareness of the metaphorical register, the inclination to glean practical details from comic and oratorical sexual metaphors remains fairly dominant among classical scholars.[57] It is not that these metaphorical maneuvers fail to indicate anything at all about sex in classical Athens, but rather that the referential ranges of the vehicles are difficult to distinguish and that they appear largely to target other citizen behaviors, especially speaking in formal settings. This is what matters, after all, in the regulation of citizen behaviors: that a man be a man where it counts, not in the bed (as the modern adage has it) but in the public forums for exercising authority and sovereignty, over the self and over others. Thus references to some sorts of sexual postures or activities serve as the vehicles—again, in the technical workings of metaphor—for pinpointing and ridiculing the targeted behaviors, which are almost always verbal practices.

This poses a problem for those who, apparently following Winkler's influential essay "Laying Down the Law," aim to use comic or other abusive

---

57. E.g., Hubbard 1998; Davidson 2001, 2007; Papageorgiou 2004; commentaries on Aristophanes also tend to sustain such equations.

imagery to recover actual sexual attitudes and behaviors. Winkler himself appears quite aware that the policing of sexual behaviors (however stringent it actually was) in fact primarily targeted verbal practices, particularly public speaking. Further, he begins his essay with this caution: "Simply knowing the protocols does not tell us how people behaved" (1990: 45). Surveying material from the same sources I have offered here, he paints a compelling if somewhat tendentious picture of a city that practiced what he terms "anus surveillance," with the goal of keeping overly indulgent practitioners out of the citizen ranks and offices (54–64). My difference with Winkler is twofold: not only do I have doubts about whether we can actually know the "protocols"; but the realm in which this discourse operates is also largely that of figuration and very specialized, both in its aesthetic scheme and in its ritual setting. Thus comic imagery (and its appropriation in oratory) may be suggestive, but it does not definitively delineate specific attitudes, let alone behaviors and practices.

One might, in the end, want to retreat even further from using Foucault to make claims about ancient sexual practices, and recognize with Kristina Milnor that Foucault's own work is not fundamentally about sex (or madness, etc.). "It is," she says, "about power and the mechanisms of social systems" (2000: 305). For my more narrow purposes, what we find in comedy and oratory is a relatively limited set of terms that tells us something about social dominance and control as they are construed in relation to gender. We certainly cannot extrapolate from them a picture of homosexual practices, and not only because they are metaphors. The terms themselves point, often rather aggressively, to the ruder end of sexual excesses and target all available bodies, the more appealingly defenseless the better. Literary context can help to distinguish and locate types, but these fall far short of concrete information about how people were disporting themselves in downtown Athens. Quite tellingly, and in keeping with Foucault's emphases, the pointedly crude innuendoes of such terms as *euruprōktos* and *katapugōn* indicate very little about what ancient Athenian men were actually doing with their anuses. Instead they offer the barest edge of an intricate power dynamics and the anxieties that attend its orchestration.

BIBLIOGRAPHY

Austin, Colin, and S. Douglas Olson. 2004. *Aristophanes Thesmophoriazusae*. Oxford.

Bakhtin, Mikhail. 1984. *Rabelais and His World*. Trans. H. Iswolsky. Bloomington, IN.

Barthes, Roland. 1974. *S/Z*. Trans. R. Miller. New York. (French ed., Paris 1970.)

Bourdieu, Pierre. 1991. *Language and Symbolic Power.* Trans. G. Raymond and M. Adamson. Cambridge, MA.

Bowie, Ewen. 1986. "Early Greek Elegy, Symposium and Public Festival." *Journal of Hellenic Studies* 106: 13–35.

Boys-Stones, George R. (ed.). 2003. *Metaphor, Allegory, and the Classical Tradition.* Oxford.

Butler, Judith. 1990. *Gender Trouble: Feminism and the Subversion of Identity.* New York.

Carrière, Jean-Claude. 1979. *Le carnaval et la politique: Une introduction à la comédie grecque.* Paris.

Certeau, Michel de. 1984 [1980]. *The Practice of Everyday Life.* Trans. S. Rendell. Berkeley.

Corbeill, Anthony. 1996. *Controlling Laughter: Political Humor in the Late Roman Republic.* Princeton.

Davidson, Donald. 1978. "What Metaphors Mean," in S. Sacks (ed.), *On Metaphor,* 29–45. Chicago.

Davidson, James. 1997. *Courtesans and Fishcakes: The Consuming Passions of Classical Athens.* New York.

———. 2001. "Dover, Foucault and Greek Homosexuality: Penetration and the Truth of Sex." *Past and Present* 170: 3–51.

———. 2007. *The Greeks and Greek Love.* London.

Derrida, Jacques. 1982 [1972]. "White Mythology: Metaphor in the Text of Philosophy," in *Margins of Philosophy,* 207–71. Trans. A. Bass. Chicago.

Douglas, Mary.1969. *Purity and Danger.* London.

Dover, Kenneth J. 1978. *Greek Homosexuality.* Cambridge, MA.

Dunbar, Nan. 1998. *Aristophanes: Birds.* Oxford.

Easterling, Patricia. 1999. "Actors and Voices: Reading Between the Lines in Aeschines and Demosthenes," in S. Goldhill and R. Osborne (eds.), *Performance Culture and Athenian Democracy,* 154–66. Cambridge.

Fisher, Nick. 2001. *Aeschines: Against Timarchus.* Translated with an Introduction and Commentary. Oxford.

Foley, Helene P. 1988. "Tragedy and Politics in Aristophanes' *Acharnians.*" *Journal of Hellenic Studies* 108: 33–47.

———. 2000. "The Comic Body in Greek Art and Drama," in B. Cohen (ed.), *Not the Classical Ideal: Athens and the Construction of the Other in Greek Art,* 275–311. Leiden.

Foucault, Michel. 1985 [1984]. *The History of Sexuality.* Vol. 2, *The Use of Pleasure.* Trans. R. Hurley. New York.

Fox, Robin L. 1994. "Aeschines and Athenian Democracy," in R. Osborne and S. Hornblower (eds.), *Ritual, Finance, Politics: Athenian Democratic Accounts Presented to David Lewis,* 35–55. Oxford.

Franke, William. 2000. "Metaphor and the Making of Sense: The Contemporary Metaphor Renaissance." *Philosophy & Rhetoric* 33.2: 137–53.

Golden, Mark. 2000. "Demosthenes and the Social Historian," in I. Worthington (ed.), *Demosthenes: Statesman and Orator,* 159–80. London.

Halperin, David M. 1990. *One Hundred Years of Homosexuality: And Other Essays on Greek Love.* New York.

Heath, Malcolm. 1997. "Aristophanes and the Discourse of Politics," in G. W. Dobrov (ed.), *The City as Comedy: Society and Representation in Athenian Drama,* 230–49. Chapel Hill.

Henderson, Jeffrey. 1990. "The *Dêmos* and Comic Competition," in J. J. Winkler and F. I. Zeitlin (eds.), *Nothing to Do with Dionysus? Athenian Drama in Its Social Context,* 271–313. Princeton.

———. 1991 [1975]. *The Maculate Muse: Obscene Language in Attic Comedy.* New Haven.

Herrick, Robert. (1643 [1963]). *The Complete Poetry of Robert Herrick,* ed. J. M. Patrick. New York.

Hubbard, Thomas. 1998. "Popular Perceptions of Elite Homosexuality in Classical Athens." *Arion* 6.1: 48–78.

Jocelyn, H. D. 1980. "A Greek Indecency and Its Students: *Laikazein.*" *Proceedings of the Cambridge Philological Society* n.s. 26: 12–66.

Konstan, David. 1995. *Greek Comedy and Ideology.* New York.

Lear, Andrew, with Eva Cantarella. 2008. *Images of Ancient Greek Pederasty: Boys Were Their Gods.* New York.

Martin, Richard. 2003. "The Pipes Are Brawling: Conceptualizing Musical Performance in Athens," in C. Dougherty and L. Kurke (eds.), *The Cultures within Ancient Greek Culture: Contact, Conflict, Collaboration,* 153–80. Cambridge.

Milnor, Kristina. 2000. Review of D. H. J. Larmour, P. A. Miller, and C. Platter (eds.), *Rethinking Sexuality: Foucault and Classical Antiquity,* (Princeton 1998). *Classical World* 93: 304–5.

Möllendorf, Paul von. 1995. *Grundlagen einer Ästhetik der Alten Komödie: Untersuchungen su Aristophanes und Michail Bachtin.* Tübingen.

Moran, Richard. 1996. "Artifice and Persuasion: The Work of Metaphor," in A. Rorty (ed.), *Essays on Aristotle's* Rhetoric, 385–98. Princeton.

Muecke, Frances. 1982. "A Portrait of the Artist as a Young Woman." *Classical Quarterly* 32: 41–55.

Müller, D. 1974. "Dei Verspottung der metaphorishen Ausdrucksweise durch Aristophanes," in *Musa iocosa: Arbeiten über Humor und Witz, Komik und Komödie der Antike,* 29–41. Hildesheim.

Ober, Josiah. 1989. *Mass and Elite in Democratic Athens: Rhetoric, Ideology, and the Power of the People.* Princeton.

O'Higgins, Laurie. 2003. *Women and Humor in Classical Greece.* Cambridge.

O'Sullivan, Neil. 1992. *Alcidamas, Aristophanes, and Early Greek Stylistic Theory.* Hermes Einzelschriften 60. Stuttgart.

Papageorgiou, Nikolaos. 2004. "Ambiguities in 'Kreitton logos.'" *Mnemosyne* 4th ser. 57.3: 284–94.

Revermann, Martin. 2006. *Comic Business: Theatricality, Dramatic Technique, and Performance Contexts of Aristophanic Comedy.* Oxford.

Ricoeur, Paul. 1978. "The Metaphorical Process as Cognition, Imagination, and Feeling," in S. Sacks (ed.), *On Metaphor,* 141–57. Chicago.

Rosen, Ralph M. 1988. *Old Comedy and the Iambographic Tradition*. American Classical Studies 19. Atlanta.

Sacks, Sheldon, (ed.). 1978. *On Metaphor*. Chicago.

Scholtz, Andrew. 2004. "Friends, Lovers, Flatterers: Demophilic Courtship in Aristophanes' *Knights*," *Transactions of the American Philological Association* 134.2: 263–93.

Steiner, Ann. 2002. "Private and Public: Links Between *Symposion* and *Syssition* in Fifth-Century Athens." *Classical Antiquity* 21: 347–90.

Taillardat, Jean. 1962. *Les images d'Aristophanes: Études de langue et de style*. Paris.

Taplin, Oliver. 1993. *Comic Angels and Other Approaches to Greek Drama through Vase Paintings*. Oxford.

Wilkins, John. 2000. *The Boastful Chef: The Discourse of Food in Ancient Greek Comedy*. Oxford.

Wilson, Peter. 1999. "The *Aulos* in Athens," in S. Goldhill and R. Osborne (eds.), *Performance Culture and Athenian Democracy*, 58–95. Cambridge.

———. 2000. *The Athenian Institution of the Khoregia*. Cambridge.

Winkler, John J. 1990. *Constraints of Desire: The Anthropology of Sex and Gender in Ancient Greece*. New York.

Wohl, Victoria. 2002. *Love Among the Ruins: The Erotics of Democracy in Classical Athens*. Princeton.

Worman, Nancy. 2008. *Abusive Mouths in Classical Athens*. Cambridge.

———. Forthcoming. *Landscape and the Spaces of Metaphor in Ancient Literary Theory and Criticism*. Cambridge.

Yunis, Harvey. 2001. *Demosthenes: On the Crown*. Cambridge.

CHAPTER FIVE

Lusty Ladies
in the Roman Imaginary[1]

DEBORAH KAMEN and
SARAH LEVIN-RICHARDSON

*N*early two thousand years ago, someone scratched the words Μόλα φουτοῦτρις, "Mola the fucktress" (*CIL* IV 2204), into the wall of one of the small rooms of Pompeii's purpose-built brothel.[2] *Fututrix*, or, as here, *foutoutris*, comes from the Latin verb *futuo*, "to fuck," and the agent ending *–trix* suggests that Mola had some sort of active role in sex. In what ways might the Romans have conceptualized Mola, or any other woman, as a sexual agent?

In this chapter, we first offer a short review of how the terms "active" and "passive" have been used in scholarship on ancient sexuality, arguing that the terms ought to be disentangled from notions of penetration and refer instead to sexual agency. We turn next to three types of lusty (i.e., active) ladies—*fellatrices, tribades,* and *fututrices*—and explore what it means for these women to be agents. We demonstrate that some women in Roman culture were conceptualized as sexual agents despite being penetrated (*fututrices* and *fellatrices*), while others were conceptualized as agents *and* penetrators (*tribades*). Ultimately, this discussion illuminates

---

1. Our title was inspired by the famous San Francisco- and (now defunct) Seattle-based worker-owned strip club, the Lusty Lady. We would like to thank Ruby Blondell, Kirk Ormand, and the anonymous reviewers for their comments.

2. VII.12.18–20. All translations are our own unless otherwise noted.

not only women's sexual agency but also the role of agency (in addition to penetration) in the Romans' conceptual map of sexuality.

HISTORIOGRAPHY OF "ACTIVE" AND "PASSIVE"

The use of the modern terms "active" and "passive" with respect to ancient sexuality first came to be important in scholarship on ancient Greek homoeroticism, specifically the practice of pederasty.[3] Kenneth Dover's *Greek Homosexuality*, published in 1978, is one of the most influential of these discussions, exploring Greek literary and artistic depictions of (primarily male) homoeroticism. In discerning the rules that governed these interactions, Dover asserts that "the distinction between the bodily activity of the one who has fallen in love and the bodily passivity of the one with whom he has fallen in love is of the highest importance" (1978: 16). He glosses "active" as "'assertive,' or 'dominant,'" and "passive" as "'receptive,' or 'subordinate'" (16). The older, or higher-status, partner is (or ought to be) the "active" partner (67, 83–84, 87), in the sense that he pursues his object of desire (44) and initiates contact (91). The younger, or lower-status, partner is (or ought to be) the "passive" partner, in the sense that he is pursued. If the older lover is worthy, the younger male ought to *hupourgein*, to "render service" or "serve as a subordinate" (44, 67, 83–84, 87). The words most often used in Greek to denote these two partners—the grammatically active *erastēs* for the former and the grammatically passive *erōmenos* for the latter—replicate in their voice this distinction between lover and loved, between the active pursuer and the passive pursued. Thus, by this definition, "active" denotes the dominant pursuer, "passive" the subordinate pursued.

In volume 2 of his influential three-volume *The History of Sexuality*, Michel Foucault adopts the concepts of "active" and "passive" to describe ancient Greek sexuality, but he uses the terms differently than Dover does.[4] For Foucault, the terms have two separate sets of meanings. One defini-

---

3. For further background on the historiography of ancient sexuality, see the introduction. For a re-evaluation of Greek attitudes towards pederasty, see Shapiro (in this volume); for a comparison of visual and literary representations of Greek pederasty, among other sexual acts, see Parker (in this volume).

4. Foucault does not profess to outline the entire schema of Greek sexuality, focusing instead on sexual ethics within philosophical and medical texts of the fourth century BCE. His investigation therefore focuses primarily on the idealized sexuality of elite Greek males. For feminist critiques of Foucault by Classicists, see, e.g., Richlin 1992 [1983]; duBois 1998; Foxhall 1998; Richlin 1998.

tion, perhaps the more important one for Foucault's broader philosophical project, is "quantitative," that is, "it has to do with the degree of activity that is shown by the number and frequency of acts" (1985: 44). For one to be "active" by this definition means that one is active *with respect to one's desires*; this entails exercising mastery and control over desires, with the result being moderation of sexual activity. To be passive with respect to desires, on the other hand, as women, children, and slaves were thought to be, means that one is not able to control or master one's desires. The result of such passivity, especially in the case of women, is sexual immoderation (85).[5] Indeed, the notion that self-control was the key issue for the Greeks when it came to conceptualizing individuals' sexual behavior is shared by James Davidson (1998 and 2001), who otherwise is critical of many aspects of *The History of Sexuality*.[6] Thus, for Davidson, too, "active" means self-controlled, "passive" means being enslaved to passions.[7]

In addition to this quantitative definition, Foucault also adopts a "role or polarity specific" use of the terms "active" and "passive," one stressing the distinction between sexual subject and object, agent and "patient" (46). According to Foucault, the primary element characterizing this polarized schema is penetration:[8] in his words, sexual relations are "always conceived in terms of the model act of penetration, assuming a polarity that opposed activity and passivity" (215; see also 220). In elaborating this model of sexuality, Foucault suggests a number of additional related polarities: those who penetrate are active, masculine, dominant, superior sexual subjects, whereas those who are penetrated are passive, feminized, dominated, subordinate sexual objects (46–47, 194, 210, 215, 219–20).

It is Foucault's "role or polarity specific" definition that has been adopted by the majority of Hellenists working on sexuality.[9] A particularly

---

5. See also Parker (on Roman sexuality): "The man weak (as women are weak) in self-control, in resisting pleasures, will be pathic . . . Thus, paradoxically from our point of view, the man obsessed with women is passive" (1997: 58).

6. Ormand likewise demonstrates the importance of sexual self-control in both ancient Greece and Rome (2009).

7. For the relationship between desire for sex and other appetites, see Davidson 1998; see also Worman (in this volume).

8. Foucault was not the first to argue for this equation; see Veyne 1978. Cf. also Dover 1978, who hints at a link between "passive" and penetrated when he argues that Aristophanes and other comic poets were tolerant of the "active homosexual partner" but "intolerant of the passive" (135); here he must mean, as he explains later, those who "submit to the homosexual desires of others" (137), that is, males who are, and like to be, anally penetrated, rather than the socially acceptable *erōmenoi* discussed in Plato.

9. E.g. Winkler 1990; Halperin 1990; Ormand 2009. Cf. Davidson 1998: 167–82; Davidson 2001; Davidson 2007 passim.

good example is the work of David Halperin, who argues in "One Hundred Years of Homosexuality," with specific reference to pederasty—but with broader ramifications—that Greek sex is both polarized and hierarchical.[10] It is polarized around, in his words, "the penetration of the body of one person by the body—and specifically, by the phallus—of another" (1990: 30). In Halperin's analysis, then, the terms "active" and "passive" are used as synonyms for "penetrating" and "penetrated." These polarity-specific terms also serve as a sort of shorthand for the constellation of characteristics associated with each sexual partner: thus, the "active" partner is also the sexual agent who dominates, initiates, and obtains pleasure (with the opposite holding for the "passive" partner).

This use of terminology—as well as a focus on penetration as the main organizing principle of ancient sexuality[11]—has been taken up by scholars of Roman sexuality, as well. For example, Amy Richlin in "Not Before Homosexuality" uses the terms "active" and "passive" to refer to penetrating and penetrated males in Roman homoerotic relations. Moreover, observing that (willingly) "passive" partners were disparaged for their effeminacy as well as their desire to be penetrated, Richlin argues that they comprised a vilified subculture in Rome.[12] She expresses some reservations about using the term "passive" for "penetrated," however, pointing out that it evokes, perhaps inaccurately, a sense of "inaction" (1993: 531). Craig Williams takes Richlin's concern one step further in *Roman Homosexuality*, using the more penetration-specific terms "insertive" and "receptive" in place of "active" and "passive" (2010 [1999]: 230–31, 258, 261, 309n16).

In "The Teratogenic Grid," Holt Parker continues the prevailing trend of using "active" and "passive" for "penetrating" and "penetrated," but expands their use to encompass heteroerotic as well as homoerotic relations (1997: 47, 48, 50, 52, 64n5). He represents this paradigm of Roman sexuality with a grid (table 1), the left-hand side of which is divided into two major categories—"active" and "passive"—while at the top are the three orifices that can be sexually penetrated.

---

10. Halperin 1990; Halperin *OCD*, s.v. "homosexuality."
11. See, e.g., Richlin 1992 [1983]; Richlin 1993; Parker 1997; and Williams 2010 [1999], with further bibliography in 412n16. For a critique of this penetration model as it applies to Roman sexuality, see bibliography cited in Williams 2010 [1999]: 258–62.
12. In contrast to Foucault and Halperin (as well as Parker and Williams, discussed below), Richlin argues for an essentialist interpretation of these sexual categories: "a free passive male [in Roman culture] lived with a social identity and a social burden much like the one that Foucault defined for the modern term 'homosexual'" (1993: 530).

TABLE 1. Teratogenic Grid (adapted from Parker 1997: 49)

	ORIFICE		
	Vagina	Anus	Mouth
ACTIVE			
Activity	*futuere*	*pedicare*	*irrumare*
Person	*fututor*	*pedicator/pedico*	*irrumator*
PASSIVE			
Activity	*futui*	*pedicari*	*irrumari/fellari*
Person			
Male	*cunnilinctor*	*cinaedus/pathicus*	*fellator*
Female	*femina/puella*	*pathica*	*fellatrix*

Parker then explores the implications of this model for Roman gender norms, stating that the normative male is "active" and the normative female is "passive," whereas "passive" men and "active" women are considered abnormal. He clarifies the role of women in this model thus: "As the opposite of *vir* [normative male], the *puella* or *femina* (i.e., the normative/passive female) has open to her exactly three possible sexual passivities: to be fucked in the vagina, the anus, or mouth. She can be a *fututa* (vaginal insertee), a *pathica/pedicata* (anal insertee), or a *fellatrix/irrumata* (oral insertee)" (49). He further explains: "A woman cannot be properly active at all, since she has no penis. A woman cannot (in the Roman scheme of things) fuck a man" (50).[13] That is, a Roman woman is ideally "passive," in the sense that she is penetrated.

Parker also uses "active" in a second, quite distinct sense, meaning something akin to "lusty." For example, he writes that "the sexually active woman is the prostitute or the adulteress, who inverts the values of the society. She hunts and seeks out men to give her pleasure and uses them as toys" (58). A proper woman, on the other hand, "is forbidden to *act* at all—her only acceptable role is to be passive" (53; emphasis in original). Parker further notes the Romans' ambivalence towards this type of "activity" in women, on one hand desiring it, on the other deeming it nonnormative.[14]

---

13. The exception, Parker later states, is in the case of the man who performs cunnilingus, who (he argues) is penetrated by the woman's clitoris; hence she "fucks" him (1997: 51). For criticism of this interpretation of cunnilingus, see, e.g., Karras 2000: 1260; Williams 2010 [1999]: 261.

14. "Not only do lovers (e.g., the elegiac poets) prefer sexually active, loving women to cold fish, but so do some husbands . . . Feminine passion, to satisfy cultural expectations, must be simultaneously active . . . and passive, still under the control of the husband" (Parker 1997: 56); "The anoma-

Moreover, the representation of female sexual agency has the additional effect, he argues, of creating "the willing victim": Romans could more easily justify acts of sexual violence or aggression by suggesting that their sexual objects wanted it (54).

SCHOLARS have thus used the terms "active" and "passive" in a number of different, and sometimes contradictory, ways. Most common is the use of the term "active" to refer to the person who penetrates, with the implication of a number of related traits (e.g., masculinity and dominance). In other contexts, "active" has been used to refer to the party who initiates and desires (e.g., Dover's *erastēs*, Parker's prostitutes). Finally, we have also seen "active" taken to mean "active with respect to passions," or self-controlled. This broad range of uses by modern scholars obscures what the Romans themselves may have meant when, for example, they called Mola a *fututrix*.

To access this conceptualization, we propose building from an emic model based on Latin grammar.[15] For example, Charisius, a fourth-century CE grammarian, glosses the terms *activum* and *passivum* in this way:[16]

> *Activum est quod facere quid significabit, ut "lego," <vel> corporis motum significans, ut "salio," vel animi, <ut> "provideo" . . . passivum est activo contrarium, quod pati quid significat, ut "uror."* (Char. 211.27, 29; text Schad 2007: 12, 292)

> Active is that which will indicate doing something, like "I say," indicating a motion either of the body, like "I mount," or of the mind, like "I foresee" . . . Passive is the opposite of active, [and is] that which indicates enduring something, like "I am burned."

If we apply these definitions to the sexual realm, "activity" should refer to more than just penetration; it should encompass, for example, performing a sex act, moving one's body during sex, or moving one's soul (i.e., desiring). Redefining "active" and "passive" along the lines of the Romans' use

---

lous woman, the woman active in any sense, is attacked as sexually active and hence monstrous" (Parker 1997: 59).

15. The following three paragraphs are modified from Kamen and Levin-Richardson 2015.

16. Grammarians on the meaning of *activus*: Plin. ap. Pomp. 5.227.25; Macr. *exc.* 5.652.21; Diom. 1.336.26; Sacerd. 6.430.18; Char. 211.27; Cled. 5.18.35; Prisc. 2.373.15 (cited in Schad 2007: 12). On the meaning of *passivus*: Plin. ap. Pomp. 5.227.26; Macr. *exc.* 5.652.22; Diom. 1.336.32; Char. 211.29; Cled. 5.18.36; Prisc. 2.374.1 (cited in Schad 2007: 292). We thank Curtis Dozier for his insights on the Latin grammarians.

of grammatical voice—that is, to indicate agency (or lack thereof)—illuminates a facet of sexual behavior *independent from penetration,* allowing for a more nuanced understanding of Roman sexuality.

In recent work, we have explored the representation of penetrated males in Roman culture as "active" or "passive" based on the definitions above (Kamen and Levin-Richardson 2015). Through examination of Roman literature and graffiti, we argued that some penetrated males (the *irrumatus* and the *pedicatus/fututus*) were conceptualized as passive, while others (the *fellator* and the *cinaedus/pathicus*) were characterized as active.[17] We then proposed a revised model for Roman sexuality that adds an axis of agency (active versus passive) subordinate to the main axis of penetration (penetrating versus penetrated).

Building from Parker's model, we replaced his terms "active" and "passive" with the more specific terms "penetrating" and "penetrated,"[18] and clarified his category "activity" by renaming it "verb."[19] Next, we divided penetrated males into "active" and "passive" based on their agency, supplementing Parker's model with the bold entries below (table 2):

TABLE 2. Penetration–Agency Model for Male Sexuality (Kamen and Levin-Richardson 2015: 456; modified from Parker 1997: 49)

	ORIFICE		
	Vagina	Anus	Mouth
PENETRATING			
Verb	*futuere*	*pedicare*	*irrumare*
Person	*fututor*	*pedicator/pedico*	*irrumator*
PENETRATED			
Verb	*futui*	*pedicari*	*irrumari/fellare*
Person			
Male (passive)	—	***pedicatus/fututus***	***irrumatus***
Male (active)	—	***cinaedus/pathicus*** (?)	***fellator***
Female	*femina/puella*	*pathica*	*fellatrix*

---

17. Since the term *pathicus* is related to *patior,* "to endure," we expected the *pathicus* to be a passive penetrated male. However, despite the etymology, the evidence suggested that at least some *pathici* were agents (Kamen and Levin-Richardson 2015: 455).

18. Cf. Williams 2010 [1999]: 230–31, 258, 261, 309n16.

19. We also corrected the verb *fellari* to *fellare* in the category of oral penetration, and removed the entry *cunnilinctor* [*sic*] in the "penetrated male—vagina" category (see further Kamen and Levin-Richardson 2015).

The question remains, where do active women like Mola *foutoutris* fit in this model of Roman sexuality?

LUSTY LADIES

> All night long I had a lusty girl, whose naughtiness no man can conquer. Tired by a thousand different positions, I asked for the boy routine; before I begged or started to beg, she gave it in full. Laughing and blushing, I asked for something more indecent; she exuberantly promised without hesitation.[20]

—Martial IX.67.1–6

It is not unusual in Latin literature and graffiti for women to be described as playing an active role in sex.[21] For example, the (nameless) woman described in the epigram above is the subject of active verbs (*dedit; pollicita est*), she moves her body in every way imaginable (*mille modis; illud puerile; totum . . . dedit*), and she wants it (cf. *lascivam; cuius nequitias vincere nemo potest; ante preces . . . dedit; luxuriosa*).

Rather than exhaustively survey every instance of female sexual agency, we focus here on three specific types of women: *fellatrices, tribades,* and *fututrices*. We do not suggest that these are sexual identities, but use the terms heuristically to explore different manifestations of sexual agency. In the close readings that follow, we pay particular attention to markers of sexual activity as established above (based on the model of Roman grammarians): performing a sexual act, moving one's body during sex, and expressing desire.

---

20. *Lascivam tota possedi nocte puellam, / cuius nequitias vincere nemo potest. / fessus mille modis illud puerile poposci: / ante preces totum primaque verba dedit. / improbius quiddam ridensque rubensque rogavi: / pollicita est nulla luxuriosa mora.* The poem continues *sed mihi pura fuit; tibi non erit, Aeschyle, si vis / accipere hoc munus condicione mala,* "But so far as I am concerned, she was undefiled; she won't be so far as you are concerned, Aeschylus, if you choose to accept this present on bad terms." As interpreted by Housman (1972: 725), after the woman has performed numerous sexual acts, the poet asks for fellatio ("something more indecent"). The woman promises to deliver on the condition that he reciprocate (the "bad terms" of the last line). Because the poet is unwilling to accept these terms, she thus remains "undefiled" by fellatio. Aeschylus, on the other hand, who is reputed to enjoy cunnilingus (Martial IX.4), would happily agree to the terms. All text and translations of Martial are from Shackleton Bailey 1993, with modifications.

21. Representations of female sexual agency can also be found in Greek literature. In this volume, see Gilhuly on the agency of the *hetaira* (in the context of Lesbos's association with female homoeroticism), and Boehringer on the agency of the female characters in Lucian's *Dialogue of the Courtesans* 5 (which she argues is a result of Lucian's "metadiscursivity").

Fellatrices

The term *fellatrix* is a compound of the verb *fello*, "to suck"—that is, to perform fellatio[22]—and the feminine agentive ending *–trix*. A *fellatrix*, then, is a woman who performs fellatio. The specific title is used only in graffiti, with Latin literature using active forms of *fello* or related verbs to indicate a woman who performs oral sex on men. The agent-noun for the male equivalent, *fellator*, is found in both literature and graffiti,[23] suggesting that the term *fellatrix* would have been easily understood as the grammatically equivalent title for a female practitioner of fellatio.

Literary depictions of women who fellate can be found in invective, where accusations or insinuations of fellatio functioned to mock the practitioner. Performers of fellatio were doubly stigmatized: not only was the performer's mouth penetrated by the act (which rendered the performer— regardless of gender and status—as feminine and servile), but the act was also thought to be particularly reprehensible for the pollution caused by oral contact with genitals.[24] Performing fellatio is often paired with other undesirable character traits, as, for example, in Catullus 59: "Rufa of Bononia sucks (*fellat*) her Rufus—Rufa, Menenius's wife, whom you have often seen in the graveyard grabbing the baked meats from the very pyre, and while reaching for a loaf rolling down out of the fire getting pounded by a half-shaven corpse-burner."[25] Not only does Rufa practice fellatio, but she does so on someone other than her husband, making her an adulteress. In addition, Catullus mocks her for the impious act of stealing food from a funeral pyre, and calls attention to her degraded social standing by representing her as beaten (or fucked[26]) by the lowest-of-the-low: the runaway slave of an undertaker.[27]

Martial, too, uses accusations of fellatio to slander women. In II.73, for instance, he attacks Lyris as both a drunk and a willing practitioner of fellatio: "Lyris is always saying that she doesn't know what she is doing when

---

22. See Adams 1982: 130–34. On fellatio, see also Krenkel 1980. For female performers of fellatio in Greece, see, e.g., Gilhuly (in this volume).

23. For *fellatores*, see, e.g., Kamen and Levin-Richardson 2015: 452–53.

24. See, e.g., Richlin 1992 [1983]: 27, 69; Williams 2010 [1999]: 218–24. See also Martial I.94 and III.87.

25. *Bononiensis Rufa Rufulum fellat / uxor Meneni, saepe quam in sepulcretis / vidistis ipso rapere de rogo cenam, / cum devolutum ex igne prosequens panem / ab semiraso tunderetur ustore.* Text and translation by Cornish, revised by Goold 1988, with modifications.

26. For the sexual use of *tundo*, see Adams 1982: 148.

27. For the identification of the half-shaven corpse-burner as a runaway slave of an undertaker, see Goold 1983: ad loc.

she is drunk. Lyris wants to know what she does? The same as when she's sober. She sucks (*fellat*)."[28] Sometimes Martial substitutes less specific verbs for *fello*,[29] as in VI.69: "I am not surprised, Catullus, that your Bassa drinks water (*potat aquam*). I *am* surprised that Bassa's daughter drinks water,"[30] or IX.40.3–5, where he says that Philaenis "made a vow for her man's return, namely to lick (*lingeret*), innocent girl, what even chaste Sabine women love [i.e., cock]."[31] Likewise, in III.97, Martial discusses the possible retribution of Chione—whom he has accused in other epigrams of practicing fellatio—against her lover: "I charge you, Rufus, don't let Chione read this book. She has been hurt by my verse, and she too can hurt (*laedere*)."[32] Although Shackleton Bailey (1993: ad loc.) suggests that Chione can hurt by kissing or bathing with Rufus, thus polluting him, a more likely scenario (and one more in keeping with the meaning of *laedo* as "to wound" or "to injure") involves hurting Rufus *during* the act of fellatio. For our purposes, however, it is sufficient to note that here, and in all of the cases above, the female subject is presented as *active*—that is, as the grammatical subject of an active verb (*fello*, *lingo*, etc.), and therefore as an active sexual participant.

Women are portrayed as practitioners of fellatio in graffiti, as well.[33] Most common are short statements that pair a female name with the verb *fello*. In Pompeii's purpose-built brothel, for example, we find *Fortunata fellat*, "Fortunata sucks" (*CIL* IV 2259, 2275), written twice, as well as *Nice fellat*, "Nike sucks" (*CIL* IV 2278). This type of statement wasn't restricted to brothels, but can be found in a variety of locations. Some can be found along streets, as in *Rufilla felat*, "Rufilla suks" (*CIL* IV 1651), written next to an altar to the neighborhood Lares on the Vicolo dei Soprastanti, and *Fyllis felat*, "Fyllis suks" (*CIL* IV 7057), extending over a meter of wall space near the back door of the House of Epigrams.[34] Oth-

---

28. <*Quid faciat se scire Lyris negat ebria semper.*> / *quid faciat vult scire Lyris? quod sobria: fellat.* For commentary, see Williams 2004: 231. For other examples of the verb *fello* with a female subject, see Martial II.50, IV.84, and IX.4.

29. For other possible innuendos of women performing fellatio, see, e.g., Martial X.95, XI.40, and XII.26 (27).

30. *Non miror quod potat aquam tua Bassa, Catulle: / miror quod Bassae filia potat aquam.*

31. *vovit pro reditu viri Philaenis / illam lingeret ut puella simplex / quam castae quoque diligent Sabinae.* For a similar use of *lingo*, see Martial XII.55.

32. *Ne legat hunc Chione, mando tibi, Rufe, libellum. / carmine laesa meo est: laedere et illa potest.*

33. This section focuses on Pompeian graffiti. For female practitioners of fellatio at Pompeii, see Levin-Richardson 2013, on which parts of this section are based.

34. Lararium: VII.7.22; back door of the House of the Epigrams: V.1.11–12. Misspellings in the graffiti have been retained and translated accordingly.

ers were written in houses, as in *Methe fela,* "Methe suk" (*CIL* IV 4434), from inside the doorway of the House of Eutychus.[35]

Other graffiti further describe or qualify the act of fellatio. One, from the purpose-built brothel, enhances the standard formula with an adverb: *Murtis · bene / felas,* "Murtis, you suk well" (*CIL* IV 2273, Add. 216). Some list prices for fellatio, as in *Lahis / felat / a(ssibus) II,* "Lahis suks for 2 *a(sses)*" (*CIL* IV 1969, Add. 213), from the building of Eumachia.[36] The image of a female face scratched next to *Mula fellaat Antoni / Fortunata aa II,* "Mula suucks at Antonius. Fortunata for 2 *aa.*" (*CIL* IV 8185), draws further attention to the female subjects—Mula (who may be our Mola *foutoutris,* with a misspelled name) and Fortunata—rather than the named male recipient.[37] The desire to accentuate the female agent's role can likewise be seen in a conversation between two graffiti in the purpose-built brothel. While the graffito *vere / felas,* "you truly suk" (*CIL* IV 2266),[38] leaves the practitioner unknown, a nearby graffito, by a different writer, may have claimed this act for Fortuna (perhaps a misspelling of Fortunata, mentioned above): *Fortuna sic,* "Fortuna in this way" (*CIL* IV 2266).

Finally, we come to attestations of the agent-noun *fellatrix* itself. In the purpose-built brothel, only Murtis earns the title: *Murtis · felatris,* "Murtis the cock-suker" (*CIL* IV 2292). The epithet is used five other times at Pompeii. On a crowded section of wall along the Vicolo del Labirinto, we see both *Timele · felatris / Timel,* "Timele the cock-suker; Timel" (*CIL* IV 1388, Add. 207), and near it *Nympe felatrix,* "Nympe the cock-suker" (*CIL* IV 1389), perhaps representing competition between the two women.[39] We find the title inside houses as well, as in the House of M. Terentius Eudoxus, where someone wrote *Amarillis fellatri,* "Amarillis the cock-sucker" (*CIL* IV 1510, Add. 208).[40] *Secundilla / felatrix,* "Secundilla the cock-suker" (*CIL* IV 9228), appears under a drawn phallus in the atrium of the Villa of the Mysteries, and *[?]ecidia fellatrix,* "[]ecidia the cock-sucker" (*CIL* IV 4192), was inscribed on one of the peristyle columns in the House of the Silver Wedding.[41]

Regardless of the original intentions of whoever wrote these statements—advertising the sexual acts of these women, expressing admiration

---

35. VI.11.8.
36. VII.9.1.
37. From the so-called tavern of Felix Pomparius: I.8.1.
38. We use Fiorelli's reading of the first line of the graffito as *vere* (at *CIL* IV 2266).
39. The graffiti are located on the wall between VI.11.14 and VI.11.15.
40. Also known as the House of the Forno; main entrance: VI.13.6.
41. V.2.i.

for or pride in their sexual acts, or disparaging the women by calling attention to their penetrated and polluted status[42]—the women are either the subjects of the active verb *fello* or described with the agent-noun *fellatrix*, and as such their sexual agency is highlighted.

The use of *fello* and associated terms in both graffiti and literature gains added significance when one considers the potential uses of the Latin verb *irrumo*. This verb refers to a male forcing someone to perform fellatio upon him, and translated colloquially, it means "to face-fuck."[43] For example, Martial responds to an accusation of senectitude thus: "Why do you keep calling me an old man, Thais? Nobody is an old man, Thais, when it comes to face-fucking [*irrumandum*]" (IV.50).[44] Martial's choice to say that he face-fucks (with the implication that the object of his threat is Thais), rather than to say that Thais fellates (as he accuses her of doing in IV.84), focuses the reader's attention on *his* action and agency, rather than on hers.

This suggests that there was an important conceptual difference between women as agents of fellatio and as objects of *irrumatio*. A graffito like *Nice fellat* (above) stresses *female* action, whereas describing a woman as "face-fucked" emphasizes *male* action. Likewise, a woman who is "face-fucked" is likely to be an unwilling participant (as *irrumo* was often a hostile act; see, e.g., Richlin 1992 [1983]) or a sexual object (e.g., Thais above), whereas Nice and other women who fellate are often conceptualized as sexual subjects.

Tribades

A second class of active woman in the Roman imaginary is the *tribas*. Literally, the term should refer to "a woman who rubs," but generally it is used to describe women who penetrate.[45] The first-century CE fabulist Phaedrus describes the origin of both *tribades* and effeminate men (*molles*) thus (4.16): a drunken Prometheus put women's genitals (*virginale*, 12) on the

---

42. For pride, see Levin-Richardson 2013; for disparagement, see Levin-Richardson 2011.
43. See further Krenkel 1980; Adams 1982: 125–30. See also Richlin 1981.
44. *Quid me, Thai, senem subinde dicis? / nemo est, Thai senex ad irrumandum.* For commentary, see Moreno Soldevila 2006: 364–65. For other uses of *irrumo* in Martial, see II.47, 70, 83, IV.17, 50; for *irrumo* in Catullus, see 10, 16, 21 (the noun *irrumatio*), 28, 37, 74; for *irrumo* in these authors, see especially Richlin 1981. For *irrumo* in graffiti, see *CIL* IV 1529, *CIL* IV 1931, *CIL* IV 2277, *CIL* IV 4547, *CIL* IV 8790a, *CIL* IV 8790b, *CIL* IV 10030, *CIL* IV 10197, *CIL* IV 10232a, *CLE* 1933 (Belgium), *AE* 1949: 00003 (Rome). See also Varone 2002 [1994]: 78 and 138.
45. For other verbs of rubbing used metonymically for sexual penetration, see Adams 1982: 183–85.

race of men, creating *molles,* and men's genitals (*masculina membra,* 13) on the race of women, creating *tribades.* The precise sexual acts of *tribades* are not described, but presumably penetration is involved, since *tribades* are thought to have *masculina membra.* Phaedrus ends the fable by drawing attention to the gender-inappropriate desire of these individuals: "thus lust now enjoys depraved joy" (*ita nunc libido pravo fruitur gaudio,* 14).[46]

The masculinity, or rather failed masculinity, of *tribades* is seen in many other literary sources, as well.[47] Seneca the Elder quotes a comment about a man who, after catching his wife in bed with another woman, first seizes the "man" (ἄνδρα) (*Controversiae* 1.2.23). Interestingly, although both women are called *tribades,* only one of them is a "man"—perhaps because she's the one thought to penetrate, or perhaps because by default the person sleeping with your wife is a man.[48] Seneca the Younger, in turn, speaks of women who "match men in their lust" (*libidine vero ne maribus quidem cedunt*) (*Moral Epistles* 95.21), though he does not use the word *tribas.*[49] These women, instead of being penetrated as they are born to be (*natae pati,* 21), actually penetrate men (*viros ineunt,* 21)![50]

Tribades also appear a few times in the poems of Martial. One tribad is called Philaenis, the same name Martial gives to a personified penis in another poem (II.3). In one epigram (VII.67), Martial writes that Philaenis penetrates both boys[51] (*pedicat pueros,* "she sodomizes boys," 1) and girls (*undenas dolat in die puellas,* "she drills eleven girls a day," 3). Not only that, but she also performs cunnilingus (*plane medias vorat puellas,* "she clearly devours girls' middles," 15), thinking, incorrectly (17), that cunnilingus is more manly than fellatio (14). Moreover, the fact that her practice of cunnilingus is common knowledge (*plane,* 15) makes things worse: she's not even hiding this disgraceful act. Indeed, both literary sources and graffiti heap extra abuse upon those who don't hide their depraved sexual acts.[52]

---

46. See also Williams 2010 [1999]: 233–34, 405–6n278 on this passage. For an alternate reading of this myth, see Boehringer 2007: 261–67.

47. For the masculinization of "lesbians" in Latin literature, see Hallett 1997 [1989]. See also Brooten 1996: 42–50; Boehringer 2007, s.v. "*tribade*"; and Williams 2010 [1999]: 233–35 and 238–39 on tribadism in Latin literature.

48. On this passage, see also Hallett 1997 [1989]: 258–59; Boehringer 2007: 267–71. For the Roman inability to conceptualize sex between women without penetration, see, e.g., Kamen 2012.

49. These women are said to equal men in other appetites (drinking and eating), as well, and partake in traditionally male activities (e.g., wrestling).

50. On this passage of Seneca the Younger, see also Williams 2010 [1999]: 238–39, and 407n296.

51. Hallett 1997 [1989]: 271n14 suggests that Philaenis might be a bilingual pun: *Phil-* + *anus,* "Anus lover."

52. In literature, see e.g., Cicero *Pro Caelio* 47 and Martial I.34. In graffiti, see e.g., *CIL* IV 2257: *Froto plane / lingit cun/num,* "Froto clearly licks cunt," and *CIL* IV 2400: *Satur noli cunnum · lingere / extra porta set intra porta . . . ,* "Satur, don't lick cunt outdoors, but indoors."

Elsewhere, Martial terms the same Philaenis "the tribad of tribads" (*tribadum tribas*, VII.70.1), who rightly calls whom she fucks (*futuis*) her girlfriend (2). In both poems, the *active* nature of Philaenis is stressed by the verbs *pedicat, dolat, vorat,* and *futuis*, and this activity, inappropriate for a woman, is the object of ridicule.

In another poem (I.90), we hear of a woman named Bassa whom Martial calls a *fututor*, "[male] fucker" (6): "You dare to join (*audes committere*) two cunts and your *prodigiosa Venus* feigns masculinity (*mentiturque virum*)" (7–8). *Prodigiosa Venus* is probably a double entendre meaning both "monstrous love," that is, inappropriate desire, and "monstrous organ" referring to an oversized clitoris (as Shackleton Bailey 1993 ad loc. takes it).[53] Either way, the poem draws attention to Bassa's active sexual role, highlighting her agency (the agentive *fututor*; *audes committere*) and sexual acts (i.e., implied penetration), all of which are condemned as gender non-normative (the masculine *fututor*; *mentitur virum*).

In sum, tribads are active in that they are the agents of sexual activity (and on a grammatical level, the subjects of active verbs). This agency generally takes the form of penetration—whether vaginal (girls) or anal (boys)—but might also take the form of cunnilingus. Apart from the last sexual act, which is unacceptable even for men, the tribad's other acts—those of penetration—are completely normative for men, but inappropriate ("monstrous") for women.

Fututrices

Finally, we come to the third type of lusty lady, *fututrices*, which brings us back to Mola *foutoutris*. *Fututrix* is a rare epithet that scholars have interpreted in two ways.[54] The first way, adopted by the editors of the *Thesaurus Linguae Latinae* among others, is to equate it with *tribas* (VI.1.1664.60–64).[55] By this interpretation, for a woman to be active in *fututio*, she must penetrate someone. The connection between *tribas* and *fututrix* is tenuous, however: in Latin literature, tribads are never described as *fututrices* (see above), and graffiti do not mention tribadic activities (penetrating a man or

---

53. See also Adams 1982, s.v. "*Venus.*"
54. In graffiti, *fututrix* is used only of Mola and *Miduse fututrix*, "Miduse the fucktress" (*CIL* IV 4196), inscribed in the House of the Silver Wedding in Pompeii. Cf. a possible instance of *fututrix* [*fotor*] on a curse tablet from Campania (*Def. Tab.* 191, on which, see Audollent 1904: 252–53). *Fututrix* also appears twice as an adjective in literature (discussed below).
55. See also Varone 2005: 96.

woman, or performing cunnilingus) in association with named *fututrices*.[56] On the contrary, Mola is represented elsewhere in the brothel as sexually penetrated. In one graffito, Mola's name is penetrated by a drawn phallus (*CIL* IV 2237, Add. 215), and another graffito claims: *futui Mula<m> hic,* "I fucked Mula here" (*CIL* IV 2203, Add. 215). Most scholars take Mula to be the same woman as Mola, and take her to be the accusative object of *futui*.[57] The only other mention of Mola (or Mula) in Pompeii, discussed above, again refers to her in a nontribadic capacity: *Mula fellaat,* "Mula suucks" (*CIL* IV 8185).

The other approach is to gloss *fututrix* as *ea quae fututitur,* "she who is fucked," as J. N. Adams has done in *The Latin Sexual Vocabulary* (1982: 122). The supposition in this case seems to be that a woman cannot be an active partner in *fututio*.[58] By converting the agentive noun to a passive construction, Adams has in essence restored Mola to her gender-normative (i.e., passive) role. We argue instead that *fututrix* should be interpreted in the same way as other female agentive nouns. Just as *fellatrix* means "she who fellates," not "she who *is* fellated," by analogy, *fututrix* ought to mean "she who fucks,"[59] not "she who *is* fucked." If someone wanted to convey the idea "Mola, she-who-is-fucked," or "Mola was fucked," he or she could have written *Mola fututa,* akin to another graffito from the brothel: *fututa sum hic,* "I (a woman) was fucked here" (*CIL* IV 2217).[60] There is no prima facie reason to doubt that the agentive ending of *fututrix* is significant and meant to capture Mola's *active* role.

One common assumption underlies both of these interpretations: that a woman cannot simultaneously be active *and* penetrated. If she is active, she must penetrate, or if she is penetrated, she must be the passive partner. As we argue above, the agency of a woman (whether she is active or passive) was conceptualized separately from her role in penetration (whether she is penetrated or penetrating). In what ways could a *fututrix*—or any other female participant in *fututio*—be active, then, if she didn't penetrate?

Close reading of the two attestations of *fututrix* in Latin literature, both in book XI of Martial's epigrams, helps provide an answer. In the first

---

56. Nor, as Boehringer (in this volume) points out, is tribadism associated with female prostitutes in antiquity.

57. Such as Zangemeister at *CIL* IV 2204 and 2203. The lack of final –m in graffiti need not indicate the nominative case (Väänänen 1959: 73).

58. Cf. Prisc. 2.487.1, 2.556.13 (cited in Varone 2005: 107n22).

59. See also Williams, who translates *Mola foutoutris* as "Mula [sic] is a fucker" (2010 [1999]: 297).

60. See also Levin-Richardson 2013; cf. Williams 2010 [1999]: 294, 428n25. For other graffiti with *fututa*, see *CIL* IV 2006 and *CIL* IV 8897.

instance, the poet warns his readers against fondling boys' genitals, since doing so hastens their puberty and, with it, their transformation away from sexual-object status (XI.22.1–6):

> That you rub snow-white Galaesus's soft kisses with your hard mouth, that you lie with naked Ganymede—it's too much, who denies it? But let it be enough. Refrain at least from stirring their groins with your fornicating hand (*fututrici . . . manu*). Where smooth boys are concerned, the hand is a worse offender than the cock; the fingers make and precipitate manhood.[61]

In this poem, *fututrix* is used as an adjective modifying the feminine noun *manus*; the hand is active presumably because it moves up and down on the boy's penis.[62]

In the second instance of *fututrix* (XI.61), Martial attacks a certain Nanneius for performing cunnilingus. About this Nanneius, Martial writes (1, 6–13):

> Husband with his tongue, adulterer with his mouth . . . he that lately used to go through all the inner tubes and declare confidently as of personal knowledge whether boy or girl was in a mother's belly (rejoice, cunts; this is to your advantage) cannot raise his fornicating tongue (*linguam . . . fututricem*). For while he was stuck deep in a swelling womb and heard the infants wailing inside, an uncomely disease relaxed the greedy member.[63]

Nanneius's *fututrix lingua* is active because it moves (*ibat*) through women's bodies. There are indications that this tongue also has agency: it is described as *gulosa*, "greedy," implying that it has its own sexual desires. From these two literary examples, then, we see that *fututrix* as an adjective seems to imply desire, agency, and movement.[64]

---

61. *Mollia quod nivei duro teris ore Galaesi / basia, quod nudo cum Ganymede iaces, / —quis negat?—hoc nimium est. sed sit satis; inguina saltem / parce fututrici sollicitare manu. / levibus in pueris plus haec quam mentula peccat / et faciunt digiti praecipitantque virum.*

62. See also Kay 1985 ad loc., who suggests that *fututrici manu* "indicates that the hand belongs to the person performing the active role."

63. *Lingua maritus, moechus ore Nanneius, / . . . modo qui per omnes viscerum tubos ibat / et voce certa consciaque dicebat / puer an puella matris esset in ventre, / —gaudete cunni; vestra namque res acta est— / arrigere linguam non potest fututricem. / nam dum tumenti mersus haeret in vulva / et vagientes intus audit infantes, / partem gulosam solvit indecens morbus.*

64. As an adjective modifying a feminine noun, *fututrix* can be used to describe either the party being penetrated (as in the *manus*) or the party penetrating (as in the *lingua*). When *fututrix* is used to label a woman, however, she is apparently not conceptualized as a penetrator (see above).

Descriptions of prostitutes and other lusty ladies in Latin literature further illuminate how a *fututrix* can be active. In Martial XI.7, a woman who is said to perform *fututio* (*placet ire fututum,* 13) is described as a serial adulteress with an itch (*scabies,* 6) for sex, highlighting her desire.⁶⁵ More often we find descriptions of women moving their bodies during sex. Martial twice describes prostitutes as wagging their bottoms (*crisat*) in an arousing or seductive way (*blandior, blandum*).⁶⁶ In the Priapic Corpus, a certain prostitute named Quintia is described as "very skilled at shaking ass" (*vibratas docta movere nates,* 27.2), and the prostitute Telethusa is praised for her gyrations (19): "Should the bare-ass pavement-pounder (*circulatrix*) Telethusa (who can shake it [*motat*] higher than her guts are churning) put her bumps and grinds in motion (*crisabit . . . fluctuante lumbo*), her technique would set atremble not just you, Priapus; she could even turn on Phaedra's stepson."⁶⁷ Telethusa's agency is stressed first with the agent-noun *circulatrix,* then with a description of her lusty movements (*motat, crisabit, fluctuante lumbo*).

Furthermore, the agency and movement of prostitutes stood, ideologically, in contrast to the behavior of proper wives.⁶⁸ As Lucretius claims (4.1268–77):

> Lascivious movements (*molles . . . motus*) are of no use whatever to wives. For a woman forbids herself to conceive and fights against it, if in her delight she herself thrusts (*retractat*) against the man's penis with her buttocks (*clunibus*), making undulating movements (*ciet . . . fluctus*) with all her body limp; for she turns the share clean away from the furrow and makes the seed fail of its place. Whores indulge in such motions for their own purposes, so that they may not conceive and lie pregnant, and

---

65. N. M. Kay comments that the active verb form of *ire fututum* suggests that the woman "is brazen and voracious" (1985: ad loc.).

66. Martial X.68.9–12, to Laelia, who sprinkles her speech with Greek: "Do you wish to know how you talk, you, a respectable married woman? Could a waggle-bottom be more blandishing (*numquid, quae crisat, blandior esse potest*)? You may learn all Corinth by heart and reproduce it, but, Laelia, you will not be altogether Lais." See also Martial XIV.203, about a girl from Gades, probably a slave-prostitute: "Her waggles are so tremulous (*tam tremulum crisat*), her itch so seductive (*tam blandum prurit*) that she would make a masturbator out of Hippolytus himself." Cf. Martial VI.71.1–2, where a woman is described as "skilled to match lusty gestures (*lascivos . . . gestus*) and dance to the measures of Gades."

67. *Hic quando Telethusa circulatrix / (quae clunem tunica tegente nulla / extis scitius altiusve motat) / crisabit tibi fluctuante lumbo, / haec sic non modo te, Priape, possit, / privignum quoque sed movere Phaedrae.* Text and translation Hooper 1999. For *criso,* see also Adams 1982: 136–38 and Williams 2010 [1999]: 178.

68. Cf. Gilhuly (in this volume).

at the same time that their intercourse may be more pleasing to men; which our wives evidently have no need for.⁶⁹

Proper wives, according to Lucretius, hardly move their bodies during sex, since doing so would make it harder for them to conceive. Prostitutes, on the other hand, gyrate in all sorts of ways (*molles motus, clunibus retractat, ciet fluctus*),⁷⁰ both because they don't want to conceive and also because they know that doing so arouses their clients. Robert D. Brown notes, moreover, that Lucretius's word choices in this passage suggest the prostitute's "active . . . participation" and "initiative" (1987: 366).

As for Martial, however, in his ideal world wives *should* be more like prostitutes—at least in bed. The narrator of epigram XI.104 claims to want his wife to be a Lucretia by day, a Lais (i.e., a prostitute) by night. She would then have sex fully naked and illuminated by light, give seductive (*blandas*, 9) kisses, "help the business along by movement of voice or fingers" (*motu . . . opus . . . voce iuvare . . . digitis*, 11–12), and let the narrator anally penetrate her.

In sum, despite the limited use of the word *fututrix*, literary evidence seems to suggest that women can be active in *fututio* in two main ways: by expressing desire for the act, and by exhibiting movement during sex.

BROADER IMPLICATIONS

As we have seen, lusty ladies—*fellatrices, tribades*, and *fututrices*—share the traits of desiring and performing sex acts, as well as moving their bodies during sex. In these ways, all three groups transgress gender norms that prescribe passivity for women, but this is not to say that they occupy the same conceptual space within the Roman imaginary. *Tribades*, because they are active and penetrate, are depicted as unambiguously negative, as an antitype: they are monstrous pseudo-men. *Fellatrices* and *fututrices*, on the other hand, are both disparaged and highly sought after for their whorish lustiness and sexual prowess. Moreover, because of their status as penetrated women, *fellatrices* and *fututrices* are aligned more closely with

---

69. *nec molles opu' sunt motus uxoribus hilum; / nam mulier prohibet se concipere atque repugnat, / clunibus ipsa viri Venerem si laeta retractat / atque exossato ciet omni pectore fluctus; / eicit enim sulcum recta regione viaque / vomeris atque locis avertit seminis ictum. / idque sua causa consuerunt scorta moveri, / ne complerentur crebro gravidaeque iacerent, / et simul ipsa viris Venus ut concinnior esset; / coniugibus quod nil nostris opus esse videtur.* Text and translation Smith 1975, with modifications.

70. For the sexual connotations of these terms, see Brown 1987: ad loc.

Roman gender norms than *tribades* are, although *fellatrices* bear the stigma of oral pollution. Regardless of the ways in which the activity of lusty ladies could be vilified, fetishized, or used to justify sexual violence (cf. Parker 1997, discussed above), there remains a clear conceptualization of some women as *active* in sexual encounters.

We therefore propose revising the conceptual map of Roman sexuality to reflect female sexual agency.[71] In addition to our already suggested replacement of the major categories "active" and "passive" with the more precise terms "penetrating" and "penetrated" (2015; see tables 1 and 2 above), we now divide the penetrated female category into both passive and active, and divide the penetrating person category into male and female, adding the bold entries to the grid.[72]

TABLE 3. Penetration-Agency Model for Roman Sexuality[73]

	ORIFICE		
	Vagina	Anus	Mouth
PENETRATING			
Verb	*futuere*	*pedicare*	*irrumare*
Person			
Male	*fututor*	*pedicator/pedico*	*irrumator*
Female	*tribas/**fututor***	*tribas*	—
PENETRATED			
Verb	*futui*	*pedicari*	*irrumari/fellare*
Person			
Male (passive)	—	*pedicatus/fututus*	*irrumatus*
Male (active)	—	*cinaedus/pathicus*(?)	*fellator*
Female **(passive)**	*femina/puella/**fututa***	*pathica*(?)	***irrumata***
Female **(active)**	***fututrix***	—	***fellatrix***

---

71. A similar revision to current models of Greek sexuality may be in order.

72. The Romans do not seem to have conceptualized penetrating women (or men) as anything but active; therefore, we do not further subdivide the category of penetrating female.

73. A few terms in the grid warrant further explanation. For a female penetrator as a *fututor*, see, e.g., Bassa in Martial I.90. The adjective *fututa* is not of the same register as the nouns *femina* and *puella,* as it draws attention only to a woman's sexual role, rather than to her social role(s). The term *pathica* is rarely used: there are some hints that *pathicae* express desire (e.g., *Priapea* 25.3, 73.1; cf. Williams 2010 [1999]: 196), whereas other examples are more ambiguous (e.g., *Priapea* 40.4, 48.5). The position of *pathica* under "passive" may therefore need to be re-examined. The term *irrumata* is not attested to describe women in extant literature or graffiti, but women who were the object of *irrumo* certainly existed, as suggested above. Cf. the male equivalent, *irrumatus*, found in Catullus 21.13, *Priapea* 70.13, and Martial II.70.3 (metaphorical); see also Kamen and Levin-Richardson 2015: 450–51.

This modified grid not only includes normative females, who are penetrated and passive, but also accounts for *fututrices* and other lusty ladies who are active, whether they penetrate (as in the case of *tribades*) or are penetrated. In the end, the most salient axis for sexual acts remains penetration, as proponents of the penetration paradigm hold. What we hope to have shown is that *in addition to* penetration, there was a subordinate but still important axis, one emic to Roman society, of agency.[74]

In addition, our analysis contributes to scholarship illuminating the agency that subordinated groups (like women and slaves) could exercise within the constraints of Roman society.[75] Though our chapter has focused on the Roman imaginary, an imaginary driven for the most part by elite male authors for an elite male audience (with the exception of graffiti), we can nevertheless suggest that real opportunities for sexual agency existed for women in Roman culture.

In this light, we return to the graffito with which we began this chapter, *Mola foutoutris*. Sexual metaphors relying on *mola*, "grindstone," and *molere*, "to grind," are not uncommon in Latin literature, and generally the woman is the one "being ground."[76] The juxtaposition of the name Mola with the title *foutoutris* might have served in this case to reclaim her agency: the grindstone fucks back.

BIBLIOGRAPHY

Adams, J. N. 1982. *The Latin Sexual Vocabulary*. Baltimore.

Audollent, Auguste. 1904. *Defixionum Tabellae*. Paris.

Boehringer, Sandra. 2007. *L'homosexualité féminine dans l'Antiquité grecque et romaine*. Paris.

Brooten, Bernadette. 1996. *Love Between Women: Early Christian Responses to Female Homoeroticism*. Chicago.

Brown, Robert D. 1987. *Lucretius on Love and Sex: A Commentary on* De rerum natura *IV, 1030–1287, with Prolegomena, Text, and Translation*. Leiden.

Davidson, James. 1998. *Courtesans and Fishcakes: The Classical Passions of Classical Athens*. New York.

———. 2001. "Dover, Foucault and Greek Homosexuality: Penetration and the Truth of Sex." *Past & Present* 170: 3–51.

---

74. Another possible axis (although one more relevant, arguably, to Greek sexuality) is relationship to one's passions. The two options on this axis could be called "self-controlled" and "lacking self-control."

75. See, e.g., Joshel 1992; Levin-Richardson 2013.

76. See Adams 1982: 152–53. For more on the possible connections between prostitution and bakeries, see Panciera 2001: 104–11.

———. 2007. *The Greeks and Greek Love: A Radical Reappraisal of Homosexuality in Ancient Greece.* London.

Dover, Kenneth J. 1978. *Greek Homosexuality.* Cambridge, MA.

duBois, Page. 1998. "The Subject in Antiquity after Foucault," in David H. J. Larmour, Paul A. Miller, and Charles Platter (eds.), *Rethinking Sexuality: Foucault and Classical Antiquity,* 85–103. Princeton.

Foucault, Michel. 1985. *The History of Sexuality.* Vol. 2, *The Use of Pleasure.* Trans. Robert Hurley. New York.

Foxhall, Lin. 1998. "Pandora Unbound: A Feminist Critique of Foucault's *History of Sexuality*," in David H. J. Larmour, Paul A. Miller, and Charles Platter (eds.), *Rethinking Sexuality: Foucault and Classical Antiquity,* 122–37. Princeton.

Goold, G. P. 1983. *Catullus.* London.

———. 1988. *Catullus, Tibullus, Pervigilium Veneris.* Cambridge, MA.

Hallett, Judith P. 1997 [1989]. "Female Homoeroticism and the Denial of Roman Reality in Latin Literature," in Judith P. Hallett and Marilyn B. Skinner (eds.), *Roman Sexualities,* 255–73. Princeton.

Halperin, David M. 1990. *One Hundred Years of Homosexuality and Other Essays on Greek Love.* New York.

Hooper, Richard W. 1999. *The Priapus Poems: Erotic Epigrams from Ancient Rome.* Urbana.

Housman, A. E. 1972. *The Collected Papers of A. E. Housman. Volume 2: 1897–1914.* Ed. James Diggle and Francis R. D. Goodyear. Cambridge.

Joshel, Sandra R. 1992. *Work, Identity, and Legal Status at Rome: A Study of the Occupation Inscriptions.* Norman, OK.

Kamen, Deborah. 2012. "Naturalized Desires and the Metamorphosis of Iphis." *Helios* 39.1: 21–36.

Kamen, Deborah and Sarah Levin-Richardson. 2015. "Revisiting Roman Sexuality: Agency and the Conceptualization of Penetrated Males," in Nancy Rabinowitz, James Robson, and Mark Masterson (eds.), *Sex in Antiquity: Exploring Gender and Sexuality in the Ancient World,* 449–60. London.

Karras, Ruth M. 2000. "Active/Passive, Acts/Passions: Greek and Roman Sexualities." *The American Historical Review* 105: 1250–65.

Kay, N. M. 1985. *Martial Book XI: A Commentary.* London.

Krenkel, Werner A. 1980. "Fellatio and Irrumatio." *Wissenschaftliche Zeitschrift der Wilhelm-Pieck-Universität Rostock* 29: 77–88.

Levin-Richardson, Sarah. 2011. "*Facilis hic futuit*: Graffiti and Masculinity in Pompeii's 'Purpose-Built' Brothel." *Helios* 38.1: 59–78.

———. 2013. "*fututa sum hic*: Female Subjectivity and Agency in Pompeian Sexual Graffiti." *Classical Journal* 108: 319–45.

Moreno Soldevila, Rosario. 2006. *Martial, Book IV: A Commentary.* Leiden.

Ormand, Kirk. 2009. *Controlling Desires: Sexuality in Ancient Greece and Rome.* Westport, CT.

Panciera, Matthew. 2001. "Sexual Practice and Invective in Martial and Pompeian Inscriptions." Ph.D. diss., University of North Carolina at Chapel Hill.

Parker, Holt N. 1997. "The Teratogenic Grid," in Judith P. Hallett and Marilyn B. Skinner (eds.), *Roman Sexualities,* 47–65. Princeton.

Richlin, Amy. 1981. "The Meaning of *Irrumare* in Catullus and Martial." *Classical Philology* 76: 40–46.

———. 1992 [1983]. *The Garden of Priapus: Sexuality and Aggression in Roman Humor.* Rev. ed. New York.

———. 1993. "Not Before Homosexuality: The Materiality of the *Cinaedus* and the Roman Law Against Love Between Men." *Journal of the History of Sexuality* 3: 523–73.

———. 1998. "Foucault's *History of Sexuality*: A Useful Theory for Women?" in David H. J. Larmour, Paul A. Miller, and Charles Platter (eds.), *Rethinking Sexuality: Foucault and Classical Antiquity,* 138–70. Princeton.

Schad, Samantha. 2007. *A Lexicon of Latin Grammatical Terminology.* Pisa.

Shackleton Bailey, D. R. 1993. *Martial* Epigrams. Cambridge, MA.

Smith, Martin F. 1975. *Lucretius* De Rerum Natura. Cambridge, MA.

Väänänen, Veikko. 1959. *Le latin vulgaire des inscriptions pompéiennes.* Berlin.

Varone, Antonio. 2002 [1994]. *Erotica Pompeiana: Love Inscriptions on the Walls of Pompeii.* Trans. Ria P. Berg. Rome.

———. 2005. "Nella Pompei a luci rosse: Castrensis e l'organizzazione della prostituzione e dei suoi spazi." *Rivista di studi pompeiani* 16: 93–109.

Veyne, Paul. 1978. "La famille et l'amour sous le Haut-Empire romain." *Annales économies, sociétés, civilisations* 33: 35–63.

Williams, Craig A. 2004. *Martial* Epigrams *Book Two.* New York.

———. 2010 [1999]. *Roman Homosexuality: Ideologies of Masculinity in Classical Antiquity.* Rev. ed. New York.

Winkler, John J. 1990. *The Constraints of Desire: The Anthropology of Sex and Gender in Ancient Greece.* New York.

CHAPTER SIX

The Illusion of Sexual Identity in Lucian's *Dialogues of the Courtesans* 5

SANDRA BOEHRINGER[1]

"This is not a pipe," Magritte declared in his painting *The Treachery of Images*. "Are these courtesans?" we may be tempted to ask when reading Lucian's *Dialogues of the Courtesans*. The question may seem peculiar, but it is a useful one for tackling Lucian when we are ignorant, or nearly so, of the real-life context in which these dialogues were performed. The question will serve as a vade mecum to help us avoid (or at least hope to avoid) the snares and ambushes of an author who spoke and wrote multiple languages, an itinerant sophist whose native tongue was Syriac, who wrote in Greek in a world under Roman rule, and is known for his humor, sophisticated learning, and exceptionally metadiscursive writings.[2]

One of Lucian's most seductive snares may be found in the fifth dialogue of this minor work. *Dialogue* 5 presents us with two women, one of whom describes to the other a remarkably erotic evening spent with two rich foreign women. Long neglected by scholars because of the

---

1. I would like to thank Ruby Blondell and Kirk Ormand warmly for letting me participate in this volume. Thanks to Ruby for her generosity, and the care and time she devoted to translating this article. Thanks also to her and Kirk for their careful reading, comments, and good advice. I am responsible, of course, for any errors or inaccuracies that remain.

2. On Lucian, see König 2009: 27–40 for a recent synthesis. On the metadiscursivity of Lucian's work, see Briand 2007.

253

group's "trivial" overall theme of sex for pay (the *Dialogues of the Dead* and *Dialogues of the Sea-Gods* are preferred), *Dialogue* 5 has recently—and rightly—had its moment in the sun, thanks to recent work both on its genre and on ancient sexuality.[3] In fact, after the publication of many works on male sexuality, when historians are facing the challenges posed by less explicit and more complicated texts about sex between women, this dialogue has seemed to some a veritable godsend: a long and complete account of a night of love among women. It seems not only to present us with erotic scenes among women that could have been taken from modern porn movies, scenes revealing gendered roles (one woman masculine and active, another feminine and passive), but to offer us, in so doing, the possibility of getting to know the representations and practices of the ancients a little better.

The goal of this chapter is to reconsider this justified enthusiasm just a little: not to deny that *Dialogue* 5 gives us information about ancient representations, but to try and understand how Lucian *uses* the erotic practices that he dramatizes for us in this way. This dialogue arouses an uncanny sense of familiarity in the reader, to the point where it seems legible and instantly comprehensible by anyone, whether or not they are an expert in the ancient world. As we all know, however, it is absolutely essential to mistrust such feelings when they are provoked by texts that are almost two millennia old. It is this necessary mistrust that underpins the historian's or anthropologist's critical sense; it is this that keeps us from imposing modern categories on ancient texts.[4] Yet when it is a matter of love, sex, and desire, lo and behold, we can be credulous enough to think that Lucian is talking to *us,* and to believe him when he says, "This is sex."

THE ILLUSION OF A MODERN DIALOGUE

Lucian's fifteen *Dialogues of the Courtesans,* composed in the 160s, belong to a group explicitly identified as such by the author. In addition to his

---

3. It is important to emphasize that after so many years of silence and lack of interest in female homoeroticism among classicists, the present volume includes three essays which partly tackle the subject.

4. On transcultural translation see Calame 2002. On the idea of exploring antiquity with the tools of anthropology and the use of "fuzzy sets" (a mathematical term) which enable us to avoid conflating categories anachronistically, see the introduction to Dupont 2010. See also Ormand and Blondell's illuminating introduction to this volume, on the evolution of research on ancient eroticism, the influence of Foucault, and new theoretical tools available to scholars of antiquity.

many satirical philosophical dialogues, Lucian composed three groups of dialogues that are distinguished by the identity of the speakers: sea-gods, courtesans, and famous dead people. According to one modern classification, these groups make up the set of "lesser dialogues."[5] Why "lesser"? Because they are short, but also because, according to some, they are not inspired by the same sources. Their influences are limited to mime, comedy, or the idyll, and their tone is, it is thought, far from that of philosophy or Menippean satire. Specialists in source-criticism have found in them significant reuse of motifs from Greek comedy of the third and second centuries BCE.[6] Yet the use of the particular techniques of a particular genre does not give us strong reason for believing that a work composed in this way will adhere strictly to the rules of that genre, and in the case of Lucian, this is highly unlikely.

The *Dialogues of the Courtesans* are short farces that seem to offer us a kind of survey of character-types from the world of commercial sex in "golden age" Athens—a reconstituted world that the educated public of the second century liked to imagine. In order to avoid misinterpreting these works, it is important to bear in mind that they are the products of this half-admiring, half-ironic infatuation with a classical Athens that was "made in the imperial period." We cannot use them as direct documents about the lived sexuality of Athenians or the conditions of the real lives of female prostitutes in the fifth century BCE.[7] The characters are not drawn from life, but developed using the techniques of a genre well known to apprentice orators: ἠθοποιΐα.[8] This was a progymnasmatic exercise that consisted in placing in the mouths of given speakers a discourse that was both as realistic as possible and as well adapted as possible to the character (ἦθος) of the person in question.[9] In creating type-characters, the author generates a group identity (based on geographical origin, occupation, or social status) by using *topoi,* predictable and superficial responses that he expects to match his audience's shared prejudices.

---

5. I am referring to—without necessarily endorsing—Bompaire's classification in the introduction to the first volume of the complete Budé edition of Lucian (in progress) (Bompaire 1993: XXIV). The *Dialogues of the Dead* are not classified as "lesser" because they seem more like the (longer) Menippean dialogues.

6. Note, however, that no one has yet been able to establish such an influence for *Dialogue* 5 (see, e.g., Legrand 1907 and 1908 and Bompaire 1958).

7. On Lucian's work as a historical source, see the summaries of different approaches and of the controversy on this issue in Anderson 1994: 422–26; Macleod 1994: 1362–421.

8. According to Reardon (1971), the rhetoricians do not seem to have used dialogue as such, but dialogue incorporates progymnasmatic elements.

9. On ἠθοποιΐα, see Amato and Schamp 2005, and especially Heusch 2005: 11–33.

Dialogue 5, the one that concerns us here, aroused no special interest prior to the twenty-first century. One reason, probably, is that its subject—sex between women—has often been thought of as merely a variation on the theme of prostitution. Numerous erotic novels, starting in the nineteenth century, do indeed evoke the private lives of courtesans and their love affairs with each other. Plenty of contemporary texts likewise link sex for pay with homosexuality (the unifying theme being debauchery). In the ancient world, however, as recent work has clearly shown, sex between women is *not* a *topos* associated with prostitution.[10] From the eighth century BCE to the second century CE, when Lucian was writing, there is no allusion to sex between women in works that mention female prostitution. The sense of déjà vu that a contemporary reader may experience—influenced, perhaps, by erotic videos of our own time—is an anachronistic reaction that should be resisted. Sex among women is far from a familiar erotic motif for the ancients.[11] It may be a cliché for us, but it was not for them, and we must *not* treat this aspect of *Dialogue* 5 as transparent or self-explanatory. It is also important to bear in mind that within the fiction of the dialogue the two central players, Megilla and Demonassa, are not, themselves, courtesans. In keeping with the theme of these fictional dialogues as a group, Leaena and Clonarium are indeed sex workers, but Megilla and Demonassa clearly are not. Lucian does not call them courtesans; they do not refer to themselves as courtesans; and indeed, there is nothing in the text to suggest that this is what they are.[12]

Let us look at Lucian's own words:[13]

> CLONARIUM: We've been hearing strange things about you, Leaena: that Megilla, the rich woman from Lesbos, is in love with you (ἐρᾶν) as if she were a man, and that you spend time together (συνεῖναι) doing (ποιούσας) I don't know what with each other. What's this? Are you blushing? Tell me, is it true?

---

10. Many studies of this dialogue, and also of Philaenis in pseudo-Lucian's *Erotes*, have concluded, wrongly in my opinion, that there is a link between prostitution and female homosexuality. For a summary and criticism of these approaches see Boehringer 2007b: 275–311 and Boehringer 2014. In her essay in this volume, Gilhuly illuminates the interconnection in our texts among oral sex (fellation), the island of Lesbos, and the profession of courtesan: these contexts are not concerned with "homosexual" women.

11. See Dover 2002 on an epigram by Asclepiades (*Anth. Pal.* V. 207) and the interpretations to which it has given rise. On the absence of this theme from "pornographic" ancient images, see Boehringer 2007b: 143–56.

12. On Leaena's account, Megilla and Demonassa have money and seem to lead independent lives. If they frequent the world of prostitution it is as clients, not as women who sell themselves. They also have a "conjugal" life outside this context.

13. The translation is by Ruby Blondell.

LEAENA: It's true, Clonarium. But I'm ashamed, because it's something (τί) unusual (ἀλλόκοτον).
CLONARIUM: By the child-rearing goddess, what is this business (πρᾶγμα). What does the woman want? What do you actually do (πράττετε) when you're together (συνῆτε)? You see? You don't love (φιλεῖς) me! Otherwise you wouldn't be concealing such things.
LEAENA: I love you, if I love any woman; but she is terribly manly (ἀνδρική).
CLONARIUM: I don't understand what you mean, unless she is a *hetairistria* (ἑταιρίστρια). For they say there are such women in Lesbos, masculine looking (ἀρρενωπούς), not willing to have it done to them (πάσχειν) by men, but preferring to associate with women (πλησιαζούσας) as men do.
LEAENA: Something like that.
CLONARIUM: Tell me this then, Leaena: how did she first try to seduce you (ἐπείρα), how were you persuaded (συνεπείσθης), and what happened after that?
LEAENA: She and Demonassa, the Corinthian woman, who is also rich and has the same skills (ὁμότεχνος) as Megilla, were organising a drinking party and had taken me along to play the cithara for them. After I had played, when it was late and time to sleep and they were both drunk, Megilla said, "Come on, Leaena, it's time to go to bed. Sleep here in the middle between the two of us."
CLONARIUM: And did you sleep? What happened after that?
LEAENA: At first they were kissing me just like men do, not just pressing their lips to mine but opening their mouths a bit, and embracing me and feeling my breasts. Demonassa was also biting me in the middle of (μεταξὺ) kissing me. I couldn't tell what the whole business (πρᾶγμα) was. After a while Megilla, getting rather heated, took off her wig—which was very realistic and fit as if it were natural—and I saw that she had her head shaved like the most manly-seeming (ἀνδρώδεις) of athletes. I was shocked at the sight.

But she said, "Leaena, have you ever seen such a handsome youth?"

"But I don't see a youth anywhere here, Megilla," I said.

"Don't feminize me," she said, "for my name is Megillus; I have been married (γεγάμηκα) to Demonassa here for a long time (πρόπαλαι), and she's my wife."

I laughed, Clonarium, and said, "Well, Megillus, we didn't realize you were really a man, just like Achilles when he was hidden among the girls (παρθένοις). Do you have what men have, and do you do to Demonassa what men do?"

"I don't have *that*, Leaena," she said, "but I don't need it at all. You'll see me associating with a woman in a way of my own that is much sweeter."

"But," I said, "You surely aren't a Hermaphroditus, as many people are said to be—people who have both kinds of things (ἀμφότερα)?" For I still knew nothing about the business (πρᾶγμα), Clonarium.

"No," she said, "I'm completely a man." I said, "I heard the Boeotian flute-girl Ismenodora telling hearth-side tales from her home, how someone at Thebes became a man after being a woman, someone who was also an excellent prophet, called Tiresias, I think. Surely you haven't experienced something like that?"

She said "No, Leaena, I was born female like the rest of you, but I have the mind (γνώμη) and desire (ἐπιθυμία) and everything else of a man."

"Is desire enough for you?" I said.

She replied, "Give yourself to me, Leaena, if you don't believe me, and you'll find out that I don't fall short of a man in any way; for I've got something instead of what men have."

I did give myself to her, Clonarium, when she begged me a great deal and gave me an expensive necklace, and a dress made of fine linen. Then I embraced her (περιελάμβανον) as if she were a man, and she went into action (ἐποίει), and kissed and panted and seemed to me to be enjoying herself incredibly (ἐς ὑπερβολὴν).

CLONARIUM: What did she do (ἐποίει), Leaena, and how did she do it? That's what I most want you to tell me!

LEAENA: Don't ask about the details, for they are shameful (αἰσχρά). So by the heavenly goddess, I won't tell!

At first glance, it is true, various aspects of this text have a familiar air. It is therefore vital to identify which of them overlap with modern stereotypes. One result of such stereotyping is the casting of Megilla as the protagonist.

IS MEGILLA THE STAR?

When *Dialogue* 5 is mentioned in general studies of Lucian, the context is usually speculation about its possible comic sources. This text serves as a site of disagreement between those who see in Lucian a talented imitator, who reworked pre-existing material, and those who give a more important role to creation and innovation in his work. Such scholars are concerned with sexuality only to the extent that, according to most of them, the theme of sex between women does not "suit" the genre of comedy.[14] The dialogue is also often cited in studies of erotic vocabulary because it includes so many sexual motifs in one place; but this just means adding a noun or verb used by Lucian to a list of usages by earlier authors. Such linguistic surveys do not provide a general account of Greek society, and the lack of any comprehensive picture, prior to these studies, of the system for categorizing sexual practices, sometimes leads to anachronistic interpretation of the women known as "tribads."[15] Moreover these scholars are only interested in Megilla's sexual practices, thus seeming, by implication, to exclude Leaena's caresses and Demonassa's biting kisses from the field of the erotic.

In more extensive studies of ancient sexuality *Dialogue* 5 features as one of the longest accounts of sex among women that have come down to us. Here again, however, it is not given extended analysis, since the scholars in question are interested primarily in male–female sex or in sex between men. According to most such discussions, Megilla exemplifies the female homosexual type, masculine and active (it is implied that sex between women involves one masculine woman and another, the feminine and passive partner, who should not properly be called homosexual). Lucian is portraying a relationship that is polarized in the way that a relationship between men would be (on the ἐραστής/ἐρώμενος model), and where the partners have specific gender identities defining them as different. Thus Dover, in the brief section on women in *Greek Homosexuality,* calls Megilla "a very masculine homosexual woman" (1978: 183). Cantarella, who sees in Megilla a "transvestite" and "man-woman," comments, "Homosexual women lose the natural characteristics of their sex, becoming a sort of caricature of maleness and appearing as a phenomenon in nature which reveals its monstrosity at first sight" (1992: 93).

Megilla's "masculine" identity is usually tied closely to her use of the term νεανίσκος to characterize herself and to her avowed possession of

---

14. Legrand thinks Lucian was not inspired by a scene from comedy, "given the theme of the dialogue" (1907: 62), but by pornographic writings or mimes like those of Herondas (1908: 231). Anderson likewise thinks there is no parallel for this dialogue in New Comedy and insists on its resemblance to the works of Herondas (1976: 95). Helm presents the dialogues as derived from New Comedy, but makes an exception of *Dialogue* 5 (1927, col. 1730). But we should beware of arguments ex silentio. Note, too, the comic fragment of Amphis (fr. 46, K-A) which mentions the special relationship between Artemis and Callisto.

15. Note, however, that this word does not appear in Lucian's dialogues. For the occurrences of this term in Roman and then Greek literature, see Boehringer 2003 and 2007b: 261–303. See also the contribution to this volume by Deborah Kamen and Sarah Levin-Richardson (though their interpretation differs in some ways), chapter 5.

"something instead of what men have." The latter has been interpreted in various ways. Brooten, who focuses on Megilla's "masculine" behavior and defends the active/passive interpretation, sees the "something" as representing Lucian's desire to affirm the importance of imagination and wit ("the mind") in sexual intercourse, and not as the use of a dildo (1996: 52, 154). But she is an exception. Anderson, writing some years earlier, says "Megilla boasts about having some kind of dildo" (1976: 95–96).[16] Winkler, who speaks of bringing a relationship between two women into "the determinate field of meaning" constituted by "the system, penetrator vs. penetrated," describes the scene as follows: "one shaven-headed prostitute straps on a dildo to mount another woman" (1990: 39–40 and 40n). According to Johnson and Ryan, Megilla's activities, as described by Leaena, constitute "active, dominant and sexually aggressive behavior"; she "represents transvestism as well as tribadism" (2005: 135). They explain Megilla's "something instead" as either an enlarged clitoris (i.e., an abnormal bodily structure), or a dildo.[17] (Either option, they say, explains the shame felt by Leaena, who only agrees to sexual union on condition that she is compensated.) Skinner, writing the same year, connects Lucian's dialogue with the construction of "freaks" in ancient literature and with Romans' fascination with the phallus, the tribad embodying the possibility of pleasure without a penis.[18]

The "official" bond between Megilla and her companion, suggested by her talk of "marriage" (γαμεῖν), has also aroused comment. Sirugo thinks that Megilla simply wants to show that they have a stable relationship, and that perhaps we can see here "an anachronistic allusion to the famous practices of Lesbos and Sparta" (Pellizer and Sirugo 1995: 163n32). Boswell seems to regret that Megilla does not provide details about the legal aspects of the union (1994: 82). Davidson compares their tie with the relationships between women found in Sappho and Alcman. He thinks we have good reason to believe that their relationship is officially sanctioned, or at least public, and that we should regard such bonds as fulfilling the same social functions as sexual relationships between men (2007: 405–9).

The verb γαμεῖν raises certain questions, however. Cameron, in a critical article challenging Brooten's translation of this verb as "marry" (in a text by Clement of Alexandria), shows that the word is often used euphe-

---

16. Anderson also declares, "We are in the same world as Herondas." That is inaccurate, however, insofar as in Herondas not the least suspicion hangs over female sexuality; most importantly, Herondas repeats clichés (already developed in Aristophanic comedy) to create an effect of comic realism, whereas Lucian puts clichés into perspective and plays with them, which is quite different.
17. I shall return to this interpretation below.
18. Skinner 2005: 252–53 (she calls it a "shaggy-dog story," 253).

mistically, and usually means "to have sex with."[19] He thinks that in this passage of the *Dialogues of the Courtesans* the verb should be taken *exclusively* in its sexual sense. The import of the conversation and Megilla's desire to win over Leaena prevent us, in his view, from taking it as "marry." According to him, γεγάμηκα (in the active) is used by Megilla to indicate in concrete, physical terms that she and Demonassa have sex together and that it is she who plays the masculine role. "There would be no point in introducing the idea of marriage at this stage of the negotiation" (1998: 142).[20] Yet the use of the perfect tense indicates a state; moreover, the temporal adverb (πρόπαλαι) makes it clear that this state has continued for a long time. If Megilla simply wants to inform Leaena that she has had sex with Demonassa, this adverb is unjustified. Nor is there any need for a euphemism (a cruder and more explicit term would not have been shocking in Megilla's mouth). Moreover the sentence continues in a way that prevents us from deciding unequivocally in favor of the sexual sense of γαμεῖν. Megilla says, "She is my wife," which indicates (within the fiction of the dialogue) a permanent bond as much as a sexual relationship.

Two recent articles offer a deeper analysis of *Dialogue* 5. Since they take into account both the dialogue's form and the scholarship on ancient sexuality from the 1990s, they are much more fully developed than the brief remarks by twentieth-century scholars. In her 2002 article, "Lucian's 'Leaena and Clonarium': Voyeurism or a Challenge to Assumptions?" Haley sets out to read this text using the queer tools of "pomosexuality" (postmodern sexuality).[21] Gilhuly, in her 2006 article, "The Phallic Lesbian: Philosophy, Comedy, and Social Inversion in Lucian's *Dialogues of the Courtesans*," shows that Lucian's work as a whole is pervaded by identification between the orator and the prostitute.[22] In all these discussions, whether shorter or

---

19. On the use of Greek and Latin terms for marriage to denote sexual union, cf. Adams 1982: 159–61. For the numerous Greek euphemisms for sex, see Henderson 1975: 154–61.
20. Cf. Cameron 1998: 143: "It is not the permanence of her relationship with Demonassa that needs to be spelled out."
21. Haley sees aspects of Demonassa and Megilla that shed light on the ancient social construction of gender and sexuality. She also raises the question of Lucian's attitude towards his characters (voyeurism? identification?) and finds striking similarities both to the polyamorous experiences of contemporary communities and to "butch" and "femme" identities (2002).
22. Gilhuly connects the author's specific cultural identity (as an "outsider") with the generic hybrid identity of the comic dialogue; she also notes that the dialogue is pervaded by an Athenian cultural norm: "the relentless focus on phallic sexuality" (2006: 282). According to her, we should understand Megilla's "something instead" in symbolic terms, to denote power and strength, what Judith Butler calls the "lesbian phallus." By examining the historical, philosophical, and mythic figures with whom Megilla (an "unprecedented portrait of a female homosexual" [2007: 275]) is implicitly or explicitly compared, she argues that Megilla shares a transgendered/transgeneric character with the

more fully developed, the analysis is essentially about Megilla, whether it concerns the sexual act or the social act of marriage. Even though the overall meaning of the dialogue and its significance have received very varied interpretations, there is a general consensus as to the paramount importance of this character. But Megilla is not, strictly speaking, one of the two participants in the dialogue. And most importantly, she is not the only woman involved in the relationship. If there is a circulation of eroticism in this text, then it is about much more than just one straightforward portrait of a "butch lesbian."

TALKING ABOUT SEX

Let us examine the language used in the dialogue to describe erotic practices and to characterize persons engaging in those practices. Clonarium's first speech begins *in medias res,* describing the relationship between Leaena and Megilla without preliminaries.[23] The plural verb, "we have been hearing" (ἀκούομεν), tells us that she is speaking not just for herself but as one of a group. She is thus presented from the outset as the mouthpiece of a larger group of which she is representative (betraying evidence of ἠθοποιΐα). Leaena is the object of the group's interest, and therefore the actual subject of the dialogue.

Leaena is rumored to be in a relationship with Megilla, who is "in love with" her (ἐρᾶν). The Greek verb is unequivocally erotic, devoid of the potential ambiguity of the English word "love."[24] Clonarium's inquiry is strongly focused on activity ("you are . . . doing [ποιούσας] I don't know what"). The common verb ποιεῖν, "make" or "do," can be used in an erotic sense,[25] and συνεῖναι confirms that the relationship is definitely sexual.[26] This verb, which has the basic meaning "be together, spend time together," is often used as a euphemism for "have sex with." It does not imply life as a couple. Clonarium's use of the present tense for all three verbs (ἀκούο-

---

genre of dialogue. Gilhuly's argument is much clearer and more convincing in her study of *Dialogue* 6, published the following year (2007).

23. On the double embedding of the opening speech, cf. Andrieu 1954: 308–11.

24. The addition "as if she were a man" (ὥσπερ ἄνδρα) makes this clear. Conversely, when Leaena says to Clonarium, "I love you," it denotes friendly affection (the Greek verb is φιλεῖν).

25. In comedy it can be the equivalent of βινεῖν ("fuck"). The Latin equivalent *facio* is used for sex in the imperial period in a very general way: the subject can be a woman as well as a man, or either member of a male couple (cf. Adams 1982: 204).

26. See, e.g., Henderson 1975: 159 and 214. Most translators render it as "live together," but that does not suit the way the relationship is presented within the dialogue.

μεν, ἐρᾶν, συνεῖναι) implies that the relationship is current, showing that it is not just a matter of a one-night stand: the two women have a regular erotic relationship. Her second speech reiterates these themes: "What do you do (πράττετε) when you're together (ὅταν συνῆτε)?" The grammatical construction (ὅταν plus subjunctive) again expresses repetition, letting us know that the women see each other regularly and will no doubt do so in the future ("What do you do *each time* you are together?"). The dialogue is, from the outset, focused on *acts*.[27]

We hear more about Megilla both from gossip and from Leaena herself. Clonarium has already heard that she is "from Lesbos." In many satirical and humorous texts, and especially in Lucian, geography functions as a shorthand for traits of character.[28] Here, Lesbos could allude to the island's general reputation for lubricity and debauchery,[29] and thus to unbridled sexuality, or indirectly to Sappho, and thus her sexual tastes.[30] The ambiguity is soon resolved, however, when Clonarium reports the current rumor about women in Lesbos who have sex with other women. An explicit link is made here—for the very first time in our surviving texts—between the island of Lesbos and the practices of women known in English as "lesbians." But Clonarium does not call them that.[31] She uses the substantive ἑταιρίστρια.

It is difficult to suggest a good translation for this word because it only appears three times in our surviving texts. It was probably invented by Plato in the *Symposium*: "Each of us," says Aristophanes, "is the complementary half of a human, because we were cut in half like flatfish, making two out of one" (*Symp*. 191d). He characterizes as ἑταιρίστριαι a subset of the "halves" that resulted from splitting the original female. As Kate Gilhuly also explains in her essay for this volume,[32] the word therefore definitely does not mean "homosexual" or "lesbian" here.[33] Given its place in the structure of Aristophanes' myth, it denotes, rather, an intensification of the idea of "women oriented towards women." ἑταιρίστριαι are, presum-

---

27. Note also her use of the words πρᾶγμα or τί, which are repeated several times throughout the dialogue, and can also be sexual in meaning (cf., e.g., Plato, *Symp*. 182a5).
28. See also the analysis of the proper names in the dialogue in Mras 1916.
29. See Henderson 1975: 163. The term λεσβιάζειν generally means "fellate." For a summary of scholarship on the connotations of Lesbos in the archaic and classical periods see Boehringer 2007b: 61ff.; see also Gilhuly's chapter in this volume.
30. It is only in this period that texts start to mention the particular character of the love affairs in her poetry. See Boehringer 2007b: 211–14 ("Le paradoxe saphique").
31. In Greek, the adjective "Lesbian" never signified anything other than "person from Lesbos." As for the term "Sapphic," it was used for Sappho's musical mode.
32. See Gilhuly, chapter 2.
33. See the analyses of Halperin 1997 and 1998 (and the expanded 2002 version).

ably, those women derived from the original female who do not behave in a conventional or measured fashion.³⁴ As for Clonarium's usage, she defines the word herself: "they say there are such women in Lesbos,³⁵ masculine looking (ἀρρενωπός), not willing to have it done to them (πάσχειν) by men, but preferring to associate (πλησιάζειν) with women as men do." The verbs πάσχειν and πλησιάζειν are unambiguously sexual,³⁶ and the rumors surrounding this kind of activity have a gendered aspect: these women are "masculine seeming" (ἀρρενωπούς).

Clonarium insists on hearing about every stage of the encounter. Her language draws on the traditional Greek vocabulary of seduction and the division of roles, into pursuer and pursued, that is involved in that tradition: "How did she first try to seduce you (ἐπείρα), how were you persuaded (συνεπείσθης)?" The two verbs (πειρᾶν, πείθειν) are drawn from the classical vocabulary of erotic courtship, as used, for example, by Pausanias in Plato's *Symposium* (182b). Here, however, the traditional roles are reversed: confronted with the enterprising Megilla, Leaena, the professional seducer, finds herself an object of pursuit.

Leaena is persuaded and submits—to Clonarium's request. She tells her the story of what took place during that first encounter. It all started with a party that was apparently a regular occurrence, even though in reality, where women were concerned, such behaviors (organizing a soirée, drinking late into the night, paying musicians) were strongly condemned by society. The hostesses were Megilla and Demonassa, who, we are told, "has the same skills" as Megilla (she is ὁμότεχνος). Leaena's status shifts in the course of the party: invited as a musician, she finds herself drinking with the other two women, then Megilla proposes that she spend the night with them. The ambiguous expressions "go to bed" and "sleep" leave us momentarily uncertain as to the exact nature of this proposition.³⁷ Then, after a final interjection from Clonarium, the narrative picks up speed. Leaena describes each woman's movements in detail and names specific body parts (lips, mouth, breasts), conveying the enthusiasm that seizes the three woman by means of a long sentence where action-verbs in the plural come thick and fast, and using the adverb μεταξύ (biting "in the middle

---

34. For this reason it should not be called simply the "myth of the androgyne" but rather the "myth of the three primordial beings." For a study of the word ἑταιρίστρια in this context, see Boehringer 2007c and Gilhuly in this volume.

35. See Gilhuly's analysis in chapter 2 of this volume of the semantic interplay between sexuality and the island of Lesbos.

36. Πάσχειν is the equivalent of the Latin *patior,* which is likewise a euphemism for the role of a man's sexual partner. Πλησιάζειν means "be near to" or "have sex with."

37. See the analysis of erotic vocabulary in comedy in Henderson 1975: 160–61.

of" kissing) to reinforce the impression of an explosion of activity. The body parts to which she refers are rarely mentioned in ancient erotic texts. Breasts (μαστοί) are not typically regarded as an erogenous zone, but usually linked to nurturing (not necessarily of a "maternal" kind).[38] Nor do Greek and Latin texts usually give detailed descriptions of kissing (elaborated here by the mention of light biting).

Leaena's account is thus unusually specific in its description of sexual activity. The fact that this activity is among women makes it still more remarkable. Moreover, if we read the *Dialogues of the Courtesans* carefully as a group, we find no descriptions of the kind of sex that we would expect to find, given the overall theme, namely erotic relations between these women and their male clients. With the exception of *Dialogue 5*, there is nothing about erotic pleasure, mutual love, or successfully consummated sex. The overall mood is gloomy, pervaded by jealousy (a feature of almost all the dialogues), violence—whether threatened[39] or fulfilled[40]—gruesome war-stories,[41] the ruthless pursuit of profit,[42] lies and malicious gossip,[43] sorrow, empty hopes, and thwarted expectations. The women, whether they are very young[44] or older, deceive their clients and are themselves faced with deception. Few passages describe pleasure that is genuinely felt, either by the client alone or by two people in each other's arms: sexual connection is faked[45]—out of jealousy[46] or spite—hoped for but unfulfilled,[47] or even

---

38. This word is used for animals' udders and for women's nursing breasts. The poetic term for the breast is μῆλον, which denotes a round fruit.

39. Polemo has returned from war and is furious to find Pannychis with Philostratus and threatens the latter (*Dial.* 9.5).

40. For Ampelis, slaps and blows are proof of love (*Dial.* 8.1–2); Parthenis has been hit by Dinomachus, who has also dragged a peasant by his hair and beaten him bloody (*Dial.*15.1).

41. The proud Leontichus boasts at length of his war exploits (*Dial.* 13.1–2).

42. This is obviously to be expected in works set in the world of prostitution. See, e.g., *Dial.* 6.4, 8.3, 9.2, 14.2–3.

43. Musarium's mother tries to convince her daughter that Chaereas's promises are ruses (*Dial.* 7.4); Tryphena, to get Charmides back, paints a hideous portrait of the woman he loves (*Dial.* 11.3); Leontichus's war stories are pure invention (*Dial.* 13.6).

44. *Dialogue* 6 portrays a mother giving advice to her very young daughter who is just entering the profession.

45. Philinna kisses Lamprias in revenge, after her lover Diphilus avidly kisses the beautiful Thais in front of her to provoke her: desire does not motivate any of these kisses (*Dial.* 3).

46. Ampelis says the only way to make men loving is to make them jealous (*Dial.* 8.3).

47. Glycera does not come to terms with the loss of her lover, who has gone off with Gorgona, and keeps hoping for his return (*Dial.* 1); Drosis, whose lover Clinias has been taken in hand by a philosophy professor, reads his letter sadly and tries to find a way to get him back (*Dial.* 10).

withheld.[48] A kiss is no more than a way to make someone else jealous,[49] and the *only* scene describing real pleasure is in the sole dialogue from which men are completely absent. This is, moreover, the only three-way that is mentioned in the *Dialogues of the Courtesans*. Every other erotic triangle involves jealousy (and definitely not group sex), resulting from the assumption that a binary partnership is desired. In fact, nearly all the other dialogues involve jealousy of some kind. *Dialogue 5* is thus unique for its eroticism. In this context, its portrayal of sex among women is best understood as an ἀπροσδόκητον—something unexpected, intended to arouse the surprise that every good orator tries to provoke in his audience.

LIES AND TRUTH: A SOCRATIC INQUIRY

The three bodies are tangled up in movement, the tension at its height, when something unexpected intervenes, triggering a dialogue within the dialogue: Megilla's wig. When this wig (which no one remarked on beforehand) is removed, Leaena sees that Megilla has her head shaved bare (ἀποκεκαρμένη). The perfect tense underlines the fact that her baldness results from a voluntary act, as opposed to ill health or a congenital defect.[50] Even before Megilla asks to be called Megillus, her baldness shocks Leaena. So great is the symbolic weight of the cultural code that this simple modification of a body part *completely* transforms a person's appearance. The bald head, exposed in its nakedness, is specifically masculine, because it recalls "the most manly-seeming" (ἀνδρώδεις) of athletes,[51] or, as we are told elsewhere in Lucian, because it is a feature of Spartan dress (*Runaways* 27). Similarly, in *Dialogue* 12, when Lysias sees someone with a shaved head in his mistress's bed he immediately thinks she is cheating on him with

---

48. Philinna refuses herself to Diphilus (*Dial.* 3.3); the jealous Lysias refused himself for a long time to Joessa, whom he believed unfaithful; Joessa expresses her sorrow (*Dial.* 12.1).

49. Diphilus kisses Thais to provoke Philinna (*Dial.* 3.2).

50. Elsewhere in these Dialogues, to discourage Charmides, Triphena says that Philematium has numerous blotches on her skin, is old, and wears a wig (*Dial.* 11, 3). The courtesan Pythias, according to Joessa, wears a wig because her hair fell out as a result of illness (*Dial.* 12, 5; for the probable echo of *Dialogue 5* see below).

51. In Greek representations athletes usually have short hair, or heads shaved round the edge, leaving hair only on the crown of the head (this is called the σκαφίον). The adjective ἀρρενωπός, "manly looking," used earlier by Clonarium for the Lesbian women who have sex with women, appears eight times in Lucian's oeuvre, and is associated with a bald or shaved head in half the cases. In addition to *Dial. of the Courtesans* 5, 2 see *Hermotimus* 18; *The Runaways* 27; *The Double Indictment or Trials by Jury* 20 (ἐν χρῷ κέκαρμαι).

another man.⁵² Megilla likewise, as Leaena tells it, sees her own shaved head as sufficient reason for thinking that one might regard her as a handsome youth (νεανίσκος) and call her Megillus.⁵³ (Note that she is not an ἀνήρ—a mature man—a point to which I shall return.) This specificity regarding both her age and the gender of her name is joined by an important social specificity: Megilla is the husband of Demonassa, because she "has married" her: the latter is her "wife."⁵⁴

This announcement arrives as a coup de théâtre. The feverish sexual activity stops and a serious discussion ensues, using the question and answer form associated with Platonic dialogue. This discussion is more about Megillus's masculinity than her claim to be "married." Leaena offers an initial interpretation by mentioning the episode in myth where the youthful Achilles was dressed as a girl and hidden among king Lycomedes' daughters.⁵⁵ The comparison is highly amusing: Megilla is being likened to one of the greatest Greek heroes, and the courtesans to virginal young girls (παρθένοι) of noble family. But the idea that Megilla is actually a cross-dressed Megillus is a rationalistic explanation. On this interpretation Megilla's *feminine* appearance would be deceptive and she would be, in reality, a man. Baldness is not enough to prove a sexual identity, however, since it is only a matter of appearances. As a woman who knows men, Leaena wants to know two more things to confirm her theory. One of her questions is about the body (does Megilla have what men have [τὸ ἀνδρεῖον]?) and the other is about behavior (does she do to Demonassa what men do?).

Leaena continues with her inquiry in an extremely logical manner. When Megilla responds negatively to the first question, and affirmatively to the second, the next step is to propose a different explanation. This time she suggests a possibility drawn not from reason but from the realm of miracles (θαύματα). By alluding to the mythic figure of Hermaphroditus,

---

52. *Dialogue* 12 provides a humorous echo of *Dialogue* 5. Joessa does not understand why her lover Lysias is neglecting her. He replies that one evening he came to see her and thought she was cheating on him because he surprised in her bed a young man with a shaved head (ἐν χρῷ κεκαρμένον, 12.4, the same wording as in *Dialogue* 5). He feels sad and deceived. Joessa denies the charge: the person in her bed was her female friend Pythias, who is bald because of an illness and wears a wig during the day. The explanation she gives Lysias makes sense, but the audience knows only what Joessa wants her lover to hear. After what Leaena has revealed to Clonarium, Lucian's audience is alerted: there was indeed no man in Joessa's bed, but that does not mean she has not cheated on Lysias.

53. A Megillus appears in Lucian's *The Downward Journey* 22.2, where he is described as καλός.

54. On γαμεῖν, see above.

55. Note too that in myth the young hero, while using a feminine name and dressed accordingly, falls in love with Deidameia, the king's daughter, and fathers a child with her.

whose body was merged with that of a nymph to create a creature of both sexes (Ovid, *Met.* IV, 271–388), Leaena suggests that Megilla suffers from a physical abnormality. On this theory, for reasons either rationally explicable (accident of birth) or supernatural (divine transformation), Megilla would have the physical attributes of both sexes (ἀμφότερα).

When the object of her inquiry replies in the negative, Leaena moves squarely into the realm of the supernatural. Perhaps Megilla was transformed by a divinity, like Teiresias, who "became a man after being a woman"? According to the best-known version of this myth Teiresias was, in fact, born male. It was his first metamorphosis—the temporary transformation of a man into a woman—that lingered in the Greek imagination.[56] But Leaena reverses the order, to highly comic effect, either out of ignorance, or to make the myth correspond more closely to Megilla's situation. Lucian's humor is particularly subtle here, since Leaena makes it clear that she does not know the famous myth directly. There is, moreover, a rather rare variant (which Lucian certainly knew) whereby Teiresias was a woman first, before being transformed into a man.[57] This is typical of Lucian's humor, to present his audience with a prostitute endowed, despite herself, with remarkable learning, while subtly introducing into his discussion the theme of female pleasure.[58]

When Megilla denies this explanation too, Leaena introduces the last stage of this dialogue within the dialogue, which concerns sexual identity: the two women start debating what it is that makes a man a man. For Leaena, it is the male sexual organ, for Megilla it is "mind" (γνώμη) and "desire" (ἐπιθυμία). (Were we not on our guard, we might think the two courtesans were inventing the sex/gender distinction . . .) Leaena wonders whether desire, by itself, is "enough," but Megilla assures her that she does not need a penis because she has "something instead."

With this exchange we leave the embedded dialogue and return to the narrative frame. Leaena describes—briefly but unambiguously—sexual intercourse between herself and Megilla. Leaena fulfilled her courtesan's role as a purveyor of pleasure, while Megilla too "went into action" (ποιεῖν, here unambiguously sexual), and experienced a pleasure both extreme and externally manifest. Nor did Leaena remain passive: she embraced Megilla

---

56. For the different versions of the myth of Teiresias, see Brisson 1976.

57. See Eustathius, *Commentarii ad Homeri Odysseam* X. 494 and the fragments of Ptolemy Chennus. Cf. Brisson 1976: 78–81, esp. 78n1.

58. According to one version of the myth, Teiresias was transformed because he revealed the difference between male and female sexual pleasure. For the various versions see Brisson 1976, Appendices.

(περιλαμβάνειν) and made love to her as if to a man. Περιλαμβάνειν is definitely erotic in meaning. Alan Cameron, in the discussion of γαμεῖν mentioned earlier, talks about this verb too. Relying on a study by Louis Robert (1965: 184–89), he suggests the translation "fondle" or "cuddle" (Cameron 1998: 144). The verb appears in a funerary inscription from Aphrodisias offering what Robert calls "advice for a good life." The deceased addresses the passerby and exhorts him to enjoy life: "Eat, drink, enjoy yourself, and περιλάμβανε."[59] Robert compares this with other similar exhortations: "Eat, drink, live voluptuously, make love (ἀφρωδίασον),"[60] and "Eat, drink, fuck (βείνησον),"[61] and infers from this popular advice that περιλαμβάνειν can be erotic in meaning. In fact, Cameron's examples allow us to take the verb in an even more strongly erotic way than he proposes. I suggest that περιλαμβάνειν in our dialogue refers not merely to an embrace, but to sexual intercourse.

Once Leaena has finished her story, her audience—Clonarium—wants to know more about the women's methods (τρόπος)—their techniques for the production of pleasure; but the dialogue ends with the impression of a well-kept secret and an opaque air of mystery.

Everything has led us to expect a scene of erotic persuasion, in which Megilla would praise the charms and attributes of the woman she is courting. Instead, the audience is treated to a parody of philosophical dialogue, with a sequence of questions and answers proceeding by logical steps. As I have argued elsewhere, Plato's dialogues, especially the *Symposium,* are central to a proper understanding of Lucian's purpose.[62] Megilla gives information to Leaena little by little, making the argument proceed in the manner of Platonic συζητεῖν or joint inquiry. The structure of the inquiry resembles that of many Platonic dialogues, with one partner proposing a series of explanations, each of which is rejected by the other. As in Platonic dialogue, the speakers make use of myth and analogy. And the ending is aporetic, a little frustrating no doubt, in Socratic style.

The fundamental importance of Platonic dialogue is further reinforced by more specific allusions to the *Symposium* and *Laws*. I have already mentioned—as Kate Gilhuly does in this volume (see chapter 2)—Clonarium's use of the word ἑταιρίστρια, and Leaena's employment of the vocabulary

---

59. Funerary inscription from Aphrodisias n° 569, 5–6 (cf. Robert 1965: 184).
60. From an epitaph from Kios (cf. Robert 1965: 189n1).
61. From an epitaph from Azanoi (cf. Robert 1965: 189n2). Robert also cites CIG 7299 and Machon (Gow, frag. 16) for an intransitive use of the verb.
62. See Blondell and Boehringer 2014, which develops the argument about Plato summarized here.

of courtship.⁶³ The very form of the work, which evokes the philosophical dialogues of the classical period,⁶⁴ primes the audience to pick up on these resonances. If there are sources and a subtext to be uncovered here, they are to be found, contrary to the traditional classification that I mentioned earlier, not in comedy or mime, but in philosophy.⁶⁵

CONFUSION IS NOT REVERSAL

The expression "gender-confusion" is frequently used in discussing ancient sex roles. It often serves to indicate a "reversal" of genders: a woman acts "like a man," or a man has "feminine" characteristics. But quite apart from the need to be clearer about the influence of contemporary notions on our judgment of what counts as "masculine" and "feminine" in ancient sexuality, this accepted use of the term is not adequate to the text of Lucian. What he provides is not a reversal but a confusion in the strict sense, one that is, moreover, a confusion *within* a confusion, since in the midst of what appears to be reversed or confused we find elements that seem to make sense. It is thus not a matter of disturbing a defined field—the field of gender—but of placing in question the very assumption that we should try to make rational sense of this confusion of gendered codes. Since the list of sexual motifs that Lucian takes up and distorts in *Dialogue* 5 is too long to detail here, I shall confine myself to developing three points that exemplify this confusion—as opposed to reversal—of conventional assumptions.

"Something Instead"

According to Leaena, Megilla, who likes to think of herself as Megillus, is "terribly manly" (ἀνδρική). At first glance her meaning seems simple: Megilla will play the "active" role in relation to both Demonassa and Leaena, while they are both assigned the "passive" role. Yet Demonassa—who, we should recall, has "the same skills" as Megilla—also behaves "just like men do" in embracing Leaena, and Leaena herself takes the initiative too. There is thus no active–passive or masculine–feminine reversal.⁶⁶

---

63. For other Platonic allusions see Gilhuly 2006, and Blondell and Boehringer 2014.
64. On the philosophical dialogue generally see Andrieu 1954; on Plato's use of dialogue form see esp. Blondell 2002.
65. *Pace* Bompaire, who writes, "here the Lucianic dialogue has no contact with philosophy" (1993: XXV). I shall return to this point below.
66. In this respect I do not agree with every aspect of Kamen and Levin-Richardson's discussion

Lucian sows even more doubt by leaving us uncertain as to what exactly Megilla has "instead of what men have." The author leaves open two different possibilities. Either Megilla has an ὄλισβος (a dildo) that replaces the penis,[67] or her specific practices are veiled in mystery. Leaena plays the part of someone who thinks sex between women is impossible without a phallus (she never stops asking openly incredulous questions). But the end of the dialogue brings no clear answer; instead, it leaves any listener who may have believed in the active/passive division of roles (with the "manly" and active woman using a dildo) mired in perplexity.

A third (modern) theory, that she has an abnormally large clitoris, is definitely ruled out for several reasons, starting with the fact that there is no evidence for it in the text. More importantly, the ancients do not attribute such a physical abnormality to "homosexual" women.[68] But this interpretation of what Megilla "has" does not reflect ancient ideas about women having sex with women, or even about dominant, sexually active women, and thus does not supply a "rational" answer to Clonarium's questions. Greek texts from the archaic, classical, and Hellenistic periods provide no support for this view.[69] As for the Roman period, none of the evidence that has been adduced actually supports this hypothesis.[70] Later medical writers recommend and describe ablation of the clitoris for women whose organ has grown abnormally large,[71] but there is no mention, in these passages, of sexual behavior among women.[72] It is obviously anachronistic to supply an implication for Lucian based on the medieval and modern reception of Greek and Latin medical texts.

---

of the word *tribas* in their rich study in the present volume: the representation of active/passive symmetry (and the degree to which it is appropriate to attribute sexual activity and passivity to such representations) is not always firmly established or identical across discursive contexts.

67. Note, however, that neither this word nor any equivalent appears anywhere in the text.

68. The belief that they do is based on erroneous interpretations of two of Martial's epigrams, Epigram I, 90 and VII, 67. See Howell 1980: 298; Sullivan 1991: 206. For the application of this idea to Megilla, see Vorberg 1965: 654. A passage in Seneca *Ep.* 95 has been interpreted similarly (see Adams 1982: 79, 97, 122). Krenkel 1979: 171 and Vorberg 1965: 655 cite this same passage of Seneca as representing female homosexual behavior. But Seneca only talks about women who have sex with men; there is nothing in his entire oeuvre about sex between women. This view persists in recent work on sexuality (see, e.g., Parker 1997: 49; Halperin 1990: 166n83; Brooten 1996: 143–73).

69. See Boehringer 2007b, esp. 333–35.

70. See Boehringer 2011 (on Martial); Boehringer 2007b: 314–21 (on Petronius, *Satyrica,* 67, 11–13); 295–307 (on Pseudo-Lucian, *Amores,* 27–29). On Phaedrus, IV. 16, see Boehringer 2007b: 261–68, which develops an interpretation of the poem countering the image of the phallic woman and the vulvic man (contra Williams 2010: 232–33, and note 278).

71. Soranos (early second century), Caelius Aurelianus (fifth century), Mustio (fifth or sixth century), then Paul of Aegina (seventh century). See Brooten 1996: 143–73.

72. Noted also by Clark 1993: 90. Hanson makes it clear that clitoridectomy was sometimes prescribed in cases of enlargement of the clitoris that caused "hypersexuality," as opposed to active sexuality or sex with women (Hanson 1990: 333–34).

The claim that dildos were used by "ancient lesbians" has also been used to interpret *Dialogue* 5. But the ὄλισβος is not, in ancient texts or images, a sign of sex between women.[73] Dildos are often shown in vase-painting in scenes of sex among men and women.[74] With the exception of just two not very explicit vases,[75] however, ὄλισβοι are not used by women together. In texts dildos are a comic motif, a stock theme for satirizing women, who are typically presented as excessively prone to sex and incapable of self-control. References to ὄλισβοι in Aristophanes contain no allusion to homosexual behavior.[76] The same applies to the term βαυβῶν, perhaps connected to the name Baubō,[77] which has the same meaning,[78] and also appears in comedy but with no suggestion of homosexual activity.[79] None of the women portrayed here envisages for a moment sharing the object in question or using it together. At Rome the dildo appears occasionally in texts, but again without any such connotation.[80] We should

---

73. See Boehringer 2007b: 146–50.

74. E.g., a maenad, with a satyr, brandishing an ὄλισβος (cf. Dover 1978, R 227; *ARV*²: 135 and *App.*: 88); a group of men and women with a man about to penetrate a woman with an ὄλισβος (cf. Dover 1978, R 223; *ARV*²: 132 and *App.*: 88).

75. These are a red-figure kylix with two women dancing round a phallus-bird, c. 510–500 BCE, in the Louvre (cf. Dover 1978, R. 152; *ARV*² 85.1; *Para.*: 330; *Add.*: 84), and a red-figure kylix showing a group of women, some of whom are taking ὄλισβοι out of a basket and one of whom seems to be wearing an ὄλισβος round her waist (cf. Vorberg 1965: 409; Dover 1978, R 1163; Kilmer 1993, R. 141.3). Kilmer (1993: 29–30; 98) and Rabinowitz 2002: 142, fig. 5.21 and 5.22) think these relate to female homoeroticism. But this identification of the woman as wearing a dildo seems unlikely; we have only a sketch of it, made from a lost vase in a private collection, reproduced by G. Vorberg. Not only has it not been authenticated, but the image does not fit at all well into the thematic field of reciprocal female love. The scene shows a kind of catalogue of possible positions (ὄλισβος aimed at the mouth, at the vagina, at the sex-organs, waved in the air, etc.), in male–female sexual relations. Similarly, in the scene with the phallus-bird, nothing indicates that the painter wanted to suggest a past or future sexual interaction between the two women (cf. Boehringer 2007b: 149–50).

76. See Aristoph., *Lys.*, 108, *Eccl.* 915–18. For occurrences of this term in comedy, see Henderson 1975: 221–22.

77. See Olender 1985 and Vernant 1990: 118–19.

78. In an article on masturbation, Krenkel (1979: 167) gives as additional synonyms the words γερρόν and φάλης, but the form of the words and the contexts both suggest that these refer not to objects but to the male sex organs. See Aristophanes, *Lysistrata*, 771 and *Acharnians*, 263.

79. It is used in one of the *Mimes* of Herondas, where two women are shown exchanging the address of a dildo-seller (*Mimes*, VI, 19). The situation is very similar to a scene in the fragmentary comedy *Thesmophoriazusae Secundae*. See P. Oxy. II 212 = Pack² 156. The relevant fragment is fr. 44 (see D. L. Page in vol. 3 of *Select Papyri* [Cambridge, MA: Harvard University Press, 1941]). The papyrus dates from the first century CE and the text is hypothetically attributed to Aristophanes under the title *Thesmophoriazusae Secundae*.

80. The expression *scorteum fascinum*, "leather phallus," is found in Petronius, at *Satirica* 138.1, but in this passage it is an old woman, Oenothea, who handles it and it is intended to rekindle the passion of a young man. In Roman painting, as G. Clarke notes, these objects never appear (Clarke 1998: 227–28).

be clear—this is important—that in the whole of surviving Greek and Roman literature, only two short passages mention the use of such an object by women together.[81] It is therefore a serious mistake to consider the ὄλισβος (or other similar objects) as the "equipment" of the "ancient lesbian" (a category, in any case, that does not exist). It is, rather, a symbolic element in the representation of sexual activity in general, and cannot by any means be considered, in Greek antiquity, as a marker or element connoting sexual relations among women. Leaena's question "Do you have what men have?" may include an allusion to the dildo as a possibility, but it is not there to activate a contemporary cliché. Role-reversal (a woman taking the role of a man) is *not* the way to explain sex between women, as shown in this dialogue, where what is culturally and socially "masculine" (gender) circulates among three women without completely or permanently characterizing any one of them.

Masculine How?

When Leaena says Megilla is "terribly manly" she is definitely not talking about an obvious aspect of her appearance, visible to everyone. She is describing either a temporary state or a behavior. Megilla is not a woman of masculine physique, whose "virility" would shock a viewer at first glance. The wig, whose existence Leaena discovers later, is undetectable (it was "very realistic and fit as if it were natural"), and although Leaena has been right next to Megilla all evening, she is extremely surprised when the latter asks to be called by a masculine name. This is important: Megilla is not a woman who resembles a man in all situations. Besides, she presents herself as a νεανίσκος, a "youth," like, for example, Narcissus or Hermaphroditus, whose "femininity" is emphasized in our texts. She does not resemble a *mature* man. The cultural mark of a νεανίσκος is precisely the *absence* of confirmed physical signs of virility, and retention of the softness and sexual indeterminacy of childhood. Not only is a νεανίσκος too young for a "real" marriage, but the term also connotes a different kind of relationship, the pederastic relationship between ἐραστής and ἐρώμενος, thus adding new

---

81. In the first of these, a school case imagined by Seneca the Elder (*Controversiae*, I, 2, 3. 1–8), an orator suggests that a tribad surprised in bed with another tribad be examined to see if she used artificial means to play the active role. The text is corrupt and hard to interpret (see Boehringer 2007b: 267–71 and Kamen and Levin-Richardson in this volume). In the second, in Pseudo-Lucian's *Erotes* (28), Charicles, in a hyperbolic discourse, mentions the androgynous behavior of women using a strap-on, but with no further details (see Boehringer 2007a).

potential polarities within the couple, and evoking the confusions introduced by Plato's interpretation of ἔρως.[82]

Nor must we allow ourselves to be deceived by certain adjectives that Lucian humorously puts in the mouths of Clonarium and Leaena. The term ἀρρενωπός, formed from the adjective ἄρρην, "masculine," and the root *okʷ- "see"), which Clonarium uses to characterize the so-called ἑταιρίστριαι of Lesbos, does not have exactly its etymological meaning in Greek. In actual use, it refers to ethical qualities, that is, to characteristics designated (culturally) as masculine, such as courage. In a passage of the *Laws,* for example, assigning different musical modes to men and women, the Athenian constructs a parallelism whereby ἀρρενωπός is simply the male equivalent of θηλυγενής for women (*Laws* 802e). This adjective, derived from θῆλυς and the root seen in the verb γίγνομαι, shows no sign of a visual or physical dimension. The equivalence of the two terms shows that ἀρρενωπός refers to gender and does not necessarily imply visible physical traits. The same goes for the adjective ἀνδρώδης,[83] used by Leaena in the wig passage for the athletes with shaved heads. ἀνδρώδης normally means "manly," "strong," or "brave." Note too that in our dialogue both words are used in comparisons, and do not directly characterize Megilla.

What Lucian really insists on is not Megilla's appearance, but her "manly" (ἀνδρική) behavior, and here the wig episode is significant. Just as the reference to Hermaphroditus is used to underline the irrelevance of his physical structure to sex between women (Megilla says clearly that she is *not* a creature of this kind), similarly, an androgynous physical feature—baldness—is immediately explained as resulting from an intentional *act* of masculinization. This kind of artificial baldness—the shaved head—is characteristic of male athletes, slaves, and Spartans. It is thus coded as masculine, giving women with shaved heads a manly appearance. It is not, however, an exterior mark of a particular sexuality. The woman abducted in Lucian's little work *The Runaways,* for example, is "masculine looking" (ἀρρενωπός) because of her close-cropped hair (*Runaways* 27), but her sexual behavior does not elicit any authorial comment. Her husband looks forward to getting her back and taking her home again as his wife. Lucian plays with this cultural code. In general, a wig is there to hide natural baldness or hair loss. As we saw earlier, it is a device used by aged or diseased

---

82. On erotic reciprocity in Plato see Halperin 1986. I shall return below to this superimposition of possible readings.

83. This word is constructed from ἀνήρ and –ωδης, a suffix formed from the root ὄζω, "emit an odor," which in actual use quickly comes to mean "resembling." See Chantraine 1999, s.v. "ὄζω."

prostitutes to retain clients, and to say that a person wears one is insulting. Megilla, by contrast, is sometimes androgynous and sometimes feminine: she does not have a "masculine" physique. Nor does Leaena mention any physical signs of masculinity in Demonassa, who is also actively involved in the sexual encounter. The dialogue mentions the women's bodies only in connection with this wig, which is worn because of a specific behavioral choice.

It is thus character and behavior that are emphasized by these terms. Neither Demonassa (even though she is said to be ὁμότεχνος, to have "the same skills as" Megilla) nor Leaena (who is involved in this sexual relationship) is presented as "masculine." As for Megilla, she is not mannish or masculine in physique: she is ἀλλόκοτος, as Leaena puts it; that is, she is "unusual."

Three Is Not Two

This dialogue does not portray just one sexual act between two people. There is sex between Leaena and Megilla, sex between Megilla and Demonassa, and sex among the three women—this last an exceptionally erotic encounter that prevents us from drawing any clear conclusions. At the end of the evening Megilla invites Leaena to stay with Demonassa and herself, and sleep between them. Both these women embrace Leaena "just like men do" and feel her breasts. There can be no doubt at all that Demonassa is "active" here as well as Megilla. Lucian is careful to make this clear, when he has Leaena say, "Demonassa was also biting me in the middle of (μεταξύ) kissing me." Nor is there any doubt about the nature of their embraces: these are not chaste, friendly kisses, but sexual kisses, with open mouths (what are sometimes called "French kisses"). If both these women are behaving "like men," should we think of both of them, using Clonarium's earlier definition, as ἑταιρίστριαι, that is, women who are exceptionally strongly attracted to women? No answer is provided. The author is spreading hopeless confusion.

The scholarly argument that Lucian is relocating sex between women into a "field of significance" intelligible to the ancients, that is, into the framework of a binary active/passive relationship, is therefore untenable. Everything in the dialogue contributes to derailing any such line of argument and confounding the categories on which it is based—even the categories of "gender-inversion." Does this mean Lucian is protesting against the stereotypical view of "lesbians"? That he has a "queer" or unusually open view of sexuality? We cannot address such questions without taking into account both the genre and the particular formal structure of *Dialogue* 5, half of which consists of a dialogue within the dialogue—an embedding that turns out to be a mise en abyme.

A DIFFERENT GENRE OF DIALOGUE

Like many of Lucian's minor works, *Dialogue* 5 presents itself as a direct transcription of the conversation between its interlocutors. This form was not new in Lucian's time. As we saw earlier, he was drawing on the philosophical dialogues of the classical period. But what about the performance of such works? Were the practical conditions in Lucian's time the same as in the classical period? The circumstances of performance? The audience? Scholars agree that the answer to all these questions is No. The "spectacular" and public dimension of compositions from the Second Sophistic made their performance different from what little we know about the reading of Plato's dialogues.[84] Given the limitations of our sources, however, the best we can do is speculate from remarks in the works themselves (despite the obvious problems attending this practice).

In a well-known passage of *The Double Indictment or Trials by Jury*, Lucian implies, metadiscursively, that his dialogues result from the invention of a new genre.[85] In this lighthearted work, "Dialogue" accuses "the Syrian" of having broken the philosophical wings on which he, Dialogue, used to soar (with clear reference to Plato's *Phaedrus*), and forced him to keep company with comedy and satire. "The most monstrous thing of all," he says, "is that I have been mixed up into an absurd blend . . . To those who hear me I seem like an alien apparition, put together out of disparate parts like a centaur."[86] The Syrian replies that it is thanks to him that this scrawny and unattractive creature has been transformed by his association with comedy and won the favor of the audience. The genre that Lucian claims to have invented is, then—according to his own character—a hybrid between philosophical dialogue and comedy, a genre in which the approval of the audience plays an important role.

---

84. For Plato see Blondell 2002: 14–52.
85. On the genre of Lucian's dialogues, see Briand's very thorough article on the *Dialogues of the Dead* (Briand 2007).
86. *The Double Indictment or Trials by Jury* 33. On this passage see Briand 2007. Gilhuly refers to it too in her study of the *Dialogues of the Courtesans* (2006).

Recent scholarship has outlined the cultural context in which such works were performed, and what it may have meant for the orator and his audience.[87] Scholars have debated whether the dialogues had one or two performers, but Maud Gleason's convincing work, which emphasizes what was at stake for the sophists in such epideictic "self-presentation," leads me to believe they were performed by a single person. Be that as it may, there were no masks (in contrast to the theater) to provide information about a character's identity. And if there was indeed just one performer, then changes of speaker would not be immediately obvious to the audience. Modulation of both voice and facial expression were therefore crucial to this kind of performance. Nor must we lose sight of the fact that one purpose of these works was to allow the author/actor to making a living—that is, to make money—whether from the displays themselves or from the training in eloquence that they provided. As with the courtesan, enjoying the approval of the audience is vital to the orator's professional success.

The *Dialogues of the Courtesans* make a particularly "natural" impression when read, as if they were transcriptions of real conversations between courtesans. In performance, however, the conditions of utterance would immediately belie this impression of "naturalness," of dialogue taken unedited from life. The "uttered enunciation" of the characters within the dialogue does not correspond to the speech-act that occurs at the moment of performance;[88] it is a dialogical fiction, a genre that immediately displays its artificiality, in a pact to which the audience agrees. In the case of *Dialogue 5*, the author also had to make clear to his original audience the difference between Leaena at the time of her conversation with Clonarium (Level 1) and Leaena the interlocutor of Megilla (Level 2).

This embedding has several important consequences. The fact that the erotic drama is set within an external frame means that Leaena (who knows how things turned out) could have modified the story of her experiences at the moment of telling it to Clonarium (as is typical of retrospective first-person narratives). Clonarium is, moreover, the target audience for the speech that contains the reported dialogue. Again, this means that Leaena as speaker could be adapting her story, depending on what she wants to convey to her target audience or to make her believe. Should we actually *believe* Leaena, then, when she says decorously that at first she did not understand what was going on? Are we certain that she "really" asked for

---

87. See Gleason 1995, and on Lucian more specifically, Ureña Bracero 1995: 39–56.
88. For "uttered enunciation" (énonciation énoncée) and performance, I am relying on the work of Claude Calame. See further Calame 1986.

gifts? Or is this an excuse for Clonarium's benefit? Did she "really" embark on a learned dialogue right in the middle of a feverish embrace? Does she "really" think it is all "shameful" (αἰσχρά), as she alleges in order to explain why she will not answer Clonarium's last question? Or to put it differently, should our interpretation rest on an assumption of psychologically plausible characterization, as if Lucian were offering us a realistic picture of the feminine psyche or of the mercenary motives of real prostitutes? By making Leaena report a direct dialogue, Lucian makes the exchange between Megilla and Leaena look like an unmediated factual narrative taken directly from life; but the information we receive is actually delivered from the point of view and in the voice of just one person. To approach the character of Megilla through the details supplied in this embedded dialogue, and take what Leaena says about her at face value, is to fall into a very obvious trap.

A PARADOXICAL DISCOURSE MAKES NO SENSE

If we set aside, for a moment, the description of that wild night which has so fascinated modern readers, and focus exclusively on the conversational frame (Level 1), we may reach a better understanding of the embedded dialogue (Level 2). It is immediately obvious that Clonarium presents a most eager listener, and that Leaena organizes the elements of her narrative skillfully, deciding what will and will not be said. She does not simply report the evening's events but *performs* the two characters for Clonarium, and puts words into their mouths. The mise en abyme is clear: Lucian is staging the kind of relationship that typically binds the author to his public. His audience is like Clonarium, kept in suspense by her interlocutor's skill; meanwhile Leaena, like Lucian himself, composes dialogue marked as fictive speech and knows how to satisfy her audience. They both exercise the power of language by using sexual vocabulary, the play of suspense, and an accumulation of *topoi*. The last of these is, to be sure, a technique of all ἠθοποιΐα, but here the *topoi* come so thick and fast that we can see the strings by which the marionette is operated.

No ancient text concerned with sex between women employs such a large number of *topoi*.[89] Martial and Juvenal use stereotypes in the service of satire designed to disparage and condemn; they combine selected traits into coherent exempla which are intended to promote sexual morality by portraying its opposite. Lucian, by contrast, uses *topoi* in *Dialogue* 5 pre-

---

89. For a study of all the evidence see Boehringer 2007b.

cisely *because* they are immediately identifiable as such, and because the dramatic setting he has chosen confuses them, making it impossible to take a definite position as to what the embedded dialogue is about. Moreover, it is important not to lose sight of the fact that the entire dialogue between Megilla and Leaena is embedded in the outer dialogue between Clonarium and Leaena, and that this embedding functions as a mise en abyme where the pleasure of staging *topoi* is itself staged.

It is a mistake, then, to see Leaena and Megilla as embodying sexual roles that made sense in the ancient world. The character of Leaena is not "less lesbian" than the others, nor does any of the three figures she dramatizes embody an ancient view of female homosexuality. They are nothing but characters in a dialogue by Lucian. A constructionist approach to ancient sexual categories must be complemented by analysis of the literary structure and performance conditions of our texts.[90] Lucian is not a moralist like Juvenal, but neither is he an activist denouncing phallocentrism.

Dialogue 5 of the *Dialogues of the Courtesans* does not refer to anything coherent, or even to anything potentially clear-cut. In this respect it resembles Lucian's *True History*.[91] In that work, the moon people are constructed as non-earth-people: Lucian confuses the traits of terrestrial humanity, but without creating a reversed coherence (by means of inversion, as used to be thought) or a new kind of coherence. There is no utopia here, nor is there the construction of a possible world with possible beings. It is likewise impossible to see in our dialogue a questioning of the active/passive binary, a reconsideration of masculinity and femininity, or a promotion of gender fluidity. Neither the *True History* nor the fifth *Dialogue of the Courtesans* functions by referring to reality (of "real" humans or "lesbians" respectively)—it functions through dialogue with a subtext: the *Odyssey* in the case of the *True Histories,* the *Symposium* in the case of *Dialogue 5*. Megilla, Leaena, Demonassa, and Clonarium seem by turns to take on the voice or the role of a Socrates or an Alcibiades, of a lover or a beloved, of a wise person or an ignorant one; the only fluidity to be seen is that of the

---

90. Gilhuly's analysis of *Dialogue* 6 (2007) demonstrates this perfectly. See, more generally, the work of Claude Calame and Florence Dupont, and also the publications resulting from their seminar *Antiquité au Présent* (Université de Paris VII & École des Hautes Études en Sciences Sociales).

91. The comparison with the *True History* underlines the kinds of paradox and inventiveness that are characteristic of Lucian. If *Dialogue 5* is thematically integrated with the other *Dialogues of the Courtesans,* and resembles formally other short dialogues (like the *Dialogues of the Sea-Gods*), it is nevertheless distinguished from them by its hybrid character, its distinctive structure (a dialogue completely embedded in another dialogue), its paradoxographical creativity, and the accumulation of ἀδύνατα.

characters: voices, words, and tones are mingled, bringing great pleasure, no doubt, to the audience.

In a way, this paradoxical discourse remains coherent in its paradox because it does not produce a result. To see in it an accurate reflection, a solidly constructed and sincere account, or, again, the image of a different world, a different gender, a different eroticism, is an optical illusion, helped along by a chance intersection of ancient and modern stereotypes. It is a lovely illusion, one that tells us little about ancient women and eroticism, but a great deal about the importance of Lucian's metadiscursivity. I shall simply note, in conclusion, that his choice of a place (*topos*) in which to dramatize (by way of a long mise en abyme) the performance of his own dialogues involves an erotic scene among three women within a "feminine" group of dialogues. But are the characters really women? The only answer we can give is that their gender is probably Lucian's: just ἀλλόκοτος (different).

BIBLIOGRAPHY

Adams, James N. 1982. *The Latin Sexual Vocabulary.* London.

Amato, Eugenio and Jacques Schamp. 2005. *Ethopoiia. La représentation de caractères entre fiction scolaire et réalité vivante à l'époque impériale et tardive.* Salerno.

Anderson, Graham. 1976. "Lucian: Theme and Variation in the Second Sophistic." Supplements to *Mnemosyne* 41: 94–96. Leiden.

———. 1994. "Lucian: Tradition Versus Reality." *Aufstieg und Niedergang der römischen Welt* II.34.2: 1422–47.

———. 1999. "Performing Lucian." *Classical Review* 49: 32–33.

André, Jacques. 2001. *Le vocabulaire latin de l'anatomie.* Paris.

Andrieu, Jean. 1954. *Le dialogue antique, structure et présentation.* Paris.

Baldwin, Barry. 1961. "Lucian as Social Satirist." *Classical Quarterly* 11: 199–208.

———. 1973. *Studies in Lucian.* Toronto.

Bellinger, Alfred R. 1928. "Lucian's Dramatic Technique." *Yale Classical Studies* 1: 3–40.

Billault, Alain (ed.). 1994. *Lucien de Samosate (Actes du Colloque International de Lyon, 30–9/1-10-1993).* Lyon and Paris.

Blondell, Ruby. 2002. *The Play of Character in Plato's Dialogues.* Cambridge.

Blondell, Ruby and Sandra Boehringer. 2014. "Revenge of the *Hetairistria*: The Reception of Plato's *Symposium* in Lucian's Fifth *Dialogue of the Courtesans.*" *Arethusa* 47: 231–64.

Boehringer, Sandra. 2003. "L'homosexualité féminine dans le discours antique. Les relations sexuelles et amoureuses entre femmes dans la construction culturelle et les représentations littéraires des catégories sexuelles grecques et romaines." Doctoral diss. Paris: EHESS.

———. 2007a. "Comparer l'incomparable. La *sunkrisis* érotique et les catégories sexuelles dans le monde gréco-romain," in B. Perreau (ed.), *Le choix de l'homosexualité. Recherches inédites sur la question gay et lesbienne,* 39–56. Paris.

———. 2007b. *L'homosexualité féminine dans l'Antiquité grecque et romaine.* Paris.

———. 2007c. "Comment classer les comportements érotiques? Platon, le sexe et érôs dans le *Banquet* et les *Lois.*" *Études Platoniciennes* 4: 45–67.

———. 2011. "Le corps de Philaenis ou les ravages du sexe dans les Épigrammes de Martial," in L. Bodiou, V. Mehl, and M. Soria-Audebert (eds.), *Corps outragés, corps ravagés de l'Antiquité au Moyen Age,* 231–48. Turnhout.

———. 2014. "What Is Named by the Name 'Philaenis'? The Gender, Function and Authority of an Antonomastic Figure," in Nancy Rabinowitz, Mark Masterson, and James Robson (eds.), *Sex in Antiquity: New Essays on Gender and Sexuality in the Ancient World,* 374–93. New York.

Bompaire, Jacques. 1958. *Lucien écrivain. Imitation et création.* Paris.

———. 1993. *Introduction à l'édition et à la traduction de Lucien. Opuscules 1–10.* Paris.

Boswell, John. 1994. *Same-Sex Unions in Premodern Europe.* New York.

Briand, Michel. 2007. "Les Dialogues des morts de Lucien, entre dialectique et satire: une hybridité générique fondatrice," in A. Eissen (ed.), *Dialogue des morts. Otrante* 22: 61–72.

Brisson, Luc. 1976. *Le mythe de Tirésias. Essai d'analyse structurale.* Leiden.

———. 1997. *Le sexe incertain. Androgynie et hermaphrodisme dans l'Antiquité gréco-romaine.* Paris.

Brooten, Bernadette. 1996. *Love Between Women: Early Christian Responses to Female Homoeroticism.* Chicago.

Calame, Claude. 1986. *Le récit en Grèce ancienne. Énonciation et représentation des poètes.* Paris.

———. 1996. *L'Éros dans la Grèce antique.* Paris.

———. 2002. "Interprétation et traduction des cultures. Les catégories de la pensée et du discours anthropologique," *L'Homme* 163: 51–78.

Calame, Claude, Florence Dupont, Bernard Lortat-Jacob, and Maria Manca (eds.). 2010. *La voix actée. Pour une nouvelle ethnopoétique.* Paris.

Cameron, Alan. 1995. "Asclepiades' Girlfriends," in *Callimachus and His Critics,* 494–519. Princeton.

———. 1998. "Love (and Marriage) Between Women." *Greek, Roman and Byzantine Studies* 39: 137–56.

Cantarella, Eva. 1992. *Bisexuality in the Ancient World.* Trans. Cormac Ó Cuilleanáin. New Haven.

Chantraine, Pierre. 1999. *Dictionnaire étymologique de la langue grecque.* Paris.

Clark, Gillian. 1993. *Women in Late Antiquity: Pagan and Christian Lifestyles.* Oxford.

Clarke, John R. 1998. *Looking at Lovemaking. Constructions of Sexuality in Roman Art (100 BC–AD 250).* Berkeley.

Davidson, James. 2007. *The Greeks and Greek Love: A Radical Reappraisal of Homosexuality in Ancient Greece.* London.

Dover, Kenneth J. 1978. *Greek Homosexuality.* Cambridge, MA.

———. 2002. "Two Women of Samos," in M. C. Nussbaum and J. Shivola (eds.), *The Sleep of Reason: Erotic Experience and Sexual Ethics in Ancient Greece and Rome*, 222–28. Chicago.

Dupont, Florence. 1994. *L'invention de la littérature. De l'ivresse grecque au texte latin.* Paris.

———. 2010. Introduction to Claude Calame, Florence Dupont, Bernard Lortat-Jacob, and Maria Manca (eds.), *La voix actée. Pour une nouvelle ethnopoétique*, 7–20. Paris.

Dupont, Florence and Thierry Eloi. 2001. *L'érotisme masculin dans la Rome antique.* Paris.

Faraone, Christopher A. and Laura K. McClure (eds.). 2006. *Prostitutes and Courtesans in the Ancient World.* Madison, WI.

Foucault, Michel. 1976. *Histoire de la sexualité.* Vol. 1, *La volonté de savoir.* Paris.

———. 1984a. *Histoire de la sexualité.* Vol. 2, *L'usage des plaisirs.* Paris.

———. 1984b. *Histoire de la sexualité.* Vol. 3, *Le souci de soi.* Paris.

Frontisi-Ducroux, Françoise. 1998. "Le sexe du regard," in Paul Veyne, François Lissarrague, and Françoise Frontisi-Ducroux (eds.), *Les mystères du gynécée*, 199–276. Paris.

Gilhuly, Kate. 2006. "The Phallic Lesbian: Philosophy, Comedy, and Social Inversion in Lucian's *Dialogues of the Courtesans,*" in C. A. Faraone and L. K. McClure (eds.), *Prostitutes and Courtesans in the Ancient World*, 274–91. Madison.

———. 2007. "Bronze for Gold: Subjectivity in Lucian's *Dialogues of the Courtesans.*" *American Journal of Philology* 128: 59–94.

Gleason, Maud W. 1995. *Making Men: Sophists and Self-Presentation in Ancient Rome.* Princeton.

Haley, Shelley P. 2002. "Lucian's 'Leaena and Clonarium': Voyeurism or a Challenge to Assumptions?" in Nancy S. Rabinowitz and Lisa Auanger (eds.), *Among Women: From the Homosocial to the Homoerotic in the Ancient World*, 286–303. Austin.

Hallett, Judith P. 1989. "Female Homoeroticism and the Denial of Roman Reality in Latin Literature." *Yale Journal of Criticism*, 3: 209–27.

Halperin, David M. 1986. "Plato and Erotic Reciprocity." *Classical Antiquity* 5: 60–80.

———. 1990. *One Hundred Years of Homosexuality: And Other Essays on Greek Love.* New York.

———. 1994. "Historicizing the Subject of Desire: Sexual Preferences and Erotic Identities in the Pseudo-Lucianic *Erotes,*" in J. Goldstein (ed.), *Foucault and the Writing of History*, 19–34. Cambridge.

———. 1997. "Response: Halperin on Brennan on Brooten." *Bryn Mawr Classical Review* 97.12.3 (December 5).

———. 1998. "The First Homosexuality?" *GLQ: A Journal of Lesbian and Gay Studies* 4.4: 559–78, re-edited in 2002 in M. C. Nussbaum and J. Sihvola (eds.), *The Sleep of Reason: Erotic Experience and Sexual Ethics in Ancient Greece and Rome*, 229–68. Chicago.

Halperin, David M., John J. Winkler, and Froma I. Zeitlin (eds.). 1990. *Before Sexuality: The Construction of Erotic Experience in the Ancient Greek World.* Princeton.

Hanson, Ann Ellis. 1990. "The Medical Writers' Woman," in D. M. Halperin, J. Winkler, and F. Zeitlin (eds.), *Before Sexuality: The Construction of Erotic Experience in the Ancient World*, 309–38. Princeton.

Helm, Rud. 1927. "Lukianos," in Pauly-Wissowa (ed.), *Real-Encyclopädie der klassischen Altertumswissenschaft*, 8:1725–77.

Henderson, Jeffrey. 1975. *The Maculate Muse: Obscene Language in Attic Comedy.* New Haven.

Heusch, Christine. 2005. "Die Ethopoiie in der griechischen und lateinischen Antike: von der rhetorischen Progymnasmata-Theorie zur literarischen Form," in E. Amato and J. Schamp (eds.), *Ethopoiia. La représentation de caractères entre fiction scolaire et réalité vivante à l'époque impériale et tardive*, 11–33. Salerno.

Howell, Peter. 1980. *A Commentary on Book One of the Epigrams of Martial*. London.

Hubbard, Thomas K. (ed.). 2003. *Homosexuality in Greece and Rome: A Sourcebook of Basic Documents*. Berkeley.

Johnson, Marguerite and Terry Ryan (eds.). 2005. *Sexuality in Greek and Roman Society and Literature: A Sourcebook*. London and New York.

Jones, Christopher P. 1986. *Culture and Society in Lucian*. Cambridge.

Keuls, Eva C. 1985. *The Reign of the Phallus: Sexual Politics in Ancient Athens*. New York.

Kilmer, Martin F. 1993. *Greek Erotica on Attic Red-Figure Vases*. London.

Krenkel, Werner. 1979. "Masturbation in der Antike." *Wissenschaftliche Zeitschrift der Wilhelm-Pieck-Universität Rostock* 28: 159–78.

Legrand, P. E. 1907. "Les *Dialogue des courtisanes* comparés avec la Comédie." *Revue des Etudes Grecques* 20: 39–79.

———. 1908. "Les *Dialogue des courtisanes* comparés avec la Comédie (suite)." *Revue des Études Grecques* 21: 176–231.

Lissarrague, François. 1987. "De la sexualité des satyres." *Métis* 2: 63–90.

McLeod, Matthew D. 1994. "Lucianic Studies since 1930." *Aufstieg und Niedergang der römischen Welt*, II.34.2: 1362–421.

Mras, Karl. 1916. "Die Personennamen in Lucians Hetärengesprächen." *Wiener Studien* 38: 308–42.

Nesselrath, Heinz-Günther. 1999. "Lukianos (1)," in *Der neue Pauly. Enzyklopädie der Antike*, vol. 7, col. 493–501.

Olender, L. 1985. "Aspect de Baubô." *Revue de l'histoire des religions* 202: 3–55.

Ormand, Kirk. 2009. *Controlling Desires: Sexuality in Ancient Greece and Rome*. Westport, CT.

Ozanam, Anne-Marie. 2009. Introduction and notes to *Lucien: Voyages extraordinaires*, trans. Anne-Marie Ozanam and Jacques Bompaire. Paris.

Parker, Holt N. 1997. "The Teratogenic Grid," in Judith P. Hallett and Marilyn B. Skinner (eds.), *Roman Sexualities*, 47–65. Princeton.

Pellizer, E. and A. Sirugo. 1995. *Luciani, Dialoghi delle cortigiane*. Introd. and trans. E. Pellizer, comment. A. Sirugo. Venice.

Pomeroy, Sarah B. 1975. *Goddesses, Whores, Wives and Slaves: Women in Classical Antiquity*. New York.

Rabinowitz, Nancy S. and Lisa Auanger (eds.). 2002. *Among Women: From the Homosocial to the Homoerotic in the Ancient World*. Austin.

Reardon, Bryan P. 1971. *Courants littéraires des II et IIIèmes siècles après J.-C*. Paris.

Robert, Louis. 1965. *Hellenica, Recueil d'épigraphie, de numismatique et d'antiquités grecques*. Vol. 13, *D'Aphrodisias à la Lycaonie*, 184–89. Paris.

Schöpsdau, Klaus. 2002. "Des repas en commun pour les femmes: une utopie platonicienne." *Revue Française d'Histoire des Idées Politiques* 16: 331–40.

Skinner, Marilyn B. 2005. *Sexuality in Greek and Roman Culture*. Oxford.

Sullivan, John Patrick. 1991. *Martial, the Unexpected Classic*. Cambridge.

Ureña Bracero, Jesús. 1995. *El diálogo de Luciano: ejecución, naturaleza y procedimientos de humor*. Amsterdam.

Vernant, Jean-Pierre. 1990. *Figures, idoles et masques*, 137–207. Paris.

Vorberg, Gaston. 1965. *Glossarium Eroticum*. Hanau. Reprint, orig. Stuttgart, 1928–32

Williams, Craig A. 2010. *Roman Homosexuality: Ideologies of Masculinity in Classical Antiquity*. 2nd ed. New York and Oxford.

Winkler, John J. 1990. *The Constraints of Desire: The Anthropology of Sex and Gender in Ancient Greece*. New York.

CHAPTER SEVEN

Sculpting Antinous

Creations of the Ideal Companion

BRYAN E. BURNS

The survival of ancient bodies into modern times, whether sculpted in stone or preserved through seemingly miraculous means, can fuel surprisingly intimate connections with the classical past (Gross 1992; Dwyer 2010; Ingleheart 2014). Accumulations of decontextualized objects, artfully restored and unencumbered by provenance, make exhibition halls places where idealized forms make appealing but often unapproachable representatives of Greece and Rome. A range of literary creations, however, attest to viewers' ability to rewrite the possibilities for interacting with classical and classicizing figures, and few figures have proven more adaptable than the sculptures identified as Antinous, the sexual partner of the emperor Hadrian.

An exhibition at the Henry Moore Institute in Leeds crowned Antinous "the face of the Antique," prompting the London *Times* reviewer to compare the Roman era's "pouter extraordinaire" with the commercial appeal of Calvin Klein models and David Beckham (Irving 2006). Indeed, Antinous appears to have been a popular, adaptable model, surviving in one hundred portrait statues, recognizable even in the guise of a dozen deities. Yet the Leeds exhibit wisely pulled back from an extreme close-up and focused not just on Antinous as a commodity but also on the consumption of his image and the crucial participation of an active viewer in constructing that commodity (Vout 2006). Despite his haughty reputation, an apparent satisfaction with his own famous face, and the suspicion that he took his own life, the story of Antinous is never that of the youth in isolation. Rather, Hadrian's deification of his beloved companion created new opportunities for interaction, as a proliferation of statues attracted countless admirers who were able to reimagine Antinous, both living and sculpted. Biographers, poets, and playwrights have all taken the opportunity to sculpt Antinous anew, inventing novel accounts of how the statues were made, how well they capture the essence of the deceased, and how they provide new companionship to the viewer who often finds that "the marble in which you are immortalised speaks for itself" (De Unger 1950: 105).

Antinous is a complicated character, whose legacy as a historical person is enriched, if not overwhelmed, by his status as a god. His fame derives from his intimacy with the emperor Hadrian, who reigned from 117 to 138 CE. The emperor encountered an adolescent Antinous in Bithynia, along the Black Sea's southern coast, during extended travels in the eastern Mediterranean. The sexual nature of their relationship is described only obliquely in ancient texts, but Hadrian's devotion to the younger man took manifest form after the latter's death by drowning in the Nile in the year 130. The third-century historian Cassius Dio gives a typical account, with competing explanations of Antinous's death and of Hadrian's motivation for extraordinary acts of commemoration, including the founding of the city of Antinoopolis:

> καὶ οὕτω γε τὸν Ἀντίνοον, ἤτοι διὰ τὸν ἔρωτα αὐτοῦ ἢ ὅτι ἐθελοντὴς ἐθανατώθη (ἑκουσίου γὰρ ψυχῆς πρὸς ἃ ἔπραττεν ἐδεῖτο), ἐτίμησεν ὡς καὶ πόλιν ἐν τῷ χωρίῳ, ἐν ᾧ τοῦτ' ἔπαθε, καὶ συνοικίσαι καὶ ὀνομάσαι ἀπ' αὐτοῦ. καὶ ἐκείνου ἀνδριάντας ἐν πάσῃ ὡς εἰπεῖν τῇ οἰκουμένῃ, μᾶλλον δὲ ἀγάλματα, ἀνέθηκε. καὶ τέλος ἀστέρα τινὰ αὐτός τε ὁρᾶν ὡς καὶ τοῦ Ἀντινόου ὄντα ἔλεγε καὶ τῶν συνόντων οἱ μυθολογούντων ἡδέως ἤκουεν ἔκ τε τῆς ψυχῆς τοῦ Ἀντινόου ὄντως τὸν ἀστέρα γεγενῆσθαι καὶ τότε πρῶτον ἀναπεφηνέναι. (69.11.3–4)

> He honored Antinous, either because of his love for him or because the youth had voluntarily undertaken to die (it being necessary that a life should be surrendered freely for the accomplishment of the ends Hadrian had in view), by building a city on the spot where he had suffered his fate and naming it after him; and he also set up statues, or rather sacred images of him, practically all over the world. Finally, he declared that he had seen a star which he took to be that of Antinous, and gladly lent

an ear to the fictitious tales woven by his associates to the effect that the star had really come into being from the spirit of Antinous and had then appeared for the first time. (Cary 1914: 445–47)

Dio's text—with its equivocation between Hadrian's emotions and obligations as the motivating force, between what he said and really felt—reflects an interplay between fact and fiction that will continue to mark the tales of Antinous. Although there is a clear linkage between Antinous's death and the production of statues, Dio's ambiguity extends to the status of the sculptures, as likenesses (ἀνδριάντας) of the deceased and also as objects of worship (ἀγάλματα). Because they were the focus of a new cult, the statues became a touchstone for the scorn that early Christian fathers exhibited toward the figure of Antinous, but as we shall see, they were also essential to later writers' praise of his beauty and attempts to understand his character.[1]

Sarah Waters (1995) has shown that fantasies about Antinous became especially vivid in the late nineteenth century, when he surpassed the mythical Ganymede as the most prevalent classicizing icon of male beauty, and as a central figure for developing gay identities. The physical beauty of Antinous was fundamental to these literary visions, not just as a general attribute but in a particular form that became explicitly eroticized. Art historical catalogues and scholarly essays provided the framework for the identification of Antinous not as just as a romantic figure from ancient history but with sculpted forms that persisted into the present day. These nineteenth-century assessments and interpretations secured an iconic status for Antinous that was further developed in poems, plays, and scholarship of the early twentieth century. This chapter focuses on narratives from that period and beyond, which reinvent his physical form through statues that take an active role in their relationship with the viewer, ancient or modern. As such, the marble form is not simply a representation of Antinous's beauty but a lasting preservation of his personality. Yet it is a troublesome Antinous who looms large in Victorian biographies, art-historical analyses, and literary fantasies, a sculpted object resisting possession.

Contemporary visions of the historical figure have been profoundly shaped by Margarite Yourcenar's novel *Memoirs of Hadrian,* with its characterization of Antinous as a dreaming, narcissistic youth—a vain, self-destructive teenager. Just the kind of celebrity that fascinates the modern

---

1. The powerful meanings carried by the Antinous statues in the Roman era are assessed by Gregg 2000: 122–64 and Vout 2007.

world. Yourcenar's description of the young man's physical beauty reflects not just one ancient statue but a whole catalogue of varied forms that she encountered in publications and museums (Rovira Guardiola 2008). As the emperor narrates, Antinous embodied multiple deities through his poses, activities, and touch:

> The youth half reclining on a couch, knees upraised, was that same Hermes untying his sandals; it was Bacchus who gathered grapes or tasted for me the cup of red wine; the fingers hardened by the bowstring were those of Eros. (Yourcenar 1954: 176–77)

Yet Yourcenar's Antinous lives on not only in Hadrian's memory but also in the many sculptures of the lost youth she describes in every room of Hadrian's Villa at Tivoli. She emphasizes the emperor's desire to conjure a perfect replica of the youth's beauty in marble, but makes clear that the image in its own right, with "that dangerous countenance and its elusive smile," soon overpowered the viewer (1954: 231).

It is this sculpted Antinous, the marble presence with a strange power over the viewer, that features heavily in gay history and imagination. Because he exists from the start as a replicated image, the potential symbolism extends well beyond the particulars of the short life of the historical Antinous and even beyond Hadrian's program of commemoration. The many statues of Antinous have inspired new compositions, new narratives of his life and relationship with the emperor Hadrian, in texts that celebrate the statues for their beauty, interrogate them as historical representations, and reshape—both literally and figuratively—the relationship between the sculpted presence and his ardent lover.

Ancient portraits of Antinous, and modern restorations, have inspired historians, biographers, and poets alike to describe him as an elusive and complex figure. Descriptions abound in which the statues of Antinous are presented as enigmatic and mysterious, yet a strong will and a markedly sexualized identity were found in the Antinous of late nineteenth-century narratives (cf. Waters 1995). Through both scholarship and the arts, the character of Antinous was most vividly conjured amid Victorian fascination and fear of the homosexual—an identity constructed in its contemporary form at precisely this period (Halperin 1990; Mader 2005). In the analysis below, I identify a recurring theme in modern presentations of his sculpted form: the marble statue as enduring witness to and provocateur for same-sex desire. The face recognizable for its pensive beauty is complicated through readings of pose and physique, which combine to reveal his character, temperament, and even morality in ways that are informed by his homosexuality. This study might be termed a biography of objects, in that it follows ancient works into their modern contexts, in which the statue's history informs the viewer's appreciation (Kopytoff 1986). Yet, just as the line between personal memoir and fiction has become blurred in recent times, we recognize contrivances in both the creation and reception of these particular antiquities.

Victorian narratives of Antinous built on prior fictions, sometimes consciously, by relying on ancient statues that had been heavily restored in earlier centuries. Lorentz Dietrichson was the first scholar to comprehensively assess the many images of Antinous, with a fairly discerning review of excessive, imaginative restorations.[2] For example, a statue of Antinous as Hercules in the Louvre (see fig. 7.1) combines a portrait head with a separate body that was not its original (Dietrichson 1884: no. 88). The Antinous as Ganymede in Liverpool's Lady Lever Gallery was identified as such in the eighteenth century because of the jug held in the figure's left hand and the cup of Jupiter raised high in his right (Dietrichson 1884: no. 100). It is clear, however, that the key attributes of cup and jug are both eighteenth-century restorations (Waywell 1986: 21–22). No particular mythic or divine identity can be given to this figure, aside from the name Antinous. Finally, a statue of Antinous with a "water plant" clutched in his right hand seems to conflate the historical youth's death by drowning with the mythological seizure of the young argonaut Hylas by water nymphs (Dietrichson 1884: no. 103). Unfortunately, the extensive restorations made to this statue include both arms—and thus the essential attribute of Hylas—as well as the head of Antinous (cf. Marconi 1923: 193).

Contemporary agendas clearly guided both the artistic reconstruction and scholarly interpretation of iconographic and stylistic details, as the personal history and psychological character recognized through sculpted forms enabled the expression of Victorian desires and anxieties. Across a broad range of writing, from scholarly description to fanciful reinterpretation, diverse representations are unified by a shared response to Antinous's very presence. As we shall see in the next section, the marble Antinous is never a figure in isolation, but rather is consistently represented in conjunction with its supposed creator, an enthralled viewer, or a devoted admirer. The artist-viewers in Victorian poetry and scholarship are often presented as substitutes for Hadrian himself—Antinous's original admirer, viewer,

---

2. Modern scholarship, of course, continues to discuss the authenticity of individual statues, most recently in the comprehensive catalogue by Hugo Meyer (1991) and the more synthetic work of Royston Lambert (1984).

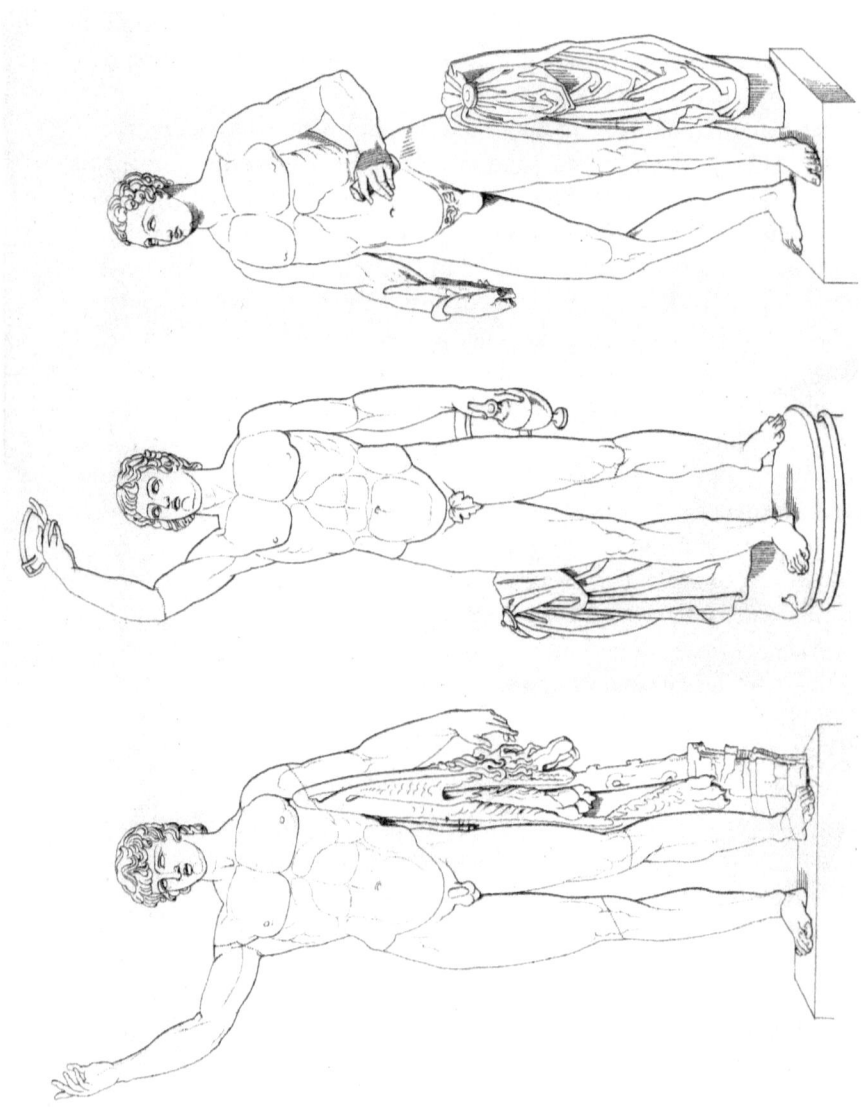

FIGURE 7.1. Drawings of Antinous restored as Heracles, Ganymede, and Hylas (Dietrichson 1884: fig. 24, 32, 35)

and sculptor—whose artistic agency is thought to underlie the beauty of Antinous, as it still survives in stone.

ANTINOUS CAPTURED

Antinous's current title as the "face of the antique" echoes Oscar Wilde's invocation of the ancient Bithynian as a counterpart for the ever youthful Dorian Gray. The artist who paints the novel's infamous portrait, Basil Hallward, describes each man as "a new personality for art. . . . What the invention of oil-painting was to the Venetians, the face of Antinous was to late Greek sculpture, and the face of Dorian Gray will some day be to me" (Wilde 1891: 14). That this new inspiration is dangerously seductive is suggested in Hallward's earlier description of his first vision of Dorian Gray: "I had come face to face with some one whose mere personality was so fascinating that, if I allowed it to do so, it would absorb my whole nature, my whole soul, my very art itself" (1891: 9). This new Antinous projects a personality with the potential to overwhelm, not through extended dialogue but from the first recognition of his physical presence.

Wilde's use of Antinous is furthered in his description of the various personas that Hallward gives to Dorian Gray, posed as a range of mythological heroes and deities, with Antinous among the mix:

> I had drawn you as Paris in dainty armour, and as Adonis with huntsman's cloak and polished boar-spear. Crowned with heavy lotus-blossoms, you had sat on the prow of Adrian's barge, gazing across the green, turbid Nile. You had leant over the still pool of some Greek woodland, and seen in the water's silent silver the marvel of your own face. (1891: 170)[3]

Wilde's characterization emphasizes the vanity of youth, appropriate for his own narrative, and his choice of classical parallels places Antinous side by side with mythical male figures that do not conform to typical models of masculine sexuality. Although Paris and Adonis figure in myths of heterosexual attraction, they are nonetheless typified as effeminate beauties, and alongside Narcissus and Antinous they figure as aestheticized and eroticized objects.

Wilde was able to bring the historical figure of Antinous into this mythic web of pretty boys because of an accepted status he held by the end

---

3. "Adrian" is a common alternate spelling for the emperor "Hadrian" in nineteenth-century English.

of the nineteenth century. The few details known about Antinous's short life were considered visible in the statues themselves: seduction, death, and continued afterlife. Viewers of marble Antinouses emphasized several elements, each of which was essential to Wilde's distillation of the eroticized icon. The supernatural element of "divine" beauty was paired with some sinister fate, adding an element of danger to his appeal. The homosocial companionship provided to numerous modern viewers by an enduring statue was therefore colored by an element of anxiety. The marble form appears to have captured the personality of Antinous, and many modern viewers could not resist playing the role of a new Hadrian to the ancient statue.

Antinous's established sexual allure and lasting presence in myth and sculpture made him an icon among the Victorians not just for antiquity but for an ancient homoeroticism. This particular function of the famed beauty was perhaps first realized by Karl Heinrich Ulrichs, who included a verse narrative of Antinous's death among his essays that documented "male love" as a natural element in cultures from antiquity to the present day. Writing under the pseudonym Numa Numantius, Ulrichs identified the sexual identity of the *Urning* as a male who desires men, typified by the Uranian love described in Plato's *Symposium* and also found in communities across the world. For Ulrichs, Antinous was not simply another example among the many from Greece and Rome but an enduring icon that mediated between historical fact and divine inspiration. As an appendix to his 1865 publication *Ara Spei* (*Altar of Hope*), he embraced and dramatized the supernatural elements surrounding the death of Antinous. He envisioned those same mythical nymphs that seized Hylas as swimming across the Mediterranean to find their new quarry on the Nile. Echoing the tradition described by Cassius Dio of a new star's appearance at the moment of Antinous's death, Ulrichs imagined the astral Antinous outlasting even marble statues, as a dazzling presence who "soothes and awakens yearning, a witness to Uranian love" (1994: 256–57). Desiring something closer than the stars and "charmed by these lines of beauty in stone," Ulrichs also carved his own image of Antinous in alabaster to bring the physical presence into his own life (Kennedy 2002: 225). A decade later, John Addington Symonds devoted much of his time to the contemplation of the beauty in stone, and produced an extended essay on the statues of Antinous. For him it was no complicated matter. It was the lived reality behind the sculpted figures of Antinous that drew the modern viewer: "no phantom of myth, but a man as real as Hadrian . . . as real as any man who ever sat for his portrait" (1879: 48).

For these viewers, the sculpted image reflected the youth's true physical form and apparently fraught psychological state. By the late nineteenth century, it had been well established by art historians that his beautiful face projected a personality that was melancholy, withholding, and almost certainly cruel (Laban 1891). But perhaps more important was the notion that this somber mood was not only represented by, but even embodied in, Antinous:

> Schmerz und Lebensgenuss, Dunkel und Licht, Tod und Jugend begegnen sich in diesen Zügen und prägen ihnen jenen unendlich ergreifenden Ausdruck auf, welchen wir am besten bezeichnen, wenn wir sagen, dass mit dem Antinooskopf die Melancholie ihren Einzug in die antike Kunst gehalten hat. (Dietrichson 1884: 150)

> Pain and enjoyment of life, darkness and light, death and youth meet in these features and form in them that infinitely moving expression, which we define best, when we say that with the head of Antinous, melancholy made its entry into ancient art.

The sadness perceived in the statues of Antinous was often linked to the notion that his death was a suicide, and moreover that it was his only manner of escape from a limited existence as the emperor's beloved. This adds a new dimension to the ancient accounts that speculated about his death, reflecting a particularly Victorian discomfort with homosexual behavior that continued into adulthood and formed the basis for new gender identities. Fictional accounts and scholarship of the nineteenth century portrayed the youth suffering under the controlling demands of the emperor, obsessed with possessing him (e.g., Taylor 1882; Laban 1891; cf. Waters 1995). Despite the pain supposedly seen in his face, however, certain viewers could not resist the charms of Antinous. Viktor Rydberg wrote of the statues depicting "the youth with dejected head and dreaming look" (1879: 188), but in his private writings imagined a more intimate relationship: "The one who Antinous grows attached to, is never forsaken by him" (Brummer 1992: 56). The same Antinous that Dietrichson and others saw as reluctant, passive, and melancholy was imagined by Rydberg as both loving and actively faithful.

Despite the repeated emphasis on the countenance of Antinous, his full corporeal presence is an obvious part of his appeal. Scholars tend to read the head and body as separate pieces, not just in obvious cases of creative restoration. My aim here, however, is to fuse face and body, for that is how they were viewed, accepted, imagined, even if not originally sculpted. The result is a statue for nearly every fantasy, and the various mythic attributes and exotic costumes sustain a chimerical identity that dominates interpretation of our historical figure.

More than any features of portraiture or physiognomy it was the languorous pose of the body that distinguished the appeal of those statues first identified as Antinous by modern viewers. Hogarth's *Analysis of Beauty* featured the Belvedere Antinous (fig. 7.2) among canonical works of the day, as an exemplum of the "utmost beauty of proportion" (1753: 81), the perfect medium between a slim Mercury and unwieldy Atlas. In his descriptions, Hogarth emphasized the figure's sinuous curves with a quotation of DuFresnoy's description of "its serpent-like and flaming form," and with an illustration that exaggerated the pose of the sculpture (1753: vi, plate I). Although the Belvedere statue would soon be stripped of its title as Antinous, since the sculpted face does not match that recognized in the expanded corpus, the notion of his body's "gracefully turned attitude" and "easy sway" (1753: 19–20) would live on.

The body itself was seen as capturing the personality of Antinous, and a sculpture's physique and posture were significant criteria for identification, even without the virtue of his famous face. For example, a sculpted torso from Antinoopolis (found in 1818, subsequently lost in Cairo) was recognized as a portrait although it preserved no head. Its find-spot, of course, heavily influenced how the object was perceived, but the original identification was presented on the merits of a "certain vigor" in the body and its "attitude . . . of softness full of grace" (Gillispie and Dewachter 1987: 326). Similarly, the statue known as the Capitoline Antinous (fig. 7.3) was so designated because it was found at Hadrian's villa in Tivoli (Haskell and Penny 1981: 143–44). This statue also does not actually bear a recognizable face of Antinous, and was subsequently interpreted as an image of Hermes. Yet it was so widely known as Antinous in the eighteenth century that other fragmentary statues were restored with copies of its head (cf. Dietrichson 1884: no. 106). The curving torso, moreover, has become so established as a defining characteristic of Antinous that the interpretation of the Capitoline statue as Antinous still has supporters (cf. de la Maza 1966: 250). The influence of Freudian theories of sexual development and also the role of photography in the documentation of deviant bodies (Seitler 2004) underlie Jiri Frel's analysis of a torso in the collection of the Metropolitan museum. Frel claimed the Capitoline Antinous as an important parallel for the compelling piece in New York, which he identified as Antinous strictly through the body's posture:

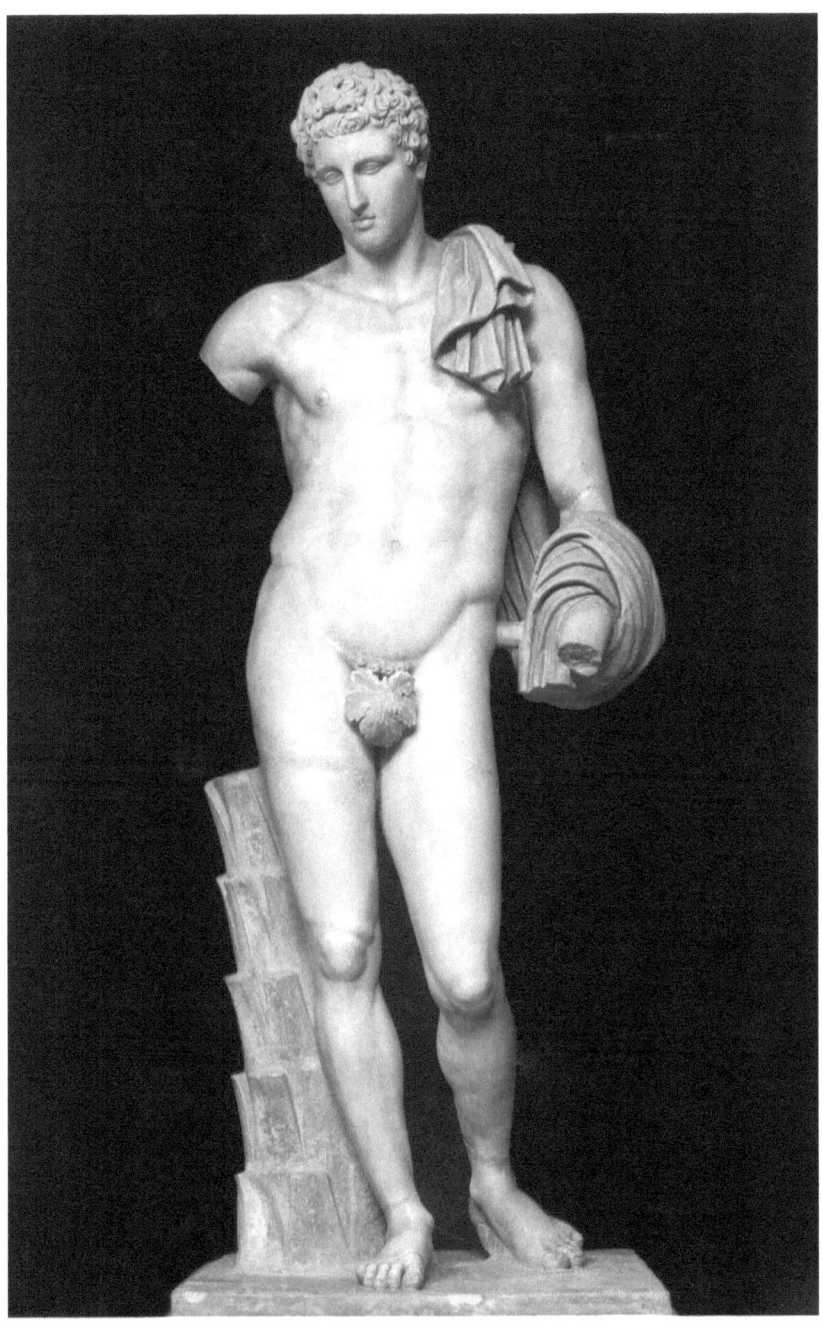

FIGURE 7.2. The Belvedere "Antinous" (Art Resource / Alinari)

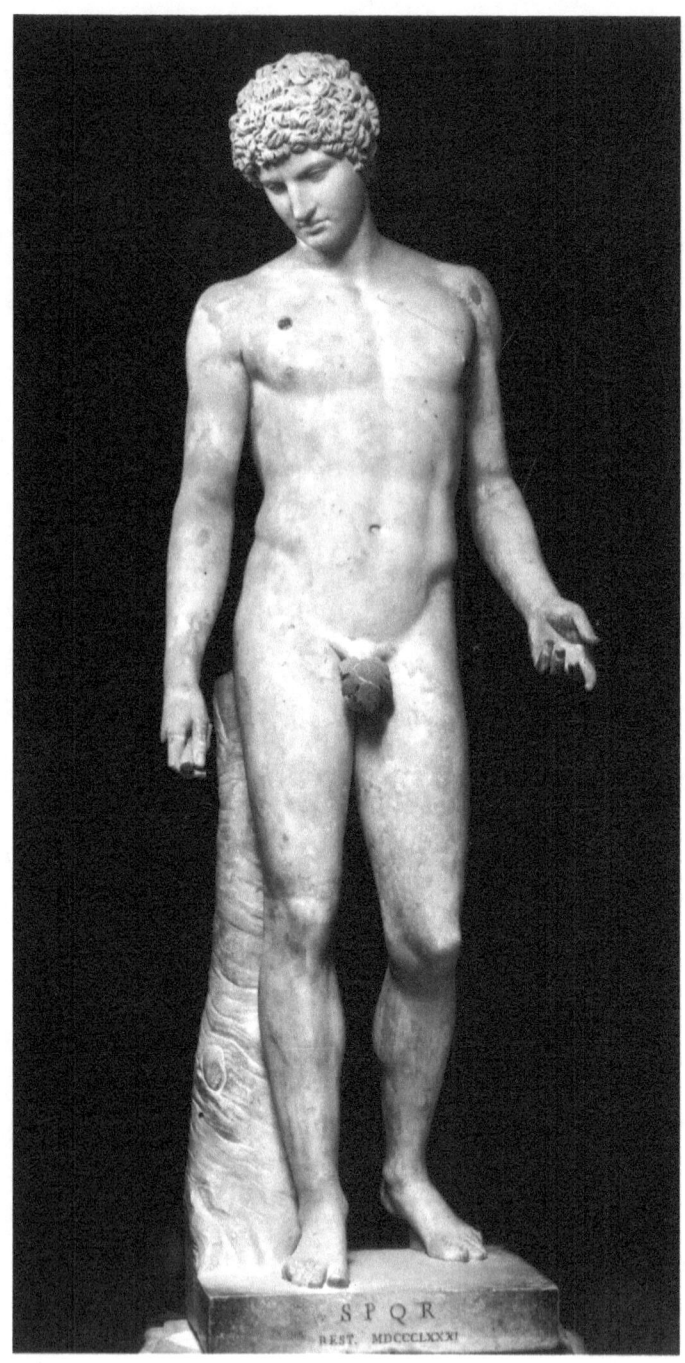
FIGURE 7.3. The Capitoline "Antinous" (Art Resource / Alinari)

The beauty of the New York youth is glamorous rather than fresh, and no modesty is evident—the head, which was bent forward, suggests rather a self-conscious introversion. Effeminate delicacy is combined here with the awkward charm of a 'Narcissus' who, though still very young, is already tired. For such a person Antinous inevitably comes to mind. (1973: 128)

The simultaneous identification of Antinous with narcissism and also the specific body type and posture are not based on visual parallels alone. Rather, perceptions of effeminacy and vanity encourage some viewers to find the icon of homosexuality in even fragments of ancient stone, to recognize not only a stereotype but his specific personality.

As these examples show, many of those who discerned a mood or psychological state in Antinous's familiar face also perceived a "type" of man in his corporeal presence. It was in this way that the perceived personality of Antinous, and the tragedy of his early death, could be linked with homosexual identity more broadly. The combination of grace and beauty with something sinister was easily extended from Antinous to other men who did not conform to normative gender types. Whether his death was characterized as self-destructive or as an act of rebellion, it resonated with the Victorian anxiety surrounding same-sex activity. Despite the danger, however, viewers who identified as *Urningen,* scholars, and museum curators all desired to have Antinous near them in whatever way they could.

ANTINOUS REANIMATED

The same statues of Antinous that proved historical realness to Symonds have also inspired narratives that go far beyond the template recorded in ancient texts. For it is through the sculptures that modern viewers have mythologized the relationship of Hadrian and Antinous as an exemplum of Greek pederasty's long endurance, the universality of sexual emotion, and the inevitably tragic nature of homosexuality. Even though their engagement with history often faltered, fantasies of Antinous rely on the notion of the sculpted image as the preserving medium of an ancient identity and a homoerotic subject that transcends historical bounds.

Ella Sharpe Youngs was an English poet who published several volumes of poetry, many of which followed classical themes, in the 1870s and 1880s. For her dramatic text *The Apotheosis of Antinous,* Youngs cited two statues as her inspiration: the Capitoline Antinous, and the Eros Centocelle, widely known in her day as the "Genius of the Vatican" (1887: 5). Her play revolves around a stone image of Antinous that inspires an obsessive artist by its unrivaled beauty, in a historical setting that actually precedes the Hadrianic era by some five hundred years. Set in classical Athens (with Plato and Socrates among the characters), Youngs's story follows the ambitions of the master sculptor Amphion, who had already gained great fame for his statue of Ganymede—Greek myth's famous object of homoerotic passion. Frustrated, anxious to surpass his own past works, Amphion enters into a mystical pact with the divine Demogorgon, who appears as a monstrous sculpture that is the accumulation of each era's lack of success in "its strife after the perfect and the high ideal" (1887: 8). This figure is, then, the antithesis of the statue of Antinous, which will come into being not through artistic skill as such, but after an invocation of the Spirits of Love and Spirits of Sculpture allows Amphion to "petrify" the mortal of his choice. The critical action required of the Athenian sculptor is, first symbolically then more literally, to grasp the object after which he yearns. He is instructed to seize a "serpent of flame" that becomes a bracelet of stone, but like the statue of Antinous it will create, the bracelet writhes because "some life is in it" (1887: 15). Once again, the sinuous curve of fire and serpent extolled by DuFresnoy (above) denote beauty, life, and danger.[4]

A noble Athenian youth named Antinous stands out among the ephebes of the gymnasium, and once the sculptor is able to lure this orphan to his studio, he places the charmed bracelet on his arm at a moment that freezes him in the pose of the Capitoline statue:

> His pallid feet netted within the pool
> Which was his bath, like silver-glancing fish.
> His godlike head, impetuously proud,
> Raised questioningly to the eyes of Life;
> Then, as if he had something sad to tell,
> Drooping in sudden wistful prescience;
> Arms drooping likewise. (1887: 21–22)

Amphion aims to sculpt his own copy using the petrified original as his perfect model, but he proves to be something of a stand-in for the obsessive, controlling Hadrian. For the sculptor's desire prevents him from releasing the captive youth, either by reanimating the stone, or by permitting Antinous's tortured soul to leave the marble, lest the statue "would grow / In shape less perfect" (1887: 37).

---

4. Youngs's choice of symbolism and language appear directly indebted to DuFresnoy's description of the Belvedere Antinous, which circulated widely through Hogarth's 1753 publication.

The Athenian context for Youngs's Antinous places the homoerotic icon in the setting most directly associated with male love of a sophisticated nature, and also marks the importance of the Capitoline Antinous as sculpture of the highest quality, specifically classical *Greek* art. In this sense, Youngs's approach would be more in line with the scholarly identification of the Capitoline statue as a Roman copy of an earlier work, recognized by most as the god Hermes rather than the mortal Bithynian. Once the youth's beauty has taken sculpted form, however, it becomes like Hermes, an object of worship for all who see it. The sculptor Amphion recognizes the divine quality of the sculpture, and celebrates the immortality and fame that the youth will now possess as a work of art:

>   Ah, sweet my god Antinoüs!
> Through whom myself shall reign a demi-god
> For ever in the annaled Art of Greece!
>   *I* know alone that *Art* immortal is;
> And that Antinoüs, my glorious gift
> To Greece, immortal shall for ever be! (1887: 44–45; emphasis in original)

Though Amphion seeks to increase his own fame as sculptor by presenting the stone Antinous as his own creation, the youth's destiny as an undying object makes him available for admiring gazes of all eras.

The cruelty of leaving Antinous petrified is underscored by those who grieve for the missing youth. Amphion's possession of the statue and account of its creation are challenged by the sisters of the Athenian Antinous, who recognize the beauty that lived in their brother when they "on the instant meet Antinoüs / Marbled" (1887: 26). An ensuing dispute for possession of the work is taken to the Aereopagus for a public judgment of each party's claim to the marble beauty. The sisters' description of the living and sculpted youth resonates with the Antinous of the Roman era, and the reception of his portraits as historically and personally descriptive:

> His body is as free from fleck or flaw
> As is a virgin's cheek; alone we knew
> Him by his perfect beauty. (1887: 63)

The recognition is instant, based not on any particular feature but rather on the unique perfection of his body and face. Like the artist absorbed by that beauty, however, the Athenian citizens are so taken by Antinous as art, as a sculpted object of worship and delight, that they deny the sisters' appeal. Only after the spirit Demogorgon reveals the truth is Amphion compelled to confess, but with a final plea in which he still claims authorship of the marble Antinous. If not sculpted by his tools, the divine Antinous was created by his desire:

> O boy, I am thy lover,
> Creator too. From Inspiration's loins
> Into the womb of Thought thou, my best work,
> And last, didst pass ineffable and dear.
> And through the travail terrible and strong
> Of arduous activity, and toil
> Promethean, thou standest forth to Greece
> Untrammeled, unexampled; perfect Youth
> And perfect Beauty—god above all gods! (1887: 85)

The apotheosis in Youngs's drama, however, is not permanent. Amphion is compelled to remove the serpentine bracelet and release Antinous from his marble state. Bereft of his alluring companion, and unable to sculpt a true replacement, Amphion resolves to take his own life.

The sinister element in another living statue fantasy is centered specifically on Antinous in Kate Everest's poem the "Dreaming Antinous," published some two decades later. Everest wrote two suspense novels under the pseudonymic title of "a Peeress," and published a wide-ranging collection of poetry that begins with Antinous and ends with Iphigenia (1912). Aside from these bookends, classical references are rare in Everest's work. Several poems, however, address another woman with an affectionate, even desirous tone that parallels the homoerotics found in her story of Antinous. And as Waters (1995: 212–13) has emphasized, male couples from classical antiquity functioned as important models for female homoeroticism of the Victorian era, given the relative paucity of lesbian icons from antiquity.[5]

Like Youngs, Everest exposes Antinous to a male gaze that is filled not only with longing, but more specifically with a desire to re-create the beauty of Antinous in a form that could outlive antiquity. Her Antinous poem resembles Youngs's "Apotheosis" in featuring a classical statue by Praxiteles, thus a work significantly older than the Hadrianic era. Nonetheless, this

---

5. Lesbian identifications did, of course, invoke the poet Sappho, and also made use of the fictional poetess Bilitis, on which see Valentine 2008 and also C. K. Prince's abstract for a paper delivered at the APA meeting in Boston, 2005, entitled "Pierre Louÿs, Les Chansons de Bilitis and the Queered Lyric Voice," http://apaclassics.org/sites/default/files/documents/abstracts/prince.pdf.

sculpture is supposed to be a representation of the Bithynian youth, and its description is strongly suggestive of the Capitoline Antinous:

> The soft light fell athwart the graceful limbs
> Gleaming in their white beauty. 'Twas a form
> Of perfect loveliness; the head was drooped,
> A smile, half-mocking, half-caressing, curved
> Those proud young lips, serene in their still rest. (1912: 10)

A contemporary artist, a painter, attempts to copy the statue's unique charm, but fails to capture on his canvas "the living beauty, all that served to make / The breathless marble live" (1912: 10). Frustrated, the painter gives voice to a dangerous wish, bargaining "I would give / My life to see you for a short hour's space / in all your living beauty face to face!" (1912: 11). The marble indeed turns to flesh and spends a full hour posing for the artist while singing of the Black Sea shore, Adrian's court, "of youth, of life, of love" (1912: 13). Though Everest's painter seeks an innocent pleasure, compared to Young's Amphion or even Wilde's Dorian Gray, there is a consequence to the fulfillment of his wish. Before Antinous resumes his place on the pedestal, he chastely caresses the lips of the artist, who falls to his death "in silent rest, and everlasting sleep" (1912: 15). Thus, the desiring male is left in a state not unlike the "Dreaming Antinous" himself.

Whatever mystical intervention enabled this transformation from marble to flesh is not identified, but we might well surmise that the spirit or personality of Antinous already or always resides in the sculpted object. This is a common trope of narratives that feature a statue coming to life (Gross 1992), and it marks an important distinction between these Antinous stories and the ancient myth of Pygmalion. In that tale, most fully preserved in Ovid's *Metamorphoses* (10.243–97), the sculptor satisfies his desire with an animated version of his own creation. Both Youngs and Everest, by contrast, imagine the marble containing the personality of Antinous as it already exists, and thus lending the stone its unparalleled beauty. Further, both authors deny their artists the ability to replicate the enchanted statue, and the transformation between flesh and stone that enables a more intimate knowledge or a more satisfying possession is only temporary. Desire remains unfulfilled.

While Everest and Youngs elaborated fantastic poetic versions of Antinous's vacillation between flesh and marble, intimating an eternal life through stone, a number of scholars concentrated on another sculpture that captures Antinous in a compelling narrative. The San Ildefonso statue group unites a pair of male figures on a single statue base, creating a scene that has invited further consideration of the relationship between another sculpted Antinous and his companion (fig. 7.4). Although the figures may have originally been sculpted during the first century CE, the work took on a new meaning when the head of Antinous was added to the figure on the viewer's left, presumably in the second century (Palma et al. 1986: 88–93). The sculpture group was discovered in seventeenth-century Rome, where it circulated among a number of papal and private collections under the identification of the twins Castor and Pollux (Haskell and Penny 1981: 173). The work was eventually sold to Philip V of Spain, who displayed it at his Madrid palace of San Ildefonso, whence it ultimately came to the Prado museum.

The San Ildefonso group's complex history of ownership is matched by its intricate composition, which pairs Antinous with an anonymous partner in a grouping that has provoked a range of interpretations. The youthful male figures lean languorously towards one another. The curvature is more distinct in the left-hand figure—the one with Antinous's head—who drapes an arm around the other. The right-hand youth extends a torch down to a small altar between them, while keeping a second torch behind his back. These actions, coupled with the presence of the altar and a small image of Persephone to the right, have evoked various musings on death and immortality (Haskell and Penny 1981: 173–74). The pose is similar to paintings of Orestes and Pylades, in which the companions have been bound for sacrifice and brought before the altar of Artemis at Tauris. The variance between the two torches could represent the different fates of the Dioscuri: Castor's inevitable death represented in the extinguished flame of the downcast torch, contrasted with the ever-burning immortality of Pollux. It is was under such a mythological identity that the sculptural group gained fame in the modern era, as its image was replicated in drawings, numerous copies, and even a pair of fanciful paintings, now lost, which presented the San Ildefonso pair as the homosocial counterpart to Eros and Psyche (Davis 2001: 256–58). Yet the group also has a clear association with our historical lovers of the Roman era. Although not part of the original composition, the portrait head of Antinous was already part of the group at the time of its discovery.

The recognition of Antinous's familiar countenance as an ancient restoration to the San Ildefonso group inspired new, allegorical interpretations of the ephebic pair. The beardless face and slim physique of the statue on the right are not easily recognized as belonging to the emperor Hadrian, but the nineteenth-century sculptor Friedrich Tieck (1868) suggested that

FIGURE 7.4. The San Ildefonso group (Art Resource / Alinari)

this torch-bearing figure be seen as the genius of the emperor. Symonds made much of Tieck's interpretation and considered this explanation the key to the very "mystery of Antinous" (1879: 84–86), since it spoke to the eternal spirit of both imperial mates, represented by the two torches. This reading also recast the nature of the erotic relationship between Hadrian and Antinous, suggesting a more equal status, rather than the distinct hierarchical roles of *erastēs* and *erōmenos*.

The reading of Antinous as an erotic peer for Hadrian, in sculpted form if not lived bodies, opened the relationship to identification with contemporary views of gay relationships by later writers such as Sulamith Ish-Kishor. She relied on the evidence of numerous statues to determine the character of Hadrian, as well as that of Antinous, in a biography that was meant "to demonstrate the origin, growth, and final tragedy of the homosexual temperament" from Hadrian to Njinsky. She wrote of the emperor and Antinous as emblematic of same-sex dynamics: "Their relationship was *typical of all such relationships,* and *its end typical"* (Ish-Kishor 1935: 11; emphasis added). Ish-Kishor was careful to describe this particular relationship as nonsexual:

> Hadrian's sensitive egoism and his devotion to Platonic ideals combine to strengthen the assumption that his behavior never transgressed the bounds of the Lycurgan code, which permitted to friends the demonstration of affection but not of passion. (1935: 11)

Nonetheless, Ish-Kishor portrays the emperor as obsessed with his younger companion, intent to control his development as he matures.

To illustrate this intensity of Hadrian's love, and his desire to shape the youthful Antinous to fit his own vision, Ish-Kishor imagines the scene behind the creation of a number of surviving statues. Her first is the Landsdowne Antinous, a bust that bears a heavy wreath of grapes and drapery around the shoulders, in which she sees the youthful, obedient Antinous cajoled into his pose:

> How exquisitely these sittings to his sculptors must have been staged— perhaps by the aesthetic Hadrian himself. . . . Here Antinous stands, all the light of the studio gathered upon him. An attendant has parted the clasp off the jeweled fibulla [*sic*] at his shoulder, the pin hangs open, for a moment the white tunic, as though held by his breathing, adheres to his spacious and faintly undulated breast. (1935: 91)

For Ish-Kishor, the sculpture's breathing form tells the story of its creation, in which she sees the guiding hand of the emperor. Her detailed accounts of Antinous's beautiful form narrate Hadrian's desire, yet his appreciative gaze is counterpoised with a personal agenda that marks the sculptures as enduring proof of his drive to recast Antinous in his chosen image.

Ish-Kishor takes her theories further with the San Ildefonso sculptures, which she imagines Hadrian not merely commissioning but himself carving.[6] Her description of the statue group emphasizes the shame of Hadrian, whom she takes to be concealing and extinguishing the torches that represent the vital force of male sexuality, both his and Antinous's. Thus in her account Hadrian created the object of his narcissistic desire and also destroyed that very love, through the act of sculpting Antinous. The younger partner died, she explained, "because the psychological mechanism of a male cannot function as that of a female and no degree of social tolerance can alter that fact" (1935: 11). The historical Hadrian, like the fictional artists, is deprived of his object of affection. Once again, the sculpted image serves to demonstrate a homosexual desire that goes unfulfilled.

This study of the numerous interpretations and fictions of the nineteenth and twentieth centuries brings home the fact that the creation and control of Antinous have not been Hadrian's alone. The continued function of Antinous as a symbol, whether face or body, has clearly gone far beyond his role as Hadrian's partner and his divine status in the Roman world. He is not defined by the narrow facts that historical and archaeological studies provide, but is open to further invention and new relevance. Despite the changing politics and preferences that contribute to gay identities, Antinous has been resculpted to suit each generation. Renewed as an object of desire for artists and admirers in classical Greece or the present day, Antinous is reimagined as a timeless companion. A gulf remains, however, between the Bithynian youth and his admirers, between classical antiquity and the modern world. As much as the statues endure, gathering devotees in each new century, they can only spark a desire that cannot be fulfilled. Texts that relate the forceful impression yet impenetrable nature of the sculpted Antinous, the inability of artists to replicate his beauty, and the cruel fate that his lovers endure, all reinforce the iconic status of Antinous as an object that cannot be possessed, an elusive figure that sustains desire.

---

6. Ish-Kishor was confused by the eighteenth-century relocation of the group to Spain (Haskell and Penny 1981: 173–74), and speculates that Hadrian had the work sent to his native land.

BIBLIOGRAPHY

Brummer, Hans-Henrick. 1992. "'Among the Shining Antique Marbles': Viktor Rydberg's Essay on Antinous," in T. Hall (ed.), *Docto Peregrino: Roman Studies in Honour of Torgil Magnuson*, 51–77. Stockholm.

Cary, Earnest. 1914. *Dio's Roman History.* Volume 8 of 9. London.

Davis, Whitney. 2001. "Homoerotic Art Collection from 1750 to 1920." *Art History* 24: 247–77.

De Unger, Edmund. 1950. *To Antinous*. Ilfracombe.

Dietrichson, Lorentz. 1884. *Antinoos: Eine kunstarchäologische Untersuchung*. Christiania.

Dwyer, Eugene J. 2010. *Pompeii's Living Statues: Ancient Roman Lives Stolen from Death*. Ann Arbor.

Everest, Kate. 1912. "The Dreaming Antinous," in K. Everest, *The Dreaming Antinous and Other Poems*, 9–15. London.

Frel, Jiri. 1973. "In the Shadow of Antinous." *Metropolitan Museum Journal* 7: 127–30.

Gillispie, Charles C. and Michel Dewachter. 1987. *Monuments of Egypt: The Napoleonic Edition: The Complete Archaeological Plates from "la Description de l'Egypte."* Princeton.

Gosse, Edmund. 1914. *Portraits and Sketches*. New York.

Gregg, Christopher. 2000. "Homoerotic Objectification in Roman Art: The Legacy of Ganymede." Ph.D. diss., University of North Carolina, Chapel Hill.

Gross, Kenneth. 1992. *The Dream of the Moving Statue*. Ithaca.

Halperin, David M. 1990. *One Hundred Years of Homosexuality: And Other Essays on Greek Love*. New York.

Haskell, Francis and Nicholas Penny. 1981. *Taste and the Antique: The Lure of Classical Sculpture, 1500–1900*. New Haven.

Hogarth, William. 1753. *Analysis of Beauty*. London.

Ingleheart, Jennifer. 2014. "Responding to Ovid's Pygmalion Episode and Receptions of Same-Sex Love in Classical Antiquity: Art, Homosexuality, and the Curatorship of Classical Culture in E. M. Forster's 'The Classical Annex.'" *Classical Receptions Journal* 6: 1–18.

Irving, Mark. 2006. "Perfectly Divine: Rome's Gay Pin Up." *The Times*, May 13: 34.

Ish-Kishor, Sulamith. 1935. *Magnificent Hadrian*. New York.

Kennedy, Hubert. 2002. *Karl Heinrich Ulrichs, Pioneer of the Modern Gay Movement*. San Francisco.

Kopytoff, Igor. 1986. "The Cultural Biography of Things: Commoditization as Process," in A. Appadurai (ed.), *The Social Life of Things: Commodities in Cultural Perspective*, 64–91. Cambridge.

Laban, Ferdinand. 1891. *Der Gemütsausdruck des Antinoos*. Berlin.

Lambert, Royston. 1996. *Beloved and God: The Story of Hadrian and Antinous*. New York.

Mader, Donald H. 2005. "The Greek Mirror: The Uranians and Their Use of Greece." *Journal of Homosexuality* 49: 377–420.

Marconi, Pietro. 1923. "Antinoo, saggio sull'arte dell'età Adrianeo." *Monumenti Antichi* 29: 161–300.

Maza, Francisco de la 1966. *Antínoo. el último dios del mundo clásico.* Mexico.

Meyer, Hugo. 1991. *Antinoos. Die archäologischen Denkmäler unter Einbeziehung des numismatischen und epigraphischen Materials sowie der literarischen Nachrichten.* Munich.

Palma, Beatrice, Lucilla de Lachenal, and Marisa Elisa Micheli. 1986. *Museo Nazionale Romano: Le Sculture: I marmi Ludovisi dispersi.* I, 6. Roma.

Rovira Guardiola, Rosario. 2008. "Museums and Literature: Marguerite Yourcenar's *Memoires d' Hadrien*," in Pepa Castillo, Silke Knippschild, Marta Garcia, and Carmen Herreros (eds.), *Imagines. La Antigüedad en las Artes Escénicas y Visuales*, 387–94. Logroño.

Rydberg, Victor. 1879: *Roman Days: From the Swedish of Viktor Rydberg.* Trans. Alfred C. Clark. New York.

Seitler, Dana. 2004. "Queer Physiognomies; Or, How Many Ways Can We Do the History of Sexuality?" *Criticism* 46: 71–102.

Symonds, John Addington. 1879. "Antinous," in John Addington Symonds, *Sketches and Studies in Italy,* 47–90. London.

Taylor, George. 1882. *Antinous: An Historical Romance of the Roman Empire.* Trans. Mary J. Safford. New York. (Originally published as *Antinous: Historischer Roman aus der römischen Kaiserzeit* [Leipzig 1880].)

Ulrichs, Karl Heinrich. 1994. *The Riddle of "Man-Manly Love": The Pioneering Work on Male Homosexuality.* Trans. Michael A. Lombardi-Nash. Buffalo. (Originally published as *Forschungen über das Räthsel der mannmännlichen Liebe* [Leipzig 1864–80].)

Valentine, Jody. 2008. "Lesbians Are From Lesbos: Sappho and Identity Construction in *The Ladder.*" *Helios* 35: 143–69.

Vout, Caroline. 2006. *Antinous: The Face of the Antique.* Leeds.

———. 2007. *Power and Eroticism in Imperial Rome.* Cambridge.

Waters, Sarah. 1995. "'The Most Famous Fairy in History': Antinous and Homosexual Fantasy." *Journal of the History of Sexuality* 6: 194–230.

Waywell, Geoffrey B. 1986. *Lever and Hope Sculptures: Ancient Sculptures in the Lady Lever Art Gallery, Port Sunlight and a Catalogue of the Ancient Sculptures Formerly in the Hope Collection.* London.

Wilde, Oscar. 1891. *The Picture of Dorian Gray.* London.

Williams, Craig. 1999. *Roman Homosexuality: Ideologies of Masculinity in Classical Antiquity.* Oxford.

Youngs, Ella Sharpe. 1887. "The Apotheosis of Antinoüs: A Lyrical Drama," in Ella Sharpe Youngs, *The Apotheosis of Antinoüs and Other Poems,* 4–95. London.

Yourcenar, Marguerite. 1954. *Memoirs of Hadrian.* Trans. Grace Frick. New York. (Originally published as *Mémoires d'Hadrien* [Paris 1951].)

EPILOGUE

Not Fade Away

DAVID M. HALPERIN

In the course of a recent plea for "a little humility" in our sexual politics and theory, Gayle Rubin cites "Meg Conkey, an archaeologist at Berkeley," who "likes to tell her students that 'today's solutions are tomorrow's problems.'" Rubin then goes on to point out the "corollary" to that statement: "today's problems are often yesterday's solutions" (Rubin 2009: 370).

One way to diagnose the problems we are having with our current ways of thinking, including our ways of thinking about "ancient sex," is to recognize that they may represent the solutions, sometimes brilliant solutions, that yesterday's scholars have bequeathed to us—solutions, in particular, to problems that had plagued the work of previous generations. As they come to show their age, to reveal their own limitations, and to fail to answer the new questions that we put to them, the once-dominant intellectual and methodological solutions that we have inherited, and that we have often embraced ourselves, come to constitute the obstacles we must now somehow surmount or evade in order to advance our thinking. What we may not grasp right away is the systematic extent to which we labor under the burden of earlier paradigms: far from being the victims of some previous failure of thought, we are often the prisoners of its past successes.

For classicists of my generation, those who came of age in the 1960s and 1970s, the enemy turned out to be the humanism that we eagerly took over from our pioneering and daring elders, and that we once championed, treating it as a badge of enlightenment and the embodiment of progress. That humanism, in its turn, was the solution to the problems that the previous generation of scholars had identified in the earlier paradigm that had dominated *their* intellectual formation—namely philology, or what we might now call the Old Historicism. In time, the humanistic reaction against philology ceased to represent a world-historical triumph of revolutionary thought and came to be the principal obstacle to the kinds of social history and cultural critique that my colleagues and I hoped to advance through the study of the ancient Mediterranean world. Current problems of method and theory in the history of ancient sexuality, which the contributors to this volume dramatize in a number of striking ways, make sense when they are set in the context of this extended genealogy.

What had been objectionable to our elders about classical philology was not only its seemingly excessive positivism, its subordination of literary criticism to textual criticism, its occasional philistinism (Wilamowitz called the *Iliad* a "wretched patchwork" [qtd. in Whitman 1965: 2]), its refusal to move beyond hard evidence to questions of meaning and feeling, its confidence in the hermeneutic value of supposedly determinative facts about an author's political or ideological affiliations (Virgil's Augustan loyalties) and its corresponding distrust of the interpretative results produced by the newer literary techniques of close reading, literary criticism, and formalist analysis (the *Aeneid*'s anti-Augustan subversions). The target of humanism's critique of philology was also its historicism, its narrow insistence on local context, its obsession with social, religious, and linguistic difference, all of which humanists associated with the particularisms intrinsic to the hierarchies and social exclusions of traditional European culture—to that culture's old identity politics of class, of race and ethnicity, and of gender, now seen as complicit in the atrocities of world history in the first half of the twentieth century. In the new Free World that emerged from World War II, with its discourse of universal human rights, its victorious sense of having triumphed over the various parochialisms that had led to racism, segregation, and enslavement, when the last remnants of the European empires and monarchies appeared to be finally giving way before the military and political success of the mass democracies, the time seemed right for a new, modern, humane approach to classical studies. This new approach would champion the human value and wisdom of classical texts, promote their objectivity, demonstrate their cosmic vision, and celebrate their universal greatness, a greatness rooted no longer in the intrinsic superiority of European culture and civilization but in a secular vision of humanity as a universal condition, comic or tragic as the case might be—a vision which we moderns now shared with the ancients.

A number of developments reinforced the universalizing humanism of the postwar period. The rise of psychoanalysis promoted a model of the human subject as the product of developmental vicissitudes resulting from the play of endogenous, biological drives that were largely outside the specificities of history and culture. It was now possible to see Euripides' Pentheus as sexually repressed, just like J. Edgar Hoover. The success of modern medicine and of other emerging forms of technology advanced a one-size-fits-all model for alleviating suffering in various parts of the world, reinforcing the belief in a universal, culture-free human nature. And in the United States, the G.I. bill, the expansion of public education, the opening of universities to populations beyond the élite (both students who came from the working class and professors who now earned proper salaries and no longer had to come from the leisured class), the new production of paperback books (begun during the war so that wounded soldiers recovering in hospitals could read with one hand), and the vast proliferation of classical translations (along with the decline of language-based classical education as the sole means of access to classical texts) all contributed to a renewed understanding of ancient Greek and Roman culture as a common human possession (at least among the educated members of the middle class), a culture whose value resided in its expression of universal truths.

In this atmosphere, the instruments of the New Criticism, forged in the 1930s, revealed a new utility. Though classical scholarship still required philological expertise, New Critical methods could bring out the form and content of the texts themselves, focusing on their internal organizing principles and formal coherence rather than their social and historical location, thereby resisting the earlier philological tendency to make textual meaning depend on contextual, extraliterary factors (linguistic, historical, biographical, social)—as if knowing the circumstances in which a text was produced sufficed to pin down its meaning and unlock its interpretation. B. M. W. Knox could now read Sophocles for his imagery the way Cleanth Brooks read Shakespeare. "The unit of poetry," Cedric Whitman explained in 1958, speaking of Homer, "is not idea, or fact, but image" (2).

The great literary critics of the period—Knox, Whitman, Adam Parry, and their students like Michael Putnam and Charles Segal—were quickly reinforced by William Arrowsmith, D. S. Carne-Ross, J. P. Sullivan, and the Young Turks responsible for creating the journal *Arion,* which began publication in 1962. *Arion* sought to recover the "humaneness" of the classics from the "narrowly philological" concerns of classicists and from an increasingly "sterile positivism" that had showed itself indifferent to the recent "revolution in criticism and poetry" (a revolution that went well beyond the New Criticism); it strove to make the classics relevant once again to the larger "community of letters" and integral to literary modernism ("Editorial" 1962: 3–4). An ebullient sense of exhilaration, of shaking off the dust of scholasticism and "*mere scholarship*" ("Editorial" 1962: 5),[1] was palpable in the journal's pages, never more so than when *Arion* gleefully reprinted, in its third issue, the words with which William Calder, speaking for "us fogies" in *The Classical World,* had fussily objected to *Arion*'s "public ridicule of" its "elders and betters" (Editors 1962: 105).

Sexuality played a decisive role in grounding the new humanism. Humanism looked to sexuality, understood as a basic human drive, at once biological and psychological, for proof of the universality of its reach. Psychoanalysis had revealed the presence of sexuality at the core of the human subject, central to the formation of the personality in all times and places, as well as a repressed force whose effects could be discerned through the decipherment of encrypted signs and symptoms in any and all cultural discourses. To recover the humaneness and universality of the classics, then, was to recognize how eloquently and how lucidly the ancient Greeks and Romans had testified to the experience of sexuality, how they had anticipated us in perceiving it as a driving force in human life, how aware they were of the "irrational" factors that shaped society and the individual.[2] Scholars did not need to find positive proof in the ancient record that sexuality had existed, hard evidence of the sex lives of the Greeks and Romans (personal letters or diaries, say, or semen samples taken from the bodies of mummies), any more than they needed inscriptions documenting the collapse of buildings to know that gravity had existed. Sexuality was now understood to be a universal fact, and so its presence in the ancient world could be assumed as well as constantly demonstrated and illustrated, to the abundant satisfaction of progressive scholars and their audiences.

The ancients, it turned out, had left plentiful evidence of their sexuality. All classical scholars had to do was to lift the ban that Victorian

---

1. Italics in original. "We use the phrase advisedly," the Editors added, in case a reader might have missed their scandalous emphasis.

2. Hence the importance in the period of the magisterial work of Dodds 1951, originally delivered as the Sather Classical Lectures in 1949–50.

philologists had imposed on the explicit analysis of sexual matters. Once that censorship and repression were overcome, it was possible to study the representations of sexual behavior on Greek vases and Pompeian frescoes, to restore four-letter words to the texts of Attic comedies (as Arrowsmith did in his translations of *The Birds* [1961] and *The Clouds* [1962], belatedly justified by Jeffrey Henderson's 1972 Harvard dissertation),[3] to catalogue the obscene graffiti inscribed on Roman siege bullets (Hallett 1977) and on the rock faces of Thera, to overhear discussions between ancient women about where to get the best dildos (Herodas 6), and of course to conduct at last an authoritative scholarly study of "Greek homosexuality" (Dover 1978), a topic previously known mostly from casual allusions in the dialogues of Plato. In place of an old-fashioned, musty historicism, there emerged the new field of psychohistory (e.g., Richlin 1983). Now that was progress for you!

The rough sketch I have drawn is admittedly simplistic—classical scholars had been writing about sex in the ancient Mediterranean world for centuries, albeit in largely antiquarian ways (see Orrells 2011 for some aspects of this tradition)—but the crude picture I have offered is, I think, basically accurate. The new progressive classical scholarship from the late 1940s to the late 1970s presupposed a materialist or biological model of the human subject, grounded in a secular humanism thoroughly informed by liberal values, scientism, psychological universalism, sexual realism, and many other postulates of the surrounding, pervasive psychotherapeutic culture, which had been given new legitimacy by the sexual revolution.[4] In such a context, innovative developments in poetics and literary theory could sometimes obtain a hearing from progressive classicists who, for example, spent much of the 1970s trying to figure out what to do about structuralism. Deconstruction could eventually have an impact on the analysis of classical texts: it had got its start in 1968, after all, in the form of a reading of Plato's *Phaedrus* (Derrida 1983). And the emerging, highly politicized interdisciplinary fields of black studies or women's studies were eagerly taken up by some classicists from the early 1970s, so long as they continued to be humanistic and to focus on persons.[5] Gay studies that followed

---

3. Published by Yale University Press in 1975 as Henderson 1975.
4. For a brilliant analysis of the ideological and political tendencies that gave rise in this period to a new culture of heterosexual love, see Jagose 2013.
5. Snowden 1970 won the Goodwin Award of Merit from the American Philological Association in 1973. The Women's Classical Caucus was founded in 1972.

the earlier humanistic examples set by black studies and women's studies also gained a certain legitimacy. Just as it was now possible to study "blacks in antiquity" or "women in classical antiquity," so one could write about "homosexuals in history" or "gay people in western Europe from the beginning of the Christian era."[6]

By contrast, the new identity politics of sexual, social, racial, ethnic, and gender difference that emerged in the 1980s in response to the rise of the New Right and the neoliberal counterrevolution appeared to many leftist humanists, including many progressive classicists, much too much like the old identity politics of sexism, racism, and class hierarchy (see Bloom 1995, 1999 for an extremely enlightening analysis of an adjacent scholarly field). The developments that led to queer theory and critical race studies remained largely unknown to classicists. As for historicism—understood as a designation for the empirical human sciences of social and cultural difference—well, classicists had already been there and done that. Historicism therefore had little chance of making a valid comeback. When the New Historicism emerged in early modern and Renaissance studies at the beginning of the 1980s, inspired by the work of Michel Foucault and by a literary turn in cultural anthropology,[7] it did not acquire much of a following among classicists, certainly not by the end of the decade, except in the work of Peter Brown, John J. Winkler, Maud Gleason, and myself. It took another decade for classicists to start catching on.[8]

In this context, the social constructionist approach to the history of homosexuality that Mary McIntosh pioneered in 1968 and that reflected larger intellectual developments already underway but manifested most visibly in the following decade in the work of British and American sociologists like John Gagnon and William Simon, Jeffrey Weeks, Kenneth Plummer, and Stuart Hall, American anthropologists like Esther Newton and Gayle Rubin, as well as British and American social historians like Carroll Smith-Rosenberg, Robert Padgug, George Chauncey, and Alan Bray—that approach was ignored by most classicists.[9] It ran shock-

---

6. I am quoting from the titles or subtitles of Snowden 1970, Pomeroy 1975, Rowse 1977, and Boswell 1980.

7. The bible of the New Historicism was Geertz 1973; also highly influential was Rubin 1975. The early monuments of the New Historicism were Greenblatt 1980, Montrose 1983, and Mullaney 1988.

8. See, for example, Ormand 1999 and Kurke 1999. When Jack Winkler published an important article on Greek tragedy (Winkler 1985) in *Representations,* the flagship journal of the New Historicism, a classicist to whom I showed the essay remarked what a pity it was that the piece had appeared in such an obscure journal where no one would ever see it.

9. See McIntosh 1968; Gagnon and Simon 1973; Weeks 1976, 1977, 1981; Plummer 1975, 1981; Hall 1974; Newton 1972; Rubin 1975; Smith-Rosenberg 1975; Padgug 1979; Chauncey 1982–83; Bray 1982.

ingly counter to generally accepted truths about the universality, ubiquity, objectivity, scientificity, materiality, naturalness, goodness, and empirical psycho-physical reality of sexuality. Far from being a natural drive—perhaps even a source of positive, life-giving energy—that hierarchical societies had exploited, repressed, and suppressed, sexuality emerged from this body of work as social by its very definition, as inextricably bound up with social organization, social interaction, and social stratification, and as irretrievably historical. Sexuality was inseparable, in short, from power and history. Then, in 1978, the English translation of Foucault's 1976 introduction to his *History of Sexuality* issued a sweeping, defiant, immensely counterintuitive challenge to what had been for decades the progressive understanding of sexuality: Foucault claimed that sex and sexuality, far from being at the core of human nature, were recently developed instrumental devices integral to modern strategies of social domination. Foucault elaborated his thesis by means of two 1984 volumes devoted to the history of sexuality in Greek and Roman antiquity; they appeared in English in 1985 and 1986. It is probably not surprising that classical scholars universally rejected them at the time: I was the only professional classicist in North America to give the second volume of Foucault's *History* a favorable review (Halperin 1986).

When I was an undergraduate and a graduate student, B. M. W. Knox and Adam Parry were my heroes. I still revere their work. I loved the impertinence, the humaneness, the literariness of *Arion*. I found the insights of psychoanalysis and the psychological and sexual realism that flowed from them to be immensely enlightening for the study of the ancient world. All of those developments seemed both intellectually and politically progressive, a welcome and bracing rebuke to the naïveté, intellectual poverty, philistinism, and authoritarianism of the old philology, whose learning and utility admittedly remained beyond dispute. But I had gone into classics because I was interested in cultural and historical difference, and I had lived in Europe and Asia as well as the United States throughout my childhood, so I was alert to social variation. The work of Foucault, of radical sociologists, and the new social history offered a more systematic way of understanding and representing cultural difference over time than I had previously encountered. That work was the first to provide me with an effective analytic framework for making sense of ancient writings about sex and love and for resolving the problems that classicists perennially encountered when trying to couch their descriptions of sexual life in ancient Greece in the modern vocabulary and categories of "sexuality." But in order to take advantage of social constructionist hermeneutics, to define ancient sexual attitudes and practices in all their specificity and particularity, I had to become a historicist again, which is to say I had to break with the protocols of biologism, psychohistory, and a universalizing, psychological humanism. I had to turn against the worldview that had shaped my relation to the classics and incarnated for me progressive, enlightened social and political values.

It is with a little humility, then—not a lot of humility, obviously, but some—that I have observed among younger scholars the signs of an increasing impatience with New Historicist approaches to the history of sexuality in the ancient world as well as with the paradigm of social construction. Are social construction and the New Historicism now yesterday's solutions to the materialism, universalism, and authoritarianism of the old liberal humanism of the 1960s? Are they responsible for the problems we encounter today when we try to think systematically about sexual life in the ancient Mediterranean world?

There have certainly been plenty of suggestions to that effect. A humanist rejection of historicism can be discerned in Britain in works as different as Rictor Norton's 1997 *Myth of the Modern Homosexual* and James Davidson's 2007 *The Greeks and Greek Love*. The essays collected in this volume, however, imply that the time of historicism is not yet up. Kate Gilhuly's discursive prising apart of "lesbian" and "Lesbian" is a case in point. Sandra Boehringer's strenuous defamiliarization of Lucian's three-way female sex scene in *Dialogues of the Courtesans* 5, and her differentiation of "lesbian" from *hetairistria,* is another. To be sure, "social construction" remains a deeply unfashionable term and concept, which the contributors to this volume systematically avoid, as I once tended to do myself in favor of "historicism" (Halperin 2002: 11). Reading this collection of essays, however, emboldens me to wonder whether diehards like me shouldn't dig in our heels more firmly and insist that social construction's day is not over.

Social construction, admittedly, has spawned a number of excesses as well as some conceptual and methodological confusions.[10] But a method, a theory, or a hypothesis does not have to be faultless in order to be viable. Social constructionist approaches to the history of sexuality have enabled us to see many things in the social and historical record that we would

---

10. See Hacking 1999, a critique of social construction by one of its most distinguished exponents.

never have seen otherwise. They also account for the empirical evidence better than essentialist approaches. And they have encouraged us to dust off philology and find new, progressive uses for it. There are of course difficulties with social constructionist hypotheses which should not be glossed over or effaced; it is the duty of scholarship to highlight pieces of evidence that seem not to fit them or even to contradict them, to propose alternate models for theorizing continuity and change in the history of sexuality, or to work out different approaches to time and temporality, which is precisely what recent work on queer temporality has done (more on that trend in a moment). But just as the issues that continue to bedevil Darwinian evolutionary theory are not likely to return us to a time before the discovery of natural selection, genetics, plate tectonics, and continental drift—a time when we believed in continents forever anchored to one place in the earth's crust and species permanently fixed in their anatomy and identity—so are we not likely to revert to a belief in transhistorical and transcultural sexualities, or in the existence of heterosexuals and homosexuals in classical antiquity, or in unchanging, invariable sexual identities.[11] In that sense, social constructionist approaches to the history of sexuality, for all that they are now showing their age and producing their own interpretative problems, are probably here to stay, at least for a while longer. Or so the articles gathered here seem to suggest.

Interpretative problems remain, unsurprisingly. Nancy Worman highlights the metaphorical nature of the sexualized language of abuse, invective, and insult in Athenian politics, oratory, and especially Aristophanic comedy. She casts doubt in particular on whether it is possible "to use comic or other abusive imagery to recover actual sexual attitudes and behaviors" (226–27)—a highly perilous undertaking indeed—or "to distinguish . . . the referential ranges of the vehicles" of sexual metaphors, which in any case "target other citizen behaviors" than sex—"the regulation of citizen behaviors" in various "public forums," not in the bedroom, being really "what matters, after all" (226). At the same time, Worman recognizes that the *meaning* of "the vehicles" can be understood only by recovering the Athenians' attitudes to anal and oral sex, to the love of boys, and to notions of bodily integrity and inviolability versus openness and

---

11. I am paraphrasing here some remarks made by Gayle Rubin at a forum on a similar collection of essays, Spector, Puff, and Herzog 2012, at the Institute for Research on Women and Gender, University of Michigan, Ann Arbor, on March 18, 2013.

penetrability, since they alone explain why "the open-holed body generally receives the biggest share of mockery" (220). In other words, while questioning "whether we can actually know [what Winkler called] the 'protocols'" governing ancient sexual discourses and while insisting that "comic imagery (and its appropriation in oratory) . . . does not definitively delineate specific attitudes, let alone behaviors and practices" (227, a point no one would contest who gives weight to the hedging adverb "definitively"), Worman herself has to rely on what we now know, thanks to social constructionist historians, about ancient attitudes to sex in order to frame her interpretations. She admits that "ancient comedy . . . perpetuates dominant discourses" (217), just as Greek oratory produces "normative rhetoric" about "the proper citizen" (217). What modern interpreters have to decipher, according to Worman, is an entire "sexual semiotics" (209). I couldn't agree more. But such a statement implies that in order to interpret ancient texts with any degree of confidence, we need first to establish "the protocols" that governed the discourses that pervade them. Worman does an excellent job of identifying some of those protocols.

It is of course quite true, as Holt Parker also emphasizes, that we are unable at this remove in time to determine what the ancients did in bed; as he rightly insists, we don't even know much about what our contemporaries do in bed (34). Worman's "deflationary thesis" is (like Parker's) welcome, especially for its argument that sexual "behaviors and practices" in classical antiquity, and "what ancient Athenian men were actually doing with their anuses" (227), remain forever beyond the capacity of insults like *euruprōktos* and *katapugōn* to disclose (though neither should we ignore what Parker calls "the plain sense of *katapugōn*" [55n87], which he relates to the fact that "when the sources, both literary and popular, are explicit, they assume that anal penetration is the only form of intercourse between males" [54]; this seems to sound quite a different note from Worman: "Although an ancient comic abusive term such as *katapugōn* ["ass inclined"?] may well have retained some more visceral associations with the body part to which it draws attention, its usage in comedy covers quite wide-ranging notions of behavioral excess" [54]).[12] At the same time, we can reconstruct a fair amount about the social-semiotic system that generated sexual categories and concepts. Worman contests "Foucault's emphasis on the oppositions active/passive and dominant/submissive (following Dover 1978), which both Halperin (e.g., 1990: 30) and Winkler (e.g., 1990:

---

12. See also the important discussion of *euruprōktos* by Carnes 2011: 6–7, which Worman strangely omits to factor in to her account.

70) accept as generally descriptive," arguing that "metaphors that appear to indicate submissive roles in sex in fact may index a wider array of excesses; and these are not only more broadly construed than soft, passive, or vulnerable, they are not even all sexual, but can include appetites for drink and/or food as well" (212–13).

Once again, I would not disagree. I would only point out, as I did in *One Hundred Years of Homosexuality*, that the importance of the active/passive and dominant/submissive oppositions lies not in what they reveal about how real people in classical antiquity went about having sex, what such people thought about when they were having it, how they regarded the objects of their desire, or how they represented to themselves the nature of their erotic relations with their sexual partners. Those hierarchical dualisms are significant because of how they informed the organization of sexual taxonomies and the very definitions of gender, sex, and status—how, that is, they structured ancient sexual discourses and social practices (including erotic practices), thereby shaping "the social articulation of sexual categories and the public meanings attached to sex" (Halperin 1990: 32n). That hierarchical ordering of gender and of sexual relations was operative whether or not ancient subjects experienced it consciously as such.

The distinction between consciousness and social structure that we seem to have such a hard time grasping when it comes to ancient sex is not one we fail to make in interpreting our own erotic lives. Heterosexuality today, for example, necessarily involves a relation between social unequals (women and men—and often, in practice, younger women and older men), but heterosexuals do not typically represent their romantic lives to themselves as expressions of social inequality. Nor do they always conceptualize the desirability of their sexual partners in terms of explicit power hierarchies or age hierarchies. Married love, in most people's conception, does not inevitably depend on the overt play of domination and submission in the attitudes of husband and wife—notwithstanding the celebration of "normal sadomasochism" by such philosophers of heterosexuality as Roger Scruton (1986). That's not how we tend to think about our sexual lives. But that doesn't mean that ordered social hierarchies are irrelevant to them. Rather the contrary.

The reason for feminists, for Foucault, and for sociologists and social constructionist historians to analyze sex/gender systems in terms of power, inequality, and stratification, then, is not in order to produce a picture of human relations that resembles "a sado-masochistic sex club in 1970s San Francisco, all domination and humiliation, role-playing and sex acts," as

James Davidson, who is too young in any case to have entered such a club and shouldn't knock it if he hasn't tried it, contends with his usual scholarly sobriety (Davidson 2007: 4). The reason for taking such an approach to ancient sex/gender systems is the same reason for analyzing the political or economic system, the kinship system, and many other aspects of social organization in terms of power, inequality, and stratification—namely in order to describe their political economy and social articulation. The point is not to get at the consciousness or intention of individuals but to get at the structures of their societies. Sexual relations for many people in the ancient world, as for many people in the modern world, were surely not *about* power, penetration, or hierarchy, but they were nevertheless organized and *structured,* then as now, by differences between the sexual partners in power, status, age, and sexual role.

Although as historians we may need to focus on the specificity of ancient social structures and do what we can to reconstitute their "emic" meanings (to invoke a bit of terminology that recurs in a number of the essays collected here), we are under no obligation to believe in the categories or identities that we have reconstituted; we have no reason to accord any reality to the taxonomies in which the ancients themselves believed.[13] That, after all, is the point of showing those realities to have been socially constructed. Gilhuly sounds rather like an essentialist caricature of a social constructionist when she concludes that "discourse creates sexuality and not the other way around"; she also speaks of "the reality [i.e., the real objects] that representations create" (173). Her ontological insistence, however, is intended to prevent us from taking constructions for things independent of the human mind and, therefore, from investing our belief in the ancient meanings she has so carefully recovered.

That is also why Deborah Kamen and Sarah Levin-Richardson go to such trouble to disaggregate the binary oppositions of active/passive, insertive/receptive, dominant/submissive, superordinate/subordinate, masculine/feminine, man/woman, phallus/no phallus, and penis/no penis. Rather than reproduce and reinforce the masculinist protocols of the ancient sociosexual system by upholding the ideality of its central terms, with their naturalizing amalgamation of different oppositions into the supreme binary of gender difference, we should preserve a sense of those terms as constructions, whose effect is to associate gender with social articulations of power and other differentiae that have no essential connection

---

13. For the distinction between "emic" and "etic" orders of meaning as they apply to sexual categories in different societies, see Herdt 1991. For the origin of those terms, see Parker 2001: 318.

to it (cf. Halperin 1990: 113n, 117n, 164–65n7, 166n83, and note the consistent use of scare quotes around the words "active" and "passive" in those passages from *One Hundred Years of Homosexuality*). This is very much in keeping with previous social constructionist approaches to the history of sexuality in the ancient world, which also sought to map the slippages among the various oppositions which ancient sexual discourses often tried to amalgamate, jockey into alignment, and fuse into a perfect isomorphism. Kamen's and Levin-Richardson's analysis of the words *fellatrix* and *fututrix* illustrate a point that other scholars have made about the figure of the *kinaidos* or *cinaedus*: in both cases, we have a personage defined by an *active* desire to play a *receptive* sexual role, which is one of the reasons for the mockery, horror, and/or outrage with which the ancients regarded such figures (Halperin 2002: 122).[14]

Perhaps that is why I believe Boehringer goes too far when she says, of Lucian's Fifth *Dialogue of the Courtesans*, "There is thus no active–passive or masculine–feminine reversal" (270). A woman who is *andrikē*, who shaves her head like a male athlete (in what Boehringer herself calls "an intentional *act* of masculinization": 274), who prefers to identify herself by a masculine version of her name, who says, "I am all man" (*to pan anēr eimi*), who boasts of having "the mind and desire and everything else of a man," and who takes the lead in making love to a woman is certainly reversing her conventional gender identification by ancient standards. The fact that she has a "wife" who also plays an aggressive sexual role with another woman, and a female sexual partner who responds to her lovemaking and participates in the action, does somewhat confuse, as Boehringer argues, the strict polarity of roles and gender identities. But it doesn't obscure the gender transgression that Lucian dramatizes, nor does it blur or alter conventional definitions of gender. Just as a woman who actively seeks to play a receptive sexual role does not totally erase her gender identity or her status as "passive" in the sense of penetrated and penetratable, by ancient criteria, so the various ways in which Megilla/us engages in erotic exchanges with her partners does not undo the masculine gender coding on which s/he insists. I have no wish to dispute, however, Boehringer's important point about how masculine attributes circulate among the three women in the story.

---

14. Cf. Halperin 1990: 36n: "I must point out, once again, that I am speaking about Greek canons of sexual propriety, not about the actual phenomenology of sexual life in ancient Greece. It would be easy to come up with many counter-examples to the generalizations I am making here in order to show, for example, that women sometimes were considered capable of pursuing men. Thus, in Euripides's *Hippolytus*," etc., etc.

Worman's salutary refusal to see through sexual rhetoric to sexual reality is nicely echoed by Parker's rejection of scholarly readings of vase paintings that see those paintings as transparent windows onto social reality rather than as images constructed according to a complex semiotics of their own. In this way, Parker wittily dispatches a number of farfetched interpretations of pederastic "courting scenes"; he also refutes the naïvely documentary approach to the paintings by some scholars of ancient sexual life. I am grateful to Parker for arguing that some scenes that seem to show mutual erotic interest between adult males of similar ages imply no such thing. Though my references in the addendum to *One Hundred Years of Homosexuality* to some images attributed to a painter dubbed The Affecter did not in fact constitute a "palinode," as Parker extravagantly puts it (let alone, as Boswell 1994: 58n20 preferred, a "retraction"), only an honest discussion of some evidence that seemed to challenge my views and that I had no wish to conceal—evidence that (as I maintained even at the time) was "relatively scanty and in need of careful interpretation" (Halperin 1990: 225)—I am happy that I can now abandon those scruples and need no longer linger over the possible trouble those images might cause my framework for understanding sex and sexual representation in classical antiquity.

I am also happy that Julia Shapiro (along with Parker 2011: 129–31) has finally put an end to the claim that pederasty in classical Athens expressed exclusively the sexual tastes of a small social élite and that the great mass of citizens regarded it with distaste and contempt. The apparent ubiquity and ordinariness of male brothels argues against such an interpretation (Halperin 1990: 91–92), as Shapiro notes. She takes the argument much further by carefully showing that Aeschines' speech *Against Timarchus*, when attentively read, also testifies to the existence of a widespread and widely accepted ethic of *good* pederasty (*dikaios erōs*), and that a number of other passages in comedy and oratory do the same.

In an inverse procedure, Bryan E. Burns shows how the figure of Antinous was overtaken in modern times by universalizing notions of homosexuality. The divinity whom Mark Simpson has called "the gay Jesus" was, according to Burns, *literally* constructed by modern restorers, before being made the object of endless, and various, erotic projections. (More recent appropriations of Antinous for gay male spirituality can be found on a number of websites, which make him the focus of a sacred cult and even the source of a set of scriptures.)[15] Burns's Antinous is thus a fitting meta-

---

15. See http://www.sacredantinous.com/ST-Epistles/oooIntroduction.html, http://templeofthedivineantinous.blogspot.fr, http://enlightenedmale2000.com/2010/03/07/antinous-

phor for the way the classical world, and its sexual life, continue to function as objects of desire for us moderns, including modern classical scholars (see Dufallo and McCracken 2006: 1–7). It is our sexuality, not theirs, that is all too often the real subject in contemporary histories of ancient sex.

※

Social constructionist approaches to the history of sexuality in classical antiquity have come in for their most serious challenge not from essentializing work on the part of classical scholars, which (as the essays contained in this volume indicate) is now largely discredited, but from more recent explorations of "queer temporality." The latter have usefully critiqued social constructionists' emphasis on historical discontinuity, rupture, and difference, arguing that it denies historical subjects the possibility of making identifications across time, of championing various forms of deviance in different societies, and of celebrating premodern instances of resistance to sexual norms (aka queerness).[16] Critics have also claimed to find in social constructionist models an implicit teleology, according to which modern sexualities represent the end point of a long process of sexual change, the outcome towards which sexuality has been evolving; they discern behind that teleology a kind of chauvinism that privileges a gay masculinist ideology of a homosexuality without gender (e.g., Freccero 2006, Rohy 2009). A further defect of thinking about the history of sexuality in such teleological terms is the racist implication that the versions of heterosexuality and homosexuality currently hegemonic within modern Western industrialized democratic societies are historically advanced with respect to earlier age-structured, role-specific, or gender-polarized forms of sexuality—all of which carries the further implication that contemporary societies in which such "premodern" forms of sexuality still exist are equivalent to the historically prior and socially primitive societies from which modern Western industrialized societies evolved (thereby echoing

---

in-his-own-words (all accessed on May 26, 2013): I have not had the patience to determine how much of this material gets recycled from one website to another.

16. For a recent survey and comprehensive bibliography, see Traub 2013, to which add Dinshaw 2012. Richlin 1993 had earlier complained that social constructionist approaches to the history of sexuality prevent modern homosexuals from identifying with ancient homosexuals; Richlin, however, was not working from a queer-temporality paradigm, which seeks to relate instances of social deviance in historically distant societies *despite* the different ways such deviance is expressed: rather, her approach, as she insisted (Richlin 1992: xx), is distinguished by its "essentialism" and "materialism" (her terms), precisely the values that advocates of queer temporality are trying to resist.

earlier racist theories that contemporary "primitive" societies reveal the childhood of European man).[17]

Against such noxious historicism, proponents of queer temporality now champion a deliberate anachronism. The most extreme of them call for "dechronolization"—that is, "a temporal version of decolonization"— whose effect would be to "destroy chronology as the basis for what we do," thereby liberating scholars at long last to "tak[e] anachronism seriously and defy[ ] difference as the underwriter of history" (Menon 2006). No professional historians have yet jumped on the bandwagon of this New Unhistoricism (as Valerie Traub has dubbed it), so far as I know, but then they weren't all that keen on the New Historicism to begin with, whose most incautious applications after all authorized literary critics to invent history out of literature, just when a new generation of social historians had warned them against doing exactly that.

I have responded to some of these critiques by arguing that historicism is not incompatible with queer temporality. Identification is motivated by the erotic appeal of difference and distance as much as by a sense of shared identity, so it is not blocked or baffled by a recognition that same-sex behaviors in the past were differently organized from the dominant ways in which they are organized in many modern societies today. Nor is historicism intrinsically teleological: to describe the historical process whereby a discursive category achieves dominance, I have contended, is not to participate in historical triumphalism but to undermine it. I have also conceded that a mature social constructionist brand of historicism must take account of continuities no less than ruptures and discontinuities in the history of sexuality (Halperin 2002: 13–23, 104–10; see, also, Traub 2013).

Nonetheless, my work, and social constructionist histories in general, have been accused of "alteritism," a tendency to fetishize "otherness" as the essence of historical difference. In my case, this accusation has included the claim that I treat ancient Greek societies not only as different from modern postindustrial societies in their sexual attitudes and practices (which I do), but also that I present them as "absolutely other." Thus, Richard C. Sha, commenting on my approach, makes the following objection: "Just as imposing our notions of sexuality onto the Greeks leads to blindnesses, so too does insisting that the Greeks were absolutely other" (Sha 2006, section 15). Similarly, Jonathan Goldberg and Madhavi Menon,

---

17. See the works cited by Traub 2013 and see, generally, Chakrabarty 2000, whose powerful and salutary critique of historicism, as I have argued (Halperin 2002: 158n25), implies an understanding of "historicism" very different from the one I advocate and defend.

in what they claim to be a rejoinder to my arguments, "call for acts of queering that would suspend the assurance that the only modes of knowing the past are either those that regard the past as wholly other or those that can assimilate it to a present assumed identical to itself" (Goldberg and Menon 2005: 1616).

Did my solution to the "homosexuals in history" paradigm, in particular my insistence on seeing radical discontinuities in the history of sexuality where others had seen gay and straight people in the ancient world, bequeath in its turn a new and unforeseen problem to these later scholars, a problem which they have had to wrestle with as best they could? Or have they in fact invented a problem where none existed? Fifteen years before Goldberg and Menon published their article, I explicitly inveighed against what I called "a kind of ethnocentrism in reverse, an insistence on the absolute otherness of the Greeks, . . . an ethnographic narcissism as old as Herodotus—a tendency to dwell only on those features of alien cultures that impress us as diverging in interesting ways from 'our own'" (Halperin 1990: 60). And I have continued to urge that in historical matters "a sensitivity to difference should not lead to the ghettoization or exotification of the Other, to an othering of the Other as an embodiment of difference itself"; I have also argued that we cannot reconstitute the otherness of the Greeks "by an insistent methodological suspension of modern categories, by an austerely historicist determination to identify and bracket our own ideological presuppositions so as to describe earlier phenomena in all their irreducible cultural specificity and time-bound purity" (Halperin 2002: 17, 107). Instead, I have called for an approach to the history of sexuality that could balance the claims of identity and alterity, both in our apprehension of the past and of the present.[18]

Long before the queer critique of "alterism," then, constructionist approaches to the history of sexuality were already sufficiently queer in their procedures to have refused the stark alternatives of difference and identity, of either seeing the past as "wholly other" or assimilating it to "a present assumed identical to itself."[19]

The new work on queer temporality has immensely enriched and complicated historians' sense of our relation to time. It productively elaborates the theoretical paradox that attaches to the historical enterprise itself—

---

18. For a more detailed defense of my position on this question, see Halperin 2006; also, Coviello 2007; Traub 2007, 2013, and 2015.

19. For an astute critical response to my work that seeks to continue its impulse to derealize sexuality and to pluralize its constituent elements, see Seitler 2004.

namely its simultaneous location in different periods, in the past as well as the present. Historians, after all, live in two worlds at once: the past, which they try to reconstruct as accurately as they can, and the present, which shapes their outlook and which they shape in turn through their research. The history of sexuality, and of homosexuality, has a divided loyalty, dedicated both to telling the truth about the past and to changing attitudes in the present.

What makes historical temporality queer is precisely our inability to produce an account of the past that can abolish the paradox of our multiple locations in time—by, say, effecting through a single, unconflicted discourse both a definitive historical recovery of what happened and a compelling address to our contemporaries in our own language. The tension between identity and difference in our relation to the past cannot be resolved once and for all, and recent work on queer temporality has given us a newly acute understanding of the multiple temporal locations queer historical scholarship necessarily occupies. But queer theory is no substitute for historical scholarship, and it does not spare the historian the chore of producing the most accurate accounts of the past that can be achieved within the limits of our own cultural blinders. For that purpose a historicist, or social constructionist, hermeneutic remains, for now—or so the work contained in this volume suggests—the starting point, though certainly not the end point, for scholarship on the history of sexuality in the ancient Mediterranean world.[20]

BIBLIOGRAPHY

Bloom, Lisa. 1995. "Ghosts of Ethnicity: Rethinking Art Discourses of the 1940s and 1980s." *Socialist Review* 94.1–2: 129–64.

———. 1999. "Ghosts of Ethnicity: Rethinking Art Discourses of the 1940s and 1980s," in L. Bloom (ed.), *With Other Eyes: Looking at Race and Gender in Visual Culture*, 19–43. Minneapolis.

Boswell, John. 1980. *Christianity, Social Tolerance, and Homosexuality: Gay People in Western Europe from the Beginning of the Christian Era to the Fourteenth Century.* Chicago.

———. 1994. *Same-Sex Unions in Premodern Europe.* New York.

Bray, Alan. 1982. *Homosexuality in Renaissance England.* London.

Carnes, Jeffrey S. 2011. Review of Davidson 2007. *Iris: The Newsletter of the Lambda Classical Caucus,* Fall: 5–12.

---

20. In terms of theory and method, the state of the field has not in fact progressed beyond Parker 2001, which it is tempting to call definitive. No one should be allowed to write about sex in classical antiquity who has not first read that article.

Chakrabarty, Dipesh. 2000. *Provincializing Europe: Postcolonial Thought and Historical Difference.* Princeton.

Chauncey, George Jr. 1982–83. "From Sexual Inversion to Homosexuality: Medicine and the Changing Conceptualization of Female Deviance." *Salmagundi* 58–59: 114–146.

Coviello, Peter. 2007. "World Enough: Sex and Time in Recent Queer Studies." *GLQ* 13.2–3: 387–401.

Davidson, James. 2007. *The Greeks and Greek Love: A Radical Reappraisal of Homosexuality in Ancient Greece.* London.

Derrida, Jacques. 1983. "Plato's Pharmacy," in *Dissemination,* trans. Barbara Johnson, 61–171. Chicago.

Dinshaw, Carolyn. 2012. *How Soon Is Now? Medieval Texts, Amateur Readers, and the Queerness of Time.* Durham, NC.

Dodds, E. R. 1951. *The Greeks and the Irrational.* Berkeley.

Dover, Kenneth J. 1978. *Greek Homosexuality.* London.

Dufallo, Basil and Peggy McCracken (eds.). 2006. *Dead Lovers: Erotic Bonds and the Study of Premodern Europe.* Ann Arbor.

"Editorial." 1962. *Arion* 1.1: 3–7.

The Editors. 1962. "Autolycus II." *Arion* 1.3: 104–5.

Freccero, Carla. 2006. *Queer/Early/Modern.* Durham, NC.

Gagnon, John H. and William Simon. 1973. *Sexual Conduct: The Social Sources of Human Sexuality.* Chicago.

Geertz, Clifford. 1973. *The Interpretation of Cultures: Selected Essays.* New York.

Goldberg, Jonathan and Madhavi Menon. 2005. "Queering History." *PMLA* 120: 1608–17.

Greenblatt, Stephen. 1980. *Renaissance Self-Fashioning: From More to Shakespeare.* Chicago.

Hacking, Ian. 1999. *The Social Construction of What?* Cambridge, MA.

Hall, Stuart. 1974. "Deviance, Politics, and the Media," in Paul Rock and Mary McIntosh (eds.), *Deviance and Social Control,* 261–305. London.

Hallett, Judith. 1977. "*Perusinae Glandes* and the Changing Image of Augustus." *American Journal of Ancient History* 2: 151–71.

Halperin, David M. 1986. "Sexual Ethics and Technologies of the Self in Classical Greece." *American Journal of Philology* 107: 274–86.

———. 1990. *One Hundred Years of Homosexuality: And Other Essays on Greek Love.* New York.

———. 2002. *How to Do the History of Homosexuality.* Chicago.

———. 2006. "That Obscure Object of Historical Desire," in Richard C. Sha (ed.), *Historicizing Romantic Sexuality. Romantic Circles Praxis Series,* http://romantic.arhu.umd.edu/praxis/sexuality/halperin/halperin.html.

Henderson, Jeffrey. 1975. *The Maculate Muse: Obscene Language in Attic Comedy.* New Haven.

Herdt, Gilbert. 1991. "Representations of Homosexuality: An Essay on Cultural Ontology and Historical Comparison, Parts I and II." *Journal of the History of Sexuality* 1: 481–504, 603–32.

Jagose, Annamarie. 2013. *Orgasmology.* Durham, NC.

Kurke, Leslie. 1999. *Coins, Bodies, Games, and Gold: The Politics of Meaning in Archaic Greece.* Princeton.

McIntosh, Mary. 1968. "The Homosexual Role." *Social Problems,* 16.2: 182–92.

Menon, Madhavi. 2006. "Reply" to Carolyn Dinshaw and Karma Lochrie. Forum: Queering History. *PMLA* 121: 839.

Montrose, Louis. 1983. "'Shaping Fantasies': Figurations of Gender and Power in Elizabethan Culture." *Representations* 2: 61–94.

Mullaney, Steven. 1988. *The Place of the Stage: License, Play, and Power in Renaissance England.* Chicago.

Newton, Esther. 1972. *Mother Camp: Female Impersonators in America.* Englewood Cliffs.

Ormand, Kirk. 1999. *Exchange and the Maiden: Marriage in Sophoclean Tragedy.* Austin.

Orrells, Daniel. 2011. *Classical Culture and Modern Masculinity.* New York.

Padgug, Robert A. 1979. "Sexual Matters: On Conceptualizing Sexuality in History." *Radical History Review* 20: 3–23.

Parker, Holt N. 2001. "The Myth of the Heterosexual: Anthropology and Sexuality for Classicists." *Arethusa* 34.3: 313–62.

———. 2011. "Sex, Popular Beliefs, and Culture," in Mark Golden and Peter Toohey (eds.), *A Cultural History of Sexuality in the Classical World,* 125–44, 229–47. New York.

Plummer, Kenneth. 1975. *Sexual Stigma: An Interactionist Account.* New York.

———, (ed.). 1981. *The Making of the Modern Homosexual.* London.

Pomeroy, Sarah B. 1975. *Goddesses, Whores, Wives, and Slaves: Women in Classical Antiquity.* New York.

Richlin, Amy. 1983. *The Garden of Priapus: Sexuality and Aggression in Roman Humor.* New Haven.

———. 1992. *The Garden of Priapus: Sexuality and Aggression in Roman Humor.* Rev. ed. New York.

———. 1993. "Not Before Homosexuality: The Materiality of the *Cinaedus* and the Roman Law Against Love Between Men." *Journal of the History of Sexuality* 3: 523–73.

Rohy, Valerie. 2009. *Anachronism and Its Others: Sexuality, Race, Temporality.* Albany.

Rowse, A. L. 1977. *Homosexuals in History: A Study of Ambivalence in Society, Literature, and the Arts.* London.

Rubin, Gayle. 1975. "The Traffic in Women: Notes on the 'Political Economy' of Sex," in Rayna R. Reiter (ed.), *Toward an Anthropology of Women,* 157–210. New York.

———. 2009. "A Little Humility," in David M. Halperin and Valerie Traub (eds.), *Gay Shame,* 369–73. Chicago.

Scruton, Roger. 1986. *Sexual Desire: A Moral Philosophy of the Erotic.* New York.

Seitler, Dana. 2004. "Queer Physiognomies; Or, How Many Ways Can We Do the History of Sexuality?" *Criticism* 46.1: 71–102.

Sha, Richard C. 2006. "The Uses and Abuses of Historicism: Halperin and Shelley on the Otherness of Ancient Greek Sexuality," in R. Sha (ed.), *Historicizing Romantic Sexuality. Romantic Circles Praxis Series,* http://www.rc.umd.edu/praxis/sexuality/sha/sha.html.

Smith-Rosenberg, Carroll. 1975. "The Female World of Love and Ritual: Relations between Women in Nineteenth-Century America." *Signs* 1.1: 1–29.

Snowden, Frank M. Jr. 1970. *Blacks in Antiquity: Ethiopians in the Greco-Roman Experience.* Cambridge, MA.

Spector, Scott, Helmut Puff, and Dagmar Herzog (eds.). 2012. *After the History of Sexuality: German Genealogies with and beyond Foucault.* New York.

Traub, Valerie. 2007. "The Present Future of Lesbian Historiography," in George E. Haggerty and Molly McGarry (eds.), *Blackwell's Companion to LGBT/Q Studies*, 124–43. Malden, MA.

———. 2013. "The New Unhistoricism in Queer Studies." *PMLA* 128: 21–39.

———. 2015. *Making Sexual Knowledge: Thinking Sex with the Early Moderns.* Philadelphia.

Weeks, Jeffrey. 1976. "'Sins and Diseases': Some Notes on Homosexuality in the Nineteenth Century." *History Workshop*, 1: 211–19.

———. 1977. *Coming Out: Homosexual Politics in Britain from the Nineteenth Century to the Present.* London.

———. 1981. *Sex, Politics and Society: The Regulation of Sexuality since 1800.* London.

Whitman, Cedric H. 1965 [1958]. *Homer and the Heroic Tradition.* New York.

Winkler, John J. 1985. "The Ephebes' Song: *Tragôidia* and *Polis*." *Representations* 11: 26–62.

———. 1990. *The Constraints of Desire: The Anthropology of Sex and Gender in Ancient Greece.* New York.

CONTRIBUTORS

RUBY BLONDELL is a Professor of Classics at the University of Washington in Seattle. She has published widely on Greek literature and philosophy, and on the reception of myth in popular culture. Her books include *The Play of Character in Plato's Dialogues* (Cambridge UP, 2002), *Women on the Edge: Four Plays by Euripides* (co-authored) (Routledge, 1999), *Helping Friends and Harming Enemies: A Study in Sophocles and Greek Ethics* (Cambridge UP, 1989), and most recently, *Helen of Troy: Beauty, Myth, Devastation* (Oxford UP, 2013). She is currently writing a book on the portrayal of Helen in film and television.

SANDRA BOEHRINGER holds the position of Maîtresse de Conférences in Greek History at the University of Strasbourg (France) and is the author of articles on ancient sexuality and culture and the following books: *L'homosexualité féminine dans l'Antiquité grecque et romaine* (Les Belles Lettres, 2007) and *Dika, élève de Sappho, Lesbos, 600 av. J.-C.* (Autrement, 1999). She is the co-editor of *Homosexualité. Aimer en Grèce et à Rome* (Les Belles Lettres, 2010; with Louis-Georges Tin) and *Hommes et femmes dans l'Antiquité. Le genre, méthode et documents* (Armand Colin, 2011; with Violaine Sebillotte Cuchet). She has translated into French with Nadine Picard: John J. Winkler's *Constraints of Desire* (2005) and Maud Gleason's *Making Men* (2013).

BRYAN E. BURNS is an Associate Professor of Classical Studies at Wellesley College and a Co-Director of Eleon Excavations (Eastern Boeotia Archaeological Project) in Greece. His scholarship in various areas of Greek archaeology is united by an interest in the consumption of material culture and the shifting meaning of objects in new social contexts. He has explored these topics in the Late Bronze Age through his book *Mycenaean Greece, Mediterranean Commerce, and the Formation of Identity* (Cambridge UP, 2010). Burns also studies the role of art and artifacts in the construction of contemporary identity, including formulations of gender and sexuality that seek historical parallels in ancient Greece.

KATE GILHULY is an Associate Professor of Classical Studies at Wellesley College. She is author of *The Feminine Matrix of Sex and Gender in Ancient Greece* (Cambridge UP, 2009) and the co-editor (with Nancy Worman) of *Space, Place, and Landscape in Ancient Greek Literature and Culture* (Cambridge UP, 2014). She began her research on cultural geography while at the Radcliffe Institute for Advanced Study at Harvard University. She has published articles on the erotic geography of ancient Greece and is currently at work on a book on this topic.

DAVID M. HALPERIN is the W. H. Auden Distinguished University Professor of the History and Theory of Sexuality at the University of Michigan, where he is also Professor of English Language and Literature, Women's Studies, Comparative Literature, and Classical Studies. He is the author or editor of ten books, including *One Hundred Years of Homosexuality* (Routledge, 1990), *The Lesbian and Gay Studies Reader* (Routledge, 1993), *Saint Foucault* (Oxford UP, 1995), *What Do Gay Men Want?* (U of Michigan P, 2007, 2009), *Gay Shame* (U of Chicago P, 2009), and *How To Be Gay* (Harvard UP, 2012). He also co-founded *GLQ: A Journal of Lesbian and Gay Studies,* which he co-edited from 1991 to 2005.

DEBORAH KAMEN is an Associate Professor of Classics at the University of Washington. In addition to her book *Status in Classical Athens* (Princeton UP, 2013), she has published a number of articles on Greek and Roman slavery, gender, and sexuality.

SARAH LEVIN-RICHARDSON is an Assistant Professor of Classics at the University of Washington. She has published articles on Pompeian graffiti and modern receptions of Pompeii, and is working on a monograph exploring the physical, social, and emotional environment within Pompeii's "purpose-built" brothel. She has excavated at Pompeii, in the Roman Forum, and on Crete, and previously held a two-year Mellon Postdoctoral Fellowship at Rice University's Humanities Research Center.

KIRK ORMAND is a Professor of Classics at Oberlin. He is the author of *Exchange and the Maiden: Marriage in Sophoclean Tragedy* (U of Texas P, 1999), *Controlling Desires: Sexuality in Ancient Greece and Rome* (Praeger, 2009), and *The Hesiodic Catalogue of Women and Archaic Greece* (Cambridge UP, 2014), and editor of *A Companion to Sophocles* (Blackwell, 2012). He has published articles on Homer, Hesiod, Euripides, Ovid, Lucan, the Greek novel, and Michel Foucault, and is the recipient of the John J. Winkler Memorial Prize, the Barbara McManus Prize from the Women's Classical Caucus, and the Gildersleeve Prize from *American Journal of Philology*.

HOLT N. PARKER received his Ph.D. from Yale, and is a Professor of Classics at the University of Cincinnati. He has been awarded the Rome Prize, an NEH Fellowship, a Loeb Library Foundation Grant, the Women's Classical Caucus Prize (twice), and the Fowler Hamilton Fellowship from Christ Church, Oxford. He has published on Sappho, Sulpicia, sexuality, slavery, sadism, and spectacle. His book *Olympia Morata: The Complete Writings of an Italian Heretic* (U of Chicago P, 2003) won the Josephine Roberts Award from the Society for the Study of Early Modern Women. *Censorinus: The Birthday Book* (U of Chicago P, 2007), the first complete English translation, makes an attractive present. With William A. Johnson he edited *Ancient Literacies* (Oxford UP, 2009). His translation of Beccadelli's notorious *The Hermaphrodite* is out in the I Tatti Renaissance Library (2010).

JULIA SHAPIRO received her Ph.D. in Classical Studies from the University of Michigan, Ann Arbor. Her research and teaching interests include Greek social and cultural history, Athenian political ideology, Greek and Roman oratory, gender and sexuality, religion and magic, and reception of the classics in film and popular culture. She is currently working on two articles on the politics of male beauty in classical Athens. Her first book will explore criminological theories in ancient Greece and Rome.

NANCY WORMAN is a Professor of Classics and Comparative Literature at Barnard College and Columbia University in New York City. She is the author of articles and books on style, performance, and the body in Greek literature and culture, including *Abusive Mouths in Classical Athens* (Cambridge UP, 2011), and has co-edited, with Kate Gilhuly, *Space, Place, and Landscape in Ancient Greek Literature and Culture* (Cambridge UP, 2014). With Joy Connolly she is editing the *Oxford Handbook of Ancient Literary Theory and Criticism* and on her own devising a new project on "tragic bodies," which explores the aesthetics and politics of embodiment in Greek tragedy and beyond.

INDEX LOCORUM

Adespota K-A[1] (Unattributed Comic Fragments)
   12: 196n64
   465: 38n50
   1025: 83n190
Achilles Tatius
   Leukippe and Cleitophon 8.9.3: 38n52
Aelian
   Var. Hist. 12:19: 163
Aeschines
   1.26: 220
   1.31: 220
   1.80: 221
   1.84: 221
   1.132–59: 186
   1.135, 138: 45n71
   1.137: 197–8
   1.139–41: 181

---

1. *Adespota* K-A refers to the unattributed fragments of Greek Comedy, following the numbering of R. Kassel and C. Austin *Poetae Comici Graeci,* vols I–VIII. (Berlin, 1983).

   1.141: 187
   1.142: 187
   1.195: 36
   2.23: 222, 222n48
   2.88: 222, 222n48
   2.151: 222
   2.166: 202–3
   3.229: 218
Aeschylus
   frs. 135–136: 36–37
Alcaeus
   fr. 249: 151
Amphis
   fr. 15: 191
Anacreon
   fr. 358: 160
   fr. 407: 37
Anacreontea
   17.30–37: 37–38
Antiphanes
   fr. 194.17–21: 163–4

Archilochus
    196a: 32, 32 n.31
Aristophanes
    Birds
    137–42: 193
    699: 39n55
    703–7: 69
    1254: 39n55
    1254–56: 40n56
    Clouds
    960–1025: 190
    963–83: 225
    963–1008: 224
    978–80: 219
    1073: 190
    1102–4: 224–5
    Eccl.
    112–20: 225
    920–22: 148
    Frogs
    1301–8: 152–3
    1069–71: 225
    Knights
    78–79: 215
    166–67: 223
    375–81: 214
    424–28: 223, 225
    638–42: 223
    735–40: 196
    Lysistrata
    124, 137, 143: 225
    Peace
    11, 724: 55
    Thesmophoriazousae
    53–62: 216
    200: 225
    200–201: 216
    235–37: 211
    Wasps
    1023–28: 194
    1219–22: 151
    1345–50: 152
    Wealth
    149–59: 70, 192
Aristotle
    Nic. Eth. 1148b29–33: 55
    Poetics
    1457b6–7: 210
    1459a5–7: 211
    1459a7–8: 211
Athenaeus
    3.97b: 83n190
    13.599c: 160
    13.599d: 162
Cassius Dio
    69.11.3–4: 286–7
Catullus
    59: 239
Charisius
    211.27–29: 236
CIL IV[2]
    1388: 241
    1389: 241
    1510. 241
    1651: 240
    1969: 241
    2203: 245
    2204: 231, 250
    2217: 245
    2237: 245
    2259, 2275: 240
    2266: 241
    2273: 241
    2278: 240
    2292: 241
    4192: 241
    4434: 241

---

2. *Corpus Inscriptionum Latinarum*, vols. 1–17. (Berlin, 1853–2012).

7057: 240
8185: 241, 245
9228: 241
Demosthenes
   18.196: 222n48
   19.237: 186
   22.57–8: 204
Eustathius
   Commentaries on Homer 741.19–24: 147
Herodotus
   2.135: 158
Hesiod
   Works and Days 744–5: 28n21
Homer
   Iliad
      6.357–8: 158
      9.128–30: 146
Horace
   Epist. 1.19.28–29: 167
Isaeus
   10.25: 179
Lucian
   Bis Accusatus 33: 276
   Dial. Meretr.
      5: 256–8
      5.1–2: 171
      5.3: 172
   Fugitivi 27: 274
Lucretius
   4.1268–77: 247–8
Lysias
   3.3–4: 201
   3.5: 199
   3.9: 201
   3.22–5: 199
   3.44: 200
   3.39: 201
   4.8: 202
Martial
   1.90: 244

2.73: 239–40
3.97: 240
4.50: 242
4.84: 242
4.203: 247n66
6.69: 250
6.71.1–2: 247
7.67: 243
7.70: 244
9.67.1–6: 238
10.68.9–12: 247n66
11.7: 247
11.22.1–6: 246
11.61.6–13: 246
11.104.9–12: 248
Ovid
   Heroides 15.199–205: 168
   Metamorphoes
      4.271–388: 268
      10.243–97: 301
Palatine Anthology
   12.37 (Dioscorides): 38
   12.102 (Callimachus): 36
   12.179 (Strato): 35
   12.200 (Strato): 36
Phaedrus
   4.16: 242–3
Pherecrates
   fr. 145 K–A: 155
   fr. 149 K–A: 147
Plato
   Hipp. Maj. 299a: 80
   Laws 700a–701a: 149
   Phaed. 231e–32a, 234a: 35
   Protag. 347c–e: 28n21
   Republic
      373a: 83n190
      398e–99a: 150
   Symposium
      181c: 40

183c7–d2: 35
184a5–6: 36
191d: 263
191e5: 171–2
217a–22b: 35
Plautus
  Amph. 840: 38n49
Plutarch
  Demetrius 24.2: 71n144
  Amatorius 768F: 35n41
Priapeia
  19: 247
  27.2: 247
Ps.-Lucian
  Amores
  53: 38
  27: 55
Seneca the Elder
  Controversiae
  1.2.23: 243
  1.2.3.1–8: 273n81

Seneca the Younger
  Mor. Epist. 95.21: 243
Scholia to Pind.
  Pyth. 2.78a: 39n54
Solon
  fr. 23: 102
  fr. 25: 36
  fr. 26: 103
Sophocles
  fr. 345: 37
Strabo
  10.2.9: 162–3
Theognis
  2.1335–36: 45n71
  2.1253–4: 102
Theophrastus
  11.8: 80
  20.10: 80
Xenophon
  Oeconomicus 2.7: 179

GENERAL INDEX

active role in sex: adopted by Demonassa, 275–76; adopted by Megilla, 270–73; defined by agency, 236–51; defined by penetration, 4, 6, 55, 60, 61, 68, 212–13, 232–38, 260–61, 273, 318, 320; not defined by penetration, 18, 231–50, 271, 275, 319–20

Aeschines: approval of pederasty, 180–81, 186–89, 198–204, 226, 321; conflict with Demosthenes, 186, 197–98, 202–4, 217–19, 220–23; status of, 186, 188

Aesop, 157, 158

Agathon, depicted in Aristophanes, 156, 215–16, 225–26

age-appropriate behavior, 201–2

age-equality in male homoerotic sex, 24–25, 50, 66, 98–99

age-reversal in male homoerotic sex, 58, 68–69, 100–101

Anacreon, 159–62

Androtion, 203–4

Antinoopolis, 286–87

Antinous: 19, 285–305; as *eromenos* in Greek pederastic couple, 297–304; as gay icon, 19, 288–89, 292, 297–304, 321–22; in San Ildefonso group, 302–5; in Victorian narratives, 289–92, 297–302; sculpture identified by posture, 294–95; seen as effeminate, 297; seen as melancholic, 293, 297

Archedice, 158

Areopagus, court of, 188–89

Arion (classical journal), 311, 314

Barringer, Judith, 73, 79

Barthes, Roland, 209, 218

Beazley, John, 40–44, 71

Beckham, David, 285

body: as depicted in comedy, 156, 213–20; as depicted in oratory, 188, 217–27; as indicative of behaviors, 220–27; as sign of gender, 266–70; as site of metaphor, 208–27; associated with the feminine, 159–65; type, to identify Antinous, 294–99

337

General Index

Bourdieu, Pierre, 214–15, 216–17
Brooten, Bernadette, 260

Cameron, Alan 260–61, 269
Cantarella, Eva, 33, 74–75, 259
Catullus, 166–67, 169, 239
Clarke, John, 83, 84, 102
comedy, Greek: as evidence for sexual behavior, 17–18, 55, 59, 76, 95–96, 145, 146, 162–65, 190–96, 213–20, 255, 259, 260, 316–17; audience of, 178–82, 188–90; depicting Sappho, 162–65
courtesans. *See hetairai;* sex workers; vases, Greek: *hetairai* on
cross-dressing, 267–70
cunnilingus, 146, 161, 222, 235, 238, 243, 244, 245, 246. *See also* vases, Greek: cunnilingus on

Damon of Oa, 150–51
Davidson, Arnold 9–13
Davidson, James, 2, 6–7 13–14, 33, 39, 53, 55, 83, 213, 233, 260, 315, 319
deconstruction, 312
Demosthenes (orator): adoption of elitist values, 186; attitude towards pederasty, 202–4; conflict with Aeschines, 186, 197–8, 202–4, 217–19, 220–23
dildoes, 260, 271–3, 312
discourse: ancient, concerning sex, 2, 15, 18, 177–205; 262–66, 278–80; ancient, regarding Sappho, 157–69; ancient, regulating citizen behavior, 18, 182, 208–27, 316–17; modern, as constituting modern sexuality, 8–14; modern functions of, 7, 9, 309
double-consciousness, 165
Dover, K. J., 1, 3, 4, 6, 24, 31, 32, 33, 34, 39, 55, 80–81, 148–49, 183, 232, 233, 259

Ellis, Havelock, 10
embedded narration, 276–80
euphemisms for sexual activity, 39, 68, 261, 264
Euripides, as character in Aristophanes, 152–54, 215, 225–26
euruproktos, 195, 212–13, 216, 224, 225, 227, 317
Everest, Kate, 300–302
excess, of appetites, 18, 58, 63, 69, 179, 212–13, 214–15, 220–27, 272, 317–18

fellatio, 18, 25, 94, 147, 148 160–61, 216, 238–42, 243, 256. *See also* vases, Greek: fellatio on; *fellatrices*
fellatrices, 239–42, 249–50
female homoeroticism: 17, 143–73, 253–80; associated with prostitution, 169–73; likened to pederasty, 259–60, 273–75; not associated with prostitution, 256–57
flagellation, 11–13
Foucault, Michel: and the *History of Sexuality,* 1–14, 16, 20, 143–44, 209–10, 227, 232–33, 313–14; conflated with Dover, 24, 33
Frontisi-Ducroux, Françoise, 46, 51–52, 81
fututrices, 231, 236, 244–48, 250, 320

gender confusion, 270–76, 279–80, 320
gender roles, as definitive of sexual behavior 2, 4–5, 6, 15, 19, 146–74, 215, 227, 231–50, 259–70, 297
geography: meanings associated with, 144, 146–54, 166, 263; of sexuality, 17, 143–45
gifts, courting, 41, 44, 69–80, 178–79, 192–93, 321. *See also* vases, Greek: courting gifts on

graffiti, 18, 212, 231, 237–42, 243, 244, 245, 250, 312
group sex, 80–93, 253–80. *See also* vases, Greek: group sex on
gymnasium, as site of erotic attention, 45, 83, 103, 178, 180 195, 197–98, 218, 219, 298. *See also* vases, Greek: gymnasia as setting on

Hadrian, 19, 285–305
Haley, Shelly, 261–62
Halperin, David, 1, 2, 4, 5, 7, 19, 35, 144, 172, 195, 196, 197, 209, 213, 234
Harmodius and Aristogeiton, as ideal pederastic couple, 181, 196
Helen of Troy, 158
hermaphroditism. *See* intersexed identities
hetairai: 46, 80, 83–84, 103, 192; contrasted to *eromenoi*, 70, 192; in comedy, 170; in Lucian's *Dialogues of the Courtesans*, 18–19, 171–73, 253–80, 315; Music depicted as, 156–58; related to female homoeroticism, 17, 145, 170–73; Sappho depicted as, 145, 157–65, 168, 169–73. *See also* vases, Greek: *hetairai* on; sex workers
hetairistriai, 171–73, 263–64, 274, 275, 315
heterosexuality, as modern concept, 318–19
homophobia, attributed to antiquity, 5, 6
Horace, 167, 169
Hubbard, Thomas, 2, 24, 25, 45, 50, 55, 95–96, 98, 178, 186, 199, 201
humanism, as critical method, 309–10
hunting, as metaphor for erotic pursuit, 17, 72–79
Hupperts, Charles, 41, 59, 98
hybris, sex as, 31, 40, 197, 199–201

intercrural intercourse. *See* interfemoral intercourse

interfemoral intercourse: 17, 31–54, 55, 106–13, 126. *See also* vases, Greek: interfemoral intercourse on
intersexed identities, 2, 258 267–68, 273–74
irrumatio, 242

katapugon, 55, 212, 216, 221, 225, 227, 317
Keuls, Eva, 51, 66, 81, 87, 103
Kilmer, Martin, 24, 25, 48–49, 56, 58–59, 82, 85–88, 100–101
kinaidos, 148, 222, 320
Kleisthenes, character in Aristophanes, 211–12
Kleitagora, author of drinking-song, 152
Koch-Harnack, Gundel, 71–72, 75–76
Krafft-Ebing, Richard von, 10, 12
Kurke, Leslie, 83–4, 90, 158, 159

Lear, Andrew, 33, 45, 46, 55, 58, 67–68, 74, 76, 77, 79, 81–82, 100, 102
lesbianism: and modern Lesvos, 143; modern construction of, 17, 18, 143–73, 262–63, 279; related to Sappho, 143–73. *See also* Lesbos
Lesbos: associations of in antiquity, 146–57, 263; associated with musical style, 149–157; gendered feminine 151; known for eroticism, 146; known for fellatio, 147–49, 152; known for female homoeroticism, 160–61, 170–73, 256, 257, 260, 263; known for manual stimulation, 147–48; known for women's work, 146
Lewis, Sian, 80, 81–85, 88, 96, 102
Lissarrague, François, 53–54, 81–82

marriage: heterosexual, 159, 168; imagined between women, 260–62, 267, 273

Megilla, 18, 172–73 256–80, 320

Meibom, John Henry (Johann Heinrich), treatise of, 11–12

metaphors: Aristotle's treatment of, 210–11, 218; hunting, as representing pederastic pursuit, 72–79; sexual, functions of, 18, 208–9, 210–20, 226, 250, 316, 318; spatial, 144

Misgolas, 190

New Criticism, 310–11

New Historicism, 19, 313, 315, 323

New Music: controversy concerning, 17, 149–57; Euripides associated with, 153–54

Oakley, John, 24

oratory, Greek, 18, 95, 177–81, 185–88, 197–204, 217–22, 317, 321

orgies. *See* group sex

Ovid, 167–69, 301

Paeléothodoros, Dimitris, 96–97, 104

passivity: as marker of inferior status, 4, 6, 212–13, 234–35, 317–18; as sign of femininity, 254, 259, 270; depicted as natural for women, 233–35, 243, 320; expressed by being penetrated, 4, 196, 232–35; not defined by penetration, 18, 231–50; not indicated by oral or anal sex, 212–13; unusual for adult males, 60, 68

pederasty: Achilles and Patroclus portrayed as example of, 187–88; and hunting, 72–79; as a marker of proper behavior, 178, 180–82, 186–89, 191, 194–95, 197–204; aspiration to by lower classes, 179–80, 188–89, 205; criticized by lower classes, 178–79 196, 197–204; depicted in comedy, 190–96; depicted in oratory, 197–204, ideal of as non-commercial, 178, 182, 191–3, 200–201; not confined to elites, 17–18, 26–28, 72–73, 96, 177–205, 321; portrayed as democratic, 180–81, 187–88; requiring wealth and leisure 178–79, 188–89, 204–5. *See also* vases, Greek: as evidence for sexual behavior

penetration: as defining sexual activity/passivity, 4, 232–36; as not defining sexual activity/passivity, 231–50; as shameful for man penetrated, 4, 31–35, 54–55, 58–60, 66–67, 68–69; 195–96, 212, 216, 225, 233; by women, 243–44, overstated in modern scholarship, 6. *See also* vases, Greek: anal intercourse on

perversion, invention of, 9–13

Philaenis, 240, 243–44

philology, as critical method, 23, 309–10

Platonic dialogue: favorable to pederasty, 7, 24, 72–73, 80, 148, 171–72, 177, 178, 180, 181, 184–85, 191, 193, 195, 196, 292; parody of, 170–71, 269–70, 276–80

popular morality in Athens, 182–96

Post, Emily, 71

Prins, Yopie, 165

prostitutes. See *hetairai*; sex workers

queer temporality, 19–20, 316, 322–25

Rhodopis, 157–59

Rubin, Gayle, 308, 313, 316

Sappho: as a muse, 156–57; as masculine, 167, 169; as object of masculine desire, 159–60, 169; associated with female homoeroticism, 17, 144–45, 167, 169, 260, 263; associated with New Music,

149; as subject of heteroerotic desire, 162–65, 167–68; depicted as *hetaira*, 156–65, 168, 169–73; depicted in Attic comedy, 162–65; imagined relationship with Anacreon, 159–62; in Roman literature, 166–73; relationship with brother, 158–59

Schnapp, Alain, 53–54, 73

sculpture, 19, 285–305

second sophistic, 170–73, 253–80

Sedgwick, Eve, 5

self-control, as ancient ideal, 1, 4, 5, 18, 35 233, 272

sex workers: female: 202–4; Lucian's depiction of, 256, 265, 268; male, 198–200; orators likened to, 221–22, 247–48, 261. See also *hetairai;* vases, Greek: *hetairai* on

sexuality: as modern development, 2, 3–6, 8–14, 68, 314–15; denaturalized in present, 5, 20; forms of in antiquity, *passim;* relation to new humanism, 311–12

Shapiro, H. Allen, 44, 60, 101–2

Skinner, Marilyn, 260

social class: anti-elitist attitudes, 151, 178, 196, 197–204; as aspect of pederasty, 17, 18, 26–27, 96, 180–82, 196, 321; definition of elite in Athens, 183–84; in relation to symposia, 28, 96, 180, 209; of audience for drama, 178, 188–89; of audience for oratory, 178, 182–89; of audience for Plato and Xenophon, 179, 184–85; of audience for vases, 26–28; of persons depicted on vases, 34. See also pederasty: aspiration to by lower classes; pederasty: criticized by lower classes; pederasty: not confined to elites

social constructionism, 315–16, 317, 319–20, 322

Stewart, Andrew, 24, 48, 181

Sutton, Robert, 29, 45, 57, 61–62, 81, 84–85, 86, 97

Symonds, John Addington, 292–93, 297, 304

symposia: as elite, 17, 25, 27–28, 84, 178, 184, 185, 209; as common site for pederastic relationships, 17, 25, 48, 58, 82–84, 93, 97, 103, 178; flute-players at, 83, 87, 151–52; *hetairai* attending, 170; in comedy, 151–52; as not limited to elites, 27, 28, 96, 180–81, 185–86. *See also* vases, Greek: symposia on

thighs, as erotic, 32, 36–40, 54

Thornton, Bruce, 39, 40

threesomes. *See* group sex

Topper, Kathryn, 25

tribades, 18, 242–44, 249–50, 259, 260, 273

truth, as product of discourses, 9, 13–14

Ulrichs, Karl Heinrich, 292

Uranian love, 292

vases, Greek: age reversal on, 68–69; anal intercourse on, 54–68, 115–16, 125–26; as evidence for sexual behavior, 16–17, 23–126; bestiality on, 101–2; Beazley's typology of homoerotic sex on, 40–44; catalogue of, 106–26; courting gifts on, 41, 69–80, 103, 116–17; cunnilingus on, 94–95, 117; dancing on, 46, 62, 88; diachronic changes in, 48–51, 54, 95–97; Eurymedon vase, 66–67; export of to Etruria, 28–30, 84; fellatio on, 94; from known Attic gravesites, 124; group sex on, 46, 80–93, 103, 118–21; gymnasia as setting on, 45, 51, 52, 58, 74, 75, 76, 103; *hetairai* on, 83–84, 87, 96, 103, 104; homoerotic sex rare on, 40–41; interfemoral intercourse on, 32–54, 106–113; komast scenes on, 56–57, 60–62, 90; observers of scene on, 46–48, 51–53, 82, 87, 90; problems in reading conventions of, 24–32, 48, 53–54, 63, 74–79, 80–93, 97–101, 106; symposia on, 25, 87, 88, 96, 103; uncertain gender of characters on, 62–63; up-and-down gesture on, 41, 97–101; use of space on, 81–93, 100–102; wedding vases, 104–5

vases, named painters of: Affecter, 97–100; Antiphon Painter, 86, 87, 88; Beldam Painter, 81; Brygos Painter, 50, 91; Dikaios Painter, 88; Dinos Painter, 63; Eucharides Painter, 50–51; Goltyr Painter, 56; Guglielmi painter, 56–57, 59, 60, 68; Hare Hunt Painter, 79; Nikosthenes Painter, 90; Onesimos Painter, 86, 88; Pedieus Painter, 63, 90; Penelope Painter, 66; Prometheus Painter, 57; Shuvalov Painter, 63; Siren Painter, 77; Syriskos Painter, 70; Thalia Painter, 90, 94; Thanatos Painter, 79; Timiades Painter, 56, 61, 68; Triptolemos Painter, 54. *See also* vases, Greek: catalog of

Victorian reception of classical sculpture, 287–90, 297–304

wigs, as gender marker, 172, 257, 266, 273–75

Wilde, Oscar 291–92

Winkler, John J., 1, 2, 4, 7, 144, 165, 210, 213, 227, 260, 313, 317

women as sexual agents, 231–50, 253–80. *See also* active role in sex; passivity: not defined by penetration

Yatromanolakis, Dimitrios, 145, 157, 162, 172

Youngs, Ella Sharpe, 297–300

Zeitin, Froma, 1

CLASSICAL MEMORIES/MODERN IDENTITIES
Paul Allen Miller and Richard H. Armstrong, Series Editors

Classical antiquity has bequeathed a body of values and a "cultural koine" that later Western cultures have appropriated and adapted as their own. However, the transmission of ancient culture was and remains a malleable and contested process. This series explores how the classical world has been variously interpreted, transformed, and appropriated to forge a usable past and a livable present. Books published in this series detail both the positive and negative aspects of classical reception and take an expansive view of the topic. Thus it includes works that examine the function of translations, adaptations, invocations, and classical scholarship in the formation of personal, cultural, national, sexual, and racial formations.

Ancient Sex: New Essays
  EDITED BY RUBY BLONDELL AND KIRK ORMAND

Odyssean Identities in Modern Cultures: The Journey Home
  EDITED BY HUNTER GARDNER AND SHEILA MURNAGHAN

Virginia Woolf, Jane Ellen Harrison, and the Spirit of Modernist Classicism
  JEAN MILLS

Humanism and Classical Crisis: Anxiety, Intertexts, and the Miltonic Memory
  JACOB BLEVINS

Tragic Effects: Ethics and Tragedy in the Age of Translation
  THERESE AUGST

Reflections of Romanity: Discourses of Subjectivity in Imperial Rome
  RICHARD ALSTON AND EFROSSINI SPENTZOU

Philology and Its Histories
  EDITED BY SEAN GURD

Postmodern Spiritual Practices: The Construction of the Subject and the Reception of Plato in Lacan, Derrida, and Foucault
  PAUL ALLEN MILLER

www.ingramcontent.com/pod-product-compliance
Lightning Source LLC
Chambersburg PA
CBHW030105010526
44116CB00005B/107